Time Regained
World Literature and Cinema

Delia Ungureanu

BLOOMSBURY ACADEMIC
NEW YORK · LONDON · OXFORD · NEW DELHI · SYDNEY

BLOOMSBURY ACADEMIC
Bloomsbury Publishing Inc
1385 Broadway, New York, NY 10018, USA
50 Bedford Square, London, WC1B 3DP, UK
29 Earlsfort Terrace, Dublin 2, Ireland

BLOOMSBURY, BLOOMSBURY ACADEMIC and the Diana logo are trademarks
of Bloomsbury Publishing Plc

First published in the United States of America 2022

Copyright © Delia Ungureanu, 2023

For legal purposes the Acknowledgments on p. xii constitute an extension of this copyright page.

Cover design by Eleanor Rose
Cover photograph: a still from Raül Ruiz's *Time Regained* (1999) © Le Petit Bureau

All rights reserved. No part of this publication may be reproduced or transmitted in any form or by any means, electronic or mechanical, including photocopying, recording, or any information storage or retrieval system, without prior permission in writing from the publishers.

Bloomsbury Publishing Inc does not have any control over, or responsibility for, any third-party websites referred to or in this book. All internet addresses given in this book were correct at the time of going to press. The author and publisher regret any inconvenience caused if addresses have changed or sites have ceased to exist, but can accept no responsibility for any such changes.

Library of Congress Cataloging-in-Publication Data
Names: Ungureanu, Delia, author.
Title: Time regained : world literature and cinema / Delia Ungureanu.
Description: New York : Bloomsbury Academic, 2021. | Includes bibliographical references and index. | Summary: "Over the past 30 years, the fields of world literature and world cinema have developed on parallel but largely separate tracks, with little recognition of their underlying similarities and the ways that each can learn from the other. *Time Regained* does not move from literature to cinema, but exists simultaneously in both fields. The 7 filmmakers selected here, Andrei Tarkovsky, Akira Kurosawa, Martin Scorsese, Raúl Ruíz, Wong Kar-wai, Stephen Daldry, and Paolo Sorrentino, are themselves also writers or people with literary training, and they produce a new type of world cinema thanks to their understanding of the world simultaneously through literature and film. In the process, their films produce new readings of literary texts that world literature studies wouldn't have been able to achieve with its own instruments. *Time Regained* examines how filmmakers build on literature to reconfigure the world as a landscape of dreams and how they use film to reinvent the narrative techniques of the authors on whom they draw. The selected filmmakers draw inspiration from the French surrealists, modernists like Marcel Proust, Virginia Woolf, and Marguerite Yourcenar, and predecessors such as Dante and Cao Xueqin. In the process, these filmmakers cross the borders between film and literature, nation and world, dream and reality"-- Provided by publisher.
Identifiers: LCCN 2021018251 (print) | LCCN 2021018252 (ebook) | ISBN 9781501355790 (hardback) | ISBN 9781501355806 (epub) | ISBN 9781501355813 (pdf) | ISBN 9781501355820
Subjects: LCSH: Motion pictures and literature. | Film adaptations--History and criticism. | Time in motion pictures. | Time in literature.
Classification: LCC PN1995.3 .U54 2021 (print) | LCC PN1995.3 (ebook) | DDC 791.43/657—dc23
LC record available at https://lccn.loc.gov/2021018251
LC ebook record available at https://lccn.loc.gov/2021018252

ISBN:	HB:	978-1-5013-5579-0
	PB:	979-8-7651-0349-4
	ePDF:	978-1-5013-5581-3
	eBook:	978-1-5013-5580-6

Typeset by RefineCatch Limited, Bungay, Suffolk
Printed and bound in the United States of America

To find out more about our authors and books visit www.bloomsbury.com
and sign up for our newsletters.

"... for everything must return in time"
MARCEL PROUST, *THE CAPTIVE*

CONTENTS

List of Illustrations viii
Acknowledgments xii

Introduction: The Fabric of Dreams 1

1 From Automaton to Movie Camera: Méliès, Selznick, Scorsese 21

2 The Vast Structure of Recollection: Tarkovsky, Proust, Yourcenar 47

3 In That Sleep of Death What Dreams May Come: Van Gogh, Kurosawa, Yourcenar 85

4 The Dark Hollow at the Back of the Head: Woolf and Daldry 117

5 In the Paradise of Trapdoors: Proust, André Breton, and Raúl Ruiz 151

6 Dream of the Red Chamber 2046: Cao Xueqin and Wong Kar-wai 191

7 Let This Novel Begin: Sorrentino and Proust 227

Conclusion: The Art of Time Regained: To Be Continued 265

Bibliography 271
Index 285

ILLUSTRATIONS

Black and white illustrations

0.1 Man Ray, *Marcel Proust on his deathbed* (1922) © Man Ray 2015 Trust / Artists Rights Society (ARS), NY / ADAGP, Paris, 2021.   12

0.2 Georges Méliès, poster for *Le Voyage dans la lune*, and Pablo Picasso, *Portrait of André Breton* © 2021 Estate of Pablo Picasso / Artists Rights Society (ARS), New York.   20

1.1 André Kertész, *Eiffel Tower* © RMN-Grand Palais—Gestion droit d'auteur. Paris, Centre Pompidou, Musée national d'art moderne, Centre de création industrielle. Photo © Centre Pompidou, MNAM-CCI, Dist. RMN-Grand Palais / Bertrand Prévost and still from Martin Scorsese's *Hugo*.   26

1.2 Clocks and eyes in Brian Selznick's *The Invention of Hugo Cabret* © 2007 by Brian Selznick. Reprinted by permission of Scholastic Inc.   29

1.3 Clocks and eyes in Martin Scorsese's *Hugo*.   31

1.4 The automaton draws Méliès's moon in *Hugo*.   42

2.1 Andrei in the ruins of San Galgano in Andrei Tarkovsky's *Nostalghia*.   54

2.2 Objects from Aleksei's dream in Andrei Tarkovsky's *The Mirror*.   63

2.3 Photo of Arseny Tarkovsky © Marina Tarkovskaya. Photo Credits: Lev Gornung, Musei Kino, Moscow.   66

2.4 Maria hearing her absent husband's voice in *Nostalghia*.   73

2.5 Maria opening the three window curtains in *Nostalghia*.   78

2.6 Marguerite Yourcenar, pencil drawing on the front page of her short story "Our-Lady-of-the-Swallows" in a copy of her *Nouvelles orientales*. © Courtesy of Houghton Library, Harvard.   81

3.1 Final shots of the fifth and eighth vignettes in Akira Kurosawa's *Dreams*.   89

3.2 Vincent van Gogh, *Roadway with Underpass: The Viaduct* (1887) © Photo Credit: The Solomon R. Guggenheim Foundation / Art Resource, NY and *Head of a Woman* (1883)

ILLUSTRATIONS

	© Collection Kröller-Müller Museum, Otterlo, the Netherlands, and stills from Akira Kurosawa's *Dreams*: "The Tunnel."	98
3.3	Van Gogh, *Sunflowers* (1888) © National Gallery, London / Art Resource, NY and still from Akira Kurosawa's *Dreams*: "The Weeping Demon."	99
3.4	Vincent van Gogh, *Pollard Willows and Setting Sun* (1888) © Photo Credit: Art Resource, NY and *The Bridge at Courbevoie* (1887) © Van Gogh Museum, Amsterdam (Vincent van Gogh Foundation). Photo Credit: HIP / Art Resource, NY.	102
3.5	Marguerite Yourcenar, pencil drawings for "The Man Who Loved the Nereids" and "How Wang-Fô Was Saved" in a copy of her *Nouvelles orientales* © Courtesy of Houghton Library, Harvard.	103
3.6	Drawing by Akira Kurosawa for his film *Rhapsody in August* © Ise Cultural Foundation.	104
3.7	Still from Akira Kurosawa's *Dreams*; Vincent van Gogh, *Self-Portrait* (1887); and drawing by Akira Kurosawa for *Dreams* © Ise Cultural Foundation.	110
3.8	Vincent van Gogh, *The Langlois Bridge at Arles with Women Washing* (1888) © Collection Kröller-Müller Museum, Otterlo, the Netherlands. Photo Credit: Erich Lessing / Art Resource, NY, and still from Akira Kurosawa's *Dreams*.	112
4.1	Virginia Woolf writing and drowning; stills from Stephen Daldry's *The Hours*.	123
5.1	Adult Marcel's projected shadow as he steps out of the mirror in Raúl Ruiz's *Time Regained*.	159
5.2	Funerary masks on Marcel's tombstone in Raúl Ruiz's *Time Regained*.	160
5.3	Man Ray, *Marcel Proust on his deathbed* (1922) © Man Ray 2015 Trust / Artists Rights Society (ARS), NY / ADAGP, Paris, 2021 and the dying Marcel in Raúl Ruiz's *Time Regained* (1999).	165
5.4	Marcel sees Robert de Saint-Loup at Balbec in Raúl Ruiz's *Time Regained*.	168
5.5	Gilberte's inviting erotic gesture to little Marcel in Raúl Ruiz's *Time Regained*.	174
5.6	The surreal rose in Raúl Ruiz's *Time Regained* and Salvador Dalí's *Meditative Rose* © Salvador Dalí, Fundació Gala-Salvador Dalí, Artists Rights Society (ARS), New York 2021.	175
5.7	Adult Marcel reading, young Marcel filming, in Raúl Ruiz's *Time Regained*.	179
5.8	Young Marcel becomes old Marcel in Raúl Ruiz's *Time Regained*.	181

5.9	Callipygian Venus, in Raúl Ruiz's *Time Regained*.	184
5.10	René Magritte, *Je ne vois pas la (femme) cachée dans la forêt* (1929) © 2021 C. Herscovici / Artists Rights Society (ARS), New York. Photo Credit: Banque d'Images, ADAGP / Art Resource, NY.	187
5.11	Still from Raúl Ruiz's *Time Regained* showing little Marcel (Georges du Fresne) and older Marcel (Marcello Mazzarella) in Raúl Ruiz's *Time Regained*.	189
6.1	A monk watches Mo-wan whispering his secret, in Wong Kar-wai's *In the Mood for Love*.	196
6.2	The final shot of Angkor Wat, in Wong Kar-wai's *In the Mood for Love*.	197
6.3	Characters watching through oval windows in Wong Kar-wai's *2046*.	212
6.4	Jing-wen as android inviting the Japanese traveler to whisper his secret in Wong Kar-wai's *2046*.	214
6.5	Bai Ling smoking on the rooftop of the Orient Hotel in Wong Kar-wai's *2046*.	217
7.1	Photo of Marcel Proust (1896) © Archivio GBB/Bridgeman Images. Photo Credit: HIP / Art Resource, NY.	238
7.2	Jep looking down from his terrace into a garden, in Paolo Sorrentino's *La Grande Bellezza*.	246
7.3	Fanny Ardant in Volker Schlöndorff's *Un Amour de Swann* and in Paolo Sorrentino's *La Grande Bellezza*.	257

Color Plates

1	Piero della Francesca, *Madonna del Parto* (1457) © Photo Credit: Scala / Art Resource, NY.
2	Vincent van Gogh, *Wheatfield with* Crows (1890) © Van Gogh Museum, Amsterdam (Vincent van Gogh Foundation), photo credit: HIP / Art Resource, NY, and Akira Kurosawa's drawing of the scene © Ise Cultural Foundation.
3	Vincent van Gogh, *Girl in the Woods* (1882) © Artepics/ Alamy Stock Photo, and corresponding still from Akira Kurosawa's *Dreams*.
4	Water grasses: stills from Andrei Tarkovsky's *Solaris* and Akira Kurosawa's *Dreams*.
5	Vincent van Gogh, *Starry Night over the Rhone* (1888) © RMN-Grand Palais / Art Resource, NY.
6	The red book hidden in the riverbed in Raúl Ruiz's *Time Regained*.
7	Little Marcel meets his oldest self in Raúl Ruiz's *Time Regained*.

8	The hole in the wall at Angkor Wat, in Wong Kar-wai's *In the Mood for Love*.
9	The opening shot of Wong Kar-wai's *2046*.
10	Mummified lovers and new life in Andrei Tarkovsky's *Stalker*.
11	Jep Gambardella posing as Proust in Paolo Sorrentino's *La Grande Bellezza*.
12	Raphael, *La Fornarina* (1520) © Courtesy of the Gallerie Nazionali di Arte Antica, MIBACT-Bibliotheca Hertziana, Istituto Max Planck per la storia dell'arte/ Enrico Fontolan.
13	Jep Gambardella's vision of Elisa in Paolo Sorrentino's *La Grande Bellezza*.

ACKNOWLEDGMENTS

It's become a commonplace to say that "this book wouldn't have been possible without the support of," etc. But this book really wouldn't have been possible without the support of Carmen, George, and Georgia Muşat, who welcomed me into their home and family in one of those times when one needs real friends and offered me the most amazing space I could dream of for writing this book. I am deeply grateful to Carmen for her invaluable intellectual and emotional support and to Georgia for her true friendship. Their home outside Bucharest houses the most comprehensive private art collection in Romania, and it turned out itself to be a surrealist object where I chanced upon other surrealist objects or encounters just as I was writing about them. When I rewatched Raúl Ruiz's *Time Regained*, I realized that the couch I was sitting on looked like the one that Ruiz's Marcel is sitting on at the Guermantes, preparing to start writing his book, when an involuntary memory materializes on the table next to him as a sculpture of Venus. Just then on a small table near me I saw a sculpture of Venus *pudica* of the kind we see in Paolo Sorrentino's *La Grande Bellezza*. While I worked on Tarkovsky, a surreal mist like the one in the opening of *Nostalghia* appeared in the garden every morning; it disappeared once I was done with the chapter. One morning three knocks on my bedroom door woke me up. Half awake, I told myself I was alone in the house, and immediately I recalled Proust's words that "we are sometimes violently awakened by the sound of bells, perfectly heard by our ears, although nobody has rung." (*Sodom and Gomorrah*, 516). And I realized that Ignat from Tarkovsky's *The Mirror* wasn't the only one to talk to ghosts and open doors onto times that haven't yet come to pass.

I've been dreaming and thinking about this book for five years, and it crystalized over time through seminars I taught both at Harvard in the Department of Comparative Literature (2015 and 2016) and at the Institute for World Literature in Tokyo (2018), at Harvard (2019), and via Zoom (2020). I am greatly indebted to all my students who pushed me to think through the overarching argument as well as the individual books and films, but also to my colleagues and friends Sandra Naddaff and David Damrosch, who supported me and believed in the topic when I myself wasn't yet sure of it. With his renowned generosity, David Damrosch has astutely read the manuscript and provided invaluable suggestions. His unflinching belief in

ACKNOWLEDGMENTS   xiii

this book's life when it was only a dormant statue in a block of marble gave me the confidence needed by anyone venturing on less trodden paths.

The book benefited greatly from the erudite knowledge of my readers, Dominique Jullien and Michael Wood, whose perceptive and eagle-eyed observations pushed me to think harder about nuancing and strengthening my argument. I am as ever indebted to my editor, Haaris Naqvi, who has warmly supported my work since we started working together in 2016 for my previous book.

Ever since this book was just a dream, I knew the visual aspect would be essential. I was extremely lucky to benefit from the invaluable help of two artists: Tudor Panduru, a prominent Romanian cinematographer, offered his artistic and technical expertise, and my cousin Smaranda Murarus, a very talented graphic designer, designed the marvelous cover based on a still from Raúl Ruiz's *Time Regained* that I discuss in chapter 5. A special thanks goes to Michael O'Krent, a brilliant graduate student at Harvard who helped with the complex process of tracking down and obtaining the images.

I am always grateful to my former students Maria Dabija and Colton Valentine, who have generously read the book and provided insightful comments. An immense thank you to Maria for her invaluable support with sources in Russian, but first and foremost for our conversations on Tarkovsky. Maria generously intermediated a most valuable and meaningful conversation with Marina Tarkovskaya, Andrei Tarkovsky's sister and the author of *Shards of a Mirror* (Осколки зеркала), to whom I am deeply indebted for kindly giving me permission to reproduce Lev Gornung's photo of their father, the poet Arseny Tarkovsky. Through Marina Tarkovskaya I was also able to reach Kitty Hunter-Blair, the brilliant translator of Arseny Tarkovsky's poetry. Thanks to their generosity the chapter on Tarkovsky is in the form I dreamed for it. Marilee Shaw and Georgeta Constantin never let me lose faith in the theoretical ideas behind the argument. But the real force behind this book is my family, by which I mean both the living and the dead, those with whom I share ties of blood and of spirit. No two types of support are alike. With my sister and oldest friend, Lavinia, I share our own glowing version of Combray in the endless stories of our paternal grandfather, Mihai Ungureanu, but also many meaningful conversations whose conclusions made it into the book. Recently, my niece Todo wrote a lovely story about my mother's memory returning to life from her favorite book. Just when I was finishing this book, I remembered that my aunt, Oana Chelaru-Murăruș, had given me Eugene Vodolazkin's novel *Laurus*, and I felt something in it beckoning me. It turned out to be a continuation of Tarkovsky's *The Mirror* that made me add a couple of more pages to my book.

But the most surreal and significant moment was yet to come. With the book out for review, one day I found myself looking at the shelf on which I keep old books that have sentimental value, which I've been carrying around with me for the past twenty years since I left my parents' home. They belonged to my maternal grandfather, Mihai Vasiliu, a brilliant lawyer who loved to read. One of them, bound in red, is a book of poetry by Victor Hugo. And then I realized that this was the very book that Raúl Ruiz shows us hidden in the riverbed in *Time Regained*, the same book that he has little Marcel reading in his room as he waits for his mother to come kiss him goodnight. Next to it on my shelf, I found a psychology text I'd completely forgotten about. I opened it randomly and found the following note in my grandfather's handwriting that looks a lot like mine: "All this is nonsense. I prefer Marcel Proust's analysis. External reality is just a pretext. Everything happens first in you before it's projected outside, and everything you see exists in your mind only." And I thought to myself: the idea behind this book *is* real. Nothing really ends, and everything must return in time.

Introduction

The Fabric of Dreams

In the Batignolles cemetery in Paris, the tombstone of the visionary surrealist André Breton bears an epitaph in gilded letters: "Je cherche l'or du temps"— *I'm searching for the gold of time*. But what message is conveyed by these half-effaced words, written in the present tense as if they're spoken by his ghost? Behind them we can hear Marcel Proust's search for the meaning *hors du temps*, outside of time, that would become the golden heart of surrealism, *l'or du temps*. As Proust says of his fictional self, "when sleep bore him so far away from the world inhabited by memory and thought, through an ether in which he was alone, more than alone, without even the companionship of self-perception, he was outside the range of time and its measurements" (*Sodom and Gomorrah*, 519). With Proust as one of their unacknowledged precursors,[1] Breton and his fellow surrealists sought *l'or du temps* in dreams, in poetry, in painting, photography, and film. This book reveals the complex structural relationship that brings together world literature, surrealist poetics in its broadest sense, and the dreamworld of global art cinema today.

This organic relationship has only been fleetingly observed, when it's been seen at all, by scholars in the largely separate domains of world literature and world cinema. To make this relationship visible entails breaching disciplinary boundaries and looking beyond surface references and direct adaptations of literature into film. Writers, poets, painters, sculptors, musicians, and filmmakers don't have disciplinary boundaries in mind when they create; scholars do. Artists rarely see themselves as belonging only to one category, even when they work in a given medium, but can work with anything that speaks to them. Their dialogue is with the world.

---

[1] I discussed this in my previous book, *From Paris to Tlön* (Bloomsbury, 2017), in the chapter "The Ghosts of Surrealism in the World Novel."

Time Regained is an attempt to rethink the notion of circulation at the heart of world literature and world cinema, starting from the artist's mode of creation. "The Worlds of Literature and Cinema are thoroughly commingled," as Robert Stam writes in his recent book, *World Literature, Transnational Cinema, and Global Media.* "Just as literature is deeply embedded in cinema, so the cinema is embedded in literature, even in literature that antedated the invention of cinema" (60). He notes that books such as *Madame Bovary* can be described as "proto-cinematic," from the use of props to the montage of contrasting discourses (62). My scope, however, is rather different. I aim to reveal the often invisible networks in which writers with a filmic imagination and filmmakers with literary training develop their ideas. The writers and filmmakers selected here are connected through networks of elective affinities that tell different stories from what we find in the separate histories of literature or of film. In this book, I trace the relations that have developed between a diverse range of writers and a set of filmmakers who share a common preoccupation: how to fight back against the irreversibility of time. Marcel Proust, the metacharacter who is a recurrent presence in this story, knew that to solve this problem he had to bring back to life the network of people and things past. At the end of his great novel, he realizes that "life is perpetually weaving fresh threads which link one individual and one event to another, and that these threads are crossed and recrossed, doubled and redoubled to thicken the web, so that between any slightest point of our past and all the others a rich network of memories gives us an almost infinite variety of communicating paths to choose from" (*Time Regained*, 504).

Proust wasn't alone in thinking that circulation is key to understanding the rich network of cultural and personal memories that go into the making of an artistic consciousness, whether of a poet, a novelist, or a filmmaker. Andrei Tarkovsky, whose cinematic poetics is deeply indebted to Proust, felt that

> Art is culture, culture is the soul and memory of the people. There must be the possibility to transmit, to communicate culture. . . . If you lack that which culture has given to others far from you, you are lacking something, you are not complete, you cannot truly say that you have achieved the fullness which defines a true, whole, complete man. Culture is like blood, it must circulate, and it must circulate normally everywhere. Otherwise what happens is what occurs in a body when blood does not circulate in some point: gangrene immediately develops.
>
> RONDI interview

Circulation has occurred between the disciplines of world literature and world cinema, but usually only in terms of theory and in one direction only: film scholars have periodically paid attention to literary theory, but world literature scholars have rarely looked into film theory, or into the broader history of film beyond an occasional study of the adaptation of a favorite novel. A significant exception is Dudley Andrew, who has been the major actor in the translation of world literature theory for world cinema studies. His career in film studies has built on his lifelong engagement with André Bazin, and his article "An Atlas of World Cinema" (2004) defines world cinema in terms of world literature theories developed by Franco Moretti and David Damrosch. For Andrew, world cinema is an atlas where "displacement, not coverage, matters most" (10). Since then, he has continued to develop his global interests in essays such as his contributions to Galt and Schoonover's *Global Art Cinema* (2010) and Gorfinkel and Williams's *Global Cinema Networks* (2018).

But not all film scholars are so open to defining their object of study or laying bare their theoretical sources. Stephanie Dennison and Song Hwee Lim deem the definition of world cinema irrelevant from the very opening of their book *Remapping World Cinema*: "What is world cinema? . . . perhaps this is not the right question to ask in the first place" (1). But why not, in a book that takes this phrase in the title? World literature hasn't shied away from answering the corresponding question, as can be seen as early as the chapter "What Is World-Literature?" in Hutcheson Macaulay Posnett's *Comparative Literature* (1886), more recently in Dionýz Ďurišin's *Čo je svetová literatura?* (*What Is World Literature?*, 1992), and most influentially David Damrosch's *What Is World Literature?*, published in 2003, only three years before film studies started thinking in the same direction. Dennison and Lim write that "'world cinema' is analogous to 'world music' and 'world literature' in that they are categories created in the Western world to refer to cultural products and practices that are mainly non-Western" (1). Yet in the field of world literature as it was generally understood up to the mid-1990s, world literature meant, on the contrary, only *Western* literature, and even today the major anthologies of world literature in America, and often elsewhere, are two-thirds Western in content.

While Dennison and Lim mistakenly identify world literature as purely non-Western literature, others have proposed better integrated accounts. Lúcia Nagib, one of the editors of *Theorizing World Cinema* (2012), proposes a tripartite definition of world cinema, in an essay included in Dennison and Lim's *Remapping World Cinema*:

- World cinema is simply the cinema of the world. It has no center. It's not the other, but it's us. It has no beginning and no end, but is a global process. World cinema, as the world itself, is circulation.

- World cinema is not a discipline, but a method of cutting across film history according to waves of relevant films and movements, thus creating flexible geographies.

- As a positive, inclusive, democratic concept, world cinema allows all sorts of theoretical approaches, provided they are not based on the binary perspective. ("Towards a Positive Definition of World Cinema," 35)

Though Nagib doesn't cite Damrosch, her definition has clear affinities, structurally and even typographically, to the threefold definition offered in the conclusion of his *What Is World Literature?*, in which world literature is defined as an elliptical refraction of national literatures, as literature that gains in translation, and as a mode of reading rather than a set canon of works. For his part, though he discusses literature from ancient Egypt to contemporary Serbia, Damrosch makes no use of film studies. A major purpose of the present book is to bring such divergent definitions into conversation.

Both world literature and world cinema have defined circulation within their respective media: books and film. Damrosch defines world literature as "that which circulates in translation," but he means translation into another language, not another medium. More recently, both he and Rebecca Walkowitz have discussed the internet-based work of the Korean digital art group Young-hae Chang Heavy Industries (in *Comparing the Literatures* [2020] and *Born Translated* [2015], respectively). Yet what YHCHI shows online is almost always a streaming text, without images, and so their work looks less like film than like a new take on the sheet of paper.

World cinema, on the other hand, understands the problem of circulation in a pragmatic way as a film's distribution network, or sometimes the circulation of ideas and practices between filmmakers. In his foreword to Galt and Schoonover's *Global Art Cinema*, Dudley Andrew too takes up circulation as a parameter for defining a more specific branch of world cinema he's interested in. He observes that the collection's title

> begs a question debated in comparative literature over the vexed term, dating from Goethe, of *Weltliteratur*. For David Damrosch, a text joins the community of world literature when it finds sustained reception beyond the borders of the specific community out of which it arose . . . As for the rest of writing . . . if never translated, these texts interact not at all with readers outside the community. Goethe and Damrosch would leave them alone; and so does global art cinema.
>
> vi–vii

The editors of the collection, Rosalind Galt and Karl Schoonover, give a more political meaning to the idea of circulation, seeking to "expose otherwise unseen geopolitical fault lines of world cinema" (3). Their book advances a Marxist view that takes global art cinema into the vicinity of Pheng Cheah's understanding of politically committed world literature (*What Is a World?*, 2016) and the leftist internationalism of the Warwick Research Collective's *Combined and Uneven Development: Towards a New Theory of World-Literature* (2015). In Galt and Schoonover's view: "Internationalism understands the circulation of films across national borders as

INTRODUCTION 5

a political act," and though "the Marxist history of internationalism might not always fit snugly with our analysis of global art cinema, the demand for a geopolitics of cinema remains an important spur" (12).

But what of the circulation of literature through film, or film through literature? I'm not thinking here simply of direct film adaptation, but of a circulation of ideas in their own right that become something else in a different medium. Creative ideas circulate and recirculate not just across the linguistic and national boundaries we hear so often discussed today in both disciplines, but across the boundaries of media too. To approach this topic, we'll begin with one of film's greatest theorists, André Bazin.

André Bazin's Mixed Cinema

Bazin earned a degree in literature at the École Normale Supérieure de Saint-Cloud with a thesis on Baudelaire, and he knew that artists are always open to other arts beyond their immediate practice. Half a century before Damrosch defined world literature through circulation and translation, Bazin put forth a rather different idea of *translation* as translation between media. As he says in his essay "In Defense of Mixed Cinema,"[2] "the filmmakers honestly attempt an integral equivalent, they try at least not simply to use the book as an inspiration, not merely to adapt it, but to translate it onto the screen" (66). Bazin wrote extensively on the connections between cinema and literature, cinema and theater, cinema and painting, cinema and photography, cinema and the world.

Bazin had a deep understanding of the relation of cinema with theater, and he knew that "cinema is the least likely of the arts to escape its influence. At this rate, half of literature and three quarters of the existing films are branches of theater" ("Theatre and Cinema I," 82). Bazin understood the arts organically and analogically; what he says of theater could very well work for cinema's relation to literature, thanks to the analogy with translation that illustrates this relationship: "The more the cinema intends to be faithful to the text and to its theatrical requirements, the more of necessity must it delve deeper into its own language. The best translation is that which demonstrates a close intimacy with the genius of both languages and likewise, a mastery of both" ("Theatre and Cinema II," 116–17).

---

[2]The original French title, "Pour un cinéma impur: défense de l'adaptation," could equally be translated "impure" as it sets up Bazin's critique of "pure" cinema. This is the proposal of Lúcia Nagib and Anne Jerslev, editors of *Impure Cinema: Intermedial and Intercultural Approaches to Film* (2014). I believe however that Hugh Gray's translation of "impur" as "mixed" captures the primary focus of Bazin's argument for the value of mixing different artistic modes.

Things become even more interesting when Bazin thinks of photography: if photography only "embalms time" as Bazin put it, "the cinema is objectivity in time," and "for the first time, the image of things is likewise the image of their duration, change mummified as it were" ("The Ontology of the Photographic Image," 14–15). To photography we can also add music, which brought such a major new dimension to cinema after the era of silent film, no longer a secondary, external element but now integrated into films from the outset of production. As we'll often see in the following chapters, our films' scores often have a directly literary dimension as well, from popular song lyrics to symphonic and liturgical music, to the visionary poetry of William Blake.

With the evolution of montage and the inclusion of sound, Bazin writes, "[t]oday we can say that at last the director writes in film . . . The film-maker is no longer the competitor of the painter and the playwright, he is, at last, the equal of the novelist" ("The Evolution of the Language of Cinema," 39–40). According to Dudley Andrew, "[a]t midcentury when Bazin was surveying things, cinema seemed in phase only with the novel, since both media deploy new narrative techniques, share a proclivity for realist representation, and address a mass audience. Bazin expected cinema to evolve in its cultural function, just as painting and poetry had, both of these growing progressively abstract after 1800" (Foreword to *What is Cinema?* II, xvi). Yet there's as much poetry in *Mrs. Dalloway* and *À la recherche du temps perdu* as in Van Gogh's paintings, and not all modern poetry and painting are abstract. Nor is cinema unable to develop in the direction of abstraction. As we will see in the following chapters, examples as diverse as Andrei Tarkovsky's *Nostalghia*, Stephen Daldry's *The Hours*, Raúl Ruiz's *Le Temps retrouvé*, and Akira Kurosawa's *Dreams* show that the structural relation between cinema, fiction, poetry, and painting is not as distinct as one may think.

Time Regained: World Literature and Cinema takes its cue from Bazin's deep understanding of the mutual relationship between literature and cinema, which as he saw goes far beyond direct adaptations of literature for the screen: "We are witnessing, at the point at which the avant-garde has now arrived, the making of films that dare to take their inspiration from a novellike style one might describe as ultracinematographic. Seen from this angle the question of borrowing is only of secondary importance" ("In Defense of Mixed Cinema," 64). Like Lawrence Venuti today, rejecting critiques of translation as betraying the original, Bazin argues that "It is nonsense to wax wroth about the indignities practiced on literary works on the screen, at least in the name of literature" (65). However, whereas Bazin has in mind only the case of the modern novel, I will take literature as entailing a more complex overlapping of concepts and of genres. The novel itself isn't at all a timeless or unitary concept, nor are genres ever pure; novels have their history and frequently overlap with poetry, theater, or arts like architecture, painting, sculpture. Virginia Woolf, Marcel Proust,

Marguerite Yourcenar, and Brian Selznick are all novelists, but what a difference between Woolf's poetic style, Proust's essayistic fiction written with a poet's taste for metaphor, Yourcenar's visual poetry in prose, and Selznick's graphic novel *The Invention of Hugo Cabret*, which is at the same time a silent film and a peep-show box. Even though "the novel" may seem like the common denominator of all the filmmakers I've selected in this book, this is only the most obvious framework; these artists are all poets at heart, and it is poetry with its visionary power that provides filmmakers who have a writer's eye with the logic of montage (Daldry), of cinematography (Ruiz), or of emotional atmosphere (Tarkovsky).

Bazin closes "In Defense of Mixed Cinema" by reinforcing the mutual relation between cinema and the other arts: "The time of resurgence of a cinema newly independent of novel and theater will return. But it may then be because novels will be written directly onto film. . . . the cinema draws into itself the formidable resources of elaborated subjects amassed around it by neighboring arts during the course of the centuries. It will make them its own because it has need of them and we experience the desire to rediscover them by way of the cinema" (74–5). In this book, I propose to return to Bazin's vision of art that travels the world via translation into different media, and to enlarge our understanding of the concept of circulation in both world literature and world cinema. And what better person to bring the two disciplines together than a brilliant film theorist with literary training and erudite knowledge of the other arts? It's almost prophetic that Bazin's "In Defense of Mixed Cinema," came out in a collective volume called *Cinéma: Un œil ouvert sur le monde* (Bovay et al., 1952). While world literature is sometimes "a window onto the world" (Damrosch, *What Is World Literature?*, 15), film will be the eye that looks through this window.

*

The following chapters focus on seven case studies of major film directors who, like Bazin, are themselves writers or have literary training. Their films engage with works of world literature, in two of my cases through direct adaptation, but often far more obliquely. In the process, these filmmakers act simultaneously as writers and directors, and they make a double intervention in the fields of world literature and world cinema. On the one hand, they engage with the work of other directors who were also writers; on the other, as readers and writers of world literature, they engage obliquely with world writers.

Time Regained doesn't move from literature to cinema but exists simultaneously in both realms. The filmmakers selected here produce a new type of world cinema, thanks to their understanding of the world (what Bazin would call the "real") simultaneously through literature and film. They also produce new readings of literature that world literature studies wouldn't have been able to produce on its own. World cinema studies should understand literature not as a background or source from which it once developed, but as a creative and very much alive partner for producing "global art cinema" in Dudley Andrew's sense. For their part, scholars of world literature should extend their interest in the networks of literary circulation not only in translation but also through film, which is certainly one of the major means through which literature circulates in the twentieth and twenty-first centuries. Following the success of his film *The Hours*, Stephen Daldry remarked that his greatest joy was when he heard that *Mrs. Dalloway* was back in a top position in the Amazon sales ranking. A great art film doesn't take you into a closed cinematic world, but is a window onto something else—in this case, Woolf's literary world. A window of the kind that Proust dreamed all great books should be: thresholds to a world of our own making. *Time Regained* is an attempt to think of world cinema as a new mode of reading, as *visual* world literature.

The writers and directors selected here configure a network of elective affinities as they build on each other's work, sometimes directly, other times obliquely, and with a focus on the heritage of surrealism, both in film and in the fictional worlds of Proust and his successors. This book opens with Martin Scorsese's *Hugo* (2011), a tribute film to the forefather of cinema, the magician Georges Méliès. Using clips from Méliès's actual films, Scorsese demonstrates retrospectively why they are worth looking at as world cinema. At the same time, it's significant that the journey into cinema's origins is sparked by a contemporary graphic novel, Brian Selznick's *The Invention of Hugo Cabret*, which Selznick designed on the principle of flipbooks that lay behind peep shows, which ultimately led to the filming camera. Méliès had a vision that transgresses borders through magic, and he found such a borderless world in dreams. He was the first filmmaker to define the art of cinema as the art of dreams, an understanding of cinema that we'll find with every film director discussed in this book.

The French surrealists took up Georges Méliès as a proto-surrealist, and they included him in the first transatlantic surrealist exhibition, "Fantastic Art, Dada, Surrealism," curated in 1936 at the recently founded Museum of Modern Art by the museum's young director, Alfred Barr, Jr. The catalog of the exhibition opened with Méliès's films and closed with Disney characters, as if in anticipation of Disney's collaboration a decade later with Salvador Dalí on the animated short film *Destino*, finally released in 2003. An important early alternative to the Hollywood model came from the first surrealist films, *Un chien andalou* (1929) and *L'Âge d'or* (1930), in a revolutionary form of cinema that took Méliès's oneiric films farther than even the magician could have imagined.

World cinema thus already existed from the very origins of cinema, taken up by the surrealists who defined themselves as citizens of the world and who saw in cinema the dream logic of an enriched version of reality. The surrealists' cinema transgressed all sorts of borders; it was antinationalist

INTRODUCTION

and anti-imperialist. Over time, surrealism's logic attracted very different film directors with a literary sensibility, sometimes themselves scholars of literature, like Stephen Daldry and Raúl Ruiz, or coming from a literary milieu like Andrei Tarkovsky, son of the prominent Soviet poet Arseny Tarkovsky. Others are filmmakers who trained both in literature and film and became great readers of world literature, like Scorsese, Kurosawa, and Sorrentino. Like the surrealists before them, these directors had a unified understanding of literature and film, and that's why the majority have written their own scripts.

These great filmmakers engage as authors themselves with great world writers. Scorsese draws comprehensively on surrealist literature and art in *Hugo*, in which the automaton becomes a metaphor for memory as filming camera. Daldry and Ruiz produce new readings of *Mrs. Dalloway* and *Le Temps retrouvé* that hadn't been achieved by world literature studies. Through Daldry's *The Hours*, Woolf becomes a postmodernist writer who uses a surrealist logic of the object and definition of the self, which she develops together with her literary model, Marcel Proust. Thanks to the developments in cinematography, editing, and special effects, Raúl Ruiz's *Le Temps retrouvé* gives us a Proust who anticipates the surrealists' major revolution of the object as oriented both to the past and toward the future, prophetic of reality's development.

Proust scholars usually discuss Ruiz's film as "unfaithful" to the original and use Proust's own dismissal of the art of cinema as inappropriate for narrating inner time, but they forget how much cinema has changed since Proust's time. Ruiz's main point throughout his film is that Proust's imagination functions like a filmmaker's. Entranced by the magic lantern, the peep box, and photographs seen through a magnifying glass, little Marcel is a film director in the making, and Ruiz suggests that Proust's literary mechanism for capturing images and the movements of the soul anticipate what modern cinema is able to accomplish. A point well taken by Paolo Sorrentino, whose *La grande bellezza* carries Ruiz's intuition one step further, and we learn that had Proust lived in our present time, and in Rome rather than Paris, his writing would have transmuted into filmmaking. After Ruiz, Sorrentino makes us return once more to Proust, to see how timely all his intuitions still are, about human nature, mortality, and the passage of time.

Major filmmakers who think beyond their culture's boundaries can make an intervention both within their own literature and beyond their own cultural space. Wong Kar-wai engages in *In the Mood for Love* with his Hong Kong film tradition and Chinese literary culture, but he also employs major literary references from the Western world. The sequel to *In the Mood for Love*, his film *2046* tells a story that rewrites both a classical Chinese novel, Cao Xueqin's *Story of the Stone*, and also Proust's *Recherche*. Like Ruiz and Daldry before him, Wong reads the history of literature and of film together. Even though Proust never read Cao's *roman fleuve*, Wong brings them together to create a dialogue between film and classic and contemporary literature.

Indebted to the history both of art and of literature, Andrei Tarkovsky co-writes his *Nostalghia* with the Italian poet Tonino Guerra and in dialogue with his own filmography, polaroid photos, and his father's poetry, but also with a story from Marguerite Yourcenar's *Oriental Tales*. Most likely thanks to Tarkovsky, her tales became an inspiration for Akira Kurosawa in turn. In Yourcenar's work, as well as in the surrealists' films and aesthetics, Tarkovsky and Kurosawa found a brilliant partner of dialogue who shared the belief in film and poetry as the art of dreams. Tarkovsky's *Nostalghia* and Kurosawa's *Dreams* shed new light on the close connections between Yourcenar's aesthetics and the surrealists', one that was much more intimate than Yourcenar was ready to admit. Thanks to literary film directors like Tarkovsky and Kurosawa, what Breton, in Goethe's footsteps, liked to call networks of elective affinities bring together the most unexpected combinations of artists and writers.

All the writers and directors discussed here are at once local and worldly, rooted in their culture of origin but not only in the culture of their own profession. To establish a point of comparison between their very different ways of reading literature and film, I focus on time as a common structural and thematic principle. Bazin, too, understood literature and cinema as different forms of engagement with time: the novel's "secret essence of style," he says, is "the ordering in time of fragments of reality" ("An Aesthetic of Reality," 31), while "cinema is objectivity in time" ("The Ontology of the Photographic Image," 14).

Redefining Reality

Proust, the surrealists, and then Bazin after them developed a new notion of realism, against the nineteenth-century realism that they critiqued as remaining on the surface of objects. Proust and André Breton speak in almost identical terms about our "impoverished notion of reality":

> the kind of literature which contents itself with "describing things," with giving of them merely a miserable abstract of lines and surfaces, is, in fact, though it calls itself realist, the furthest removed from reality and has more than any other the effect of saddening and impoverishing, since it abruptly severs all communication of our present self both with the past, the essence of which is preserved in things, and with the future, in which things incite us to enjoy the essence of the past a second time. Yet it is precisely this essence that an art worthy of the name must seek to express.
>
> PROUST, *Time Regained*, 284–5

INTRODUCTION 11

For Breton, a "purely informative" style "is virtually the rule rather than the exception in the novel form. . . . And the descriptions! There is nothing to which their vacuity can be compared; they are nothing but so many superimposed images taken from some stock catalogue" (*Manifestoes*, 7). Both Proust and Breton seek to expand this impoverished version of reality with one that lies beneath the skin of our habitual perception, a reality that usually passes for "magical" in the eyes of the rational, "scientific" man. From his readings in Proust and Breton, Bazin developed his trademark understanding of realism: "the problem before us is that of realism. This is the problem we always end up with when we are dealing with cinema" ("Theatre and Cinema II," 107).

Only recently has Bazin's notion of reality been reframed through surrealism as its formative context. Until the 2000s, the accepted account was that Bazin had a "'surrealist period' as he waited out the Occupation" and that he only "became for a time a fanatic surrealist, a follower of Cocteau, and an energetic practitioner of automatic writing" (Dudley Andrew, *André Bazin*). In "The Reality of Hallucination in André Bazin," Jean-François Chevrier shows that Bazin's notion of realism remained indebted to surrealism: "Bazin defines neorealism, but he is haunted by surrealism, because realism is unable to dispel hallucination which, as Flaubert notes, follows a principle of mimic or mimetic restitution" (51). Following in Chevrier's footsteps, Adam Lowenstein's *Dreaming of Cinema* (2014) revisits Bazin's conception of cinema as the art of photography, through a comparative reading of Bazin with Breton's *First Manifesto of Surrealism*. But neither Chevrier nor Lowenstein looks beyond "The Ontology of the Photographic Image" where Bazin openly references surrealism, nor do they offer a clear trajectory of how these surrealist ideas came into Bazin's theory.

More than a passing reference or a "period" in his formation, Bazin's engagement with surrealism is structural and organic. A voracious reader, Bazin closely followed the surrealists, from their magazines and articles to their social networks of friends and enemies with whom he worked. His collaborators included the early surrealist Georges Sadoul, a contributor to the surrealist magazine *Le Surréalisme au service de la Révolution*. Sadoul became a major film historian, and he was one of the first theorists to think of a world cinema as early as 1949, when he published his *Histoire du cinéma mondial: Des origines à nos jours*. The second volume of his monumental *Histoire générale du cinéma*, as well as his monograph *Georges Méliès* (1961), look at the father of cinema as a protosurrealist.

Bazin was also close with Jean Cocteau, whom Breton despised on moral and ideological grounds, even though they did intersect in some ideas. Interacting with the wider network of surrealist ideas from Breton to Sadoul, Cocteau, and Bataille, Bazin was intimately acquainted not just with the concept of surreality, but also with surrealism's conceptual network, which included the paucity of reality (*le peu de la réalité*), objective hazard (*le hasard objectif*), chance encounter (*la rencontre fortuite*), the phantom-object (*l'objet-fantôme*), and the invisible object (*l'objet invisible*). As a graduate in literature from the École Normale Supérieure de Saint-Cloud, Bazin knew that the surrealists' ideas of reality and of the object had an immediate precursor in Marcel Proust, with whom Breton and Philippe Soupault had a brief but meaningful encounter—as history would have it, a chance encounter based on elective affinities that would leave a lasting imprint on the history of art cinema.

Since the surrealists employed photography as a practice of the ghostly object, it's fitting that the famous photograph of Proust on his deathbed was taken by Man Ray, whom Cocteau fetched at the last minute (Figure 0.1). This iconic photograph stands out like one of Breton's "cryptograms of reality" that brings together artists otherwise separated by generations, by upbringing, and even by political views: Marcel Proust, who belonged to no group but was part of many different networks from the haute bourgeoisie to avant-garde artists; Man Ray, the most renowned surrealist photographer; and Jean Cocteau, the poet, artist, and filmmaker who always denied any connection to surrealism yet intimately benefited from its ideas. But what Man Ray took wasn't just a photograph of Proust; it was a virtual death mask. For Bazin, a death mask is itself a photograph, which he thinks of through the surrealists' automatic creation: "the molding of death masks ... likewise involves a certain automatic process. One might consider photography in this sense as a molding, the taking of an impression, by the manipulation of

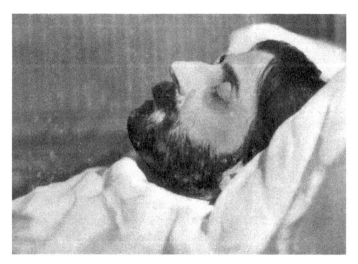

FIGURE 0.1 *Man Ray, photograph of Marcel Proust on his deathbed, November 19, 1922*

INTRODUCTION

light" ("The Ontology of the Photographic Image," 12 n.2). In Man Ray's photograph of Proust, we can read reality's prophecy of the future of art: by capturing literature through the new media of photography and then film, time can be regained and the ghost of literature summoned back from the inanimate object that forms its prison, to share our present once more.

*

The surrealists discovered the power of photography to efface the borders between reality and dream, and in this emphasis they became heirs of the proto-surrealist poet Gérard de Nerval. In the opening pages of *Aurélia*, the manuscript found in Nerval's pocket when he committed suicide in 1855, we learn that dream is a second life. Everything that Proust and the surrealists seek comes from *this* reality rather than from a beyond, which is what distinguished them radically from the Romantics and the nineteenth-century utopianists. As Sorrentino's Jep Gambardella will say, "I don't deal with what lies beyond." To capture the revolutionary aspect of the concepts of reality and realism as proposed by *le surréalisme* one should think of a double concept: a reality that is made both from something underneath the skin of our everyday reality (*la **sous**-réalité*) but also something that is added on top of it, *la **sur**-réalité*. As Bazin says,

> The photograph as such and the object in itself share a common being, after the fashion of a fingerprint. Wherefore, photography actually contributes something to the order of natural creation instead of providing a substitute for it. The surrealists had an inkling of this when they looked to the photographic plate to provide them with their monstrosities and for this reason: the surrealist does not consider his aesthetic purpose and the mechanical effect of the image on our imaginations as things apart. For him, the logical distinction between what is imaginary and what is real tends to disappear. Every image is to be seen as an object and every object as an image. Hence photography ranks high in the order of surrealist creativity because it produces an image that is a reality of nature, namely, an hallucination that is also a fact.
>
> "The Ontology of the Photographic Image," 15–16

Connecting the beginnings of cinema with the surrealists' understanding of reality, Bazin locates the specificity of cinema in photography's status as a ghostly object. But before the surrealists, it was Proust who understood the world around us as a world of ghosts imprisoned in apparently immobile objects until our imagination summons them once more into reality. As he says at the start of the *Recherche*, "Perhaps the immobility of the things that surround us is forced upon them by our conviction that they are themselves and not anything else, by the immobility of our conception of them" (*Swann's Way*, 3). Proust's poetics of the object keeps the secret of time regained:

I feel that there is much to be said for the Celtic belief that the souls of those whom we have lost are held captive in some inferior being, in an animal, in a plant, in some inanimate object, and thus effectively lost to us until the day (which to many never comes) when we happen to pass by the tree or to obtain possession of the object which forms their prison. Then they start and tremble, they call us by our name, and as soon as we have recognised them the spell is broken. Delivered by us, they have overcome death and return to share our life.

And so it is with our own past. It is a labour in vain to attempt to recapture it: all the efforts of our intellect must prove futile. The past is hidden somewhere outside the realm, beyond the reach of intellect, in some material object (in the sensation which that material object will give us) of which we have no inkling. And it depends on chance whether or not we come upon this object before we ourselves must die.

59–60

Four decades after Proust wrote these words, Bazin took up the surrealists' ghostly object as a common term of photography and cinema: "The only property inherent to cinema, he argued, is its photographic base, which keeps the subject (or referent) hovering like a ghost around its image" (Andrew, "Foreword," xv).

The invention of cinema is based, as Bazin writes, on "an integral realism, a recreation of the world in its own image, an image unburdened by the freedom of interpretation of the artist or the irreversibility of time" ("The Myth of Total Cinema," 18). In this sense, the camera is an "*objectif* objectif" (both noun and adjective in French), through which the writer sees reality. Bazin's "*objectif* objectif" has the same meaning as the surrealist concept of *hasard objectif* that reveals the *real* reality, hence a new realism, as Breton put it in the lecture he delivered in Prague in 1935, "Surrealist Situation of the Object." There he draws attention to "the problem of *objective chance,* or in other words that sort of chance that shows man, in a way that is still very mysterious, a necessity that escapes him, even though he experiences it as a vital necessity" (*Manifestoes,* 268).

The much-discussed objectivity and realism in Bazin's theory of cinema cannot be understood outside the context of surrealism that made it possible. Bazin's "objectivity" should in fact be *objectuality* or the privileging of the object as the bearer of a life of its own—something already at the heart of Proust's understanding of the reality around us and then developed further by the surrealists. For Bazin, surrealism encompasses a comprehensive and extended meaning, one that works in free variation with "the supernatural. I apologize for this equivocal word; the reader may replace it with whatever he will—'poetry' or 'surrealism' or 'magic'—whatever the term that expresses the hidden accord which things maintain with an invisible counterpart of which they are, so to speak, merely the adumbration" ("*Cabiria,*" 88).

INTRODUCTION 15

The marvelous—*le merveilleux*—was another key concept for the surrealists: "the marvelous is always beautiful, anything marvelous is beautiful, in fact only the marvelous is beautiful" (*Manifestoes*, 14). Even better, the marvelous is projected onto an invisible screen through a cinematic imagination, a "shadow theater that we have found a way to project without any apparent screen, the shadow of hands picking hideous flowers and getting pricked, the shadow of charming and fearful beasts, the shadow of ideas too, not to mention the shadow of the marvelous that no one has ever seen" ("Soluble Fish" [1924], in *Manifestoes*, 63). Three decades later, Bazin too would define cinematic realism as making the marvelous possible: "The realist destiny of cinema—innate in photographic objectivity—is fundamentally equivocal, because it allows the 'realization' of the marvelous. Precisely like a dream. The oneiric character of cinema, linked to the illusory nature of its image as much as to its lightly hypnotic mode of operation, is no less crucial than its realism" ("Tout film est un documentaire social," 12). Raúl Ruiz will return to these very passages from Breton and Bazin when using the shadow theater as one of the principles of his cinematography in the visionary "adoption," as he called it, of Proust's *Le Temps retrouvé*.

Bazin defined cinema as a hybrid intimately related to literature, painting, and poetry. Hybrid cinema isn't easy to create, however, because it needs a director who is not only knowledgeable about film history and technique, but who also has a literary sensibility and can bring the force of an age-old human practice into a new medium. As Bazin argued,

> genuine authors are rare in the cinema; the vast majority of directors, even the best of them, are far from possessing the creative freedom enjoyed by the writer. Even when he writes his own screenplay, the film maker remains primarily a director, that is to say a master craftsman who organizes objective elements. Such working conditions are sufficient to warrant artistic creation and the development of style but they lack that total identification, that biological cohesion often found in other arts— between Van Gogh and his painting, between Kafka and his novels.
>
> "The Grandeur of *Limelight*," 136–7

Such rare artists are the filmmakers included in this book.

Following in the footsteps of Pascale Casanova and Franco Moretti, engaging with world literature as with world cinema, I am interested in a range of exceptional artists who have the visionary power to change the stakes of the game. Their films can be called art films, of the sort taken up by Dudley Andrew in his early book *Film in the Aura of Art*, films that "question, change, or disregard standard film making in seeking to convey or discover the utterly new or the formerly hidden" (5–6). Explaining his selection of art films, Andrew writes that the films he analyzes have actually chosen him (xii). In the case of *Time Regained*, I can say not only that the films chose me, but the films first chose their filmmakers, who themselves were chosen by the masterpieces of literature and art that inspired their films. Harold Bloom once proposed that canonical writers like Shakespeare— or, we could add, Cao Xueqin, Proust, or Woolf—choose their followers; his idea takes on a whole new meaning when we step out of the boundaries of the art of literature. But before turning to my case studies of chance encounters between world literature and cinema, let me share one more story that chose me in a most surreal way, only after I had completed the research for this book.

Surrealism is Born at the Movies: Méliès and Breton

Writing the script for *Le Voyage dans la lune*, an icon in the history of cinema, Georges Méliès engaged creatively with major world writers, together with popular genres like the operetta. From Jules Verne's novels *From the Earth to the Moon* (1865) and *Around the Moon* (1870) Méliès borrowed the idea of a trip to the moon in a capsule that included a poet among its travelers. In Méliès's story, Verne's three travelers become six moon voyagers, all renowned scholars and astronomers. They include their leader Professor Barbenfouillis, Nostradamus, Micromégas, Omega, Parafaragaramus, and a certain Alcofrisbas.

The list of six voyagers mixes reality, fiction, pseudonyms, real names, invented names, and pen names. Barbenfouillis, French for "tangled-beard," is probably a parody of President Barbicane from Jules Verne's *From the Earth to the Moon* (*Essai de reconstitution*, 111). Nostradamus was the sixteenth-century physician and visionary from a family of converted Jews. His book *Les Prophétie*s (1555) became famous as a way to foretell the course of history, and to this day it continues to be seen so by many. Micromégas is the protagonist of a novella of that name by Voltaire, published in 1752; it is considered among the earliest examples of science fiction. An inhabitant of a planet orbiting Sirius and a great scholar, the giant creature Micromégas travels the universe together with a peer from Saturn until they reach Earth, where they are bewildered and amused by the inhabitants' ideas about the universe. Méliès names the third lunar explorer Omega, as if to tell us that his tale is the last stage of the literature of his predecessors, in this case, Voltaire. From him, he inherits irony, wit, and the belief in exploring the unknown through knowledge and reason.

Parafaragaramus is Méliès's own creation, demonstrating a kinship with one of the surrealists' predecessors, the avant-garde poet Alfred Jarry, the inventor of "pataphysics," the meta-science of studying imaginary solutions for realities beyond meta-reality. Jarry makes fun of scientific concepts in

Exploits and Opinions of Dr. Faustroll, Pataphysician (1898), in a manner that reminds us of François Rabelais. Or should we say that it reminds us of Alcofribas Nasier, the comical pseudonym used by Rabelais? The fifth traveler in Méliès's capsule is called Alcofrisbas, who doesn't appear in Jules Verne's novels, in Offenbach's operetta loosely based on Verne, or in H.G. Wells's later novel. Alcofrisbas reminds Méliès's viewer of his great predecessor in the art of exploring the space (of dreams) through knowledge: François Rabelais, who signed the opening page of *Gargantua* and the last page of *Pantagruel* with an anagram of his own name: Alcofribas Nasier, "l'abstracteur de quinte essence." Alcofribas the writer is thus a parodic alchemist, claiming to find the quintessence—or fifth essence—of life or the "philosopher's stone."

Rabelais described his work as a "Silenus box" that contains an apothecary's drugs for aiding digestion, a wink at the alchemists' analogy between the alchemical furnace and the stomach, or the body as microcosm. What resulted depended on the viewer's eye: if you were an alchemist, it was gold; if you were a vulgar mind, it was nothing more than excrement. If you were Rabelais, you realized that it isn't a matter of choosing one or the other, but of being both at the same time: the rationalist who makes fun of the literal understanding of what gold means in alchemy, but also the literary magician who knows that he could indeed find "quint-essence" in this Silenus Box where he puts all the knowledge that the moon/Selene/Silenus/Socrates has revealed to him. Almost a century after Méliès, Brian Selznick took up Méliès's character Alcofrisbas and turned him into the fictional writer and filmmaker of *The Invention of Hugo Cabret*.

Méliès himself was parodying Offenbach's operetta *Le Voyage dans la lune* (1875). He was a magician who could enchant the audience with rationally designed magic tricks, but also the alchemist who could bring together writers like Rabelais and Voltaire in dialogue with Jules Verne and H.G. Wells, in what would become the first truly world film, *Le Voyage dans la lune*. Bazin too felt that Jules Verne was the greatest writer for children because he was a poet "whose imagination is privileged to remain on the dream wavelength of childhood . . . The artist who works spontaneously for children has attained a quality of universality" ("The Virtues and Limitations of Montage," 41–2). His praise of the child's imagination as genuinely poetic shows Bazin once more as a follower of surrealism. In the first manifesto, Breton writes that childhood exhibits the surrealist logic of chance encounter and absolute freedom, as well as a Proustian self, made of infinite selves. To regain it, "Man, this inveterate dreamer" has to "turn back toward his childhood which, however his guides and mentors may have botched it, still strikes him as somehow charming. There, the absence of any known restrictions allows him the perspective of several lives lived at once; this illusion becomes firmly rooted within him" (*Manifestoes*, 3–4).

Because Verne's characters never leave their capsule once they reach the moon, other writers, including Offenbach's librettists and then H.G. Wells, could imagine what actually *was* on the moon. Offenbach's operetta tells the story of King Vlan, his son Prince Caprice, and the court's astronomer Microscope, who designs the device that gets them to the moon. There they meet with the "selenites," who include King Cosmos, his wife Poppotte, and their daughter Fantasia. The selenites live by different values than the earthlings: they don't know love, alcohol, or apples. Fantasia is fed an apple by Caprice, and this makes her fall in love with him; Cosmos is offered hard cider that perverts his thoughts and makes him fall madly in love with his wife, but his wife, offered the same liquor, falls in love with Microscope. Cosmos sentences the earthlings to death by imprisoning them in an extinct volcano. Both Poppotte and Fantasia accompany their new lovers inside the volcano, which erupts, causing a rain of fire and ash and an explosion that brings everyone back to the surface of the moon. As the operetta ends, the selenites and the earthlings contemplate the *clair de terre*—light of the rising Earth as seen from the moon.

In 1917, most of the prints of Méliès's films were melted down by the French military to make shoe heels. His films resurfaced only in the late 1920s thanks to his surrealist devotees. These included Jean-Placide Mauclaire, director of Studio 28, an avant-garde cinema theatre that showed Buñuel and Dalí's *L'âge d'or* and exhibited surrealist painters, and Jean George Auriol and Paul Gilson, who dedicated the fourth issue (October 15, 1929) of Gallimard's surrealist tribune for cinema *La Revue du cinéma* to Méliès. With Auriol editor-in-chief, *La Revue du cinéma* (1928–32) remained in the avant-garde through the 1940s (1946–49), when young André Bazin joined the team. In 1951, a year after Auriol's death, Bazin founded together with Jacques Doniol-Valcroze *Cahiers du cinéma* to continue Auriol's *La Revue du cinéma*. Surrealism's deep history goes backwards to Méliès and forward with Bazin.

Méliès was twice a predecessor for the surrealists: he put forth the reign of the imagination by making the impossible possible on screen and he was a committed Dreyfusard having created the film series *The Dreyfus Affair* (1899). Showing on the cover Méliès as Mephistophélès in *The Infernal Cake Walk* (1903), the fourth issue of *La Revue du cinéma* opened with Paul Gilson's article "Georges Méliès, Inventeur" and continued with a 1907 text by Méliès, "Les Vues Cinématographiques" followed by Méliès's script for *Voyage à travers l'impossible*, complete with a rich collection of Méliès's drawings, photographs and stills from his films. Méliès's rediscovered films were shown at the gala in Méliès's honor on December 16, 1929, at the Salle Pleyel in Paris organized by Mauclaire's Studio 28, to whom Méliès first thanked in his address. Beloved by the surrealists, Méliès stayed a major reference for them. One wonders whether Breton's 1923 poetry volume *Clair de terre* takes its title from Méliès's iconic image shown in a key moment in

INTRODUCTION

Le Voyage dans la lune: a shining Planet Earth rises to the surprise of the earthlings visiting the moon. Among Méliès's drawings for *Le Voyage dans la lune*, there is one on which Méliès wrote the title "Arrivée dans la lune. Le clair de terre," drawing reproduced in the 1929 issue of *La Revue du cinéma* dedicated to Méliès. To this day no one has been able to trace the book of astronomy that Breton cites in the epigraph to his volume: "The earth shines in the sky like an enormous luminary among the stars. Our globe projects onto the moon an intense earthlight [*clair de terre*]." Born in 1896, Breton could have seen Méliès's film as a child; it was screened from 1902 through 1908 to great acclaim both in France and abroad, especially in the US, where it circulated through piracy—which is why Méliès decided to open a New York branch of his Star Film Company to suppress future piracy of his work. In 1902, Breton was six, and in 1908 he was twelve, just the right age for a little boy—like the one in Scorsese's film and Selznick's book—to be impressed for life by the device that brought dreams into our everyday reality.

Breton's *Clair de terre* included five dreams together with poems written in 1921–2 published in the proto-surrealist magazine *Littérature*, alongside a portrait of Breton by Picasso. Breton described the portrait in a letter to his then wife, Simone Kahn, as a "portrait à l'œil terrible": "The print of my portrait is marvelous: the eye is a bit terrible, but it's just about like that" (*Lettres à Simone Kahn*, 188). No doubt Picasso was replying to Méliès's sketch for the film poster *Le Voyage dans la lune* that showed what became the iconic image from this film. Scorsese too uses Méliès's poster in his film, not only as a tribute to the first dreamer as filmmaker, but also as a metaphor for the director's eye and the round light of the projection camera, and ultimately the dreamer's eye. To reinforce the fact that the metaphor *clair de terre* is indebted to Méliès, Breton personally designed the letters on the cover of the 1923 first edition of his book. He took pains to make them look like white letters on a black background—like the letters seen on a screen in the darkness of the cinema theater.

Comparing Méliès's sketch to Picasso's pencil portrait of Breton (Figure 0.2), we see two "*yeux terribles*": one is the eye of the man in the moon who is the moon itself, when his other eye is hit by the capsule that carries the earthlings to the moon; the other eye is wide open in terror: the terror of the unknown. Picasso represents Breton in profile, with only the right eye visible, wide open onto the unknown that only he can see. Méliès the magician-filmmaker, and Breton the poet and the father of surrealism, were among the first visionaries whose "œil terrible" could clearly see *le clair de terre* that the future held: a promise of the unknown made known, impossible voyages made possible, and dreams turned real. In the scene in *Hugo* that recreates the 1929 gala held in his honor, Méliès invites us to follow him into the world of his recently restored films: "My friends, I address you all tonight, as you truly are: wizards, mermaids, travelers, adventurers, magicians. Come and dream with me!"

FIGURE 0.2 a & b *Poster for Méliès's film* Le Voyage dans la lune *(1902) and Pablo Picasso, detail from* Portrait of André Breton *(1923)*

Time itself is the artist that can make the invisible visible through its magic lantern: "These were puppets bathed in the immaterial colours of the years, puppets which exteriorized Time, Time which by habit is made invisible and to become visible seeks bodies, which, wherever it finds them, it seizes upon, to display its magic lantern upon them" (*Time Regained*, 342). This revelation doesn't come from a filmmaker but from Marcel Proust, who is already creating the cinematic literature of the future:

> The writer's work is merely a kind of optical instrument which he offers to the reader to enable him to discern what, without the book, he would perhaps never have perceived in himself ... In order to read with understanding many readers require to read in their own particular fashion, and the author must not be indignant at this; on the contrary, he must leave the reader all possible liberty, saying to him: "Look for yourself, and try whether you see best with this lens or that one or this other one."
>
> *Time Regained*, 322

With their multiple lenses, the filmmakers discussed in the following chapters will bring back the world's time, each in their own particular way.

1

From Automaton to Movie Camera

Méliès, Selznick, Scorsese

Since 1993 *Vanity Fair* has asked celebrities to take a life questionnaire of the kind that Proust liked to pose to his friends and even to strangers. In March 2010, when *Hugo* was in pre-production, it was Martin Scorsese's turn. Asked "If you could change one thing about yourself, what would it be?" Scorsese replied: "I would like to learn to read faster." His greatest regret? "Not reading more when I was younger" ("Proust Questionnaire"). Scorsese had had little exposure to literature growing up; his parents hadn't even completed grammar school. "I'm forcing myself to read as much as possible now. I'm sort of catching up on books that I should have read twenty years ago" (*Interviews*, 128). He has constantly rejected films that take literature as an elitist sign of distinction used decoratively—"I guess I'm still cowed a little by the tyranny of art with a capital A. And there has always been the tyranny of the word over the image: anything that's written has got to be better" (*Interviews*, 127). And yet Scorsese has always understood, like André Bazin, the mixed nature of genuine cinema, and he has always sought an organic understanding of the relation between literature and film.

If Pheng Cheah is right and the *world* in "world literature" should be a normative and not merely descriptive concept (*What Is a World?*, 2), then world art—be it literature or film—should do more than just copy the world around us. It should make it into something better. Cheah criticizes the field of world literature studies for operating with the *world* as a spatial rather than temporal category, thus diminishing its revolutionary potential. In a film, this visionary process materializes in the question: who or what is the camera that sees the world into being, and how does it intervene in the world? We will begin with Martin Scorsese's *Hugo* (2011), which meditates on this very theme, presenting cinema as the art of making dreams real—an art that belonged for a much longer time to literature.

Hugo brings to the screen Brian Selznick's graphic novel *The Invention of Hugo Cabret* (2007), which tells the story of a twelve-year-old who lives with his father in Paris in the late 1920s. Hugo's father works in a museum and one day stumbles upon an automaton that he and his son try to fix, but one night a fire breaks out at the museum and Hugo's father dies. The boy is left in the care of his uncle Claude, a drunkard who tends the clocks in the Gare Montparnasse and who takes Hugo to live with him there. Claude then dies, leaving Hugo alone, mending the clocks and desperately trying to fix the broken automaton, hoping that it contains a secret message from his father. In the same train station there's a booth that sells all sorts of mechanical toys, from which Hugo steals parts for his automaton. One day the seller, an old man by the name Georges Méliès, catches him red-handed, and on searching Hugo's pockets he finds a strange notebook that Hugo has inherited from his father with all sorts of drawings of the automaton's mechanism. Méliès confiscates Hugo's notebook and makes him work in his toy booth to earn it back. As the film unfolds, Hugo befriends Méliès's goddaughter Isabelle, who adores books just as Hugo adores going to the movies.

With their budding adolescent romance, Isabelle and Hugo are a metaphor for the love between literature and film that's at the heart of both Selznick's book and Scorsese's film. Through their combined knowledge of books and movies, Isabelle and Hugo discover that Georges Méliès had been a magician and illusionist who had started making movies, but when technology changed and World War I broke out he fell into oblivion, reduced to his present condition, while his celluloid films have been melted down to make shoe heels. Together, Isabelle and Hugo discover how to make the automaton work, and the secret message it contains is a visual one: the automaton can draw the poster for Méliès's 1902 film *Le Voyage dans la lune*, and can also sign his creator's name.

Selznick presents the automaton as a creation of Méliès himself, and with the ability both to write and to draw pictures, it became an intermediary between Méliès's interest in theatre and painting, and his idea of perfecting his magic tricks in a new medium. With the help of a fictitious film historian named René Tabard, who is the author of a book entitled *Inventer le rêve: L'histoire des premiers films*, Isabelle and Hugo manage to restore the real identity of the filmmaker and illusionist Georges Méliès, and the film ends with a gala in honor of the filmmaker whose films first made dreams real. At the gala, several clips from Méliès's most renowned films are shown. At the end, Hugo is adopted by Méliès and grows up to become a magician himself, but also a writer: Selznick attributes his book to Hugo's mature self, now named Professor Alcofrisbas. *The Invention of Hugo Cabret* itself isn't really a graphic novel, but more a cross between a work of literature and a silent film. Every page of text has a black frame, just like a film screen in a theatre on which a silent film is projected.

Some film scholars have been too hasty in writing off the idea of films as making dreams real: "*Hugo* is let down by its script, which lapses into Hollywood cliché … There is too much breathless talk of having an 'adventure' and cinema being a 'special place', a place 'where dreams are made'. Are dreams really made by the movie business, like so many cars rolling off a production line?" (Daniel Trilling, "Dream Tickets," 44). Quite the contrary. Scorsese, a subtle reader of literature and a film historian, presents us with a very different framing of the idea that films are dreams brought on screen, as he crosses the boundaries between literature and film, and between popular culture and high art. As Guerric DeBona has said, "The very social construction of 'Martin Scorsese' as film director/scholar/ historian would help grant an aura of authorship to *Hugo*" ("*Hugo*," 460). "Scorsese also joins the pantheon of modernist authors like James Joyce and Ernest Hemingway whose names have become synonymous with scholarly prestige" (467).

To bring a world into being in a normative rather than descriptive sense as Pheng Cheah would have it is no small thing. To understand a revolutionary film's world involves answering four questions that range from the general to the very specific: To what time and space does its world vision belong? Whose is the eye that sees this world into being? What kind of relation is there between the eye and the world it creates? What is the filming camera that makes this relation possible and what role does it play in recreating the world anew? In the case of Scorsese's *Hugo*, the answers to these questions reenact a fascinating story about the origins of cinema in the Parisian avant-garde circles of poets, painters, photographers, and filmmakers associated with surrealism. This story sheds new light on the complex back-and-forth relationship between literature and the visual arts and provides an answer to the question at the heart of this book: How can we regain a time past?

Films are Dreams Made Real:
The Avant-garde Origins of an Idea

The idea of film as dreams made real has often been dismissed as a Hollywood cliché, so how could it present us with a normative vision of the world? An important problem for the field of world cinema has been the place of Hollywood within its object of study. If in the 1980s and 1990s Third World cinema and then world cinemas in the plural were defined against the generally described "Hollywood production," more recent approaches include Holly-wood as an important node in world cinema. The "polycentric approach to film studies" (*Theorizing World Cinema*, xxii) includes Hollywood as "one part amongst many" in a view of world cinema that means "cinema of the world" (Paul Cooke, *World Cinema's 'Dialogues' with Hollywood*, 8). But what makes a film a Hollywood film? Is it the studio, the producers, the director, the script, the cast? How "Hollywood" is the cliché that cinema is the factory of dreams? A very different story emerges from a closer look into the context in which the idea of cinema as dreamworld was born.

The story of Hollywood itself actually begins in Paris, with the success of Méliès's 1902 film *Le Voyage dans la lune*, which transformed cinema from a scientific curiosity into something rich and strange. His secret lay in mixing magic and literature with the new medium of film. As the film historian and surrealist Georges Sadoul has noted, "thanks to the story borrowed from Jules Verne (and Wells) cinema becomes a spectacle" in Méliès's film ("Notes," 100). Its success led to the opening of the first cinema in Los Angeles in October 1902, which showed it in a plagiarized version, and hundreds of bootleg copies of the film were soon made by Thomas Edison's company. As Sadoul points out, "Méliès wanted to sue these pirates who reproduced his work without his authorization or paying for the copyright. He was told that foreign companies weren't protected by copyright in the USA. The only thing he could do was open his own office in New York to compete with his rivals" (101). Shakespeare's "each thing's a thief" (*Timon of Athens* IV:3) takes on a whole different meaning when it comes to the history that made Hollywood possible.

Long before Hollywood took up the theme, dreams had enjoyed a long history in the Romantic era as the logic beyond our everyday perception of the reality around us. The alternative logic of dreams took on new forms with the birth of photography and then of cinema, and became central in the Paris of Proust and the surrealists. Following in this tradition, Scorsese sees the dream as key to the nature of film: "this idea of movies and dreams I think has been overworked to a certain extent. But . . . it does feel like when Hugo in the film tells Isabelle his father described the film as like seeing your dreams in the middle of the day. Where your mind goes during the day, if you could translate that into any kind of artistic form or endeavor and it succeeds—to a certain extent—that's a wonderful thing" (*Interviews*, 219). In order to develop this theme, Scorsese locates it in a specific time and place—the Paris of the surrealists. "We took aspects of French visual culture around the late '20s, early '30s, the Dadaists, the short films they made, Man Ray and Léger and René Clair's comedies, *Under the Roofs of Paris* and *À Nous la liberté* and created a Paris that wasn't really Paris. It was an American's impression of Paris. As a joke, I kept asking, 'How are we going to know it's Paris?' Whatever the angle was, I'd say, 'Put the Eiffel Tower in there!'" (Bowe, "Martin Scorsese's Magical *Hugo*"). In the US, "Dada" and "surrealism" pass for partial synonyms, an idea that entered American culture as early as the 1936 exhibition "Fantastic Art, Dada, Surrealism" organized by Alfred H. Barr, Jr. at the MoMA, but it was the surrealists, not the Dadaists, who made the films that Scorsese has in mind. Significantly, the exhibition catalog put together by Alfred Barr includes a series of "Fantastic or Surrealist Films" that opens with Méliès's *Hydrothérapie Fantastique* (1900) and *Le Voyage dans la lune* (1902) and closes with Luis Buñuel and Salvador Dalí's *Un Chien andalou* (1929).

In the absence of a thorough knowledge of the visual culture that Scorsese alludes to in *Hugo*, critics sometimes write off the film as "an imagined, artificial vision of Paris of the 1930s full of golden light and Gothic statuary" (Annett, "The Nostalgic," 174). For an eye trained in art history, though, Scorsese's vision of Paris isn't the product of his nostalgic imagination but has direct antecedents. Aspects of the French visual culture of the 1920s and 1930s that Scorsese used included surrealist photographs and paintings or drawings for film sets. The series of photographs *Paris by Night* by one of the most renowned surrealist photographers, Brassaï (Gyula Halász), featuring a magically lit Eiffel Tower, provided Scorsese with one of his most striking representations of Paris, when Hugo takes Méliès's goddaughter Isabelle up in a clock tower and shows her Paris seen through the clock's dial. More subtly, Scorsese uses the work of another surrealist photographer of Hungarian origin, who joined the surrealist group in 1925 in Paris. André Kertész's 1929 daytime photo of the *Eiffel Tower* shows the tower from an uncanny angle, featuring only one of the tower's legs (Figure 1.1a). As a surrealist, he's interested in the ghostly apparition of objects, so his focus is on the semicircular shadow projected by the tower's artistic ironwork, shaped like a clock dial's sections, framing the people walking under the tower. When Hugo shows Isabelle Paris at night, Scorsese has them look through the giant clock dial at a landscape that includes the Eiffel Tower, metatextually turning his camera onto Kertész and his view of Paris (Figure 1.1b). Scorsese's cinematography makes Hugo and Isabelle echo Kertész's people framed by the ghostly projection of the tower's ironwork that measures a surrealist temporality.

Scorsese also used Brassaï's *Pont Neuf* (1932) and *Brouillard Avenue* (1934) to recreate the magical atmosphere of the outdoor scenes, especially in the stark contrast between darkness and artificial light. Another photograph, *Lovers in a Parisian Café near Place d'Italie* (1932), which shows a pair of lovers about to kiss reflected in two corner mirrors, comes to life in Scorsese's unlikely pair of lovers (the police inspector and the flower girl) reflected in the atmosphere of the avant-garde circles that gather in the train station café. Among them, we glimpse James Joyce (Robert Gill) and Salvador Dalí (Ben Addis), closely modeled on iconic photographs of them at the time.

Scorsese's visual sources include also the surrealist René Magritte's *False Mirror* (1929), which shows an immense eye, with the sky reflected in its iris, which Scorsese turns into a metaphor for the director's eye that reflects the world. Most significantly, Magritte's *Time transfixed* (1938) shows a locomotive coming out of a fireplace, beneath a clock reflected in a mirror

FIGURE 1.1 a & b *André Kertész*, Eiffel Tower *(1929), and still from* Hugo.

over the mantlepiece; this image stands in Scorsese's *Hugo* for the metaphor of film as a train that takes you back into the history of film—with the Lumière brothers' first film, *Arrival of a Train at La Ciotat* (1895) and Méliès's own response to it, *Arrival of a Train at Vincennes Station* (1896)—or into the future.

Scorsese's interest in the art of the surrealists, their predecessors and followers, went back to his childhood: "I remember in third grade being shown Van Gogh's *The Starry Night* and that led us, me and a few friends, to go up to the Metropolitan Museum of Art. We were fascinated by Dalí, and then Mondrian later at the Museum of Modern Art" (*Interviews*, 227). He had used paintings for his films well before *Hugo*. For *The Last Temptation of Christ* (1988), "we had Caravaggio, of course, La Tour for the light, and Hieronymus Bosch, whose painting of Jesus carrying the cross we actually copied directly at 120 frames. . . . In *The Age of Innocence* we even replicated paintings, one by Whistler and one by Sargent. There's a scene in the ball at the beginning of the film where the camera tracks and pans, and we literally place—for our own enjoyment—figures from the paintings in the compositions as the camera just went by them" (227–8).

Seen from the Moon: *In My Mind's Eye*

But whose world is it that we're seeing in *Hugo*? Who or what is the eye that engenders the world we enter? To answer these questions, we need to understand *Hugo* through its multiple meta-layers. Scorsese creates a complex equation of authorial masks that overlay Hugo, Georges Méliès, and implicitly Scorsese himself into versions of the same self. Scorsese chose to pay a tribute to the forefather of cinema because he found in him a direct precursor. Not only was Méliès an illusionist who discovered what the new medium could do; he was also a great reader of world literature. And it is in Méliès's literary references in *Le Voyage dans la lune* that we should look for the inception of the filmmaker's vision. As Georges Sadoul has written, Méliès was proud to be called "the Jules Verne of cinema" ("Notes," 101). In addition to Verne and to Offenbach's operetta based on Verne's tale, Méliès's *Le Voyage dans la lune* drew on H.G. Wells's *The First Men in the Moon* (1901), which had come out in French translation a few months before he made his film (Sadoul, "Notes,"100). As Wells's narrator reads about Mr. Bedford's voyage through outer space, he feels that he is and isn't himself:

> "This is your world, and you are Bedford" . . . But the doubts within me could still argue: "It is not you that is reading, it is Bedford—but *you are not Bedford*, you know. That's just where the mistake comes in."
> "Confound it!" I cried, "and if I am not Bedford, what *am* I?"
> But in that direction no light was forthcoming, though the strangest fancies came drifting into my brain, queer remote suspicions, like shadows seen from far away. . . . Do you know, I had a sort of idea that really I was something quite outside not only the world, but all worlds, and out of space and time, and that this poor Bedford was just a peephole through which I looked at life. . .
>
> *The First Men in the Moon*, author's emphasis

Scorsese is engaging both with Méliès and with Wells's novel by making this cinematic description the very heart of his film. More than in Selznick's silent film-flipbook, Scorsese makes Hugo the heart of the giant mechanism that is both a filming and projection camera, operated by God as the ultimate dreamer. One night, Hugo dreams of being run over by a train, and he wakes from this nightmare into another dream in which he has turned into an automaton. Hugo then wakes up to hear the ticking of his own heart, which overlaps with the ticking of the clock next to his bed. But this isn't the actual clock at all; it's the tick-tock of the movie projector that is Hugo's body. We are all filmmakers, both Méliès and Scorsese seem to tell us. Like Wells's Bedford, Hugo is a peephole through which the Director-God looks at life, like a cameraman through his camera.

With "a film preservation consciousness" (Scorsese, "Foreword," 15), Scorsese knows that Brian Selznick's book *The Invention of Hugo Cabret* can function as a flipbook or an animated photograph, an aspect noted by scholars who have looked at Selznick (Bullen et al., "Cinema and the Book"). If the drawings on Selznick's pages 38–45 are flipped at full speed, we see a camera movement from a panoramic view of Méliès's toy booth in the Gare Montparnasse to a closeup that zooms in on his face, then on his eye (Figure 1.2a). The next two pages show a clock dial, and then we cut to Hugo looking through his clock dial at Méliès. This shift of perspective is only apparent; the zoom-in movement of the camera juxtaposes Méliès's eye and the clock dial (Figure 1.2b), implying that it's literally Méliès's eye, so burdened with the passage of time that sent him and his films into oblivion. Then on an even closer closeup of the clock dial, we see the minute hand pointing to the number 5 on the dial (Figure 1.2c). It's the index finger of the filmmaker—a Prometheus or Michelangelo's Adam in the Sistine Chapel's genesis scene, as the film later shows—pointing at the "cryptogram of reality," to quote Breton's phrase from *Nadja*. Hugo himself watches Méliès from behind the opening of the 5 in the clock dial. If treated like a flipbook, Selznick's book reveals to us a secret: Hugo lives inside Méliès's eye and from there directs the film we're watching.

This reading that both Selznick and Scorsese invite us to make is mirrored in Méliès's address at the 1929 gala that aimed to restore Méliès to his rightful place as the forefather of cinema. Scorsese recreates this gala at the end of his movie, when Méliès declares: "I am standing before you tonight because of a very brave young man, who saw a broken machine, and against all odds, he fixed it; it was the kindest magic trick that ever I've seen." While he is referring to Hugo's fixing his camera-like automaton, Méliès is in fact talking about himself: brought down by old age and the oblivion cast on him and his magical movies, he had been reduced to a broken mechanism, like the giant old clock that is Hugo's home. From there, it was the boy who repaired the automaton as a way to bring back the past, connecting with his dead father. The result was to rekindle the light behind Méliès's (camera) eye, bringing him and his films back to life through the surreal logic of childhood that makes the impossible possible and can turn back time.

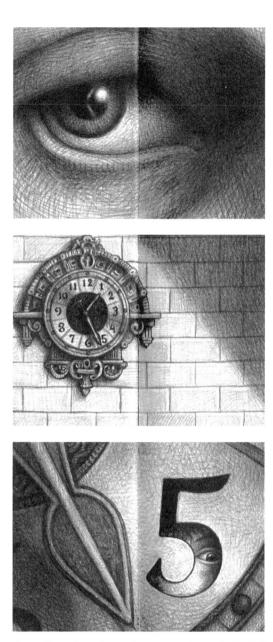

FIGURE 1.2 a, b, c *Drawings shown in consecutive order in Brian Selznick's* The Invention of Hugo Cabret *(2007)*.

Scorsese suggests this reading in two ways. Every time we plunge into the past with Hugo and he remembers his dead father, the color changes—"The autochrome had a wonderful look; it looked like Impressionist painting, and so we tried to get that particularly in the flashback scenes" (Shaw interview)—and in addition a strange sound is heard from behind Hugo. In the first scene that brings back the automaton, we initially see Hugo, crying, in a light that comes from somewhere above and behind him. The mysterious sound and what looks initially like a bluish, silvery moonlight are revealed to be emanating from the film projector in a movie theatre. We realize that we've entered Hugo's theatre of memory, as the automaton, like his father, materializes out of nowhere in front of him. The ghost in the film of his memory comes alive. Significantly, Scorsese makes a point of showing us the *direction* in which the mechanism of the film projector is rotating: like a clock that moves backwards, it makes time go back.

Then when Hugo takes Isabelle all the way up in his giant clock to show her Paris at night, the camera is above and behind them, as though some director from a larger world were watching them and the world through their eyes. Failing to understand the implicit equation between the moon and the filmmaker's eye, as well as the literary origin of this intertext in H.G. Wells's novel, Sandra Annett is puzzled by Scorsese's use of overhead shots: "there are also flagrantly unmotivated objective overhead shots of Hugo, which are not necessary to establish point of view or even narrative tension" ("The Nostalgic," 173). But that's exactly what the high angle is meant to do: to suggest the point of view from which the film is being told. Just as in the flashback scene, Scorsese uses a subtle cinematic trick to show how time is reversed in his film. In Selznick's book, as they look at Paris from behind the clock dial, Hugo tells Isabelle that they are both part of a giant mechanism: "machines never have any extra parts. They have the exact number and parts they need. So I figure if the entire world is a big machine, I have to be here for some reason. And that means you have to be here for some reason, too" (*The Invention*, 378). As we come to learn, Isabelle has the magical heart-shaped key that brings the dead automaton back to life, so that she and Hugo together form the heart of this mechanism that is the director's camera. Seen from behind the clock dial, they look as though they inhabit the eye of the director who is filming the very movie we're watching (Figure 1.3a).

As in the flashback scene, we hear the sound of the clock's escapement mechanism, which becomes the sound of the hand-cranked movie projector. On the window of the clock dial, just between Hugo and Isabelle—who are engaged in discussing the world as a mechanism—we see dimly projected the counterclockwise movement of a clock wheel or of the film projector. Scorsese shows us through a series of juxtapositions of similarly shaped objects in the same frame—a surrealist technique brought to perfection by Dalí—that we are inside the very mechanism of the camera that is both filming and projecting *Hugo*. The eye-shaped pendulum that forms part of the escapement mechanism is juxtaposed on the film projector's reflection on the clock dial window and ultimately on the shape and color of the moon in the same frame.

For Scorsese, the moon becomes the light of the film projector and of the director-god's eye turned onto us that seems to project Hugo and Isabelle themselves. We can see the technical phrase "escapement mechanism" as a metaphor for what the world of his film actually is: an escapement, Proust's *l'hors du temps* (the outside of time) and André Breton's pun on Proust's phrase, *l'or du temps*, "the gold of time." Unlike in Selznick's novel, when Scorsese's camera moves into a closeup of Méliès's eye we don't see a clock dial before us, but rather a *mirrored* one that has taken the place of Méliès' pupil (Figure 1.3b). A clock that moves backwards and that can make the lost time of his forgotten movies come back once more. A time that can make him young again through the logic praised by the surrealists from the first manifesto: the logic of childhood.

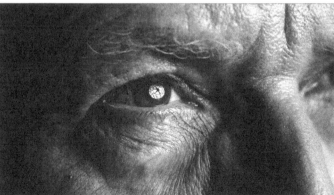

FIGURE 1.3 a & b *Hugo showing Isabelle Paris at night; closeup of Georges Méliès's pupil. Stills from* Hugo.

Rather than a nostalgic elegy for the beginning of film, as scholars such as Ian Christie have described it ("The Illusionist"), *Hugo* behaves like a surrealist object: it opens prophetically toward the future, when this past can be reborn in a different guise. When Méliès says to the police inspector who's been trying to capture Hugo to send him to an orphanage: "Monsieur, this child belongs to me," he means it literally. Hugo *is* Méliès turned young again. He is a magician and also a great reader of literature, as Selznick has Méliès give Hugo the name of one of his recurrent film characters: Professor Alcofrisbas. But this name echoes the anagrammatic penname with which Rabelais signs his *Gargantua* and *Pantagruel* ("Alcofribas Nasier, Abstractor of the Quintessence"), a reference that has been missed to date both by film scholars and by scholars of intermediality. The roots of cinema run into a deeper past than its own history; they go all the way into the imaginative literature written by revolutionaries of language, magicians of the word such as Rabelais.

Scorsese turns Méliès young under our very eyes, using a magic trick learned from Méliès himself. At the gala that brings Méliès back to life, just after he invites us to "Come and dream with me," he puts on his illusionist's hat and instantly his black-and-white films start showing behind him. Seeming to reach out for a blackboard behind the curtain, he instantly becomes a younger Méliès who draws himself on the board. Through a magic trick that literally happens "behind the magician's curtain" or off camera, Scorsese edits into his own movie the beginning of Méliès's film *The Untamable Whiskers* (1904). There, Méliès reaches out for a blackboard off camera on which he first draws and then writes words that come to life on screen. In films like *Le Livre magique* (1900), *La Lanterne magique* (1903) and *Le Palais des mille et une nuits* (1905), Méliès was bringing together into the new media of film the visionary power of literature, the secrets of illusionism, and the history of automata as memory devices.

With *Le Livre magique* (*The Magic Book*) we are in a magician's studio, equipped with magic books, a pendulum clock, and another clock on the wall. The magician displays an immense book whose characters he brings to life by making them come out from the pages under our very eyes. The characters get into a fight, and the magician forces them back into the book, even though the book itself seems to have a will of its own and falls on him, making him disappear. But lo and behold, the magician enters the stage again and carries the reluctant book away with him, as he is the god of the world we've briefly seen come to life on screen. Similarly, *La Lanterne magique* shows how a dream reality is made real by projecting images in the dark with a magic lantern, as Proust will later do in the opening of *Swann's Way*. As Dominique Jullien notes, for Proust it's the book of *A Thousand and One Nights* that's a magic lantern (*Proust et ses modèles*, 181). In Méliès's film, the magic lantern's images include the filmmaker himself, who also operates the magic lantern, a brilliant metacinematic twist that

Scorsese too performs when he uses André Kertész's photo of the Eiffel Tower and turns his camera onto Kertész's photo camera. Similarly in the gala scene, by turning his color film into Méliès's black-and-white *The Untamable Whiskers*, Scorsese reverses cinematic history. The secret in making time come back, Scorsese tells us, lies in the director's eye that is a reversed clock dial.

Voyeurism and Cinematic Imagination: Proust, Méliès, Scorsese

It made all the sense in the world when Scorsese remarked in an interview that "This is what actually got me doing the film: the way he [Hugo] is looking through the clock" (Scorsese, Stahl interview). André Bazin noted that Jean Cocteau believed that "cinema is an event seen through a keyhole" ("Theatre and Cinema I," 92). But Cocteau wasn't the first to understand the world of artistic imagination in this way; he had learned this perspective from a very close friend. Proust's filmic imagination defined literature through analogy with all sorts of optical devices—magnifying glass, magic lantern, telescope, peep box—that made him a forerunner of surrealism and cinema, an insight that Raúl Ruiz had developed a few years before Scorsese in his film of *Le Temps retrouvé*, as we will see in chapter 5.

It was Proust's perspective on the world that made him a virtual filmmaker: his voyeurism, his spying on the world from a distance, a world that he analyzes paradoxically as if through a microscope or a magnifying glass. Unseen by anyone yet seeing everything, Proust was a follower of Flaubert, who wanted to be present in his creation like God in nature, omnipresent but invisible. It's significant that Proust introduces his most striking scene of voyeurism—the whipping of the Baron de Charlus in the secret hotel during World War I—directly after Marcel identifies with Harun al-Rashid in *A Thousand and One Nights*: "losing myself gradually in the network of these dark streets, I thought of the Caliph Harun al-Rashid going in search of adventures in the hidden quarters of Baghdad" (*Time Regained*, 173). Long before Hugo would spy on Méliès from his clock in the train station, it was Proust's Marcel who spied on the world around him, in the darkness, like a filmmaker or a viewer in a cinema: "From where I stood in the darkness I could, without being seen, observe a few soldiers and two men. . . . the whole scene, in the midst of this peaceful and threatened night, was like a dream or a fairy-tale, so that it was at once with the pride of an emissary of justice and the rapture of a poet that I at length, my mind made up, entered the hotel" (*Time Regained*, 176–7).

The magic of spying through peep holes or keyholes onto forbidden or marvelous worlds is something encountered not only in Proust, but in

Scorsese's take on Méliès's films. This voyeuristic magic can be traced back to a common literary source: *A Thousand and One Nights*. Early films such as Méliès's 1905 *Le Palais des mille et une nuits* showed that the new medium could embody all the magic of these stories. Méliès's film was soon followed by Ferdinand Zecca's *Ali Baba et les quarante voleurs* (1905) and Albert Capellani's *Aladin, ou la lampe merveilleuse* (1906), with many others to follow.

A close reader of Proust, with whom he shares much more than asthma and a passion for reading, Scorsese reads the cinematic character of *A Thousand and One Nights* through him as well as through Méliès. With Proust, Scorsese shares the poetics that makes both write that their material simply "comes to them" without their control or will, a phrase that Lewis Carroll and Breton too used for their literary creations with an automatic inception. "Images would come to me as I was reading books or listening to music," Scorsese remembers about his time studying film at NYU (*Interviews*, 137). Similarly, Proust's book *comes to him* from his own past, in the absence of his control or knowledge: "And I understood that all these materials for a work of literature were simply my past life. I understood that they had come to me. . . . Like the seed, I should be able to die once the plant had developed and I began to perceive that I had lived for the sake of the plant without knowing it" (*Time Regained*, 304). There's only a small step from here to the surrealists' automatic creation.

Proust's identification with Harun al-Rashid's voyeurism makes its way into Hugo's relating to the world outside always from behind a screen, through a split or through the grates that let in enough light for us to see a closeup of Hugo's eye, filming the world outside. Secondly, Proust found in *A Thousand and One Nights* the magic spell for bringing back his lost past: "the oriental image inscribes the world of childhood in the present moment . . . This is also why the *A Thousand and One Nights* will become the privileged image of the signs of art," writes Dominique Jullien (*Proust et ses modèles*, 48). Sitting in the Guermantes' library, Marcel writes,

> I wiped my mouth with the napkin . . . and instantly, as though I had been the character in the *Arabian Nights* who unwittingly accomplishes the very rite which can cause to appear, visible to him alone, a docile genie ready to convey him to a great distance, a new vision of azure passed before my eyes . . . I thought that the servant had just opened the window on to the beach and that all things invited me to go down and stroll along the promenade while the tide was high.
>
> *Time Regained*, 258

Inspired by the same *A Thousand and One Nights* and then by Méliès, Selznick worked with a similar effect, creating motion through a succession of drawings that brings a static object to life. Sometimes he practices the flipbook effect on successive pages, but also more interestingly at a distance. Thus he places at the very heart of his book a drawing he makes of Méliès's poster for *Le Voyage dans la lune*, showing the man in the moon whose eye is hit by the space voyagers' capsule. This image relates to the opening and closing of the book, which shows respectively a full moon and a waning moon, and tells us that the man in the moon is the film director Méliès. He is like Hugo's friend Etienne, who gets a job as a cameraman and who wears an eye patch, making him perfect for the job: "Having an eye patch actually makes it easier to look through a camera—I don't have to close one eye like everyone else," Etienne tells Hugo (*The Invention*, 343).

Scorsese takes the flipbook effect one step further, and like Proust he reenacts the past, in a scene when Hugo and Isabelle discover a box of Méliès's drawings for his sets and films in a secret drawer. Isabelle accidentally drops the box on the floor, and dozens of drawings fly out of the box by themselves, miraculously coming to life: the spitting fire dragon, the fairy turning into a butterfly and spreading her wings, and the poster for *Le Voyage dans la lune*. As this last drawing comes into focus, Méliès himself opens the door, his face revealed beneath the face of the man in the moon. The drawing has come to life and a new age of the magic object has just opened up.

As Proust's Marcel approaches the end—of his life and of his book, which are one and the same to him—he identifies with a second and more important character from the *Arabian Nights*, Scheherazade: "If I worked, it would be only at night. But I should need many nights, a hundred perhaps, or even a thousand. And I should live in the anxiety of not knowing whether the master of my destiny might not prove less indulgent than the Sultan Shahriyar, whether in the morning, when I broke off my story, he would consent to a further reprieve and permit me to resume my narrative the following evening" (*Time Regained*, 324). Unlike Selznick's book, which tells the story from Hugo's perspective, *Hugo* is told from the point of view of Isabelle.

We could attribute this choice to the scriptwriter, John Logan, with whom Martin Scorsese also collaborated on *The Aviator*. However, as Logan admitted, it was Scorsese who sent him Selznick's novel to turn into a script, and they worked very closely on every change he made to the original. While the Dickensian tone and atmosphere of the film are Logan's contribution, the intertextuality with the history of film and of literature beyond Dickens is Scorsese's. As Logan said in an interview, "of course Marty Scorsese is the world's greatest cineaste. In his head he carries an archive of practically every film ever made. When we were working, astounding references would sort of tumble out of him" (Eagan interview). As his close reading of Méliès shows, Scorsese is a walking archive not only of the history of film, but also of the literature that went into these films.

Méliès's disappearing act became his trademark and appeared in almost all his films, and Scorsese could have chosen any of them to illustrate how magic tricks and illusions moved from the stage to the screen. But it was *Le*

Palais des mille et une nuits (1905) that he chose to recreate Méliès's disappearing act on screen in *Hugo*. In that film Méliès showed how he was also a writer in his own right, not only a filmmaker. He wrote an intertextual script that takes its cue from the Middle Eastern collection of tales without reproducing any of them, but rather creating something new. Méliès tells the story of the penniless Prince Sourire who wants to wed Princess Indigo, whose hand in marriage was promised to another suitor. With the aid of the goddess Siva, Sourire finds his way through a magic forest and a crystal grotto where he fights strange beings including phantom skeletons, and it's here that Méliès plays his disappearing trick on the skeletons Sourire fights with. As in *A Thousand and One Nights*, with the help of superior beings who love a pure and honest heart, Sourire is rewarded after all his trials with the hand of his beloved Indigo.

In his metatextual dialogue with Méliès, Scorsese engages simultaneously with Méliès's source text as well as with his film. Scorsese recreates Méliès's set for *Le Palais des mille et une nuits* and illustrates Méliès's discovery of the way to show the disappearing and reappearing act on screen. Méliès cut one frame, making two frames appear in succession: first one where Sourire and his men fight the skeletons, then a second where the skeletons have been removed. When the film is played, the skeletons disappear as if by magic. Ian Christie has described Scorsese's recreation of Méliès's iconic trick as lamenting the loss of a certain type of cinema: "*Hugo* also pays an elegiac tribute to the vanishing world of the film strip with a close-up demonstration of what a celluloid splice actually is" ("The Illusionist"). Colin Williamson adds that "The sequence reflects a certain enduring fascination with the capacity of early cinematic tricks to cause us to wonder" (*Hidden in Plain Sight*, 180), a view that is actually closer to the complex intertextual choice Scorsese makes. "Whereas early film audiences looked to nineteenth-century visual culture for insight into the new magic of the cinema, we in the twenty-first century can look to the *longue durée* of magic and the cinema to evaluate the 'new' magic of digital images, technologies, and techniques" (182).

But even these insightful observations don't give us the whole picture, because they are limited to the world of film or to "the shared history of magic and the cinema" (Williamson, 159). Even intermedial approaches to *Hugo* emphasize the more obvious connection between theatre, magic, and early film: "it is the more specific theatrical subgenre of stage magic, which relies on optical illusion, through which media convergence, and a genealogical relationship linking the book with both stage and cinema, can be identified" (Bullen et al., "Cinema and the Book," 76). Scorsese is doing much more than looking back nostalgically at the beginnings of cinema or reminding us that cinema is supposed to make us wonder. By choosing a literary film that recreated a major text of world literature, Scorsese is reminding us that the film's magic also comes from the magic of literature. And what better way to pay tribute to Méliès than by rereading everything that made Méliès possible in the first place? Not only to look back at the past, but especially to move cinema forward.

As the film closes, the camera waltzes us through all the film's characters, brought together at a party, and comes to rest upon Isabelle. As she sits down and opens a fresh notebook to write the story, the camera resumes moving, and we hear Isabelle's voice off camera as she writes: "Once upon a time, I met a boy named Hugo Cabret. He lived in a train station. Why did he live in a train station, you might well ask. But this isn't what the book is going to be about. It's about how this singular young man searched so hard to find a secret message from his father and how that message led his way all the way home." This wasn't the first time that Scorsese was preoccupied with a story's point of view. And it wasn't the first time that he made a point of having a female narrator used as voiceover: "I tried in *The Age of Innocence* to deal with the language. I like the way it was written, and had Joanne Woodward read the text, a female narrator, which was questioned at the time. Who is she?, they asked me. Who is she? She's the storyteller. That's who she is" (*Interviews*, 225). By making this change in the perspective from which Selznick's story is written, Scorsese takes us all the way home to literature, in a gesture that parallels both Méliès and Bazin's intuition that film will be the literature of our time.

"I wonder in the future if young people even will be reading, if they won't be using their eye," muses Doris Freedman in a 1970 interview with Scorsese (*Interviews*, 8). In a subtle but significant nod to Proust and his identification with Scheherazade as the storyteller, Scorsese makes Isabelle his writer-director, as her writing is paralleled, not replaced, by filming: as she writes and we hear her voice off camera, the camera continues to move, and when Isabelle says the word "home," the camera stops, because it has gotten home: Méliès's automaton sits quietly under the magic of the projector's moonlight, his hand frozen on the sheet of paper holding the pen, ready to start again, both to write and to draw pictures. Literature and cinema have found their way back to their common home.

Ghosts inside Objects: The Automaton as Filming Camera

As Colin Williamson has noted, "the domain of magic and technology continues not simply to entertain us but also to shape our perceptions of the cinema and, in so doing, to renew our understanding of early cinematic technologies as 'ghosted' media embedded in a landscape of optical devices, practices, and discourses that continue to cause us to wonder" (*Hidden in Plain Sight*, 184). By adding literature into the equation, we may get a more specific contextualization that would explain Scorsese's choice to turn the automaton from Selznick's book successively into Méliès, Hugo, and ultimately into the camera that brings the director's vision of the world into being, through a very specific treatment of cinematography that places Méliès not in just any Paris, but in the Paris of the surrealists.

The surrealists placed their faith in all forms of automatic art, including the automatons that Breton praised as the surrealist objects of the future in "Introduction au discours sur le peu de la réalité." The poster for the 1938 international surrealist exhibit in Paris at the Palais des Beaux-Arts showed a monstrous automaton, promising that it would make a dramatic after-hours entrance at the exhibit: "The authentic descendant of Frankenstein, the automaton 'Enigmarelle' constructed in 1900 by the American engineer Ireland, will cross the hall of the Surrealist Exhibit in false flesh and bones exactly at half past midnight." Significantly, Guerric DeBona notes that "It is very interesting that the setting of [Selznick's] book should occur in 1931, certainly a watershed for the film industry at the very beginnings of the sound era. That year would also mark Universal studio's release of a film about another 'automaton,' Frankenstein, which would not redeem, but destroy its maker and the doomed enterprise of the overreacher" (*"Hugo,"* 464). While this parallel is certainly important to understanding the workings of *Hugo* in relation to the Hollywood production, DeBona misses the more directly Parisian significance of the automaton Frankenstein.

In a nod to the surrealists' love for automata, Scorsese chose to represent his Paris as a giant mechanism that comes to life. As he told an interviewer: "With Hugo, the fantasy is very real, but it's in your head and in your heart. It has to do with the mechanisms—whether it's the clocks, the interiors, the locomotives, the trains, the automaton—with the inner workings of these objects" (Bowe interview). Breton knew that such objects could enrich our notion of reality: "There would be cleverly constructed machines that would have no use. . . . Absurd and highly developed automatons that would do everything like no one else, would be tasked with giving us a proper idea of action" ("Introduction au discours sur le peu de la réalité," 277).

From the rich history of automata, the surrealists were captivated by Pierre Jaquet-Droz's mechanical writer. Jaquet-Droz (1721–1790) was a watchmaker renowned for building three automata: the writer, the musician, and the draughtsman. The surrealists were particularly fascinated by the writer as an example of automatic creation in the absence of conscious thought: "He knows all the languages and teaches me everything I don't know," the surrealist poet Benjamin Péret wrote. "He thinks and writes for me what I don't dare to write. He dictates my thoughts" ("Au Paradis des Fantômes," 32). Colin Williamson discusses the automaton as an archival device and lists Jaquet-Droz's machine among those used to recreate the one shown in *Hugo* (*Hidden in Plain Sight*, 170), but he doesn't identify the surrealist context of its recirculation in the 1920s and 1930s. More perceptively, Guerric DeBona sees a form of the surrealists' automatic writing in the automaton's drawing and signing the name of its creator, but he explains it in passing: "the automaton appears to be exercising a kind of surrealist automatic writing, surfacing a Freudian 'return of the repressed' as it dreamily recollects a seminal, buried moment in the history of cinema" ("*Hugo*," 471). While Freud was indeed behind the attempts of the early surrealists, they had abandoned him by the late 1920s, when they moved from Freud's past-oriented interpretation of reality toward a future-oriented one through the practice of the surrealist object. The automaton was just such an object.

If the mind of the artist is inhabited by someone or something else dictating his thoughts, it follows that the self is made of many different selves, much as an automaton is made of different objects that function only when they are brought together in the assembled common self. In the 1930s, the surrealists' interest in automata was part of their larger preoccupation with the object as a manifestation of objective hazard, chance encounters, and trapdoors that reveal the cryptogram of reality. Significantly, Scorsese referred to his use of excerpts from Méliès's films as trapdoors opening onto a magical past: "I had to figure out which scenes I was going to try to recreate and what sections of which films. You know? Meaning what—like a trapdoor, how does a trapdoor work?" (*Interviews*, 219).

From the early days of surrealism in the late 1910s, Breton became very interested in Giorgio de Chirico's mannequins, in which he saw a manifestation of the apparently immobile object coming from a past that has a secret message for our present. Once the human body becomes a mannequin, it can behave like a mechanical object with a secret function, and Dalí's painting *Anthropomorphic Cabinet* (1936) or his art object *Venus with Drawers* (1935) invite us to open them and see what's inside. These would become the surrealists' being-objects or object-beings that Dalí theorized in articles published in the 1930s in the surrealist magazine *Minotaure*. But the surrealists weren't inventing anything, they were rediscovering a deep past in the history of art. Their mechanical mannequins were another version of the automata whose history goes back to the sixteenth-century clocks whose mechanism they were using, as Alfred Chapuis and Edouard Gélis showed in 1928 in their richly illustrated two-volume history, *Le Monde des automates*, glowingly reviewed by the poet Benjamin Péret in *Minotaure* ("Au Paradis des Fantômes", 3–4/1933).

But the self made of innumerable selves was no discovery of the surrealists. Proust had already set in motion the revolution in the concept of the self that the surrealists would perfect:

> Of the different persons who compose our personality, it is not the most obvious that are the most essential. In myself, when ill health had succeeded in uprooting them one after another, there will still remain two or three endowed with a hardier constitution than the rest . . . But I have

sometimes wondered whether the last of all might not be this little mannikin, very similar to another whom the optician at Combray used to set up in his shop window to forecast the weather, and who, doffing his hood when the sun shone, would put it on again if it was going to rain. I know how selfish this little mannequin is. . . . I dare say that in my last agony, when all my other "selves" are dead, if a ray of sunshine steals into the room while I am drawing my last breath, the little barometric mannikin will feel a great relief, and will throw back his hood to sing: "Ah, fine weather at last!"

The Captive, 5–6

Like Marcel, Méliès is a walking dead person, but like Proust's little mannequin, the little boy inhabiting him—Hugo—can make the chest of drawers he lives in come back to life, by fixing this broken machinery that Méliès refers to as himself in the speech at the gala that relaunched him in 1929. As Méliès becomes younger on the screen at the gala, he too can breathe a sigh of relief and say like Proust's little mannequin: "Ah, fine weather at last!".

*

Selznick's book is constructed as an automaton that generates the drawings and text of his silent-film-like tribute to Méliès. Hugo Cabret perfects his father's automaton and makes it into a magic machinery that writes and draws the very book we're reading, taking the writing of literature a step closer to filmmaking in its early days of the animated photograph and the flipbook. He's a perfected version of Jaquet-Droz's writer automaton that could write the surrealists' favorite word—*merveilleux*—and of Méliès's automaton that could draw images that would come to life in his films and sign its creator's name, too:

> The automaton my father discovered *did* save me. But now I have built a new automaton . . . When you wind it up, it can do something I'm sure no other automaton in the world can do. . . . The complicated machinery inside my automaton can produce one hundred and fifty-eight different pictures, and it can write, letter by letter, an entire book, twenty-six thousand one hundred and fifty-nine words. These words.

The Invention, 510–11

As Guerric DeBona has observed, "With its automaton rewriting a recovered history, informed by technology and magical illusion, *The Invention of Hugo Cabret* is also a story about the power of the visual to redeem and enhance the textual, that is, also to claim the genre of children's literature as a powerful and legitimate literary presence" (*"Hugo,"* 464).

Scorsese turns the surrealists' automaton into an architectural principle for the construction of Méliès, Hugo, and the film itself. He would agree

FROM AUTOMATON TO MOVIE CAMERA

with the surrealist poet Benjamin Péret, whose 1933 article on automata as the creators of the reality of the future concludes with Jaquet-Droz's writer taking over his creator through the word *marvelous*: "Today, the robot ignores us completely, us who are the gods of automata, their muscles and brain ... These mobile sphinxes continue to present man with enigmas whose solution itself invites in a new enigma [*The robot returns, making his way through the crowd. Jaquet-Droz is thrown to the ground*]. Marvelous! Marvelous! Marvelous! ..." ("Au Paradis des Fantômes," 34). In Méliès's film *Le Livre magique*, the magic book throws the magician to the ground. For Méliès, the book plays the role of Jaquet-Droz's writer automaton, providing a model for Scorsese's take on Selznick's automaton-book *The Invention of Hugo Cabret* a century later.

Both the book and the film behave like automata, because there's a constant ticking that we hear throughout. In Selznick's book it's the clock-like clicking of heels that measures the passage of irreversible time, a sound dreaded by Méliès because it summons the ghosts of his past: "Don't you know that the sound of clicking boot heels can summon ghosts? Do you want to be followed by ghosts?" (95). Méliès wasn't joking; during World War I, many of his films were melted down and turned into shoe heels. Later in the book we hear this sound turned into something else: Hugo "remembered hearing the blood beating hard in his ears, like the rhythm of a clock" (124). "He had often imagined that his own head was filed with cogs and gears like a machine, and he felt a connection with whatever machinery he touched" (126). Scorsese makes this suggestion into the striking scene of Hugo's nightmare, in which he's become an automaton trapped inside a bigger mechanism, another automaton that seems to suffocate him. This is Méliès himself, almost brought down by old age that's rusting his mechanism.

Scorsese uses two symmetrical scenes to suggest the juxtaposition between Méliès, Hugo, and the automaton, placed at the beginning and near the ending of the film. The first scene shows a depressed Méliès in his toy booth at the train station. He has caught the little thief Hugo and is looking through the notebook he has confiscated: it's full of drawings of the automaton that Hugo's father had found in a museum. Scorsese uses the effect of a flipbook, as he shows us Méliès quickly leafing through the notebook that makes the automaton come to life; Scorsese makes the automaton turn to the camera and face Méliès, the camera, and us. As he looks into Méliès's eyes, the moving drawing comes to life, and his creator is taken aback by this apparition from his past: "Ghosts" is the only word that escapes his lips. But making a drawing come to life is also Scorsese's nod to Méliès's 1900 film *Le Livre magique*, which shows a magician turning drawings in a giant book into living human beings. Symmetrically, near the end of the film when Hugo has a double nightmare, he wakes up from the first one, in which he's been run over by a train. The automaton is there next to him, looking deeply into his eyes.

The automaton is the connecting link between these two scenes, suggesting the identity between Méliès and Hugo, past and present, old age that comes back as youth. Between these scenes, at the very heart of the film Scorsese places the key scene with the automaton that's brought back to life with the help of Isabelle's heart-shaped key. Hugo is hoping that the automaton has a message from his dead father, and he himself doesn't know the extent and meaning of this thought. The message is not only from his dead father, but also from the father of cinema, the filmmaker Méliès, who will adopt him. Placing Méliès's poster for *Le Voyage dans la lune* in the middle of the narrative is something that Scorsese borrows from Selznick's book. Scorsese, too, shows us the poster of the man in the moon that the automaton draws and then signs with his creator's name, as Jaquet-Droz's automaton did too. But he adds a significant element: a round inkwell beside the drawing. Filmed from over the automaton's shoulder, Scorsese's shot makes the inkwell, with its white round margin and black center, look like an eye: the eye of the filmmaker (Figure 1.4).

Scorsese plays on a juxtaposition of similarly constructed objects brought together as if by chance to configure a different, higher meaning, a visual trick that we find in so many of Dalí's anamorphoses like *Slave Market with the Disappearing Bust of Voltaire* (1940). Scorsese juxtaposes the inkwell, the bottom of the capsule that hits the moon's eye, and the moon's eye open in terror. Like Hugo's automaton containing a secret message from his father, Scorsese's camera has a secret message for us, too. The shot shows the inkwell next to Méliès's poster and then, in the right lower corner, the automaton's hand signing the name of his creator. If read from left to right,

FIGURE 1.4 *The automaton drawing and writing in* Hugo.

the image delivers a secret message: that the magic of early films is drawn in the ink of literature by the first creator of films out of literature, Georges Méliès. If read right to left, the image delivers another message: that filmmakers like Méliès can teach us how to look differently, through the moon's camera eye, back at literature.

This scene is mirrored in a symmetrical scene. Back at Méliès's place, Hugo and Isabelle find the secret drawer in the armoire that hides all of Méliès's drawings, like stills from his films that can be brought back to life if set in motion. Frozen in a time past, Méliès has become what the surrealists would call a being-object, like his armoire with the secret drawer. It takes a surrealist's eye to open this drawer, as Dalí invites us to do in his *Anthropomorphic Cabinet* and Breton in his 1938 *Object-chest*, so that the object—the automaton—can become a being again. When the secret chest opens, a myriad of drawings by Méliès invade the room, among them a drawing of a devil that becomes a costume that Méliès wore in several of his films, including *Le Diable au couvent* (1899) and *Le Diable géant ou Le miracle de la madonne* (1902). In drawing this costume, Méliès was thinking, among others, of a drawing of a fifteenth-century mechanical devil by the engineer Giovanni Fontana, included in *Bellicorum instrumentorum liber cum figuris et fictitys litoris conscriptus*. A reproduction of Fontana's mechanical devil can be found in Chapuis and Gélis's *Le Monde des automates*. Fontana's book also included the first drawing of a magic lantern, in the devilish form of a witch. In his 1430 *Secretum de thesauro experimentorum ymaginationis hominum*, Fontana proposed several types of artificial devices that could preserve human memory. The major problem of cinema is revealed as the oldest dilemma of art: how to fight back time's irreversible passing, how to preserve a form of human memory. How to freeze for eternity a moment in time.

*

For André Breton as for Méliès time goes backward, but only to recuperate the visionary literature that will enable us to move forward, in a double movement oriented toward both the past and the future. In a manifesto for his exhibit at the Gradiva Gallery in 1937, Breton described the power of surrealist objects to make us children again, just as in Scorsese's *Hugo*:

> We dreamed of a timeless space, somewhere outside the *rational* world, where those man-made objects that have lost their utilitarian function, or haven't found it or have gradually moved away from it, and so have now a SECRET one; they would incessantly and electively emerge from the increasingly opaque river of sand that the adult's vision is and would give him back the transparency of that of the child.
>
> "Gradiva," 26, author's emphasis

The automaton is one such object, made with a mathematical or clockmaker's precision to record the poetic logic of the invisible reality around us. As Méliès and Scorsese know, this object, in the form of the film camera, will serve us all. In the darkness of the movie theatre, it will help us become children all over again, because as the surrealists know, films are waking dreams.

In the manifesto for the Gradiva Gallery, Breton describes his own position—the seeker and visionary poet—in almost identical cinematic terms to those used by Méliès and Scorsese. But with a difference: for him, this ideal location—like Hugo's spot behind the clock dial in the Gare Montparnasse—would bring back the best of visionary *art*, in a view that would make possible Bazin's theory of mixed cinema:

> Moreover, we have dreamed of the tiniest place in the world, but from where we can perceive without straining the boldest, most audacious works in progress in the minds of people, of a place from where we can *overcome the retrospective perspective* we're used to having on authentic artistic creation, for instance. Of a minuscule yet unlimited space that affords us a panoramic view on everything visionary and at the same time to tell ourselves: "We could have read Nerval's *Delfica* here, we could have seen Borel entering unexpectedly . . . or even better: Seurat would have left here one of his *Poseuses*, it is here that Henri Rousseau would have loved to sit."

> "Gradiva," 27–8

Such a minuscule place that affords a panoramic view on the world was also Scorsese's childhood view from his third-floor window. Like Proust before him, Scorsese remembers how, because of his asthma, he spent most of his time indoors reading and watching films. The distance from the world outside made Proust a dreamer, but a lucid one. Watching movies together with reading made Scorsese a filmmaker. Not able to play outdoors, he had to content himself with watching the movie of life from his window. For Flaubert's Emma Bovary, "a window, in a country town, is a substitute for the theatre or the park" (*Madame Bovary*, 113), and later for Proust it provides the perspective from which he analyzes the world through a telescope. For Scorsese it becomes the perspective that will enable him to become a filmmaker. As he said, comparing himself to Hugo: "That third floor image from my childhood offered a panoramic image of life" ("Martin Scorsese on *Hugo*").

From this privileged position, the filmmaker looks onto the world through his camera. Following Breton's cinematic intuition, Bazin defined the camera as simultaneously a microscope and telescope: "The camera puts at the disposal of the director all the resources of the telescope and the microscope" ("Theatre and Cinema II," 103). In a similar spirit to Méliès's and with a filmmaker's eye, in *Time Regained* Proust described his work as a telescope turned on the world:

FROM AUTOMATON TO MOVIE CAMERA

Even those who commended my perception of the truths which I wanted eventually to engrave within the temple, congratulated me on having discovered them "with a microscope," when on the contrary it was a telescope that I had used to observe things which were indeed very small to the naked eye, but only because they were situated at a great distance and which were each one of them in itself a world.

520

Beyond Méliès's Lunar Landscapes

How important is the nation still as a frame in world literature and world cinema? How far is Scorsese an Italian director, or an American one, and how American is Selznick's graphic novel? What about Méliès himself, and what happens when Scorsese recuperates Méliès's films? Are they French films, European films, or world films? Scorsese found in Méliès not only the father of cinema; he found a visionary who understood that great art knows no boundaries and can work with whatever means suit it best, in order to produce not only a film, or another reading of a literary text or a work of art, but rather all these elements put together in a form of art that can best be described with Bazin's concept of mixed cinema. Even though Scorsese mocked high-toned "literary" cinema as snobbish and elitist, he never dismissed reading literature when making films, only the *use* of literature to appeal to a coterie audience. In Méliès, Scorsese found someone who could transgress all artistic boundaries to no other end than illuminating another part of the great unknown territory of our world: "Méliès invented everything; he invented it all. When you look at what he did with these colored scenes it's as if you're looking at illuminated manuscripts moving" ("Martin Scorsese on *Hugo*"). It's not a matter of chance that Scorsese compares Méliès's films with illuminated manuscripts that come alive under the director's eye: a book has come to life on screen, a lesson Scorsese learned from Méliès's film *Le Livre magique*.

Like the surrealists, Scorsese knows that great art can only be born from listening to a voice beyond our rational understanding:

> When I make a picture, in my mind I'm always on the set. I'm on the set right now for my next picture, picking up images. I put myself into a certain mode. I see fewer people and I just try to stay alone. It's a freeing thing to know that you really don't know that much. The best part is the hope to learn. . . . And then you wonder how you thought it up, and you have no idea. You could also devise intellectual approaches, where a character is photographed with certain-size lenses up to a certain point in the film, then the lenses change as the story progresses. That's okay. That will work. I prefer the stuff that just comes out of nowhere. But, you

know, you've got to *get* them from out of nowhere. I don't know where that comes from.

Interviews, 129

Even though he never made a film, Proust too was always "on the set" in his mind, picking up images in the solitude of his walks and even of his social interactions, always keeping a voyeur's distance. While Scorsese discussed Méliès's films through an analogy with illuminated manuscripts brought to life, Proust examines art through an apparent analogy with painting, but his language reveals a clear interest in painting as the art of optics. Proust speaks of a writer's "vision," of a book as a lens through which one *sees* the world differently. His examples, Rembrandt and Vermeer, are two painters whose art was based on a thorough knowledge of optical instruments, including the camera obscura. He perceptively notes that "style for the writer, no less than color for the painter, is a question not of technique, but of vision," and adds:

> Through art alone are we able to emerge from ourselves to know what another person sees of a universe which is not the same as our own and of which, without art, the landscapes would remain as unknown to us as those that exist on the moon. Thanks to art, instead of seeing one world only, our own, we see that world multiply itself and we have at our disposal as many worlds as there are original artists, worlds more different one from the other than those which revolve in infinite space, worlds which, centuries after the extinction of the fire from which their light first emanated, whether it is called Rembrandt or Vermeer, send us still each its special radiance.

Time Regained, 299

Thanks to visionaries like Proust, Méliès, Selznick, and Scorsese, some of the landscapes that exist on the moon are no longer unknown.

2

The Vast Structure of Recollection

Tarkovsky, Proust, Yourcenar

Do visionaries die? Diagnosed with lung cancer at only fifty-four after having chosen exile in 1984, the poet of the screen Andrei Tarkovsky wrote his last diary entry on December 15, 1986 in Paris, two weeks before his death: "Hamlet . . . In bed all day, didn't get up at all. . . . I'm very weak. Am I going to die? . . . Hamlet . . . ? If it weren't for the pain in my arms and back, there might be some question of the chemotherapy having helped. But now I have no strength left for anything—that is the problem" (*Time within Time*, 354). Which Hamlet could Tarkovsky have had in mind? Hamlet the Father, King of Denmark, Hamlet the son, both, or maybe the play itself? And why was Hamlet so important to him in such a moment?

Tarkovsky believed there is no difference between life and art, and everything he ever created—whether films, plays, or literature—was only a natural extension of his own life, a form of realism akin to what André Bazin had in mind when he wrote that cinema had to show that reality is more than the eye can see. "Hamlet was well ahead of his time," Tarkovsky wrote in his notes for his staged version of Shakespeare's play (*Time within Time*, 379). "*Hamlet* is the one play in world literature that has not been solved. And it is eternal; unlike the plays of some of our playwrights who are still alive, but are never put on because they were born dead" (383).

Like Shakespeare before him, who wrote *Hamlet* following the death of his father and also of his son Hamnet, and who chose to play the Ghost on the stage, Tarkovsky too thought of both his father, the poet Arseny Tarkovsky, but also of his second son, Andrei. His entry shows a striking symmetry with his hero and alter ego, Aleksei, in the autobiographical film *The Mirror*, a man who could look into the mirror of time and simultaneously see his father and his unborn son. Now, Tarkovsky wrote in his next to last diary entry, just before mentioning Hamlet: "I must talk to Andriushka about cinema and literature, find out what he knows" (354). Like Shakespeare's Ghost, whose final words to his son are "Remember me!", Tarkovsky wants his son to carry on his legacy, at once cinematic and literary, after his father has entered the sleep of death.

In 1979, Tarkovsky had gone to Italy scouting locations for *Nostalghia* (1983), together with the Italian poet Tonino Guerra. *Nostalghia* tells the story of Andrei, a Russian writer who has come to Italy to research his next subject, accompanied by a beautiful translator, Eugenia, a temptress whose charm he resists. His journey becomes more and more inward and spiritual, as he feels worlds apart from his homeland, as well as from his wife Maria and his two children, whom he sees only in dreams. Andrei encounters Domenico, a homeless man who has lost his family too because he kept them locked away for ten years, hoping to save them from the corrupt world and the passage of time. The film ends with a religious gesture performed in parallel by the poet Andrei at Bagno Vignoni and by Domenico in the Piazza dei Musei Capitolini in Rome: Andrei tries to carry a lit candle over a stretch of water, while Domenico becomes the candle, setting himself on fire. This final religious gesture is only a poetic transposition of their mirrored death. Two strangers and wanderers have found their way back home via an unexpected and uncanny route.

Tarkovsky turned his location scouting trip into the documentary *Tempo di viaggio*, constructed as a dialogue between himself and Guerra on cinema. "For me, thinking of cinema through genres is an aberration," he says at some point, and now we can better understand his last words to his son about cinema and literature. Poetry too, Tarkovsky insists, isn't a genre, and it permeates everything around us. Literary scholars who worry that our globalizing age is losing sight of poetry may be relieved if they look back at Tarkovsky. In *Nostalghia*, he addresses the question of poetry and its untranslatability in a way that may provide some answers to the concerns raised by Emily Apter in her book *Against World Literature*. Tarkovsky's plea for untranslatability—both in his film's title *Nostalghia*, which he insisted is an untranslatable Russian word, and throughout the film—isn't in any way a nationalistic gesture or an elegy to the impossibility of communicating beyond linguistic borders. In the years that lead up to *Nostalghia*, Tarkovsky is immersed in Seneca and Berdyaev, and takes down extensive quotes in his diary: "'Even if we travel from end to end of every land, nowhere in the world shall we find a country that is alien to us; from everywhere it will be equally possible to raise our eyes to the sky.' (Seneca)" (*Time within Time*, July 28, 1981, 286–7). "'I have a real revulsion for nationalism, it is not merely immoral, but always stupid and ridiculous' (Berdyaev)" (August 23, 1981, 291). For Tarkovsky, his Russian cinema is meant to convey a religious sense to the world: "'Without Christ, the Slav sense of being destined to perform some cosmic feat of heroism is turned into a racist aspiration.' (Vyacheslav Ivanov)" (291). Though Tarkovsky's authorial mask in *Nostalghia*, Andrei, argues for poetry's untranslatability, his would-be lover the translator Eugenia is reading poetry in translation—and specifically the poetry of Tarkovsky's father, Arseny Tarkovsky.

Tarkovsky's films are like poems, and they each represent a single piece of a giant puzzle that forms a clear image of his world only when put together. His films establish a rich network that extends from Proust's poetic prose to his father's poetry and beyond to world writers like Eugene Vodolazkin and Norman Manea, and world filmmakers from Aleksandr Sokurov to Wong Kar-wai and Paolo Sorrentino. Tarkovsky spoke repeatedly about the impossibility of distinguishing between genres, and yet he didn't simply identify his mixed mode of cinema with literature. On the contrary, he took pains to separate literature from cinema in his theoretical essays. There are several reasons for this, and they go from the very personal to the highly theoretical. As the son of one of the major Russian poets of the twentieth century, Andrei Tarkovsky grew up with his father's poetry, yet he never forgot that this father had left his family when Tarkovsky was five. His films are haunted by the recurrent idea of a man leaving his family, and they also represent the son's need to liberate himself from this father figure in more than one way.

Tarkovsky proposed that film is a document of inner life that rarely expresses itself through words, and he found that the major difference between literature and cinema is the language used: words versus images. He readily admitted, however, that there is a "kinship between music and cinema," and he argued that this kinship "distances cinema from literature, where everything is expressed by means of language, by a system of signs, of hieroglyphics. The literary work can only be received through symbols, through concepts—for that is what words are; but cinema, like music, allows for an utterly direct, emotional, sensuous perception of the work" (*Sculpting in Time*, 176). But images themselves function like language, for to make sense of what we see, we still need to talk about it, and no one has yet developed a way of talking about cinema without words. No matter how autobiographical a film is, how "truthful" to the inner logic of the filmmaker, images never give us a *direct* access to the world of the film other than through a translation into our own interior language.

André Bazin spoke of cinema's finally matching the accomplishments of the modernist novel, implying a hierarchy between cinema and literature, to which cinema needs to "catch up." At the same time, he was preoccupied with legitimizing cinema as an art in its own right, and he emphasized its specificity in order to separate it from the other arts. So too Tarkovsky, who was keenly aware that the brevity of film's history placed it worlds behind literature: "Whether up till now cinema can actually claim any authors worthy to stand alongside the creators of the great masterpieces of world literature is extremely doubtful" (*Sculpting in Time*, 173). Turning from the novel, Tarkovsky used an analogy with poetry, and more specifically with the haiku: "If time appears in cinema in the form of fact, the fact is given in the form of simple, direct observation. The basic element of cinema, running through it to its tiniest cells, is observation. We all know the traditional genre of ancient Japanese poetry, the haiku . . . What attracts me in haiku is its observation of life—pure, subtle, one with its subject; a kind of distillation," and he added: "Since this principle was already there in haiku, however, it is clearly not exclusive to cinema" (*Sculpting in Time*, 66). Despite himself, perhaps, he remained his father's son, and he made extensive use of poetic mechanisms in his films. Yet Tarkovsky wasn't just any poet, but someone whose major poetic device for reading the world around him was analogy. And he was repeatedly drawn to the greatest master of analogy in modern French literature, Marcel Proust.

Over the past three decades, a series of articles, dissertations, and books have looked at Tarkovsky's films in relation to his father's poetry and also in relation to Proust, but they never go beyond a mere comparison that continues to privilege cinema, endowing poetry or literature only with a secondary function in his work. Maya Turovskaya's seminal *Tarkovsky: Cinema as Poetry* is framed with a promising premise: "the basic trait of 'poetic cinema,'" she says, lies in "the indirect nature of its statements, as art's attempt to capture that which logic and meaning are incapable of capturing" (10). Turovskaya, however, doesn't develop a real analysis of the organic relation between poetry and film in Tarkovsky, but uses the word "poetry" simply to mean a non-verbal "atmosphere." More recently Alexandra Smith has treated Arseny Tarkovsky's poems "as primary form, or something of a raw material that might be transformed into another narrative" ("Andrei Tarkovsky as Reader of Arsenii Tarkovsky's Poetry," 51). Emphasizing Tarkovsky's ideas about the differences between literature and cinema, scholars stress differences rather than similarities. Even when similarity is the subject, as with some recent work by students of literature and film, it's always more a *thematic* comparison than a really *structural* one.[1]

More often than not, scholars address the moments of intersection between Tarkovsky's films and his father's poetry that Tarkovsky himself references, either in his diary or in his films. Yet what about the poems he doesn't directly quote in his films, but that went into the making of his own imagery? Or the architectural constructions that impressed him in writers or poets and that came to structure his own logic of images and his rhythm of editing? When one understands the surrounding world through poetic mechanisms like analogy, the relation between literature, poetry, and cinema remains organic and multidimensional, as we will see in the balance of this chapter.

---

[1]Two examples would be: Jacob Kasel's honors thesis *Poignant Immobility: Temporality in the Works of Barthes, Lispector, Proust and Tarkovsky*, and Irena Artemenko, *The Ethics of Mourning in the Narration of the Self in the Works of Marcel Proust and Andrei Tarkovsky* (Wadham College, 2017).

The Camera's Magic Mirror, a Corridor in Time

Preoccupied like Proust by the problem of returning in time, Tarkovsky doesn't limit his engagement with poetry to the poems he quotes in his films, which give only a pale image of the extent to which he lives and breathes literature, art, religious and philosophical writings. Nor does Tarkovsky limit his interest in Proust to the theoretical dialogue in the poetics of cinema he develops in *Sculpting in Time*. Throughout his diary *Time within Time*, Tarkovsky integrates quotes from the books he's reading with the ease and naturalness with which he records his own thoughts. He almost never comments on these quotations, because he makes them his own through a shared community of ideas: "The fact that time flows the same way in all heads proves more conclusively than anything else that we are all dreaming the same dream; more than that: all who dream that dream are one and the same being" (*Time within Time*, April 23, 1978, 154). Though Tarkovsky extracted this quotation from Schopenhauer, it could well have been found in *À la recherche du temps perdu*. Beyond the instances where he cites Proust directly, it's still more rewarding to see him thinking and writing *like* Proust, or selecting passages from other writers that could have been written by Proust himself.

Preparing to film *Nostalghia*, Tarkovsky copies down a few lines that any reader might think come from Proust: "'Nothing that vanishes from our sight is destroyed—it is all hidden in nature, whence it came and where it reappears. There is an interval, but no destruction. And death, which we repudiate in terror, interrupts life, but does not put an end to it. The day will come when we appear again in the world, even though many would refuse to return had they not forgotten all about it.' (Seneca, *Letter* xxxvi)" (*Time within Time*, September 3, 1981, 292). In a mirrored gesture, Proust himself returns in his final volume to the madeleine scene to conclude in almost identical terms that "one can understand that this man should have confidence in his joy, even if the simple taste of a madeleine does not seem logically to contain within it the reasons for this joy, one can understand that the word 'death' should have no meaning for him; situated outside time, why should he fear the future?" (*Time Regained*, 265).

Tarkovsky liked Proust's idea that "the vast structure of recollection" is hidden in the objects around us, and reworked it into his own theory that objects are "imprinted time": "Proust also spoke of raising 'a vast edifice of memories', and that seems to me to be what cinema is called to do. It could be said to be the ideal manifestation of the Japanese concept of *sabi*;[2] for, as it masters this

---

[2] I am here correcting the spelling, which Tarkovsky misremembered as *saba* (*саба*); *saba* means "mackerel," which Tarkovsky definitely didn't intend. I am indebted to the Japanese participants in my seminar *Localizing Time in World Literature and World Cinema* taught at the Institute for World Literature at the University of Tokyo in 2018 for pointing out this error.

completely new material—time—it becomes, in the fullest sense, a new muse" (*Sculpting in Time*, 59). In the opening of Proust's novel, just after the madeleine scene and the quoting of the Celtic belief that there are ghosts living in the inanimate objects around us, Proust already used a Japanese analogy when he explained how the edifice of recollection can be summoned back to life from an object as small as a cup of tea:

> But when from a long-distant past nothing subsists, after the people are dead, after the things are broken and scattered, taste and smell alone, more fragile but more enduring, more immaterial, more persistent, more faithful, remain poised a long time, like souls, remembering, waiting, hoping, amid the ruins of all the rest; and bear unflinchingly, in the tiny and almost impalpable drop of their essence, the vast structure of recollection . . . And as in the game wherein the Japanese amuse themselves by filling a porcelain bowl with water and steeping in it little pieces of paper which until then are without character or form, but, the moment they become wet, stretch and twist and take on colour and distinctive shape, become flowers or houses or people, solid and recognisable.
>
> *Swann's Way*, 63–4

Tarkovsky's very notion of cinema as "imprinted time" is found in Proust's own writing: "the artist has to listen to his instinct, and it is this that makes art the most real of things, the most austere school of life, the true last judgement. This book, more laborious to decipher than any other, is also the only one which has been dictated to us by reality, the only one of which the 'impression' has been printed in us by reality itself" (*Time Regained*, 275). "Austere school of life," "the true last judgement," and reality imprinting its secret message in us—a language that would speak so closely to Tarkovsky's own religious devotion to understanding the reality beyond what the untrained eye can see: "For me reality is in general much greater than what I can find in it, much deeper and more sacred than I'm able to perceive . . . Let me use an example: there are people who can see an aura, a certain multi-colored glow around human body, those people have certain senses developed to a higher degree than most people" (Illg and Neuger interview).

If we limit ourselves to reading Proust only in Tarkovsky's direct citations, we may end up attributing to Tarkovsky what he borrows most creatively from others, and thus miss the circulation and development of ideas that know no genre boundaries. In *The Films of Andrei Tarkovsky: A Visual Fugue*, Vida T. Johnson and Graham Petrie cite Tarkovsky who writes that "For the first time in the history of the arts, in history of culture, man found the means *to take an impression of time*" (*Sculpting in Time*, 62), but they only find here Tarkovsky's polemic against Eisenstein (37). In *Mirror: The Film Companion*, Natasha Synessios misses the fact that Tarkovsky's notion of cinema as "sculpting in time" as well as the "imprint of time" are indirect citations from Proust, and contents herself with citing only what Tarkovsky himself admits: "cinema was called to raise, in Proust's words, 'a vast edifice of memories'. To do that it had to work with time. Tarkovsky's definition of cinema as 'a sculpture made of time' informs every aspect of his film-making: camera, decor, mise-en-scène, texture, rhythm and editing. Each shot, each sequence, imprints time" (48). In his "Introduction" to Maya Turovskaya's *Tarkovsky*, Ian Christie associates Tarkovsky's conception of sculpting in time to "Michelangelo's neo-platonic conception of sculpture" (xxi), but misses the structural use of Proust, as does Turovskaya herself, treating it as if the idea were Tarkovsky's own finding (65).

Proust in turn was building on Victor Hugo, the poet whose verse "temps, ce grand sculpteur" would later reappear in Marguerite Yourcenar's collection of essays *Le Temps, ce grand sculpteur* and then in Tarkovsky's poetics of cinema entitled *Sculpting in Time*. The ultimate expression of Proust's building in his work a "vast structure of recollection" and of Tarkovsky's own cinema as "the imprint of time" is the last scene in *Nostalghia*, filmed in the ruins of the thirteenth-century Abbey of San Galgano in Tuscany. In a long and very slow final shot that moves backwards—like the time in the film—from a closeup to a panoramic view, Tarkovsky shows us Andrei, sitting quietly in front of his house back home, as if in Russia. His dog is sitting next to him, the same dog that appears like a good spirit every time Andrei dreams in *Nostalghia* and that is found in his films from *Solaris* to *The Mirror* to *Stalker*. But Andrei's house, together with his dog and Andrei himself, are placed inside the roofless Gothic cathedral of San Galgano. As the camera slowly starts to move backwards, we see a puddle in front of Andrei and the dog, who are both facing the camera as if they're waiting to be photographed by the only cameraman in this film: memory. In the puddle, we see Andrei and the dog reflected, but also three ogival arches that look like prison bars (Figure 2.1).

As the camera continues to move backwards, the seeming prison bars are revealed to be the ogival arches of the ruined Gothic triptych of the altarpiece. Framing Andrei and his memory of his lost home and past, the roofless ruined Gothic cathedral becomes a metaphor for the hero's drama. Only apparently imprisoned by his past, Andrei saves himself and his memories from oblivion by turning them into something more meaningful, what Tarkovsky calls "an act of true faith," though it has no direct religious coloring. The Proustian "vast structure of recollection" here becomes the very structure of the ruined abbey. A Gothic church, as Proust writes of the church in Combray, is "an edifice occupying, so to speak, a fourth dimensional space—the name of the fourth being Time, extending through the centuries its ancient nave. . . . bay after bay, chapel after chapel, seemed to stretch across and conquer not merely a few yards of soil, but each successive epoch from which it emerged triumphant" (*Swann's Way*, 83). Tarkovsky picks up Proust's four-dimensional architecture of his cathedral-novel and turns it into an ark that saves people and their memories from oblivion. He manages this subtle reading of both Proust and

FIGURE 2.1 *The roofless cathedral of San Galgano in Andrei Tarkovsky's* Nostalghia.

his own life by literalizing Proust's and by placing Andrei and his lost home, a metaphor of the lost paradise of his past, in the nave of the cathedral.

The last scene in *Nostalghia* shows Andrei, the orphan cut off from his homeland and his family housed in this welcoming womb of the ruined cathedral. He is surrounded by reflections that invisibly connect him to his past and his future, all the generations brought together in the space that cancels the passage of time, a process foreshadowed in Tarkovsky's father's poetry:

> Live in the house—the house will not fall down.
> Whatever the century I summon up,
> I shall enter it and build a house.
> For that very reason now your children
> And your wives are with me at one table,
> One table for great-grandfather and grandson:
> The future is accomplished here and now,
> All five beams of light will then remain.
> . . .
> My immortality is all I need
> For my blood to flow from age to age.
> For some corner, safe and always warm,
> I would traffic my life willingly enough,
> Were it not for life's flying needle
> Drawing me like a thread around the world
>   ARSENY TARKOVSKY, "Life, life," *Poetry and Film*, 142–3

Life is a miracle of miracles, and on its lap
Like a lonely orphan, I lay myself down,
Alone amid mirrors, surrounded by reflections
Of seas and cities glowing in miasmic haze

"And I have dreamed of this," *Poetry and Film*, 164

Tarkovsky's reading of his father's poems—especially those *not* explicitly cited but that feed into the structure of his cinematic thought—is embodied through Proust's cathedral-ark as the vast structure of recollection that turns the mirrors and the reflections from a space of loneliness into an open space of shared community: "there existed, none the less, between the church and everything in Combray that was not the church a clear line of demarcation which my mind has never succeeded in crossing" (*Swann's Way*, 85). Tarkovsky's choice of the Gothic ruins of San Galgano mirrors Proust's description of the Combray church with a special focus—like Tarkovsky's camera—on the triptych altar windows: "the graceful Gothic arcades which crowded coquettishly around it like a row of grown-up sisters who, to hide him from the eyes of strangers, arrange themselves smilingly in front of a rustic, peevish and ill-dressed brother" (*Swann's Way*, 83). By returning to Proust's poetic prose in this passage, Tarkovsky subtly suggests, we may find a different meaning of *Nostalghia*'s last scene. Tarkovsky said in an interview that the last scene is supposed to suggest Andrei's death, but if we turn to Proust, we know that death is only a period of absence when the soul rests captive in some inanimate being: "I used to advance into the church, as we made our way to our seats, as into a fairy-haunted valley, where the rustic sees with amazement in a rock, a tree, a pond, the tangible traces of the little people's supernatural passage" (83).

Thinking of the next to last scene in *Nostalghia* may shed more light on what this architectural structure actually is. Before the final scene, Tarkovsky shows in parallel two acts of faith: Andrei carries a lit candle over the hot pool at Bagno Vignoni while his homeless double Domenico becomes the candle as he sets himself on fire in the Piazza dei Musei Capitolini in Rome, in a final attempt to raise awareness that only faith can save us from death. As Andrei manages on a third attempt to bring the lit candle across the hot pool and place it on the opposite wall, Tarkovsky's camera focuses on Andrei's hands carrying the light in a sign of prayer—a visual metaphor that continues a similar one from *The Mirror* where Aleksei's mother carries a burning twig to light the fire in the chimney. Tarkovsky's closeup of this simple gesture turns it into a visual metaphor of faith, but also of the magic object that the soul of the dead changes into. Andrei's burning candle is himself, as we know from Arseny Tarkovsky's poem cited in *Nostalghia* and later turned real onscreen in the final scene:

I'm a candle, I burnt out at the feast
Gather my wax in the morning
And this page will give you a hint
Of how to weep and where to take pride,
How to distribute the final third
Of jollity, to die easily
Then, sheltered by some chance roof,
Flare up after death like a word.

"Sight is Fading—my power," Poetry and Film, 175

And what better chance roof than the sky itself above the ruins of San Galgano, in which Andrei—both the hero and the filmmaker—teaches us to read into his wax candle a hint to another page that spoke of another burning candle in another Gothic structure, the church in Combray:

> beneath the shadowy vault, powerfully ribbed like an immense bat's wing of stone, Théodore and his sister would light up for us with a candle the tomb of Sigebert's little daughter, in which a deep cavity, like the bed of a fossil, had been dug, or so it was said, "by a crystal lamp which, on the night when the Frankish princess was murdered, had detached itself, of its own accord, from the golden chains by which it was suspended on the site of the present apse and, with neither the crystal being broken nor the light extinguished, had buried itself in the stone, which has softly given way beneath it."

Swann's Way, 84

These layers of intertextual references in *Nostalghia* move circuitously between poetry, narrative, architecture, and film, not unlike Proust's notion of individual memory as a collective memory, expressed through the analogy with geological strata that point "to differences of origin, age, and formation" (*Swann's Way*, 263). As André Breton wrote, this poetic visual language belongs to us all, and it configures the hidden patterns of reality. It is these patterns, Proust tells us, that are imprinted in us by time and dictated by reality into the book we're reading (or the film we're watching). Dictated, not inspired; created automatically, not rationally—arguments that will form the surrealists' own poetics: "When an idea—an idea of any kind—is left in us by life, its material pattern, the outline of the impression that is made upon us, remains behind as the token of its necessary truth. The ideas formed by the pure intelligence have no more than a logical, a possible truth. The book whose hieroglyphs are patterns not traced by us is the only book that really belongs to us" (*Time Regained*, 275).

Tarkovsky's camera eye becomes "a magic mirror in which one can read life and death" (Breton, "Le message automatique," 56). Taking us from the

THE VAST STRUCTURE OF RECOLLECTION

present to the past and the future in one single take, it connects all his films like pieces of a single giant puzzle but also as a trapdoor in the hidden pattern of his individual films. *The Mirror* (1975) is a highly autobiographical film that sets in motion the complicated logic of dreams as editing principle. It brings together three temporal layers: the 1930s, the 1940s, and the late 1960s and early 1970s, to tell the complex story of a mirrored self composed of Andrei Tarkovsky himself as Aleksei, of his father Arseny, and also of Tarkovsky's own son, called Ignat in the film, in reality called Andrei, just like his father. The three temporal layers are constructed on the principle of repeated history through symmetrical characters that return with every generation. Not only is his father constructed through a mirrored identity with his son and then grandson, but the same actress, Margarita Terekhova, plays Maria—the elusive Father's wife and Aleksei's mother—but also Natalia, Aleksei's wife years later. Through the complex logic of a dream narrative, Tarkovsky sets in motion a Proustian conception of time and the self that never dies but comes back with each new generation, each time with a difference, to point at the higher meaning of the pattern of reality hidden underneath the skin of our everyday lives.

The Mirror includes two scenes that bear the material pattern of Proust's idea of objects as trapdoors and gateways both to the past and future, bringing together three generations—the absent and elusive father, who left the family in 1936, Aleksei the son, who becomes a filmmaker, and his son Ignat—to suggest, like Proust, how death becomes a matter of indifference. As Seneca (whom Tarkovsky quotes in his diary) writes, death isn't an ending, but only a break in the flow of time until the past comes back to life. Andrei Tarkovsky found in his father's poetry a representation that defeats time's irreversibility, and he turned it into a structuring principle of his films.

The first scene takes place in the time frame of the second generation. We are in the house of Aleksei, now a grownup, the son of the anonymous Father who left the family in the opening of the film. Aleksei in turn has repeated his father's history and left his wife Natalya and their son Ignat (the same actor, Ignat Daniltsev, plays both Ignat and his father as twelve-year-olds). For Tarkovsky, there was no essential difference between our immediate reality and that of his films. He constantly made a point of this by choosing actors with names like the character they're playing—the case of Ignat played by the actor Ignat Daniltsev—or, more subtly, through the repetition of the same names or the same initial in different generations. Whereas Andrei Tarkovsky's father was the poet Arseny Tarkovsky, his own two elder sons will repeat his father's name and his own. Andrei Tarkovsky had three sons: in 1962, Arseny, his son by his first wife, Irma Raush, in 1970, Andrei, his son by his second wife, Larissa Tarkovskaya, and in 1986, Aleksandr, his son by the Norwegian dancer Berit. In *The Mirror*, the anonymous Father (i.e. Arseny) is played by Oleg Yankovsky, who will later play the main character, this time named Andrei, in *Nostalghia*, where he will repeat the story of the man who leaves his family. Oleg Yankovsky's son Filipp plays the five-year-old Aleksei (the second-generation son) in *The Mirror*.

In 1994, Johnson and Petrie critically observed that: "Supposed 'analyses' of the film in English, French and German abound with elementary factual mistakes whose cumulative effect is either to make the film appear virtually incomprehensible or to distort the meaning of specific, crucial scenes." Yet they themselves write that *The Mirror* is "an autobiography of the artist and a biography of two Soviet generations" (*The Films of Andrei Tarkovsky*, 116). There are in fact *three* generations, but Johnson and Petrie conflate the absent father figure and Aleksei's generation. As maddening as Tarkovsky's structure may be, it's necessary to understand this time-related logic before delving into the logic of the mirror that brings ghostly objects and different generations into the eternal present of the camera's eye.

The grownup Aleksei is never seen on screen and talks off camera to his former wife, Natalya, who has come to ask him to keep Ignat with him for a couple of weeks while she renovates her house. Tarkovsky suggests that Aleksei is his authorial mask when we see on the wall of his house a poster of Tarkovsky's 1969 film *Andrei Rublev*. When Natalya brings Ignat to Aleksei's house, his father isn't there. She accidentally drops her bag and its contents spill out on the floor. Ignat helps her put them back, but all of a sudden, he pulls back. "I felt an electric shock," he says while holding coins he's just picked up from the floor. "As if it had already happened. But I've never been here before." "Stop daydreaming," his pragmatic mother says, but we are already in fully Proustian mode. The electric shock of the coin is much more than "a kind of Platonic anamnesis" (Peter Green, *Andrei Tarkovsky*, 82) or a mere "remnant of the Proustian madeleine" (Nariman Skakov, *The Cinema of Tarkovsky*, 120). Objects are souls of the past beckoning us to bring them back to life, and the electric shock Ignat feels coming from the coins is of the same substance as the triggers of Proust's involuntary memory, which goes both toward the past and toward the future: the madeleine, the uneven paving stone, the napkin, sometimes electricity itself: "As by an electric current that gives us a shock, I have been shaken by my loves . . . It is in those invisible forces with which [the woman] is incidentally accompanied that we address ourselves as to obscure deities" (*Sodom and Gomorrah*, 719).

Ignat's mother leaves the house, and we see her in the doorway telling her son: "If Maria Nikolaevna comes, tell her to wait for me." Little does she know what her words are about to become. The door closes on her, and Ignat is now alone in the house. He randomly touches the books on the shelf next to the door, and then he looks back at the room behind him. But lo and behold, a woman is now sitting at the table as her aged maid is serving her a cup of tea, and she invites him to come in and join her. This woman is his (grand)father's nanny.[3] She appears in three scenes: early on, then at the heart of the film, and finally in the next to last scene. The first time we see her as Aleksei's nanny, carrying him lovingly in her arms in front of his childhood dacha. She is a poorly dressed peasant woman. The second time she appears to Ignat as a ghost in his father's house, but this time she's wearing an old-style dark green velvet dress with a lace collar and behaves like an authoritative tutor. She's very well educated, she knows Rousseau's and Pushkin's works and orders Ignat to read from a book. Judging by her clothes and education, she must be his grandfather's nanny. And finally, dressed in clothing that doesn't suggest a specific time, in a scene that completely overlaps the figures of Aleksei and of his absent father, she appears at his deathbed. If the first and final scenes raise no questions about her presence, the middle one does. How did she materialize there? She appears right after Ignat touches a book on the shelf. Proust again is the secret source:

> a thing which we have looked at in the past brings back to us, if we see it again, not only the eyes with which we looked at it but all the images with which at the time those eyes were filled. . . . If, even in thought, I pick from the bookshelf *François le Champi* immediately there rises within me a child who takes my place, who alone has the right to spell out the title *François le Champi*, and who reads it as he read it once before, with the same impression of what the weather was like then in the garden, the same dreams that were then shaping themselves in his mind about the different countries and about life.
>
> *Time Regained*, 284–5

As Ignat touches the book, within him there arise his father Aleksei and/or his grandfather, who as a child may have touched the same book and read from it at the request of the same nanny. And as in Proust, the nanny comes back too, and she asks Ignat/Aleksei to read her a passage from the very same book. The text he reads is from a letter by Pushkin to his friend the philosopher Pyotr Chaadayev:

> The division of churches separated us from Europe. We remained excluded from every great event that had shaken it. However, we had our own, special destiny. . . . Although I'm heartily attached to our sovereign, I'm not at all delighted with what I see around me. As a man of letters, I am annoyed, insulted, but I swear that for nothing in the world would I change my home country or have any other history than the history of our forebears such as it was given us by God.

---

[3]Nariman Skakov senses rightly that she's a ghost in this scene, but doesn't identify her as the (grand)father's nanny: "She may be a former prerevolutionary owner of the flat who enters it as a ghost" (*The Cinema of Tarkovsky*, 120). Nor do Johnson and Petrie recognize who the women are: they are just "the mysterious visitors in the 'Pushkin' scene" (*The Films of Andrei Tarkovsky*, 129).

All this time, Ignat/Aleksei hasn't entered the room but reads the text from the doorway. As he reaches the part where Pushkin rejects the idea of changing his history, Tarkovsky's camera focuses on the nanny—a contemporary version of Proust's Françoise, who brought him his tea and madeleine. As the nanny sips her tea, as from Proust's cup, there rises the "vast structure of recollection." Like the flickering of Proust's magic lantern, the camera rests for a second on a photo of Aleksei's mother—and Andrei Tarkovsky's own mother, Maria Vishnyakova—seen on the wall behind Ignat/Aleksei as he reads from the book. Another flicker of light, and as Ignat/Aleksei finishes reading, the nanny tells him to go and open the door, even though no one has knocked. We return symmetrically to the beginning of the scene when Ignat saw his mother to the door. Tracing back his and our steps—to the door and toward the past—Ignat opens the door. An old woman is sitting on the doorstep; she says, "I'm afraid I got the wrong address," and walks away. It's the same woman from the photograph, but older. She is Aleksei's grandmother from the house in the woods and the mother of the absent Father; she is also Aleksei's own mother, and finally she is Natalya, Ignat's future mother. "I have no need of dates, I was, I am, I shall be. / Life is a miracle of miracles."

Turning back, Ignat is puzzled: now the room is empty, as if no one was there a moment ago. He finally enters the room, still holding the book in his hand. The camera's eye now becomes Ignat's as we draw into a closeup of the table. There we see a round mark where the teacup had been placed by the nanny. The mark disappears gradually, like the ghost of the past that had been summoned a moment before by the book and then the tea. The portal closes, taking with it the nanny, Aleksei the boy, and the ghost of his grandmother, leaving a confused Ignat as the phone rings. At first, one would assume it's his father, Aleksei, and that we are back in the present moment. But the voice on the phone asks Ignat "Did Maria Nikolaevna come," not "did grandma come," confusing our sense of reality: this is what Ignat's grandfather, Aleksei's father, would call his former wife. The magic of reality with its significant juxtapositions that blur all borders between past, present and future never ends with Tarkovsky and it is the very heart of his representation of time: "And you will dream all that I have seen in dreams." For there is only "[o]ne table for great-grandfather and grandson."

Proust explains such inexplicable occurrences through a dreamed reality, in a passage that provides Tarkovsky with all the major elements for this scene:

> I entered the realm of sleep, which is like a second dwelling into which we move for that one purpose. It has noises of its own and we are sometimes violently awakened by the sound of bells, perfectly heard by our ears, although nobody has rung. It has its servants, its special visitors who call to take us out, so that we are ready to get up when we are compelled to

THE VAST STRUCTURE OF RECOLLECTION 61

realise, by our almost immediate transmigration into the other dwelling, our waking one, that the room is empty, that nobody has called.

Sodom and Gomorrah, 516

Tarkovsky is doing more than engaging in a dialogue with Proust; he *is* Proust turned filmmaker. He shows us how a whole lost paradise can be brought back to life through a cup of tea, and the book is a ghostly object that can summon back the dead, as *François le Champi* could for Marcel.

As the ultimate ghost summoned is Aleksei's (grand)mother who is also Ignat's grandmother, the entire scene brings to life on screen Proust's passages where Marcel muses on bringing his dead grandmother back to life. In *Sodom and Gomorrah*, after his grandmother dies, she comes back in a different shape: "as soon as I saw her enter in her crape overcoat, I realised— something that had escaped me in Paris—that it was no longer my mother that I had before my eyes, but my grandmother" (228). But the world we've just been in with Ignat is a mental, imaginary world, entirely drawn from Proust, from the bookshelves that signal the mental space we enter to the magic doors that open inside us to reveal the dead who inhabit us—future or past lovers, future or past mothers and grandmothers, superimposed in the affective memory to point at the single idea that runs through all of them. It's this idea that obsesses Proust and both Tarkovskys, because it's the idea of how to turn time on its head and defeat death:

> Two or three times it occurred to me, for a moment, that the world in which this room and these bookshelves were situated . . . was perhaps an intellectual world, which was the sole reality . . . And I might search for a hundred years without discovering how to open the door that had closed behind her. But at that moment, to my astonishment, the door opened and, with a throbbing heart, I seemed to see my grandmother standing before me, as in one of those apparitions that had already visited me, but only in my sleep. Was it all only a dream, then? Alas, I was wide awake. "You see a likeness to your poor grandmother," said Mamma, for it was she, speaking gently . . . Her disheveled hair, whose grey tresses were not hidden and strayed about her troubled eyes, her aging cheeks, my grandmother's own dressing-gown which she was wearing, all these had for a moment prevented me from recognizing her and had made me uncertain whether I was still asleep or my grandmother had come back to life.

Sodom and Gomorrah, 718–22

With a single masterful twist in the cinematography, the editing, and the set, Tarkovsky brings this very passage from Proust on screen to tell his own autobiographical story, superimposing past and future.

Tarkovsky frames all these ghostly apparitions with the doorframe: Natalya, her older self/the grandmother, the nanny, and even Ignat/Aleksei himself, who remains reading in the doorframe, not daring to enter the magic room where the ghost of the past is quietly sipping her tea. Tarkovsky uses the doorframe as a magic mirror that effaces the borders between the different layers of time, while the editing and the camera movement that follows Ignat/ Aleksei between the doorframes is a way to perform Méliès's magic trick: the disappearing act. But Tarkovsky didn't stop at this resurrection of Proust's memory, as well as his own, through the poetic treatment of similar frames. Near the end of *The Mirror*, we find another encounter with the hidden pattern in the great book that reality is. We hear offscreen the adult Aleksei speaking of a recurrent dream as we cut back to his childhood house, next to a *selva oscura* that Tarkovsky films as a living being, with the wind moving through its leaves like an invisible ghostly presence. The camera stays outside the dark wood that looks like a tunnel opening onto the unknown. It is the tunnel to his own past:

> With an amazing regularity I keep seeing one and the same dream. It seems to make me return to the place, poignantly dear to my heart, where my grandfather's house used to be, in which I was born forty years ago right on the dinner table. Each time I try to enter it, something prevents me from doing that. I see this dream again and again. And when I see those walls made of logs and the dark entrance, even in my dream I become aware that I'm only dreaming it. And the overwhelming joy is clouded by the anticipation of awakening. At times something happens and I stop dreaming of the house and the pine trees of my childhood around it. Then I get depressed. And I can't wait to see this dream in which I'll be a child again and feel happy again because everything will be still ahead, everything will be possible . . .

And indeed everything will be still ahead, for one way in which Tarkovsky's camera functions is to resurrect the past by destroying measurable time. As we hear the last words "everything will be possible," Tarkovsky's camera shows us a closeup of a broken clock gear wheel seen through a water jar that functions like a magnifying glass. Significantly, this turns the device that measures irreversible time into a spiral that goes from the past to the future and the other way around. And as the camera slowly moves backward, we see next to this spiral-opened time his mother's / his wife's knitted shawl, made of similar round structures that mirror the broken clock wheel (Figure 2.2). Such juxtapositions of multiple realities based on similar formal structures point toward a deeper pattern behind the visible reality. As Maya Turovskaya notes, "Someone remarked at the Cannes Festival that Hari's knitted shawl in *Solaris* seemed possessed of an almost magical power as if it had a life of its own" (*Tarkovsky*, 97).

FIGURE 2.2 *Spiraling time in* The Mirror.

The object that Tarkovsky was resurrecting through this scene has a complex history. Before the surrealists found that it's only our habitual force of perception that makes us think that things are themselves and nothing else, it was Proust who argued for the necessity to unthink the relations between things. With its juxtaposition of different realities, poetry could convey the exact impression—or rather the revelation—of the hidden nature of reality: "it is surely logical, not from any artifice of symbolism but from a sincere desire to return to the very root of the impression, to represent one thing by that other for which, in the flash of a first illusion, we mistook it" (*The Guermantes Way*, 574). Thus Proust advocates metaphor over symbolism, and following Proust's conceptual distinctions, Tarkovsky constantly pointed out that objects in his films are not symbols, but metaphors: "I prefer to express myself in a metaphoric way. I insist on saying metaphoric and not symbolic. The symbol intrinsically comprises a specific meaning, an intellectual formula, while the metaphor is the image itself. It's an image that possesses the same characteristics as the world it represents. Contrary to the symbol, its meaning is undefined" (Guibert interview).

With Tarkovsky, time really is out of joint; the penknife has both broken the clock mechanism and disjointed the shawl's knitted rosettes. This pattern of a broken circle turned into a spiral is Tarkovsky's visual representation of time. This spiral branches toward two histories and two futures: Tarkovsky's own previous and future films, and his own past and future. The shawl in

The Mirror is very similar to the one worn in *Solaris* by Hari, the psychologist Chris's dead wife who comes back as a phantasm of his memory on the spaceship, reflected back by the dreaming ocean, Solaris. Chris's mother—another ghost from his past—wears a dress made of this pattern; it will be resurrected in *Nostalghia* in the pattern of the lace curtains in Domenico's ruined house, in the shawl with which the woman who prays to have a child covers her head, and ultimately, the white lace veil thrown on the ground that becomes the path that leads Andrei back to his lost home in Russia, in a dream vision that ends with a white angel far in the back, slowly dragging his wings through the dust and entering his house. This is the path that connects Andrei with his lost home, but also Arseny the father with his son, Andrei; ultimately, this is the path that takes us from Arseny Tarkovsky's poetry to his son's *Nostalghia*:

> By the jasmine lies a stone,
> Beneath the stone a treasure.
> Father's standing on the path,
> It is a white, white day.
> . . .
> Never again have I been
> As happy as then.
> Never again have I been
> As happy as then.
>
> There can be no returning
> Nor has it been given
> To tell of the sheer joy
> That filled my garden heaven.
>   ARSENY TARKOVSKY, "The White Day," *Poetry and Film*, 156–7

But there *can* be a return, both *The Mirror* and *Nostalghia* say, and Tarkovsky rewrites his father's poem by opening it: irreversible time can be opened, the spiral tells us. This is Proust's feeling of bliss when tasting the madeleine, when tripping on the uneven paving stone, or when touching his lips with a napkin in the Guermantes' library as he discovers how irreversible time can be overcome, because the lost paradise isn't really lost, it's only dormant within us until a chance encounter brings it back to life. Andrei Tarkovsky revisits his father's poem "The White Day" and with Proust's logic finds the possible return in the repeated lament of the very impossibility to return: "Never again have I been/ As happy as then./ Never again have I been/ As happy as then." These multiple reworkings of his readings from his father's poetry are reflected in the working titles of the film *The Mirror*: from *Confession*, to *White Day* and significantly, *A White, White Day*. Ultimately it would be the magic mirror that can make unrepeatable time return.

THE VAST STRUCTURE OF RECOLLECTION

A second scene from *The Mirror*, closer to the end of the film, takes the time-bending apparition of ghosts one step farther: doorframes are replaced with a complex use of mirrors that effaces differences between past and future. The young Aleksei goes with his mother to Nadezhda's house to sell a pair of earrings. Aleksei is left alone in a room for a few minutes, and symmetrically to the scene with his future son Ignat and the apparition of the nanny drinking tea, something unusual happens. As he sits on a chair, he looks into an oval mirror on the wall. On the table next to him, a closeup shows a couple of peeled potatoes; from a shelf above, a few drops of milk fall steadily on the table, in a rhythm that is revealed to be Aleksei's interior rhythm, and Henry Purcell's instrumental air "They tell us that your mighty powers above" from the opera *The Indian Queen* breaks out, an air that we've heard before in the film.

While the scene with Ignat was highly verbal, this one is entirely musical. As Proust also knew, following in the steps of Goethe (a frequent reference for Tarkovsky in his diary), music is liquid architecture and architecture is frozen music. Following Purcell's instrumental music, Aleksei glides slowly into the oval of the mirror and sees there a series of three dream vignettes. A small blurry mirror, nestled amid glowing coals, shows an indistinct human face. A woman's hand slowly closes a wardrobe's mirrored door, which reflects a man whose back is turned to the camera; he wears a winter coat and quickly steps out of the frame to reveal a young red-haired woman who's holding a burning twig in front of a stove. When she looks into the camera, a quick cut suggests that someone has opened the wardrobe door again, and the mysterious woman disappears as quickly as the nanny and the tea cup disappeared in the earlier scene. As the camera focuses on the hands holding the burning twig in a gesture of prayer, the music dims and only the crackling of the fire can be heard as we cut back to the room in Nadezhda's house and we see a rather confused Aleksei blinking as if he is waking up from a dream. In the background we hear the same flickering sound that was coming from the gas lamp that gradually went out. This must have been the external factor responsible for the three dream vignettes. But could this really be all there is to them? A closer look at each of these three vignettes reveals Tarkovsky's conception about time, that once again is intimately indebted to Proust.

The oval mirror that reveals these three vignettes is a metaphor epitomizing the entire film with its three generations. Each can be traced back to a dream, a memory, or a prophecy. The first vignette showing a small burning mirror dates back to Aleksei's early childhood when there was a great fire shown in the opening of the film. The fire had been caused by the kerosene stove that feeds into the second vignette, using the logic of dream work. The face reflected in the mirror is Aleksei's at age five, as an earlier dream memory in black and white showed him playing with the same mirror and then holding a big jar with milk; it's the same milk jar we see in Nadezhda's room where Aleksei enters.

The second vignette plays with an early trick employed by Méliès for his disappearing acts—covering and uncovering the woman who disappears in a magic box (or wardrobe). This is a memory that isn't Aleksei's, but rather his father's, and it is also a prophecy for Aleksei's own future. It anticipates—or rather prophesies—*Nostalghia*, where a similar dream scene showing a hand opening a mirror-covered wardrobe reveals a strange identity: Andrei the poet is reflected as the older Domenico, who is his self in the future. For the dream vignette in *The Mirror* that shows a man wearing a coat with a fur collar, Tarkovsky was using a photo of his father from 1937. This photo showed Arseny Tarkovsky wearing the same coat as the man in the second vignette, next to a mirror that reflects his profile from a skewed angle (Figure 2.3).

FIGURE 2.3 *Lev Gornung, photo of Arseny Tarkovsky (1937).*

THE VAST STRUCTURE OF RECOLLECTION

Tarkovsky used this photo again in *Nostalghia*, to construct an entire scene of double identities and parallel time threads. Failing to recognize this reference leads Johnson and Petrie to conflate two distinct generations—Aleksei's father and Aleksei himself—into one: they suppose that the man Aleksei sees in the oval mirror must be Aleksei's "imagining of the aftermath of an encounter between the redheaded girl and the military instructor" (*The Films of Andrei Tarkovsky*, 128). In fact, the winter coat isn't representing a minor character but rather signals Aleksei's absent father.

In *The Mirror*, the second vignette is both a memory of a past that doesn't belong to Aleksei and a prophecy of his own future. At the end of the disappearing teacup scene, Ignat was interrupted from his daydream by a phone call from his father, who could as well be his grandfather, given the echoing sound of the voice as well as the estranging tone that seems to come from a distant past. The voice on the phone tells him of a red-haired woman he was in love with when he was Ignat's age, and then Purcell's air begins. Because the mirror reflects the back of Aleksei's father (i.e. Tarkovsky's own father's back), the red-haired woman may also be his father's beloved, turning the vignette into a memory that Aleksei has inherited from his father, whose life story he will repeat. Symmetrically, this vignette can be read backwards, as the camera's shifting between the two faces of the mirror invites us to do. As the man on the phone says he met the red-haired woman during the war, he could be the absent, nameless father, a version of Arseny Tarkovsky, who was a war correspondent and lost his leg to gangrene after being wounded in action in 1943. As it's the same Aleksei/Ignat who appears in the training scene in winter, and he looks about fourteen years old in what seems to be a scene during the war, he doesn't have the age of either Arseny or Andrei at the time, but is somewhere in between both. With Andrei Tarkovsky, the three temporal layers—grandfather, father, and son—arc narrated simultaneously, not in irreversible time but in simultaneous space, as in his father's poetry: "One table for great-grandfather and grandson."

Tarkovsky wasn't the first poet to see multiple selves and different existences from different moments in time in the magic fire of the mirror. The red-haired woman lighting the fire, the bearer of the magic burning twig who was loved in different existences by the father and then the son in every generation, was in a former existence Françoise, the narrator's motherly maid in the *Recherche*:

> Françoise would come in to light the fire, and in order to make it draw, would throw upon it a handful of twigs, the scent of which, forgotten for a year past, traced round the fireplace a magic circle within which, glimpsing myself poring over a book, now at Combray, now at Doncières, I was as joyful, while remaining in my bedroom in Paris, as if I had been on the point of setting out for a walk along the Méséglise way, or of going

68 TIME REGAINED

to join Saint-Loup and his friends . . . even if, in recalling them, I could see them as pictures only, they nonetheless recreated out my present self, the whole of that self . . . the child and the youth who had first seen them. There had been not merely a change in the weather outside, or, inside the room, a change of smells; there had been in myself an alteration in age, the substitution of another person. The scent, in the frosty air, of the twigs of brushwood was like a fragment of the past, an invisible ice-floe detached from some bygone winter advancing into my room, often moreover, striated with this or that perfume or gleam of light.

The Captive, 24–5

Aleksei experiences an alteration in age and a substitution of person as the red-haired woman from his father's past and from his own future appears in *The Mirror*, first in a wintery landscape and then carrying the burning twig, bringing with her "the frosty air" of "a fragment of the past." As the scent of the twig advances, the gleam of light becomes the light in the room that goes off, bringing Aleksei with it to the present moment. *The Mirror* is a highly autobiographical, personal story, and one would expect it to be unrepeatable, especially where dreams are concerned. But it was both Arseny and Andrei Tarkovsky who defined life as a repeated dream:

And I have dreamed of this, and this is what I dream
And some day I shall dream of this again.
And all will be repeated, all be made incarnate,
And you will dream all that I have seen in dreams.

ARSENY TARKOVSKY, "And I have
dreamed of this," *Poetry and Film*, 164

Before Aleksei looked into the oval mirror to find there a self made of divergent selves coming from different generations, it was Proust's Marcel who did so, one night after his grandmother's death. The inception of his dream is the same as Aleksei's, a flickering fire: "I could not get to sleep at once, for the fire lighted up the room as though there were a lamp burning in it. Only it was nothing more than brief blaze, and—like a lamp, too, or like the daylight when night falls—its too bright light was not long in fading; and I entered the realm of sleep, which is like a second dwelling into which we move for that one purpose" (*Sodom and Gomorrah*, 516). In the realm of sleep—as in Tarkovsky's mirror—we get to be androgynous: "The race that inhabits it, like that of our first human ancestors, is androgynous. A man in it appears a moment later in the form of a woman" (516). Or the other way around. The first time the red-haired young woman appears, she is a ghost in Aleksei's father's memory, associated with war, winter, and her blistered lips. The second time she appears in the magic oval mirror, her lips are clean, but Aleksei's lips are blistered. As she looks over her shoulder, it's the past that looks back to the future. "And you will dream all that I have seen in dreams," seems to be Aleksei's secret message from his absent father. In his turn, he will pass the dream on to his son, Ignat.

But the magic of Tarkovsky's oval mirror doesn't end here. The film *The Mirror* itself behaves like the oval mirror Aleksei looks into, a portal that effaces the difference between past, present and future, including the filmmakers and writers who will build on Tarkovsky's work in the future. The scene of the oval mirror, lit by the fire of memory, brings together past and future in the pages of one of the most beautiful and poetic contemporary Russian novels: *Laurus* (2012) by Eugene Vodolazkin. *Laurus* tells the story of Arseny, a healer gifted with the visionary power of faith who spends his life as a saint hoping to repay the untimely death of the woman he loves, Ustina, who had died in childbirth. Close to the ending of the novel, Arseny looks into the mirror of fire, as Aleksei did in Tarkovsky's *The Mirror*, and the child in him (and from a symmetrical earlier scene in the novel) looks back at him from the past that looks prophetically onto the future:

> Sometimes he would see his face in the fire. The face of a light-haired boy in Christofer's home. A wolf curled up at the boy's feet. The boy looks into the stove and sees his own face. Gray hair, gathered on the back of his neck, frames it. The face is covered with wrinkles. Despite the dissimilarity, the boy understands this is a reflection of himself. Only many years later. And under other circumstances. It is the reflection of someone who is sitting by the fire and sees the face of a light-haired boy and does not want the person who has entered to disturb him.
>
> *Laurus*, 311

Tarkovsky's cinema is an oval mirror filtering literature's past through Proust before returning again, in the future, through Vodolazkin.

Like Raúl Ruiz and Paolo Sorrentino after him, Tarkovsky sees Proust as a fellow filmmaker. Going back to Proust's interest in Japanese culture, Tarkovsky will associate Proust's treatment of the object as a repository of a past that can one day be resurrected, to the Japanese concept of *sabi*:

> *Sabi*, then, is a natural rustiness, the charm of olden days, the stamp of time. . . . In a sense the Japanese could be said to be trying to master time aesthetically. Here one is inevitably reminded of what Proust said of his grandmother: "Even when she had to make someone an ostensibly practical gift, when she had to give an armchair, a dinner service or a walking-stick, she would look out for 'old' ones, as if these, purged by long disuse of their utilitarian character, were able to tell us how people had lived in the old days, rather than serve our modern needs."
>
> *Sculpting in Time*, 59

Tarkovsky finds in Proust his own poetics of the object. But Tarkovsky's interest in Proust goes far beyond a theoretical one. The narrative structure of *The Mirror*, the most openly autobiographical of Tarkovsky's films, is intimately modeled on the structure of the *Recherche*.[4] Like Marcel, writing the story of his life from his deathbed in a narrative whose ending is the very beginning of the book, Aleksei's anonymous Father or Aleksei himself is seen on his deathbed (the notebooks Tarkovsky kept during *The Mirror* include a photograph of himself as the dying hero at the end, holding a bird). He is trying to rewind the film of his memory, in an attempt to make time come back and liberate him from the guilt of having abandoned his family. But his face is obscured, and we only see his naked torso and right hand. Who is it that we're seeing? And why is it that Tarkovsky chose to obscure this scene, which suggests himself as the author on his deathbed? *The Mirror* never shows the adult Aleksei; we only hear his voice off-camera. But we do twice see Aleksei's father naked from the waist up, in symmetrical black and white dream scenes showing Maria washing her hair or levitating above the marital bed. By obscuring the face of the dying man, Tarkovsky finally merges the father and son into one single being. Time turns back: the son becomes his father. This identity will be at the heart of *Nostalghia*, too: the man who leaves his mother, his wife Maria, and their two children back in Russia is clearly modeled on Arseny Tarkovsky himself. But his name is Andrei.

Next to the dying man's bed, we see the two elderly women from the disappearing teacup scene: the nanny and the aged maid. Why does Tarkovsky edit the film to imply a continuity between this scene and the next, where we see the absent father played by Oleg Yankovsky, young again, with his wife Maria at their house in the country? A second before the father dies, Tarkovsky's camera shows a closeup of his hand, holding a small bird that seems dead. A few drops of blood are on the bedsheet next to it. As he lifts his hand to liberate the bird, he dies, but his soul flies away with the bird that comes to life and disappears into the sky. From there, the camera glides down to show us Aleksei's father young again, lying on his back with Maria in a meadow, just as in the previous scene he was lying on his deathbed. He asks her if she would like to have a boy or a girl. She looks over her shoulder, and in the magic mirror of time she sees her unborn children, both a boy and a girl on the meadow, accompanied by the aged

---

[4]Film scholars miss out on how much Proust, not just other filmmakers, is behind the architectural construction. For Nariman Skakov, the film is "a complex exercise in counterpoint consisting of a series of recollections of a dying man . . . Memories of childhood and scenes from the man's present life are intermixed with dreams and 'unmotivated' leaps into the historical past by means of a documentary chronicle . . . All of these place *Mirror* in the domain of highly experimental cinematic endeavours" by Resnais, Fellini, and Bergman (*The Cinema of Tarkovsky*, 100).

mother: her mother-in-law, but also herself years later—Maria Vishnyakova, Tarkovsky's own mother. Nothing has yet come to pass, and we are back to the moment before the beginning of the film. Aleksei's dream has come true at last: "everything will be still ahead, everything will be possible . . ."

Ahead was also Eugene Vodolazkin's novel *Laurus*, born thirty-seven years later, in 2012. "There are events that resemble one another," an elder tells Arseny, now monk Amvrosy. "Remember, O Amvrosy, that repetitions are granted for our salvation and in order to surmount time." "Do you mean to say I will meet Ustina again?" asks the monk who has spent his life with the ghost of his dead lover in the hope they will meet again. "I want to say that no things are irreparable" (*Laurus*, 309).

*

Nostalghia takes the construction of time's architecture to a whole new level. No longer visible as the mirror or doorframe, it's now the camera's eye that becomes a corridor in time, allowing time to flow freely between past and future. It's the channel through which spouses and lovers communicate, a dream realm in Gérard de Nerval's and Proust's sense of dream as a second life. Attempting to reach an editing level that recreates inner time, Tarkovsky developed a way of doing so with a minimum of technical effects. The tracking shot, Tarkovsky's trademark meant to create the impression of real-time filming, is used twice in *Nostalghia* to indicate the form of time.

First, it's used in a scene that once again draws on the 1937 photo of Arseny Tarkovsky. Andrei, the Russian poet and writer who's researching his next subject in Italy, is in the house of Domenico, who is a version of what he could become if he pursued his faith in the possibility of escaping time's irreversibility. Domenico too lost his family, whom he kept locked away from the world for a decade. In Domenico's ruined, moldy house, Andrei is shown next to a mirror, looking pensive. But something attracts Andrei's attention, and the camera draws into a closeup of his face to follow him turning his gaze to his right. At that second, the *Ode to Joy* from Beethoven's ninth symphony is heard and the camera slowly glides, with Andrei's gaze, along a shelf on which a series of apparently random objects are shown, including an open book (either the Bible or Arseny Tarkovsky's volume of poetry), a broken clock, an old photo. But this isn't what has drawn Andrei's attention. In an apparently single tracking shot, the camera stops at the other end of the shelf, on the most surrealist object yet: Andrei himself, looking over his right shoulder. With his back to the camera, he is Andrei from the other side of the mirror, the self we saw reflected in the opening of the scene, itself a remake of Andrei Tarkovsky's father's photo.

A second scene from *Nostalghia* takes the tracking shot to its ultimate development in Tarkovsky. Andrei has a dream of his home in Russia that begins with his voice, off screen, calling his wife's name. Maria is in bed and wakes up, frightened by the voice. She slowly gets out of the bed, all the while looking back over her shoulder toward the camera, as if she were followed by a ghost. She opens the door onto a foggy Russian landscape, recreated from a photo that Tarkovsky had also used for his childhood house in *The Mirror*. Andrei's dog and younger son are outside, and Maria, her daughter, and the grandmother join them. They take their places in front of the camera as if waiting to be photographed, yet they constantly look back, again over their shoulders, and the camera starts tracking the scene, gliding from left to right. In a symmetrical twist to the mirror scene in Domenico's house, as the family vanishes from the frame, they reappear twice. First, in a close up, the three generations of women stand on different spatial planes, facing the camera. They all look back over their shoulder at the house. The camera continues to glide, and as the women disappear from the frame, they start appearing a second time, but farther away. The gliding camera has also moved backwards, as if departing from this dreamed memory. The scene closes as the camera rests in a still frame, showing the sunrise and the three women looking back toward the house and the rising sun, while we hear a sound like that of a departing ship. Andrei the dreamer's camera-ship that was gliding in this tracking shot returns to Italy, where he is at the present moment. We now see Andrei from behind, turning to the camera. Symmetrically to the opening of the scene, when he called Maria's name offscreen, it's now Maria who calls his name from behind the invisible camera's eye: "Andrei" she whispers, and he turns to look into her invisible eyes and into the dark eye of the camera.

Andrei is in Italy to research the life of Pavel Sosnovsky, a freed serf who went to Italy to become a composer but got so homesick that he committed suicide. Andrei's *nostalghia* is a form of illness too, and that's why he drifts into dreamland, like Proust's Marcel, soothing his "homesick heart . . . as from a journey too distant not to have taken a long time" (*Sodom and Gomorrah*, 519). Dreams provide the only moments of bliss for Andrei, for he inhabits them with Maria. More than dreaming the same dream, it is the reality they share even when they aren't together, and this reality is outside time. This reality is constructed by Tarkovsky as the eye of the camera. Sometimes we see Maria through her oval bedframe—an extension of the camera's eye—as her absent husband's voice calls her (Figure 2.4). For Tarkovsky, the eye of the camera is the dream space that allows the spouses to communicate.

Time doesn't flow in a single direction, but rather back and forth, as does Tarkovsky's visionary camera that shows us simultaneously the past and the future, like a corridor in time, shaped as the cylindrical corridor in *Solaris* or the round black opening into the "selva oscura" encountered "nell mezzo del camin di nostra vita"—the opening line of Dante's *Inferno*, which we hear quoted offscreen in *The Mirror*. Spouses, lovers, parents, and children communicate through this corridor that connects all of Tarkovsky's films.

FIGURE 2.4 *Maria hearing her absent husband's voice in* Nostalghia.

Like a genuine magic mirror, his camera effaces all differences between past and future, brought together simultaneously on screen by the poet's visionary eye. In his diary, Tarkovsky quotes Montaigne for this understanding of time:

> "We do not move in one direction, rather do we wander back and forth, turning now this way and now that. We go back on our own tracks . . ." [Montaigne, *The Complete Essays*, III, Ch. VI]. That thought of Montaigne's reminds me about something I thought of in connection with flying saucers, humanoids, and the remains of unbelievably advanced technology found in some ancient ruins. They write about aliens; but I think that in these phenomena we are in fact confronting ourselves; that is, our future, our descendants who are travelling in time.
>
> *Time within Time*, June 23, 1981, 282

The Cryptogram Reality

Tarkovsky's poetics of cinema, *Sculpting in Time* (literally in Russian "Imprinted/ Captured Time") came out first in German in 1986, only three years after Marguerite Yourcenar published with Gallimard a collection of essays on art and the passage of time, entitled *Le Temps, ce grand sculpteur*. Yourcenar's title essay had first been published in *La Revue des voyages* in 1954, and then included in the 1981 volume *Voyages*. The English title of Tarkovsky's book is appropriate, as both Yourcenar and Tarkovsky were drawing on Proust's representation of time as the sculptor of his *Recherche*;

Proust was in turn drawing on Victor Hugo's phrase "temps, ce grand sculpteur" from the fourth canto of *Voix intérieures*. For Tarkovsky,

> What is the essence of the director's work? We could define it as sculpting in time. Just as a sculptor takes a lump of marble, and, inwardly conscious of the features of his finished piece, removes everything that is not part of it—so the film-maker, from a "lump of time" made up of an enormous, solid cluster of living facts, cuts off and discards whatever he does not need, leaving only what is to be an element of the finished film, what will prove to be integral to the cinematic image.
>
> *Sculpting in Time*, 63–4

Yourcenar speaks of a double sculpture and a double time: first, it's the artist who carves the sculpture; but secondly, it is time that adds its own sculpting to the statue, changing it through its "imprint." This second stage produces an involuntary beauty, in an automatic process of creation over time. Involuntary, unconscious beauty, objective hazard and automatic creation: Yourcenar defines time's artistic effects using all the surrealists' major concepts. "Certain of these modifications are sublime. To the beauty intended by a human mind, an epoque, a particular social formation, they add an involuntary beauty, connected to the chances of history, thanks to the effects of natural processes and of time" (*Le Temps*). Exposed to time's work, these statues "no longer belong to us," Yourcenar says, quoting Ariel's song from *The Tempest*: "Like that corpse of which the most beautiful and most mysterious of Shakespeare's songs speaks, they have undergone a sea change that is as rich as it is strange."

At the heart of Tarkovsky's *Nostalghia* lies a mysterious case of sculpting in time. Andrei is guided through Italy by a beautiful translator, Eugenia, who tempts Andrei, but without success, as he is more and more immersed in an interior journey with a religious drive. He often dreams of his wife and two children back home, and throughout his journey he is followed by images of motherhood—one in particular. The film opens with a scene filmed in the San Pietro church in Arezzo, where Andrei has come to see Piero della Francesca's *Madonna del Parto* or Madonna of Childbirth (1457). However, he doesn't enter the church, only Eugenia does; she witnesses women praying next to the fresco, in front of a statue of the Virgin, so that they can be blessed with the miracle of motherhood. As his diary shows, Tarkovsky saw this scene as the heart of his film and structuring it, giving Proust's "vast structure of recollection" a whole new meaning.

Nostalghia begins by juxtaposing Piero della Francesca's *Madonna del Parto* with the face of Eugenia the temptress, and then decomposes the painting into signs that he places in key scenes: the Madonna becomes Eugenia, but more significantly, the painting is brought to life through the

THE VAST STRUCTURE OF RECOLLECTION

ritual performed in the church. Tarkovsky's visual reading of *Madonna del Parto* treats painting much as Akira Kurosawa will do in *Dreams* by bringing Van Gogh's paintings to life. In the painting, the Virgin subtly points with her right hand into the split of her dress to reveal her pregnant belly. The two angels who hold open the pavilion's curtains are a reminder of Archangel Gabriel, who brought Mary the good news of motherhood (Color Plate 1).

In Tarkovsky's *Nostalghia*, this story will take the shape of the angel seen by Andrei entering his house in Russia, and then in the church during the ritual, birds suddenly come out from the parting of the cloak worn by the statue of the Virgin. Later, Andrei meets a little girl named Angela in the Bagno Vignoni, and finally Tarkovsky shows the statue of an angel in the pool at Bagno Vignoni. For Tarkovsky, this conception was an organic development of his film *Solaris*, which showed how our entire universe is only the dream of the giant brain/ocean called Solaris, and of *The Mirror*, where life is the reflection of what we see in the magic waters of the mirror of memory. The statue of the angel seen underwater in *Nostalghia* also recalls the ending of Marguerite Yourcenar's essay "Le Temps, ce grand sculpteur": "The Neptune, a good workshop copy, destined to adorn the dock of a village where the fishermen would offer him the first fruits of their catch, has descended into Neptune's realm. The heavenly Venus and the one of the streets have become the Aphrodite of the seas" (*Le Temps*). Tarkovsky takes this vision one step further, to show how the Virgin Mary has become *la Marie des mers*, for she is after all *La Mère des Mers, La Mère des Mères*, as Yourcenar calls her in a dream in her book *Dreams and Destinies*.

With Proust, Yourcenar, and Kurosawa, Tarkovsky shared an interest in dreams as a second life. In *The Magic Lantern*, his great admirer Ingmar Bergman noticed the affinity between Kurosawa and Tarkovsky as well as their common debt to Georges Méliès:

> When film is not a document, it is dream. That is why Tarkovsky is the greatest of them all. He moves with such naturalness in the room of dreams. He doesn't explain. What should he explain anyhow? He is a spectator, capable of staging his visions in the most unwieldy but, in a way, the most willing of media ... Fellini, Kurosawa and Buñuel move in the same fields as Tarkovsky ... Méliès was always there without having to think about it. He was a magician by profession. Film as dream, film as music.
>
> 73

The scene in the opening of *Nostalghia* shows Eugenia walking into a church and stopping in front of the *Madonna del Parto*, whom she strikingly resembles. Eugenia is portrayed as a frivolous woman who isn't a believer, yet she is moved beyond words by the fresco. Tarkovsky invites the viewer to superimpose Eugenia's face on Maria's as he alternates between their expressions in a movement that gradually becomes a close-up. The second superimposition is of the painted *Madonna del Parto* onto the image of a woman who prays for a child in front of a statue of the Virgin. After she finishes her prayer, she opens the split of the Virgin's mantle, from which dozens of birds fly out, grazing her face as if they were the Holy Ghost descending on Mary as a dove to bring her the good news of motherhood. Through the superimposition of images, Tarkovsky suggests that the trivial and the frivolous—Eugenia—can find true religious feeling and fertility through the means of art.

This surreal scene, perhaps the most powerful in the entire film, isn't Tarkovsky's own creation, an "invented ritual" as James MacGillivray believes ("Andrei Tarkovsky's 'Madonna del Parto,'" 96). Maya Turovskaya writes off this scene as a touch of "local color" in a film that has generally "'de-Italianized' Italy" (*Tarkovsky*, 120). In fact, this scene is a creative transformation of at least three different sources: a poem by Tonino Guerra, who worked with Tarkovsky on the screenplay, two poems by Arseny Tarkovsky, and a source that no one has noticed: a story by Yourcenar, "Our-Lady-of-the-Swallows." As an entire year is missing from Tarkovsky's diary (May 1982-May 1983) just when he was filming *Nostalghia*, we can't know what books he was reading or what his thoughts were when he constructed this scene. But knowing his network of elective affinities as well as his reading preferences, we can put together a plausible story.

All of Tarkovsky's films variously develop the metaphor (not symbol!) of the bird. Tarkovsky always described himself as a poet, and he believed that poetry is behind all the revelations of philosophy and science. In this, he was very much his father's son. Perhaps this is why a poem that Tonino Guerra wrote for Tarkovsky, which he reads to him in the opening of their documentary *Tempo di viaggio*, spoke so intimately to Tarkovsky that he asks Guerra to read it to him again at the end of the documentary:

> What's a house? I don't know.
> A cloak? Or an umbrella if it rains?
> I've filled mine with bottles, rags, wooden ducks, curtains, fans
> As if I'd never go out again.
> So what's it then, if not a cage
> That imprisons those who stop by,
> Even a bird like you

Tarkovsky reworks the house that provides shelter from rain but also from the passage of time into the image of the Virgin's cloak that hides dozens of birds; as a cage that imprisons people, it appears literally in the house Domenico builds to protect his family from the passage of time. Yet even though it sheds some light on the ritual performed in front of the fresco,

THE VAST STRUCTURE OF RECOLLECTION

Guerra's poem doesn't explain the ultimate meaning of the scene's architecture. Closer to that come two poems by Arseny Tarkovsky, "A ghost, an empty sound" (1955) and "Swallows" (1967).

A ghost, an empty sound,
A legacy too late,
Childhood's simulacrum,
My own poor town.

My shoulders are burdened
By so many years.
This meeting is pointless
When all's said and done.

Beyond the window now
There's another sky –
Pallid, smoky-blue
And a small white dove.

A scarlet curtain
Hangs in the window,
Jarringly red
From afar.

The waxen mask
Of times long gone
Watches blank-eyed
As I pass.

ARSENY TARKOVSKY, "A ghost, an
empty sound," *Poetry and Film*, 154–5

This poem could summarize Andrei's role and trajectory in *Nostalghia*. Himself a ghost because he's mortally ill when he's away from his homeland—this is literally the Russian meaning of *nostalghia* as Tarkovsky reminds us—he finds a mirrored double, symmetrically placed at the end of the poem in "the waxen mask / of times long gone." André Bazin spoke of funeral masks as ancestors of the photograph, and *Nostalghia* is modeled on Tarkovsky's polaroids previously used in *The Mirror*. The small white dove seen through the window frame is one image that he uses in juxtaposition to Piero della Francesca's Madonna, echoed later in the film in the dream Andrei has of Maria back home. As he calls her name and she wakes up, as if hearing "a ghost, an empty sound," she goes to the triple window to open the curtains, as the two angels do in Piero della Francesca's fresco; the curtain in Arseny Tarkovsky's poem is even scarlet, as in the painting (Figure 2.5). A white dove is revealed, as Maria becomes a version of her archetype, Maria, in a contemporary setting.

FIGURE 2.5 *Maria opening the curtains in* Nostalghia.

Even more interesting is the second poem, "Swallows":

Swallows—go on flying, do not let your bills
Take up drill or saw, don't make discoveries,
Don't copy us, it's enough that you can speak
So fluently in your barbaric tongue,
That your stately retinue is blest with sharpest eyes
And the sacred joy of nascent green.

I have been in Georgia, I too made my way
By grass and shattered stones to Bagrat's church –
A broken wine-jar, above whose mouth you spread
A hanging net. And Simon Chikovani
(Whom I loved and who was like my brother)
Said he'd failed you in this world, for he'd forgotten
To write lines about your weightless convocation;
That he'd played here as a boy; that on Bagrat himself
Your clamorous speech may once have cast its spell.

In Simon's place I render you all praise.
Don't copy us, but here, in the land where Simon
Sleeps in earth, in your own language
As in a trance—sing one line of my verse.

ARSENY TARKOVSKY, "Swallows," *Poetry and Film*, 156

With this poem, we are coming a step closer to Andrei Tarkovsky's central scene in *Nostalghia*. The birds are no longer metaphoric, but recall an actual story with a clear historical setting.

THE VAST STRUCTURE OF RECOLLECTION

A response to the poetry of Arseny's friend Simon Chikovani, who was the leader of the Georgian Futurist movement, "Swallows" is a vision set in a ruined temple, the eleventh-century Orthodox Bagrati Cathedral built by the first king of the united Georgia, Bagrati III, and consecrated to the Assumption of the Virgin. Even though the cathedral was mostly destroyed by the Ottomans, a fresco of the Virgin in the southern lobby survived. Roofless until a massive restoration began in 2009, the Bagrati Cathedral looked a good deal like the abbey of San Galgano that Andrei Tarkovsky chose for his final scene in *Nostalghia*. The Gelati Monastery, founded a hundred years after the Bagrati Cathedral, was built very close to it and survived better. Like the Cathedral, the monastery is known as the Church of Virgin Mary the Blessed. Its central mosaic behind the iconostasis shows the Virgin as *Theotokos* or Bearer of God, framed by the archangels Michael and Gabriel. Mirroring his father's tribute to his Georgian friend, Andrei Tarkovsky transports his father's poem to Italy, and replaces the Bagrati Cathedral with the San Pietro church and ultimately with the ruins of San Galgano in *Nostalghia*, and in San Pietro he finds the perfect Catholic correspondence for the fresco of the Virgin in the Bagrati and Gelati cathedrals: Piero della Francesca's *Madonna del Parto*.

Arseny Tarkovsky's ode to the swallows that inspired Bagrati III to build them a cathedral makes its way into the film. Every time Andrei dreams of his lost home, we hear the chirping of birds: "in your own language / As in a trance—sing one line of my verse." But the "barbaric" tongue spoken by the swallows, apparently untraceable in *Nostalghia*, opens a whole new literary venue for Andrei Tarkovsky, one that takes us all the way back Yourcenar's "Our-Lady-of-the-Swallows," included in her 1938 volume *Oriental Tales*. Unlike the other stories in the volume, this story isn't based on a legend; Yourcenar invented it to explain the name of a chapel she visited in Greece. This means that Tarkovsky must have read Yourcenar's tale, as there was no other source on which both would have been drawing. Yourcenar doesn't give the name of the chapel in her story, but she does specify that it's on the banks of the river Cephissus or Kifisos. In the medieval period, a small and austere monastery was built there dedicated to the Virgin of the Swallow, called Panagia Chelidonas. Yourcenar became interested in Kifisia as a central part of Attica, because during the reign of Hadrian (to whom she would consecrate the fictional *Memoirs of Hadrian* in 1951) it became a center for philosophers. Aullus Gellius, who wrote *The Attic Nights*, restored a sanctuary to the nymphs there. In "Our-Lady-of-the-Swallows," Yourcenar tells the story of a monk, Therapion, who wants to purify the place by driving away nymphs who are still living in a cave. Driven by religious intolerance, he thinks it's his Christian duty to free the place from these remnants of pagan beliefs, and he builds a chapel at the entrance to their cave: "The monk feared them like a pack of she-wolves . . . they failed to arouse in him unclean longings because their nakedness revolted him like the smooth flesh of the caterpillar or the slithery skin of the grass snake" (*Oriental Tales*, 89).

In *Nostalghia*, Tarkovsky draws on this story on the levels of the plot and of the imagery. His hero wasn't the first Andrei to be tempted by a beautiful woman to stray from his religious path. Early in Tarkovsky's career, it was Andrei Rublev, the medieval monk who became one of the most renowned Byzantine icon painters, who was tempted by a similar nymph and gave into the temptation, after which he lost his faith and abandoned his art. In *Andrei Rublev*, the film that made Tarkovsky renowned worldwide, the monk carries with him the pagan woman who had made him lose everything, until in the end he finds faith again and returns to his art.

Nostalghia's Andrei knows better. When Eugenia comes to his room wearing a lacy black negligée, with the excuse that her room has run out of water, he rejects her advances. Angry that he isn't responding to her charms, Eugenia bursts into a frightening monologue that culminates with her half undressing and showing him her left breast. "What are you all after? These? Here! But not you. You're a kind of saint." Eugenia goes on to tell Andrei of a dream she had that uses imagery identical to that used by Yourcenar to describe carnal temptation—the caterpillar, the snake: "when I met you, the same night I dreamed that a soft worm with lots of legs fell on my head. It stung me, it was poisonous. I kept shaking my head until it fell off. I tried to squash it before it reached the wardrobe but it was no good because I just kept missing it . . . and since that night I keep touching my hair. Thank God there's been nothing between us!" Totally puzzled, Andrei leaves the room, saying to himself: "She's insane."

In Yourcenar's story, Therapion would feel the nymphs' "hot breath on his face, like that of an almost tame animal timidly roaming a room" (*Oriental Tales*, 89). Andrei falls asleep in the hotel room and has an erotic dream of Maria and Eugenia caught in a sexual embrace as Maria looks into the camera. We switch to Eugenia sitting on the bed next to Andrei, looking down at his face, crying silently, her hot breath on his face. Her hair runs down over him like Maria's white lace shawl, as Tarkovsky shows us a closeup of Eugenia's arm and hand that bears a strange mark, like a wound. Her fingernails are dirty, and she looks like a ghost returned from the grave. As she clasps the mattress, we cut to Maria's hand turning Eugenia's face in a sensual gesture. Oddly enough, film critics shy away from discussing this scene as erotic: Andrei "subconsciously acknowledges an attraction toward Eugenia that he represses in waking life but resolves this by having the wife and potential mistress lovingly accept each other" (Johnson and Petrie, *The Films of Andrei Tarkovsky*, 167); "The women touch each other tenderly with outstretched fingers (a gesture from Renaissance painting) almost like an echo, a faint reflection of an alien culture" (Maya Turovskaya, *Tarkovsky*, 124); "his conflicting desires for Eugenia and for home resolve themselves into a fantasy of Eugenia's reconciliation with his wife" (Robert Bird, *Andrei*

Tarkovsky: Elements of Cinema, 177). Yet as Chris Marker rightly remarked: "There is nothing more earthy, more carnal than the work of this reputed mystical filmmaker" (*One Day in the Life of Andrei Arsenevich*).

In Yourcenar's tale, one evening as the monk is guarding the entrance to the chapel, "he saw on the path a woman coming toward him . . . a strange radiance shone through [her] dark cloth, as if she had spread the cloak of night over the morning. In spite of her extreme youth, she had the gravity, the slow pace, the dignity of a very old woman, and her sweetness was that of mellow grapes or a scented blossom" (94–6). She persuades the monk to let her talk to the nymphs.

> Sharper wails were heard in the darkness, twitterings and a sound like the rustling of wings. The young woman spoke to the Nymphs in an unknown tongue, perhaps that of angels and birds. After a moment, she reappeared by the side of the monk, who had not ceased praying. "Behold," she said, "and listen." Innumerable small piercing cries came from inside her cloak. She opened it, and Therapion the monk saw that in the folds of her dress she bore hundreds of young swallows. She stretched out her arms, like a woman praying, and let the birds fly away. And then she said, in a voice as clear as the sound of a harp: "Go, my children." The freed swallows soared into the evening sky, drawing with their beaks and their wings inscrutable signs.
>
> 97–8

FIGURE 2.6 *Marguerite Yourcenar's pencil drawing on the opening page of "Our-Lady-of-the-Swallows" in a copy of her* Nouvelles orientales. *Courtesy of Houghton Library, Harvard.*

In the Italian Renaissance paintings of the Virgin and Child, the swallow sometimes appeared as a symbol of Christ's resurrection. One example is Carlo Crivelli's 1491 altarpiece *La Madonna della Rondine* (*The Madonna of the Swallow*). Like her Orthodox double, the Madonna is flanked by two saints rather than angels: Saint Jerome, who represents the scholar, and Saint Sebastian, who represents the soldier. The baby Jesus is looking at Saint Jerome, who holds a miniature chapel resting on two books symbolizing religious learning. From the chapel emerge rays of the sun (God's words as logos), as in the iconographic tradition of the Annunciation in Renaissance painting. Crivelli added an arcade to frame the Virgin and Jesus, and on the architrave, just above the miniature chapel, he placed the swallow.

In a surreal encounter, two visionary poets—Yourcenar and Arseny Tarkovsky—interpreted the swallow through a religious framing to promote religious tolerance. Yourcenar's mysterious virgin "spoke to the Nymphs in an unknown tongue, perhaps that of angels and birds," bringing peace between Christianity and the pre-Christian forms of belief. Arseny Tarkovsky's swallows "can speak / So fluently in [their] barbaric tongue," which is that of angels and poets: "in your own language / As in a trance— sing one line of my verse." When Yourcenar and Arseny Tarkovsky devised their vision of the swallow as speaking an unknown or barbaric language, they were both drawing on the ancient Greek idea that oracles and priestesses speak in tongues. As the classicist Thomas Harrison has written: "It is also because of the imagined incomprehensibility of foreign languages that the frequent analogy is drawn between foreign languages, prophecy and the sound of birds. . . . Cassandra's prophecies likewise are described as uttered in a 'barbarian language' like a swallow" ("Herodotus' Conception of Foreign Languages," 17–18).

Yourcenar's story is also based on a dream that she notes in her book *Dreams and Destinies*, entitled "Wax Candles in the Cathedral." In her dream, she enters an empty cathedral where she finds a wall covered in candles, in front of which she sees a majestic woman. "I do not know if this is a living woman, or only a statue," she writes. "She is propped against what seems to me a drapery traversed with great vertical folds, but upon a closer look I see that this is actually a dress with deep pleats, like the fluting of columns, and that the tall standing woman is propped against the legs of a tall seated woman whose immense knees overarch the church vault and vanish in all directions into the night" (39–40). Piero della Francesca's *Madonna del Parto* is constructed on a similar basis: the Madonna's split in the dress is doubled by the angels' opening the curtain of what was initially a larger structure, a tent pavilion, in which the art historian Maurizio Clavesi sees a representation of the Ark of the Covenant (*Piero della Francesca*). The Madonna herself is like the one in Yourcenar's dream: she is placed in the belly of a bigger Madonna. This is a statue, Yourcenar tells us; and from

THE VAST STRUCTURE OF RECOLLECTION 83

there, Tarkovsky places the statue of the Virgin Mary at the center of the childbirth ritual.

Like the woman in Tarkovsky's *Nostalghia*, the dreaming Yourcenar feels compelled to pray to this double goddess: "I hold myself upright before this goddess; I invoke her with arms upraised in a gesture of prayer, as are hers in a gesture of benediction. Something very deep within me advises me to name her mother, or rather *mothers*" (*Dreams and Destinies*, 40). The dream ends as the dreamer lights a candle: "I feel compelled to add a candle to that display of flames; besides, I understand that to fail in this obligation would be worse than sacrilege; this crime would bring disaster" (40). It's not surprising, then, that in *Nostalghia* the act of lighting a candle becomes Andrei's symbolic task in the film's final and longest tracking shot. As he manages to carry his lit candle over a steaming pool on a third attempt, Domenico sets himself on fire in the Piazza dei Musei Capitolini in Rome, becoming a burning candle, like the one in Arseny Tarkovsky's poem that is quoted in the film to illustrate true faith.

In his diary, Tarkovsky records a dream from 1972 that resonates with Yourcenar's dreams that show a cinematic imagination and a painter's eye. Here, like Van Gogh, to whom his father dedicated a poem, Tarkovsky perceives the texture of things, the pattern hidden underneath the skin of reality:

I had a strange dream last night: I was looking up at the sky, and it was very, very light, and soft; and high, high above me it seemed to be slowly boiling, like light that had materialized, like the fibres of a sunlit fabric, like silken, living stitches in a piece of Japanese embroidery. And those tiny fibres, light-bearing, living threads, seemed to be moving and floating and becoming like birds, hovering, so high up that they could never be reached. So high that if the birds were to lose feathers the feathers wouldn't fall, they wouldn't come down to the earth, they would fly upwards, be carried off and vanish from our world forever. And soft, enchanted music was flowing down from that great height. The music seemed to sound like the chiming of little bells; or else the birds' chirping was like music.

Time within Time, April 6, 1972, 56

Tarkovsky, "the man who saw the Angel" (Ernst Neizvestny) could show his visions to us through his camera eye, which captures our world as it once was and keeps it unchanged for eternity, defeating the passage of time and death. And this angel of the lens originates in poetry.

A fine wind blows into the heart,
And you fly on and on,
While within the film love holds
The soul fast by her sleeve.

Bird-like stealing grain by grain
From oblivion—and now?
She does not let you fall to dust,
Being dead, you are alive –

Not wholly, but a hundredth part,
In muted tone or sunk in sleep,
As if wandering through some field
In a land beyond our ken.

All that's seen and dear and living
Flies on once again,
Once the angel of the lens
Takes your world beneath his wing.

ARSENY TARKOVSKY, "Photography," *Poetry and Film*, 121

3

In That Sleep of Death What Dreams May Come

Van Gogh, Kurosawa, Yourcenar

On July 27, 1890, Vincent van Gogh set out to paint his last painting, *Wheatfield with Crows*, in the small village of Auvers-sur-Oise, where his brother Theo, his lifelong friend and constant supporter, could keep an eye on him after the repeated mental breakdowns that made painting a strenuous effort. After finishing the painting, Van Gogh put a bullet through his chest; two days later, he passed away under his brother's eyes. Theo had a last letter from Vincent dated July 23, though nothing in it gave any sign of what was about to happen. But when Van Gogh shot himself, an unsent draft of the letter was found on him. The two versions differed dramatically. The letter he ended up sending was full of everyday details related to his brother's recent marriage, telling him about his paintings in progress, and including several sketches, as he usually did in his letters to Theo, whereas the unsent draft spoke in almost ominous terms about his consuming devotion to his work and his special relationship with his brother. One sentence, though, was almost unchanged in both versions of the letter: "I'd really like to write to you about many things, but I sense the pointlessness of it" (Letter RM25, July 23, 1890). And yet, how pointed this pointlessness.

This letter carried a secret message. The draft spoke of his love for Theo, whom he credited for making his art possible, and with an ardent and consuming religious devotion to his work, Van Gogh closed his draft with an oracular, unfinished sentence: "Ah well, I risk my life for my own work and my reason has half foundered in it—very well—but you're not one of the dealers in men; as far as I know and can judge I think you really act with humanity, but what can you do" (*"mais que veux tu"*). "Ah well, really we can only make our paintings speak," he said earlier in the draft letter. But what was *Wheatfield with Crows* speaking of? A hundred years later, the

Japanese filmmaker Akira Kurosawa attempted to solve this mystery in his oracular film *Dreams* (1990). Told from the perspective of an anonymous narrator, the film is composed of a series of eight apparently unrelated vignettes based on actual dreams that Kurosawa had had. He visualized each vignette using intensely colored drawings he'd made based on paintings by Van Gogh, as with the central fifth vignette entitled "Crows," based on *Wheatfield with Crows* (Color Plate 2).

In this vignette, the narrator is in a museum looking at several paintings by Van Gogh. As he moves from Van Gogh's *Self Portrait with Palette* (1889) to his *Starry Night* (1889), to *Still Life—Vase with Fifteen Sunflowers* (1888), and finally to *Wheatfield with Crows* (1890), the viewer turns to two ghostly paintings: Van Gogh's empty chair (1889) showing his pipe and tobacco, waiting for the smoker to return, and *Vincent's Bedroom in Arles* (1888), with an empty bed, waiting for its dreamer. Between them, *The Langlois Bridge at Arles with Women Washing* (1888) opens like a trapdoor: the river turns real, and the viewer steps into the picture to find himself running after Van Gogh through landscapes that magically turn into his master's paintings. Finally he finds Van Gogh in a wheatfield, wearing his straw hat over a bandaged ear. It's a hot day and Van Gogh cuts Kurosawa's narrator short: "I have to hurry, time's running out. So little time left for me to paint." Yes, time *is* running out. It is July 27, 1890, and Van Gogh has to finish his last painting, and then himself.

If swallows spoke the language of oracles for the ancient Greeks, as well as for Arseny and Andrei Tarkovsky, do Van Gogh's crows tell us something about his suicide? And more importantly, what *is* this language? A letter he sent to Theo in 1888, during his very productive stay in Arles, sheds some light. He poses what he calls "the eternal question: is life visible to us in its entirety, or before we die do we know of only one hemisphere?" Then he continues:

Painters—to speak only of them—being dead and buried, speak to a following generation or to several following generations through their works. Is that all, or is there more, even? In the life of the painter, death may perhaps not be the most difficult thing.

For myself, I declare I don't know anything about it. But the sight of the stars always makes me dream *in as simple a way* as the black spots on the map, representing towns and villages, make me dream.

Why, I say to myself, should the spots of light in the firmament be less accessible to us than the black spots on the map of France.

Just as we take the train to go to Tarascon or Rouen, we take death to go to a star. What's certainly true in this argument is that while alive, we cannot go to a star, any more than once dead we'd be able to take the train. So it seems to me not impossible that cholera, the stone, consumption, cancer are celestial means of locomotion, just as steamboats, omnibuses and the railway are terrestrial ones.

To die peacefully of old age would be to go there on foot.
For the moment I'm going to go to bed because it's late.

Letter 638, July 9 or 10, 1888, author's emphasis

Three decades before Proust, Van Gogh dreamed of the invisible reality hidden in the railway timetable. But he wasn't thinking of actual trains that turned place names from images of desire into lived experiences, as Marcel would. Van Gogh's metaphorical trains take us beyond what the eye can see into the secret realm revealed by the cartography of the stars. Such trains are Van Gogh's *Starry Night over the Rhone* (1888) and a second *Starry Night* as seen from his asylum in 1889. On July 27, 1890, Van Gogh took death to go to his star because he couldn't wait to go there on foot.

Consumed by the beauty of the natural setting, Kurosawa's Van Gogh confesses to the puzzled dreamer: "It's so difficult to hold it inside." "And what do you do?" asks the young Japanese disciple. "I work, I slave, I drive myself like a locomotive," he replies, and Kurosawa cuts to the image of a locomotive rushing to an unknown destination, taking Van Gogh, who disappears from the wheatfield. He will appear only once more, walking on the path that cuts through the middle of his *Wheatfield with Crows* before he disappears down the hill. The camera pulls back, the scene turns into the painting, and we are back in the museum. The sound of a locomotive—departing or arriving, we'll never know which—tells us that the master has reached his beloved star. His disciple, in awe, removes his hat in a gesture of respect for this final journey. Kurosawa scholars have seen the locomotive in this vignette as a more or less random metaphor,[1] but it is actually the result of his close reading of Van Gogh's letters that reveal his suicide as taking the train to more quickly reach the world mapped by the stars. But by what circuitous routes did Kurosawa's train reach the Dutch master's star, and what stops did it include on the way? As we will see, this train stopped in unexpected stations, from Marguerite Yourcenar's *Oriental Tales* and *Dreams and Destinies*, to André Breton's 1928 *Nadja* and the early silent films, to Chopin's Preludes, Andrei Tarkovsky's films, and finally back to Van Gogh's paintings, which held a promise for the future of cinema.

From Wang Foo to Wang-Fô

One of the most striking stories in Yourcenar's 1938 *Oriental Tales* is called "How Wang-Fô Was Saved." Wang-Fô is a great artist patronized by the emperor of an unspecified dynasty. But Wang-Fô's magnificent paintings

---

[1]Noriko Tsunoda Reider, for instance, describes the locomotive as the intrusion of technology that corrupts nature ("Akira Kurosawa's *Dreams*," 263).

make reality seem poor. Upon discovering that the beauty in Wang-Fô's paintings doesn't exist in reality, the enraged Emperor brings him to the palace, together with his silent disciple Ling. The Emperor asks Wang-Fô to complete an unfinished painting he had left behind years before, and then he intends to blind Wang-Fô and cut off his hands, so that the painter can no longer have access to the world of beauty that only he could see. When Ling tries to protect Wang-Fô, his head is cut off. His master proceeds to finish the painting, which shows a river on which a boat approaches. As he completes the painting, the scene turns real, and the river floods the palace. Ling appears in the boat and saves his master, taking him into the world of the painting. As they disappear, the waters flow back into the painting, leaving the world as it was before.

When I first read "How Wang-Fô Was Saved," I had a feeling of déjà-vu. It seemed that this could have been a source for Kurosawa's Van Gogh vignette in *Dreams*. Like Ling in Yourcenar's story, Kurosawa's first-person narrator, played by Akira Terao, will follow his master into the world of painting to save himself from the corrupt, decaying world of men. The last vignette in *Dreams* shows Terao exiting the screen via a bridge across a river, which is actually the final shot in the Van Gogh vignette turned real, and we realize that we've all along been walking through the Dutch master's paintings (Figure 3.1).

But could Kurosawa have read Yourcenar's story? The resemblance was striking, and as I was soon to find out, it wasn't just surreal: it was surrealist. Yourcenar had visited Japan in 1982, and she met several times with Donald Richie, the prominent Kurosawa scholar who lived in Japan most of his life and was close friends with Kurosawa. Her *Oriental Tales* had been available in Japanese since 1980, translated by the renowned surrealist poet Tada Chimako, who also translated her masterpiece *Memoirs of Hadrian* (1964) and her books *Fires* (1983) and *The Dark Brain of Piranesi* (1986). All her books were published by Hakusuisha, a publishing house dedicated to translations of French literature. The successive translations of her works in the 1980s were likely sparked by an increasing interest in the author of *Mishima: A Vision of the Void*, Yourcenar's meditation on the life and death of Yukio Mishima, which came out in 1980 and helped inspire a revival of interest in Mishima both in Japan and in the West. Her success would have brought her to Kurosawa's attention at the right time, and as he was writing the script for *Dreams* in 1989, Hakusuisha Press brought out André Breton's *Nadja* in the translation by Kotani Saya, one of Japan's leading scholars of surrealism.

Yourcenar claimed that her story of the painter Wang-Fô was based on "a Taoist legend," and critics have identified this legend as "The Magic Paintbrush" (Du Blois 7, n.16), yet no Wang-Fô appears in that source. The basic storyline of a painting that comes to life to save the world from a greedy king does indeed come from the Chinese legend, but the name of the character hasn't been explained by any Yourcenar scholar. While I was

FIGURE 3.1 *Final shots of the fifth and eighth vignettes in Kurosawa's* Dreams: *"Crows" and "Village of the Watermills"*.

researching the possible sources of Yourcenar's story, I remembered that André Breton spoke in *Nadja* (1928) of a film that had made a strong impression on him, "in which a Chinese who had found some way to multiply himself invaded New York by means of several million self-reproductions.... This film, which has affected me far more than any other, was called *The Trail of the Octopus*" (32–7). Luckily, there is an even earlier account of Breton's seeing this film, in a 1921 letter to his then wife Simone Kahn:

> I saw yesterday the last episode of an admirable film called *The Trail of the Octopus*. It's a fifteen-week series about a formidable learned Chinese who had to find twelve daggers which, when inserted in the twelve locks of a strongbox, would unlock it and he'd be in the possession of I don't know what secret. Initially the twelve daggers were in the possession of twelve learned men. Having managed to get his hands on eleven of these daggers, this cruel man finds himself faced with his adversary, "the masked man," who threatens him with a gun. The masked man is forced

to reveal his identity. He's none other than the Chinese himself, or maybe his first astral body that managed to escape his will. Then, liberating himself from his guilty previous self, he becomes conscious of his marvelous powers and tries to invade New York all by himself. All it takes is for him to multiply himself indefinitely. We see him coming out of a gate in countless copies, one after the other. This episode is called *The House of Shadows*. I have never seen anything more beautiful.

Lettres à Simone Kahn, 143–4

So I searched for this film, which turned out to be a fifteen-episode serial from 1919 by the American director Duke Worne. It was popular at the time but was soon forgotten, so much that even Breton's synopsis was rather vague. I purchased the final part of the serial, just to see the actual scene that impressed Breton so much. The silent film is a story about a detective, Carter Holmes, who tries to save the world from being ruled by an evil man who plans to get his hands on a powerful "Secret Talisman" in Egypt. As the film unfolds, the Chinese man's identity is revealed, as we see written on the screen: "Dr. Wang Foo, played by Ernest Garcia." Fascinated with the new medium, Yourcenar and Breton clearly saw the same film in Paris in 1921. Through a series of surreal chance encounters, I had stumbled upon the actual source for the name of Yourcenar's character, and I was led unconsciously to this discovery by Breton himself.

In the film, Dr. Wang Foo is portrayed with all the racist clichés about Orientals as devil-worshippers. He plans to multiply himself through a machine and then invade the world. He can also disappear as often as detective Holmes can capture him, and he dies several times only to appear somewhere else, moving from San Francisco to New York and then to Paris. Even though Breton misremembered this particular scene, as Wang Foo is captured just before he launches his invasion, we can see why Breton was impressed: in the disappearance and multiplication of Wang Foo, he saw an occurrence of the marvelous object which he would define in the late 1920s as the "object-phantom." For the same reason, Yourcenar too borrowed his name, and she retained from the ghostly mandarin the power to disappear and to multiply reality in order to save his life.

The Chinese mandarin's disappearing act that so impressed Breton became a commonplace in early cinema, when film was still associated with the world of magic and illusionism. As we've seen, the first filmmaker and illusionist Georges Méliès turned the disappearing act into his trademark, and popular series like *The Trail of the Octopus* used it; then Tarkovsky transformed it radically in *Nostalghia*, by showing the main character, the poet Andrei, disappearing and multiplying in what appears a single tracking shot. In Kurosawa's Van Gogh episode, both the disciple and his master disappear in the painting-landscape. More recently, the disappearing act has been comically deconstructed by Woody Allen in *Magic in the Moonlight*

(2014), where the act is performed by the Chinese illusionist Wei Ling Soo in 1928, the year when Breton published *Nadja*. Wei Ling Soo, however, turns out to be the stage identity of a British magician named Stanley Crawford, played by Colin Firth.

Though Marguerite Yourcenar wasn't a member of the surrealist group, she did interact with them: she met André Breton in 1935 and was friends with Nico Calas, who joined Breton's group in the 1930s and who remained a lifelong surrealist poet, and she corresponded with him until the mid-1970s. One of the major novelists of her generation, she was the first woman elected to the Académie Française. In 1938, she published two books that would connect dreams and East Asia: *Dreams and Destinies*, based on her own dreams, and a collection of *Oriental Tales*, based in part on actual Asian sources and partly on Western Oriental fictions—and movies. As we saw in the last chapter, these books proved of interest to Andrei Tarkovsky as well.

It was no exceptional thing in Paris in the 1930s to turn to the Orient for inspiration while seeking your destiny through dreams. Following the First World War, Paris was dominated by a rising Orientalism in response to the loss of belief in Western ideologies. As early as 1924, Breton praised the Orient as a source of inspiration—even though he admitted that his "Orient" was only a projection: "Oh, Orient, triumphant Orient! You who are only a symbol for me . . . help me see your ways in the future Revolutions! . . . I'm begging you, from the depths of the kingdom of shadows! Inspire me, so that I can become one without shadow!" ("Introduction," 280). In 1929, the surrealists' Orientalism could be easily read on their "World Map in the Time of the Surrealists," published in the Belgian magazine *Variétés*. The map centers on the Pacific Ocean, with an oversized China and Easter Island, while Paris is almost falling off the map. As Naoko Hiramatsu has written about Yourcenar's *Nouvelles orientales*, her "eclectic Orient . . . is less an objective entity than a reflection of Yourcenar's interests" ("Le Dernier Amour de Prince Genghi," 91). Osamu Hayashi rightly noted that her Orient is a reflection of her vision of Europe (*"Nouvelles Orientales,"* 101). In this she is only in sync with her contemporaries, including the surrealists, rather than in opposition to them as she liked to imagine.

Wang-Fô's impressive career spans the globe. He had been born as an exoticized Oriental character played by a Mexican-American actor, Al Ernest Garcia, who was known for his long association with Chaplin. Following the Parisian circulation of *The Trail of the Octopus* Wang Foo returns in the form of the exoticized image of a Chinese painter in Yourcenar's story, mirrored in the Dutch painter Cornelius Berg from another story in Yourcenar's collection, "The Sadness of Cornelius Berg." From there, Kurosawa picks him up and makes him his own alter ego at the center of *Dreams*, projecting himself in the Dutch painter Van Gogh, who is played by none other than Martin Scorsese, one of Kurosawa's supporters and friends in later life.

From Wang-Fô to Van Gogh

But how would the Chinese-American magician Wang-Fô taken up by Yourcenar in France become the Dutch painter Van Gogh in Kurosawa's *Dreams*? The film was criticized by Donald Richie and Stephen Prince for being too indebted to Kurosawa's American fans and filmmakers—George Lucas, Francis Ford Coppola, and Martin Scorsese—who supported its production at Twentieth Century Fox. *Dreams* was poorly received both by the Western audience and the one back home. The Westerners found it incomprehensible and gratuitous, while in Japan Kurosawa was criticized for abandoning the Japanese style that had consecrated him, trying to please his Western audience by using references they could relate to. Yet neither criticism rings true, as Kurosawa, like Tarkovsky, never settled for a formula, but was in a constant quest for what they both called moments of "pure" cinema.

More recently, a number of articles have appeared discussing how Japanese *Dreams* really is. Zvika Serper has shown Kurosawa's deep engagement with the nōh theatre ("Kurosawa's *Dreams*"), while Noriko Tsunoda Reider has argued that Kurosawa connected his dream vignettes via principles of association and progression used in the Japanese anthologies of classical poetry ("Akira Kurosawa's *Dreams*," 257). Like Reider, Serper explains the poor Western reception of *Dreams* through a lack of knowledge of its Japanese context. Serper's conclusion is almost disheartening for Kurosawa's international audience. If you aren't familiar with Japanese folklore traditions you can't understand the film: "the various issues Kurosawa treats in the film, the way it is constructed, and its aesthetic elements all have deeply loaded meanings in Japanese culture, giving *Dreams* levels of meaning that Western viewers are likely to miss" ("Kurosawa's *Dreams*," 82). Yet we don't need to look that far to explain the lack of understanding, as Western film critics hardly recognize the film's European references either, namely Van Gogh's paintings or Yourcenar's stories.

Both purist approaches to *Dreams*—either as a "Western" film or as a "typically Japanese" one—could benefit from looking back at André Bazin's thoughts on Kurosawa. Even though Bazin died in 1958 when Kurosawa still had thirty productive years ahead, he sensed this complex issue underlying Kurosawa's films. Bazin explained Kurosawa's success abroad through a type of cinematic language that spoke to Western taste as early as *Rashomon* and *The Seven Samurai*. In contrast to the tendency of most film scholars to interpret these two films as typically Japanese, Bazin said that "both of these films attest to an extremely skillful and deliberate Westernism" ("Akira Kurosawa's *To Live*," 163). Usually film critics have discussed such "Westernism" only in the case of *Dreams*, but Bazin understands that the Western influence on Kurosawa is not just passive, however. He isn't merely concerned with integrating it into his work; he also understands how to profit from this influence and use it to transmit back to us an image of Japanese tradition and culture that we can assimilate mentally as well as visually. Kurosawa succeeded so well at doing this with *Rashomon* that it could be said this film opened the gates of the West to Japanese cinema.... This leaves me wondering whether, instead of considering Kurosawa's cosmopolitanism in *Rashomon* and *The Seven Samurai* as a concession to marketability—even if it is of a superior quality—we shouldn't consider such cosmopolitanism a dialectical progression that points the way forward for Japanese cinema.

163–4

Current work on Kurosawa within the frame of world cinema has forgotten Bazin's nuanced understanding of his work. Rachel Hutchinson's essay "Orientalism or Occidentalism? Dynamics of Appropriation in Akira Kurosawa" discovers what Bazin had outlined in the 1950s: that we should think about Kurosawa's films as working both within his own Japanese local context, where he interacts with the local literary and cinematic traditions which he revolutionizes, and also within the larger context where he works against Western literary and cinematic traditions. Hutchinson is right that we should think of Kurosawa as *appropriating* rather than merely adapting Western literary texts to Japanese cinema, but it's also necessary to look beyond examples of direct adaptation, such as his films based on Shakespeare or Dostoevsky. Neither a belated imitation of a Western source nor an assertion of Japaneseness against the West, *Dreams* has enough Western and Eastern cultural references to please both audiences, provided that these audiences are trained in their own culture and also have a taste for the cinematic experiments of avant-garde filmmakers like Kurosawa and Tarkovsky. To better understand Kurosawa's film, we must first turn to Kurosawa's interest in painting, in general, and in Van Gogh in particular.

Kurosawa and Painting

Until the 1930s, Kurosawa wanted to become a painter. Even after he turned to film, his way of seeing and understanding the world remained a painter's. This is shown especially in his later works, *Ran*, *Kagemusha*, *Dreams*, *Rhapsody in August* and *Madadayo*, for which he returned to painting and drawing before recreating his images on film. "I started out as a painter, not a filmmaker," he notes in the foreword to the catalog for the 1994 *Akira Kurosawa Drawings* exhibit at the Ise Foundation Gallery in New York. "But as life would have it, I embarked on a career in film. Upon entering that world, I thought of the proverb 'If you try to catch two rabbits,' you will succeed at catching neither. And so I burned all the works that I had made before" (no pagination).

Whereas Andrei Tarkovsky, whose work he greatly admired, thought like a poet, Kurosawa thought in images like a painter, and he came back to drawing and painting later in life, when he was confronted with financial difficulties for his films *Kagemusha* (1980), *Ran* (1985), and *Dreams* (1990). Having fallen out of favor with the domestic audience who accused him of having abandoned his "truly Japanese" style in order to cater to Western tastes, he struggled to secure funding for these films. Drawing became a way to save these images from perishing altogether:

> It was the film *Kagemusha* that prompted me to draw intensely. We were having difficulty financing it; and the fear that it would not be realized at all drove me to record my ideas for the film on paper. I thought that even if the images were still, I would have them to show to people. The desire to have these images to show led to my drawing the scenes for *Kagemusha* every day ... When the film *Ran*, like *Kagemusha*, took a long and arduous time before production could begin, drawing the images became, again, a consoling necessity. Then it evolved into a practice, and I have continued to do the same for the succeeding films, *Akira Kurosawa's Dreams*, *Rhapsody in August* and *Madadayo*.
>
> "Foreword"

In *Something Like an Autobiography*, he confesses that from an early age, he was "a lover of Cezanne and Van Gogh" (71), and he saw the world through the Impressionists' paintings:

> I had begun to have doubts about my own talent as a painter. After looking at a monograph on Cezanne, I would step outside and the houses, streets and trees—everything—looked like a Cezanne painting. The same thing would happen when I looked at a book of Van Gogh's paintings or Utrillo's paintings—they changed the way the real world looked to me. It seemed completely different from the world I usually saw with my own eyes. In other words, I did not—and still don't—have a completely personal, distinctive, way of looking at things.
>
> 88

But why would Kurosawa choose Van Gogh of all painters, both to represent himself in the film and as the lens through which he filters his film images? Not because he found in Van Gogh the influence of Hokusai, as Reider argues ("Akira Kurosawa's *Dreams*," 263)—Kurosawa had no need to search for his own culture through other cultures—but rather because he was interested in what Van Gogh's filtering of Hokusai's sensibility could bring back to his cinematography. Already, as Peter Wild remarks, *Dodes'ka-den*, the film that preceded *Dreams*, "owes a great deal to Van Gogh and clearly foreshadows *Dreams*" (*Akira Kurosawa*, 152).

When Kurosawa decided to place Van Gogh at the heart of his *Dreams* he was engaging with the history of cinema as well as of painting. In 1948, Alain Resnais directed a black and white short film entitled *Van Gogh*, filmed in a documentary style that focuses on closeups of Van Gogh's paintings while a narrator tells his life story. As the story comes to an end, Resnais shows us Van Gogh's last painting, *Wheatfield with Crows*. Moving across the painting from left to right, Resnais edits into the last shot another empty field by Van Gogh that continues the wheat field. A black cloud appears on the right side of the frame, and as the camera glides slowly left to right, the black cloud covers the entire screen. The film, like Van Gogh's life, has come to an end. In this final metaphoric touch, Resnais was building on earlier closeups that zoomed in twice on Van Gogh's black shadow from his self-portrait *On the Road to Tarascon*, as if to suggest that his film tells the story of Van Gogh's gradually becoming a ghost. From here, Kurosawa will bring him back to life, turning the clock backwards. His fifth vignette in *Dreams* picks up where Resnais left off, in front of Van Gogh's *Wheatfield with Crows*, which has the ability to bring Van Gogh's ghost back to life through the eyes of the young disciple, Kurosawa's authorial mask in his own film.

Kurosawa was both establishing a dialogue with Resnais's 1948 film and proving himself a close reader of Van Gogh's letters. In a letter to his sister Willemien a month and a half before committing suicide, Van Gogh wrote: "I WOULD LIKE, you see I'm far from saying that I can do all this, but anyway I'm aiming at it, *I would like* to do portraits which would look like apparitions to people a century later" (Letter 879, June 5, 1890). More than mere likenesses of people who once lived, Van Gogh's paintings carry the ghosts of thc past.

A Walk through a Gallery

Using his own dreams for his work, Kurosawa would have been interested in Yourcenar's *Dreams and Destinies*. In one of her dreams, she is looking over a set of Chinese paintings that look like real landscapes when seen close up, while all the while she remains aware that she is looking down at the paintings on her desk: she describes "the Chinese wash landscapes, which we gaze upon as you would actual landscapes glimpsed through a window, even though we are leaning over the table where they are outspread and contemplate them from above" (109). We could have here one of Kurosawa's sources for his Van Gogh vignette, from which all the other vignettes emanate. This principle can be illustrated by a short comparative analysis of the eight vignettes in relation to Van Gogh's paintings and Yourcenar's dreams.

Yourcenar believed that painters are dreamers who remember their dreams, and she cites among others Leonardo da Vinci, in whose method of painting Breton found a precedent for surrealist automatic creation via Paul Valéry's *Introduction to the Method of Leonardo da Vinci* (1894). Leonardo advised his students to look intensely at a wall until they could observe the cracks in it, and then merely copy the image in front of them, which preexists them and isn't created but discovered. In Kurosawa's film, Van Gogh tells his disciple something similar: "when that natural beauty is there, I just lose myself in it. And then, as if it's in a dream, the scene just paints itself for me. I consume this natural setting, I devour it completely and whole. And then when I'm through, the picture appears before me complete." Kurosawa was reading Van Gogh's letters when he wrote the script for *Dreams*, and his statement is reminiscent of what Van Gogh wrote to his brother in 1888: "I have a terrible clarity of mind at times, when nature is so lovely these days, and then I'm no longer aware of myself and the painting comes to me as if in a dream . . . I do landscape and colour without worrying where that will take me" (Letter 697, September 25, 1888).

Like his Van Gogh in *Dreams*, Kurosawa felt that a form of automatic creation could best manifest his idea, a belief he shared with Breton and the surrealists: "To create skillful pictures was not my intention. Rather, these are tiny fragments of my films . . . when I consciously tried to draw well, the drawing would not come out well. But when I simply translated onto paper an image I had in mind for the movie, the drawing somehow seemed to captivate viewers" ("Foreword," *Akira Kurosawa Drawings*).

Yourcenar and Kurosawa share a filmic dream imagination, and Kurosawa could have found in her dreams the means to superimpose Van Gogh's paintings, one leading into another in the fifth vignette. One of Yourcenar's dreams features a satchel of paintings: "the pictures it contains flow beneath my gaze, one after the other . . . I have the impression that the image from underneath emerges to the surface at the right moment and is superposed by itself over the preceding image . . . somewhat in the manner of those broad prospects that fill a screen during a film projection . . . Much more than painted landscapes, these are immobilized landscapes" (*Dreams and Destinies*, 13).

All the other vignettes in Kurosawa's *Dreams* emanate from the Van Gogh paintings that he uses as the basis for his immobilized images in the fifth vignette, and they turn out to be closeups of other Van Gogh paintings. Thus the first vignette, "Sunshine through the Rain," is an expansion of Van Gogh's *Girl in the Woods*, *Flowering Garden*, and *Wheatfields under Thunderclouds*. Most notably, Kurosawa provides an answer to the question underlying *Girl in the Woods*: what could the strange lights seen in the background be? Invisible immortal beings, they are the foxes that materialize on Kurosawa's film performing their wedding as they walk on the secret path in the woods. Kurosawa's childhood self, which replaces the little girl in Van Gogh's painting, spies on them from behind a plane tree (Color Plate 3).

IN THAT SLEEP OF DEATH WHAT DREAMS MAY COME   97

The second vignette, "The Peach Orchard" is based on Van Gogh's *Almond Tree in Blossom, Orchards in Blossom: Plum Trees, Peach Tree in Bloom*, and also more subtly on a detail from *Langlois Bridge at Arles*, used for the geometrical arrangement of colors in the ritual dance performed by the spirits of the peach trees. The third vignette, "The Blizzard" is based on *Head of an Angel, after Rembrandt*: a bluish surreal apparition of an Angel, the only painting he did after a painting attributed to Rembrandt, *The Archangel Raphael*. Kurosawa turns Van Gogh's angel into the ghostly Snow Woman in a scene that illustrates his take on the nōh theatre, and at the same time comes close to the surrealists' preoccupation with spectral objects.

The fourth section of *Dreams*, "The Tunnel," shows the encounter between the dreamer, now commander of a battalion in World War II, and his dead soldiers. The scene opens with a zooming into Van Gogh's *The Viaduct*. Kurosawa recreates the scene in great detail, turning the shadow we can see entering Van Gogh's tunnel into our dreamer, and then the vignette opens into what happens if one enters that tunnel (Figure 3.2a, b). In addition, the bruised figure of a dead soldier, with black circles around his eyes, is a vivid representation of Van Gogh's sketch of a *Woman's Head* turned real (Figure 3.2c, d).

Following the fifth vignette, the sixth, "Mount Fuji in Red" is based on Van Gogh's sunset colors from *The Old Tower in the Fields*, and also on a painting by Kurosawa himself. Then the seventh vignette, "The Weeping Demon," recreates the barren landscapes of some of Van Gogh's less-known paintings, like *Landscape with Pollard Willows*. But most strikingly, the dreamer encounters a giant dandelion, a mutant result of a nuclear experiment, which is the very image of Van Gogh's famous *Sunflowers* (Figure 3.3). Van Gogh's sterile mutant sunflowers are the perfect image for Kurosawa's end-of-the-world vignette.

The final episode, "Village of the Watermills," opens with a zooming into Van Gogh's *Water Wheels of Mills at Gennep* and *Watermill*. As the disciple exits the frame like Van Gogh before him, disappearing into the landscape, a final shot shows Van Gogh's *The Seine with a Rowing Boat*. Perhaps this was the boat in which Ling saved his master in Yourcenar's story, here only with one oarsman, as the dreamer in Kurosawa disappears alone into the world of painting.

In addition to being modeled on Van Gogh's paintings, at least three of the vignettes are visually close to three dreams recorded by Yourcenar. Kurosawa's "The Blizzard" shows four men walking on a snow-covered mountain, until a storm begins and three of them fall as if by magic into a deep sleep. Their captain is the only one who stays awake as a ghostly, demonic woman appears and tucks him into the snow as if it's a blanket. She comforts him that "The snow is warm," yet her movements seem to suffocate him. As she disappears into the sky, we see only her mantle like a ghostly apparition in a dream. Next the captain awakes and finds the path that saves them as they

FIGURE 3.2 a, b, c, d *Vincent van Gogh,* Roadway with Underpass. The Viaduct *(1887) and* Head of a Woman *(1883), and stills from Kurosawa's* Dreams: "The Tunnel" *(1990).*

FIGURE 3.3 *Vincent van Gogh*, Still Life: Vase with Fifteen Sunflowers *(1888) and still from Akira Kurosawa's* Dreams: *"The Weeping Demon."*

reach a military base. In "The Pathway beneath the Snow," Yourcenar tells of a dream that opens onto a "still life" winter landscape that gradually becomes threatening: "I see an affable and commanding walker" (*Dreams and Destinies*, 9). Then "the falcon from which I was just separated returns to alight on my shoulder, and I seek the homeward path with the animal of the resurrection as my companion for the roadway" (20–1).

Secondly, Kurosawa's "The Tunnel" shows the commander, who has lost his entire battalion, coming out of a black tunnel followed by the ghost of one of his soldiers, and then by the entire battalion like a terrifying army of the dead. Once the first soldier hears they're dead, they return into the black void. Yourcenar's "The Corpse in the Ravine" is a vision seen by an imprisoned dreamer who contemplates a mountain ravine filled with the bodies of Greek soldiers. Here too, the dreamer converses with a soldier who is almost dead: "I can see, all the way at the bottom, the ground strewn with rocks. I know that it is in this trench that Greek prisoners condemned to death had been massed . . . only one remains behind. . . . When I arrive level with the ground, the young soldier is already dead" (23–5).

In Kurosawa's vignette "Mount Fuji in Red," nuclear reactors on Mount Fuji have exploded. A fleeing crowd of people throw themselves into the sea, with the exception of our narrator and a mother with her two children and an engineer from the plant, before everything is swallowed up by a red fog. Yourcenar's "The Avenue of the Beheaded" speaks of men condemned to death whose heads fall into the sea as the dream scene closes on this apocalyptic image: "The sky in its entirety has turned red. And one by one, beneath the shock of who knows what invisible ax, those twenty-five heads roll on the ground . . . and rapidly descend the invisible slope that goes down to the sea" (36–7).

Kurosawa's Proustian Van Gogh

Kurosawa's fifth vignette plays on close-ups of Van Gogh's paintings; this transforms all the other landscapes we've seen in *Dreams* into paintings through which we walk, together with the narrator as the disciple of Van Gogh. Our film becomes a gallery where Kurosawa's works can be seen side by side with Van Gogh's, just as Ling, the disciple in Yourcenar's story, comes to see the world through his master's paintings: "Wang-Fô," she writes, "had just presented him with the gift of a new soul and a new vision of the world" (*Oriental Tales*, 5). As Proust wrote of Renoir, great artists have the gift to make us see the world anew, and in this respect, their works are like lenses through which the world we knew is defamiliarized:

> the original painter or the original writer proceeds on the lines of the oculist. The course of treatment they give us by their painting or by their prose is not always pleasant. When it is at an end the practitioner says to us: "Now look!" And, lo and behold, the world around us (which was not created once and for all, but is created afresh as often as an original artist is born) appears to us entirely different from the old world, but perfectly clear. . . . Such is the new perishable universe which has just been created. It will last until the next geological catastrophe is precipitated by a new painter or writer of original talent.
>
> *The Guermantes Way*, 445–6

IN THAT SLEEP OF DEATH WHAT DREAMS MAY COME   101

Women no longer look like women, or sunflowers like sunflowers, Proust remarks; they look like the work of the artist—we can say Van Gogh, Yourcenar, Kurosawa—who has created them afresh.

Van Gogh would come to identify with sunflowers as his own artistic property. As he wrote to Paul Gauguin, "if Jeannin has the peony, Quost the hollyhock, I indeed, before others, have taken the sunflower" (Letter 739, January 21, 1889). He saw in these uncanny flowers his own self: restless, unfamiliar, fiery. The next day Van Gogh wrote to his brother Theo about his sunflowers, which left Gauguin at a loss for words: "Gauguin likes them extraordinarily. He said to me about them, among other things: 'that—. . . that's . . . the flower'," adding: "To be sufficiently heated up to melt those golds and those flower tones, not just anybody can do that, it takes an individual's whole and entire energy and attention" (Letter 741, January 22, 1889). This will be the fire that Alain Resnais and then the Tarkovskys would find in Van Gogh's paintings.

In 2012, a crew of American researchers published an analysis of the two types of sunflowers painted by Van Gogh. The surprise was that Van Gogh's sunflowers turned out to be mutants, and they would have been sterile: "Sunflower mutants that show alterations in floral symmetry . . . provide an opportunity to investigate the genetic basis of this trait. . . . Interestingly, the *dbl* mutants bear a strong resemblance to the phenotype captured in Vincent van Gogh's famous 19th century sunflower paintings" (Chapman et al., "Genetic Analysis," 2). More than the "sunflowers are mine," Van Gogh tells us: "I *am* the sunflower." Mutant, at odds with a world where he didn't fit. That's why he didn't sign his *Sunflowers* in the lower corner of the painting in the usual way. Instead, he signed his name on the vase, only "Vincent," as if his name were part of the object itself, anticipating by four decades the surrealists' logic that breaks with the traditional mimetic theory of language and proposes a poetic one, as expressed in René Magritte's 1929 painting *The Treachery of Images*, on which he wrote "Ceci n'est pas une pipe." As Van Gogh tells us, *Ceci n'est pas un vase, c'est Vincent*.

The sunflower takes many different forms across his sketches and paintings, from his self-portraits, to details of sunflower heads, to the sun whose light emanates in fine grains or other times in heavy brushstrokes covering the entire landscape. A world bathed in light and fire, as Alain Resnais tells us in his film. Resnais suggests this reading by the editing and the closeups of the details he's juxtaposing: he shows in succession the light in the artist's eye from one of Van Gogh's self-portraits that gradually becomes the dark center of the sunflower or the sun in his paintings (Figure 3.4a).

Sometimes Van Gogh goes beyond even what Resnais shows and hides his eye in the secret construction of an apparently impressionist painting, like *The Bridge at Courbevoie* (1887). The second arch takes the shape of the artist's eye looking at us and making us see the world through his eyes (Figure 3.3b). Van Gogh anticipates by four decades the surrealists' notion

FIGURE 3.4 a, b *Vincent van Gogh's* Pollard Willows and Setting Sun *(1888) and* The Bridge at Courbevoie *(1887)*.

of *surréalité* that tells us the world around is more than the untrained eye can see, and also Salvador Dalí's method of critical paranoia that found hidden shapes—eyes, faces, sometimes entire bodies—in apparently perfectly realistic landscapes. Dalí's burning cypresses—a recurrent fantasy that shows up in many of Dalí's paintings and writings—were first seen by the Dutch master in paintings like *A Wheatfield with Cypresses* (1889), *The Starry Night* (1889) and *Road with Cypresses* (1890).

Moved by a painterly sensibility similar to Van Gogh's, both Marguerite Yourcenar and Akira Kurosawa resurrect in drawings the vision of the

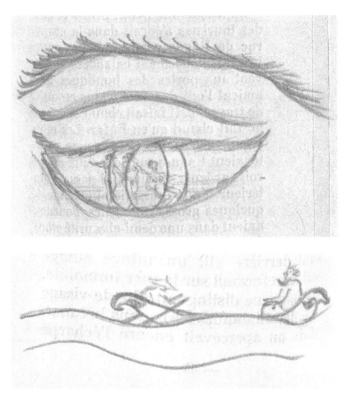

FIGURE 3.5 a, b *Marguerite Yourcenar's pencil drawings in a copy of her* Nouvelles orientales. *Courtesy of Houghton Library, Harvard.*

artist's eye as a new lens to see the world. Yourcenar added drawings to the copy of her *Nouvelles orientales* that she presented to her partner Grace Frick. In this copy, preserved in Harvard's Houghton Library, at the end of the short story "The Man Who Loved the Nereids", Yourcenar drew an immense eye, shaped like the Japanese boat she drew in the same copy at the end of the story "How Wang-Fô Was Saved," and on this eye-boat she placed three naked nereids on the banks of a river (Figure 3.5).

Akira Kurosawa painted an immense eye opened in terror rising like the sun over endless green fields, as an image for his 1991 film *Rhapsody in August* (Figure 3.6). With a sensibility akin to Yourcenar's, Kurosawa was also returning to Resnais's interpretation of Van Gogh, which equated the sunflower both with the sun and with the painter's eye looking at us. And like Van Gogh, Kurosawa too described himself as a sunflower, citing the friend with whom he wrote the script that first made him famous, *Drunken Angel*: "Uekusa Keinosuke has also said my personality is like that of a sunflower, so there must be some truth to the allegation that I am more sanguine than my brother was" (*Something Like an Autobiography*, 87).

FIGURE 3.6 *Drawing by Akira Kurosawa for his film* Rhapsody in August *(1991)*.

Kurosawa's camera lens in *Dreams* also tells us something about the three routes by which Kurosawa came to the Dutch master's paintings. First, through his direct contact with them as a young artist in love with non-academic painters like Cezanne and Van Gogh who had never had formal training. Second, through the *ukiyo-e* printmakers who heavily influenced him—Hokusai, Utagawa, Hiroshige—and who in turn were creatively interpreted by Van Gogh. In a letter sent to his brother from Arles, dated July 15, 1888, Van Gogh writes: "Japanese art is something like the primitives, like the Greeks, like our old Dutchmen, Rembrandt, Potter, Hals, Vermeer, Ostade, Ruisdael. It doesn't end" (Letter 642). He had moved to the south of France, which he saw as Europe's Japan:

> we love Japanese painting, we've experienced its influence—all the Impressionists have that in common—and we wouldn't go to Japan, in other words, to what is the equivalent of Japan, the south? So I believe that the future of the new art still lies in the south after all. . . . After some time, your vision changes, you see with a more Japanese eye, you feel color differently. I'm also convinced that it's precisely through a long stay here that I'll bring out my personality.
>
> Letter 620

In turn, Kurosawa looks back at his own world of dreams through a "Van Gogh eye," but a Van Gogh who filtered Hokusai's view of the world. Approaching the end of his immensely productive life, during which he is said to have produced 30,000 drawings, Hokusai mused on what his dream afterlife would be: "Oh, the freedom, the beautiful freedom, of wandering in the summer fields, as a body no longer, only a soul!" (in Baatsch, *Hokusai: A Life in Drawing*, 80). Hokusai's dream afterlife would include Van Gogh's burning eye and ghostly presence in the bright, endless summer fields he painted, ending with his last and most ominous one, *Wheatfield with Crows*, and Kurosawa's camera eye that haunts the landscapes of his dreams. Oh, the freedom, the beautiful freedom!

A third route through which Kurosawa looked back at Van Gogh for *Dreams* was Yourcenar's *Oriental Tales*, not only for the fifth vignette that draws on her story "How Wang-Fô Was Saved," but also for the architectural construction of his movie as a whole. Taken together, the eight vignettes constitute a giant chiastic construction that mirrored a Chinese painter as a Dutch painter, contemporary of Rembrandt. This third route is inscribed within Van Gogh's last painting, which shows a crossroads with three possible paths, but no sign of a human presence. In the film, as Van Gogh commits suicide after finishing this painting, his soul or ghost disappears in this painting and turns into black crows, as Kurosawa shows in the closing of his fifth vignette. But a still of this scene reveals that the crows aren't real: they are animated drawings added by Kurosawa.

Kurosawa was a great admirer of Tarkovsky: "Every film by Tarkovsky is marvelous . . . I always felt as if he were my younger brother" (Kurosawa, *A Dream is a Genius*). He had a particular affinity for Tarkovsky's *Mirror*:

> *Mirror* deals with his cherished memories in his childhood, and many people say again it is disturbingly difficult. Yes, at a glance, it seems to have no rational development in its storytelling. But we have to remember: it is impossible that in our soul our childhood memories should arrange themselves in a static, logical sequence. A strange train of fragments of early memory images shattered and broken can bring about the poetry in our infancy.
>
> "TARKOVSKY and *Solaris*"

Kurosawa drew extensively on *Mirror*, from the poetic logic of bringing the dream vignettes together to specific details. In the first vignette of *Dreams*, "Sunshine through the Rain," the scene follows Tarkovsky's reconstruction of his childhood dacha in the forest for the earliest autobiographical sequences in *The Mirror*. But more interestingly, Kurosawa concludes his fifth vignette by bringing together a series of artists who shared an interest in Van Gogh. Kurosawa's Van Gogh disappearing in his last painting is a nod to Georges Méliès, but also more specifically to Resnais's ghostly Van Gogh, who exited the 1948 short film as a black shadow that covered the screen. At the same time, Kurosawa interprets the crows as Van Gogh's turning literally into a ghost in his final painting, as Tarkovsky had shown Aleksei's (father's) soul rising to the sky as he frees the bird he'd kept in his hand on his deathbed.

Kurosawa particularly admired Tarkovsky's skill in filming water: "He was especially marvelous in handling the Water Element, as seen, for example, in *Solaris* and *Sacrifice*. He was somehow able to shoot a pond or water pool as transparent as to allow us to see through to the very bottom . . . I, too, wanted to shoot water as he did, in making an episode of the 'Village of the Watermills' in *Dreams*" (*A Dream Is a Genius*). Kurosawa would also have been interested in Tarkovsky's literary and poetic sources. If Tarkovsky used Marguerite Yourcenar's "Our-Lady-of-the-Swallows" to create the structuring principle of *Nostalghia*, Kurosawa turned to Yourcenar's "How Wang-Fô Was Saved" in his central vignette for *Dreams*, and to her mirrored construction of the entire *Nouvelles orientales* for his own chiastic construction of the order of the vignettes. And like Tarkovsky, who interpreted Yourcenar's story through his father's poem "Swallows," Kurosawa may have interpreted Yourcenar's Wang-Fô through Arseny Tarkovsky's poem "May Vincent van Gogh forgive me" (1958):

May Vincent van Gogh forgive me
For not being able to help.

For not spreading grass underfoot
As he walked on the scorching road,

For not undoing the laces
Of his dusty peasant shoes,

Not giving him drink in the heatwave,
Not stopping him firing his gun.

I stand here and over me towers
A cypress, twisting like flame.

Chrome yellow and Prussian blue—
Without them I would not be me.

I should debase my own speech
If I cast that load from my shoulders.

And the angel's roughness, with which
He allies his strokes with my lines,

Leads you too, through the eyes' pupils,
To where van Gogh breathes the stars.

ARSENY TARKOVSKY, Poetry and Film, 89–90

IN THAT SLEEP OF DEATH WHAT DREAMS MAY COME   107

In Arseny Tarkovsky's poem dedicated to Van Gogh, Kurosawa found expressed his own relationship with Van Gogh, whose disciple he believed himself to be. Arseny Tarkovsky structures the poet's relationship to Van Gogh through the biblical relationship between John the Baptist and Jesus. His "May Vincent van Gogh forgive me . . . For not undoing the laces / Of his dusty peasant shoes" rewrites John the Baptist's prophecy: "I baptize you with water. But One who is more powerful than I am will come. I'm not good enough to untie the straps of his sandals. He will baptize you with the Holy Spirit and with fire" (Luke 3:16). Like Resnais before him, Arseny Tarkovsky finds in Van Gogh's paintings an expression of the artist's burning eye, which is his secular interpretation of the baptism "with the Holy Spirit and with fire." For Arseny Tarkovsky, as for his son Andrei, Van Gogh typifies the artist's work as the salvation of mankind.

Van Gogh becomes one of the forms of the angel or magical bird that haunts Arseny Tarkovsky's poetry, and that his son brings into *Nostalghia* together with Yourcenar's Lady-of-the-Swallows. If the swallows' magical, unknown tongue could align them with the poet's line in *Swallows* and finally with Andrei Tarkovsky's filmmaker eye, Van Gogh's painting shows to Kurosawa's eye "the angel's roughness, with which / He allies his strokes with my lines," and with the filmmaker's images. As in the last couplet of this poem, Kurosawa shows us how his painting "Leads you too, through the eyes' pupils"—or through the camera's eye—"To where van Gogh breathes the stars." The path that Van Gogh uses to exit the frame—and life—is the central path from his last painting, which returns as a filmed scene in the closing of Kurosawa's last vignette, "Village of the Watermills." This time he shows the disciple exiting the frame as Van Gogh did before, now crossing a bridge over a river, until the camera shows us only the riverbed, just as in Yourcenar's story Ling and Wang-Fô exit the frame on their boat, leaving behind them only the salty waters, which turn into Wang-Fô's last painting as the story comes to an end.

Both Yourcenar and Kurosawa were right to think of Van Gogh in terms of paintings that come to life. As he was working on his series of sunflowers in January 1889, Van Gogh wrote to both Gauguin and Theo of his intention to have a series of seven or nine canvases in which sunflowers would alternate with a series of *Berceuses*, paintings of women with their arms brought together as if in a ghostly embrace. These were intended to remind sailors of their mother's lullabies when out on the sea. Van Gogh was playing on a French pun of *bercer*, to rock, to cradle, something that *la mer* (the sea) could do, as *la mère* (the mother) once did. Together, the canvases would alternate in a chiastic construction:

> the idea came to me to paint such a picture that sailors, at once children and martyrs, seeing it in the cabin of a boat of Icelandic fishermen, would

experience a feeling of being rocked, reminding them of their own lullabies. . . . I can imagine these canvases precisely between those of the sunflowers—which thus form standard lamps or candelabra at the sides, of the same size; and thus the whole is composed of 7 or 9 canvases.

Letter 743

Kurosawa too will use a chiastic construction for the order of his dream vignettes that turn into Van Gogh paintings brought to life.

This path leads us through Kurosawa, Andrei and Arseny Tarkovsky and Marguerite Yourcenar back to Van Gogh himself, for whom ideas travel freely between genres, disciplines, media: "All these things, family, native country, are perhaps more appealing in the imagination of such as us—who do fairly well without a native country, as well as a family—than in any reality. It always seems to me that I'm a traveller who's going somewhere and to a destination. If I say to myself, the somewhere, the destination don't exist at all, that seems well argued and truthful to me" (Letter 656). The destination is never a final one, for Van Gogh's ideas traveled through poetry, literature, and film, and who knows what other ghostly paths they will follow in the future.

The Vast Chiastic Structure of Recollection

The strange symmetry between the Dutch painter and the Japanese one can be traced back to Yourcenar's *Oriental Tale*s in the revised edition of 1978, where she changed the order of the tales. The major change was that she now opened the book with Wang-Fô's story and ended it with the story of the Dutch painter Cornelius Berg (1699–1774). In Yourcenar's tale, Cornelius stops painting because God, the painter of nature, created many monstrous things as well: "What a pity that God should not have limited himself to painting landscapes," he muses (*Oriental Tale*s, 141). In an afterword, Yourcenar explained her choice in reordering her short stories: "I could not resist the idea of placing, opposite the great Chinese painter, lost and saved within his own work, this obscure contemporary of Rembrandt's, sadly meditating on his own accomplishments" (147). This mirrored structure has been described by Ana de Medeiros as "the secret architecture" of Yourcenar's book of tales, organized in concentric circles ("*Les Nouvelles Orientales*," 192), while Luc Pauchon has observed the "oriental character of the Dutch painter, in that he can detach himself from the real" ("Voyage dans les *Nouvelles orientales*," 76). Nishimura Yūichirō has identified a similar symmetry in the order of the eight dream vignettes in Kurosawa's film, describing it as an alternation between negative and positive images ("Romantishizumu," 27 in Serper, "Kurosawa"), while Noriko Tsunoda

IN THAT SLEEP OF DEATH WHAT DREAMS MAY COME 109

Reider spoke of a "cyclical wholeness" ("Akira Kurosawa's *Dreams*," 266), an image that coincides with Donald Richie's view of the cyclical or spiral structure of Kurosawa's films (*The Films of Akira Kurosawa*, 187).

The symmetries between Yourcenar's stories and Kurosawa's vignettes, and among the vignettes themselves, take the shape of a chiasmus in *Dreams*, with the Van Gogh vignette as the center from which the symmetrical parts emanate. As John Welch has noted in *Chiasmus in Antiquity* (1999), chiasmus was initially a rhetorical figure used to organize a narrative in a mirrored thematic structure so as to be more easily remembered. As a figure of memory, chiasmus is the perfect architectural structure for Kurosawa's dream vignettes, which collect the filmmaker's favorite Van Gogh paintings in an attempt to remember, but also creatively transform, his mentor's revolutionary work.

Initially, Yourcenar wrote "The Sadness of Cornelius Berg" to serve as the conclusion to an unfinished novel. The fact that she uses it to conclude *Oriental Tales* makes the collection itself more novelistic, with the individual stories as chapters that communicate through underground connections. This is a principle of organization that Kurosawa too uses in *Dreams*, a series of apparently unconnected vignettes that communicate through the dreamer, who enters the film as a child—living in Kurosawa's own childhood house—and grows up into an artist and disciple of Van Gogh and the wise old man in the final vignette.

As Yourcenar had placed Wang-Fô and the Dutch painter in mirrored positions, Kurosawa has the painter Van Gogh and the wise man mirror each other. In the final vignette, "Village of the Watermills," the narrator visits an old man who speaks of living in harmony with nature without any interference from the world of technology. He is a Japanese version of Van Gogh from the fifth vignette: they wear the same straw hat and are filmed from the same angle. For both vignettes Kurosawa used self-portraits by Van Gogh, and also a portrait of the Japanese wise man painted by himself (Figure 3.7). The symmetry intended by Kurosawa between the two can also be seen in the central placement of the "Village of the Watermills" vignette in Kurosawa's original script, whereas in the film version, it comes at the end. A perfect chiastic relation emerges between the Asian/Dutch polarization as played out in Yourcenar's stories and Kurosawa's film.

Whereas Wang-Fô isn't interested in reality but only in its painted perfection, Cornelius Berg is deeply interested in reality, knows the futility of any human endeavor, including art, and bemoans the decay of the flesh while only nature is immortal and beautiful. Kurosawa's wise old man seems to say the same to our narrator-disciple: that man is flesh (that's why we witness a funeral in the eighth vignette), and the only thing to do is to embrace our return to the earth when death comes (the funeral procession is joyful). At the end of *Dreams* Kurosawa shows us a symmetrical image to the ending of Van Gogh's vignette: whereas the Dutch master

FIGURE 3.7 a, b, c *Still from Akira Kurosawa's* Dreams: *"Village of the Watermills"; Vincent van Gogh,* Self-Portrait *(1887); and drawing by Akira Kurosawa for* Dreams: *"Village of the Watermills."*

disappears in the landscape that becomes his last painting, in the final shot of the film the disciple departs by walking along a bridge over a river. As he exits the frame, the natural setting remains, and doesn't become a painting.

For Kurosawa, Van Gogh's last painting *Wheatfield with Crows* brought together the master and his disciple, just as in Yourcenar's tale the master and his disciple disappear together in the painting. Prophetically, this would be also Kurosawa's last major film, and so his final shot of the young narrator disappearing out of the frame corresponds to Van Gogh's last painting. So too, in what was his initial sketch for a painting, Yourcenar's Wang-Fô also finds his final completed painting, and his life comes full circle through the prophetic apparition of his disciple. Similarly, Kurosawa is Van Gogh's disciple, finding in the master's painting his own voice in a new medium: world art cinema.

IN THAT SLEEP OF DEATH WHAT DREAMS MAY COME 111

Another key link between Kurosawa's Van Gogh vignette and Yourcenar's Wang-Fô is the music that Kurosawa chose for his fifth vignette: Chopin's Opus 28, no. 15. Known as the *Raindrop* prelude, it came out of a nightmarish dream Chopin had during a storm, as his lover George Sand remembers in *The Story of My Life*:

> He confessed to me later that, while waiting for us, he had seen all that in a dream and, no longer able to distinguish dream from reality, he had calmed himself and played the piano drowsily, persuaded that he had died himself. He saw himself drowned in a lake—heavy, icy drops falling rhythmically on his chest—and when I had him listen to the drops of water falling rhythmically on the roof, he denied having heard them. . . . His composition that evening was certainly full of raindrops resonating on the tiles of the monastery, but they were perhaps translated in his imagination and in his music into tears from heaven falling on his heart.
>
> 1091–2

A repeated A flat throughout the prelude marks the sound of the raindrop and its rhythm, like that of a beating heart. By using this prelude, Kurosawa makes audible Yourcenar's climactic scene in "How Wang-Fô Was Saved," in which water covers the entire kingdom and takes Wang-Fô and Ling away with it. As they disappear in the boat painted by Wang-Fô, the castle they've left returns to its life as if nothing has happened, or as if they had all been in a dream where they saw themselves drowning, like Chopin. Van Gogh disappears and reappears several times to the confused disciple in Kurosawa's Van Gogh vignette. Every time he disappears, Kurosawa marks the moment of confusion, but also of waking up, through Chopin's recurrent A flat, the raindrop that marks the passage of time but also the rhythm of the dreamer's heart, much as Yourcenar had described:

> Upon a sign from the Emperor's little finger, two eunuchs respectfully brought forward the unfinished scroll on which Wang-Fô had outlined the image of the sea and the sky. Wang-Fô dried his tears and smiled, because the small sketch reminded him of his youth. . . . Then he painted onto the surface of the sea a few small lines that deepened the perfect feeling of calm. The jade floor became increasingly damp, but Wang-Fô, absorbed as he was in his painting, did not seem to notice that he was working with his feet in water.
>
> *Oriental Tales*, 16–17

Kurosawa opens his Van Gogh vignette with a static closeup of the *Langlois Bridge at Arles*, which the disciple contemplates in a museum, but the instant Chopin's prelude breaks in and the A flat is heard, the first drop of water

FIGURE 3.8 a, b *Vincent van Gogh,* The Langlois Bridge at Arles with Women Washing *(1888) and still from Akira Kurosawa's* Dreams: *"Crows."*

stirs the painted river and brings the scene to life (Figure 3.8). The disciple starts searching for Van Gogh, and finds himself running through his master's sketches and paintings until he finally finds him drawing in a wheat field. They start a conversation about the origins of art, which shows Van Gogh's debt to Leonardo and anticipates the surrealists' automatic creation. Then the master disappears and the disciple starts running again, his heart panting, Chopin's A flat raindrop falling with regularity and each time bringing another Van Gogh painting to life.

In Yourcenar's story, the equivalent of Chopin's A flat is the sound of the oars as the disciple comes back to rescue his master:

> The fragile rowboat grew under the strokes of the painter's brush and now occupied the entire foreground of the silken scroll. The rhythmic sound of the oars rose suddenly in the distance, quick and eager like the beating of wings. The sound came nearer, gently filling the whole room, then ceased, and a few trembling drops appeared on the boatman's oars ... The courtiers, motionless as etiquette required, stood in water up

to their shoulders, trying to lift themselves onto the tips of their toes. The water finally reached the level of the imperial heart. The silence was so deep one could have heard a tear drop . . . .

"Master, have no fear," murmured the disciple. "They will soon be dry again and will not even remember that their sleeves were ever wet. Only the Emperor will keep in his heart a little of the bitterness of the sea. These people are not the kind to lose themselves inside a painting."

Oriental Tales, 17–18

In Kurosawa's Van Gogh vignette, Chopin's repetitive A flat raindrop becomes "the beating of wings" as crows fly to the sky while the master disappears on his path and leaves the frame, and we are back in the museum with the disciple who has briefly lost himself inside the painting.

Kurosawa's eight dream vignettes are all connected to water and its imagery in one way or another. In the first vignette, "Sunshine through the Rain," it's the rain and the sun that make it possible to see the wedding of the foxes. The second vignette, "The Peach Orchard," comes out of a Proustian daydream brought about by a tea ceremony. The third vignette, "The Blizzard," shows a deadly goddess who almost suffocates the narrator by drowning him in icy water or snow. The fourth, "The Tunnel," shows an army of the dead coming out of a dark tunnel with blue faces like the deadly waters they've returned from to haunt our narrator. The sixth vignette, "Mount Fuji in Red," shows a crowd of people throwing themselves from a cliff into the ocean, seeking salvation from a nuclear catastrophe by choosing death by drowning. The seventh vignette, "The Weeping Demon," shows an apocalyptic landscape with puddles of blood mirroring the decay of the human race. And finally, "Village of the Watermills" shows the river that measures time's irreversible passing. As the disciple crosses this river on a bridge that mirrors the path on which Van Gogh disappeared, Kurosawa's camera rests on a final shot of the riverbed, which he filmed following Tarkovsky's scene from the opening of *Solaris*, as he himself has said (Color Plate 4).

But if *Solaris* is behind this imagery of Kurosawa's film, it follows that everything we've seen in *Dreams* is a projection created out of nothingness, in a Buddhist conviction that reality is only an illusion. In Tarkovsky's *Solaris*, the giant, dreaming brain—represented as an agitated ocean—can only briefly make the past return and endlessly multiply one single being: Hari, Chris's dead wife, whom he materializes on the spaceship through his dreams, close to Solaris, just like the machine in *Trail of the Octopus* could multiply Wang Foo. The final shot in *Solaris* shows how even Chris's house with its serene landscape, which we admired in the opening of the film, is only an image, a projection, dreamed by the endless thinking ocean called Solaris, that in the end swallows up the house, Chris, and everything we thought was reality.

It's only fitting that a watery universe, drowned, bathed, or soaked, be represented for Kurosawa through Van Gogh's paintings. His paintings look as if they are seen through a water screen or as if they are underwater. If the Impressionists modeled their poetics as a creative response to Japanese prints, it's Van Gogh who best illustrates the world of *ukiyo-e*: a floating, fleeting world. This imagery starts with his amazing *Starry Night over the Rhone*, at the bottom of which we can see clearly for the first time a path that looks like a river covering the water, as the brush strokes suggest a counter-direction and movement (Color Plate 5). When he structures his *Dreams* as a walk through a gallery filled with Van Gogh's paintings, Kurosawa is making a very Japanese film by placing a vision of the floating world at its heart. At the same time, this is also a very worldly film, because it's through Van Gogh and his filtering of the *ukiyo-e* aesthetic that Kurosawa rediscovers a local, culturally codified truth about the floating world.

André Bazin believed that to film paintings, as Kurosawa does, in closeup without their frame, gives them the spatial properties of cinema:

> if we show a section of a painting on a screen, the space of the painting loses its orientation and its limits and is presented to the imagination as without any boundaries. Without losing its other characteristics the painting thus takes on the spatial properties of cinema and becomes part of that "picturable" world that lies beyond it on all sides. It is on this illusion that Luciano Emmer based his fantastic aesthetic reconstructions, which have served as a starting point for the existing films of contemporary art, notably for Alain Resnais' 1948 *Van Gogh*. Here the director has treated the whole of the artist's output as one large painting over which the camera has wandered as freely as in any ordinary documentary.
>
> "Painting and Cinema," 166

Kurosawa's filmic predecessor in understanding Van Gogh's paintings was Alain Resnais, but it was from Tarkovsky that Kurosawa learned how to use painting as a structuring device for films. Tarkovsky inaugurated the device of using painting as narrative with a defamiliarizing effect in the last fifteen minutes of *Andrei Rublev* (1966), when the camera moves ever so slowly across the Russian monk's paintings, in a type of closeup we see in Kurosawa's Van Gogh episode, where we zoom in so closely that the brush strokes are thick enough to become paths through a garden for the disciple to run after his master. The last eight minutes of *Andrei Rublev* break the film's black and white minimalism with an explosion of color to express the painter's renewed faith in an art inspired by God. Similarly, Kurosawa turns his film into a spiritual rediscovery of his master Van Gogh, but also of his own initial passion for painting.

*

IN THAT SLEEP OF DEATH WHAT DREAMS MAY COME   115

Kurosawa saw that, far from rivaling or superseding painting, cinema can draw on the proto-cinematic awareness of revolutionary painters like Van Gogh. Bazin would agree:

> as it became more conscious of itself, painting absorbed something of photography. It is Degas and Toulouse-Lautrec, Renoir and Manet, who have understood from the inside, and in essence, the nature of the photographic phenomenon and, prophetically, even the cinematographic phenomenon. Faced with photography, they opposed it in the only valid way, by a dialectical enriching of pictorial technique. They understood the laws of the new image better than the photographers and well before the movie-makers, and it is they who first applied them.
>
> "Theatre and Cinema II," 119

Weaving his magic carpet from sunrays and the reality hidden underneath the skin of objects, Van Gogh explored the laws of the new image long before Akira Kurosawa's *Dreams*.

Together with Van Gogh's disciple, in *Dreams* we walk through a museum where Kurosawa has collected the paintings he loves. To see an artist's paintings projected together is like playing in the dark with a magic lantern. This is Marcel's experience when he sees Elstir's paintings collected by the Guermantes. And this is our experience of Kurosawa's *Dreams*, when we realize that it stages a retrospective exhibit of Van Gogh's paintings, serving an autobiographical end: to see the world through Van Gogh's eyes, and at the same time to draw a self-portrait of Kurosawa himself as Van Gogh. This creates a cyclical pattern of the construction—both of the observer or narrator but also of the narrative—that Donald Richie found both in Proust and in Kurosawa: "One of the few ways a narrative art may encompass a character is to circle him, to reveal one facet after another, to return continually to what is already known, to contrast what we saw then with what we know now. The most revealing of psychological fiction (Proust for example) continually circles and returns. Kurosawa's interest in character revelation insists upon a like movement—with the result of a like pattern" (*The Films of Akira Kurosawa*, 188).

As a reader of world literature and a great admirer of Tarkovsky, who based his films on Proust's poetics, Akira Kurosawa too could have found in Proust a proto-filmmaker, especially when it comes to defining the painter's brain as a magic lantern, the ancestor of the film camera. When Marcel contemplates Elstir's works, he has a revelation similar to the one experienced by Kurosawa's young narrator, Van Gogh's disciple:

> The parts of the walls that were covered by paintings of his, all homogenous with one another, were like the luminous images of a magic lantern which in this instance was the brain of the artist. . . . Among these

pictures, some of those that seemed most absurd to people in fashionable society interested me more than the rest because they re-created those optical illusions which prove to us that we should never succeed in identifying objects if we did not bring some process of reasoning to bear on them ... How often, when driving, do we not come upon a bright street beginning a few feet away from us, when what we have actually before our eyes is merely a patch of wall glaringly lit which has given us the mirage of depth. .... Surfaces and volumes are in reality independent of the names of objects which our memory imposes on them after we have recognised them. Elstir sought to wrest from what he had just felt what he already knew; he had often been at pains to break up that medley of impressions which we call vision.

The Guermantes Way, 574

To give the mirage of depth—this is the optical illusion that Akira Kurosawa constructed when he went with his camera into each painting displayed in his museum of *Dreams*. Paintings become trapdoors in the artist's brain that connect him with his predecessors, who can be poets, painters, writers, composers, or filmmakers—the sky's the limit. "Instead of complaining that the cinema cannot give us paintings as they really are," André Bazin proposed with his characteristic irony, "should we not rather marvel that we have at last found an open sesame for the masses to the treasures of the world of art? ... The role of cinema here is not that of a servant nor is it to betray the painting. Rather it is to provide it with a new form of existence. The film of a painting is an aesthetic symbiosis of screen and painting, as is the lichen of the algae and mushroom" ("Painting and Cinema," 167).

The vehicle we take to the stars doesn't matter, as long as we arrive at the destination that Van Gogh dreamed of in the map of the sky.

4

The Dark Hollow at the Back of the Head

Woolf and Daldry

On March 27, 1941, a Monday, Virginia Woolf wrote her final diary entry, the day before she drowned herself in the River Ouse. The entry describes a meeting with a physician friend, Olivia Wilberforce, whom Leonard had brought her to see, in hopes that Wilberforce could help lift the severe depression that had come upon her:

> She had a <face> nose like the Duke of Wellington & great horse teeth & cold prominent eyes. When we came in she was sitting perched on a 3 cornered chair with knitting in her hands. An arrow fastened her collar. And before 5 minutes had passed she told us that two of her sons had been killed in the war. This, one felt, was to her credit. She taught dressmaking. Everything in the room was red brown & glossy. Sitting there I tried to coin a few compliments. But they perished in the icy sea between us. And then there was nothing. A curious sea side feeling in the air today. It reminds me of lodgings on a parade at Easter. Everyone leaning against the wind, nipped & silenced. All pulp removed. This windy corner. And Nessa is at Brighton, & I am imagining how it wd be if we could infuse souls. Octavia's story. Could I englobe it somehow? English youth in 1900. Two long letters from Shena & O. I can't tackle them, yet enjoy having them. L. is doing the rhododendrons . . .
>
> *The Diary*

In an elliptical tone, the entry includes fragments of the larger puzzle of that day. Despite the apparently random notation, reminiscent of Anna Karenina's haunting soliloquy as she's on her way to the train station where she will kill herself, readers of Woolf will recognize here her main preoccupations with life, death, choice, and the problem of time. It's strange how closely she resembles Clarissa Dalloway in this last entry, to the point of using the same imagery and cutting between the multiple layers of time that intersect in the present. She remembers the visit she'd paid that day, during which she plunged, like Clarissa, into thoughts about the past. The water imagery that pervades all of Woolf's writings couldn't be absent: "Sitting there I tried to coin a few compliments. But they perished in the icy sea between us. And then there was nothing. A curious sea side feeling in the air today" (*The Diary*).

She wrote this entry in a freshly begun notebook. The blank pages following the ellipsis remained like an invisible work waiting for someone who could carry Woolf's legacy into the future, and who could imagine how it would be if we could infuse souls. Someone like Stephen Daldry, who could tell an interviewer in February 2003, when *The Hours* received nine Oscar nominations: "books change my life, but it's not a phrase you hear very often any more . . . it's about the cost of creation and whether it's valid or not. . . . The books that I read felt very powerful—not only in my adolescence but now. I still read books that inform me or change me or upset me" (Billington interview). Virginia Woolf changed Daldry's understanding of the cost of creation, and his work resonates with her idea in *A Room of One's Own* that the creative mind is always androgynous. As he told his interviewer, "I get frustrated about it because they say, 'How can a man talk about women?' I say, 'Steven Spielberg didn't need to be an alien to talk about ET. You don't need to be a dog to direct Lassie.' It seems to be a denial of the process of imagination, which is a posh word for 'guesswork'."

In 2002, Daldry released *The Hours*, based on Michael Cunningham's 1999 Pulitzer-winning novel, substantially rewritten for the screen by the playwright David Hare. The film met with a rather mixed reception from literary and film scholars alike. Suspicious of three Hollywood-based superstars being cast in the leading roles—Nicole Kidman as Virginia Woolf, Julianne Moore as Laura Brown, and Meryl Streep as Clarissa Vaughan—some wrote the film off as a commercial Hollywood melodrama, despite—or because of—the many awards (42) and nominations (125) it received, including an Oscar, a Golden Globe, and a BAFTA for Kidman's performance, the Golden Globe for best motion picture, and a BAFTA for Philip Glass's music. For their part, various Woolf scholars frowned at the film's unconventional portrayal of Woolf that deconstructed the traditional representation of a mature, melancholic aesthete.

What makes a film a Hollywood production? The director, the location, the production company, the cast, the director's commercial aesthetic? Co-produced by the British producer Scott Rudin and the American Robert Fox, *The Hours* was directed by a British stage director who has a degree in English literature and who worked in collaboration with a leading British playwright (with whom he also collaborated on *The Reader*, based on Bernhard Schlink's novel). The score is by Philip Glass, known for his work

THE DARK HOLLOW AT THE BACK OF THE HEAD   119

with the avant-garde playwright Robert Wilson and art movies such as *Koyanisqaatsi*. So it's hard to say what would qualify *The Hours* as "a Hollywood film." But as we've seen with Scorsese, whereas definitions of world cinema have often excluded Hollywood productions outright, more recent approaches have become more inclusive and more aware of the complex and diverse productions of Hollywood. Paul Cooke's collection *World Cinema's 'Dialogues' with Hollywood* (2007) "defines world cinema as a polycentric phenomenon with (often overlapping) peaks of creation in different places and periods," and "takes world cinema to mean 'cinema of the world', in which Hollywood is one part amongst many" (8).

Even Cooke, however, sees Hollywood's art films less as part of world cinema than as a kind of hostile takeover:

> Hollywood is simply the best at giving audiences what they want, namely action-driven fictions, produced in the "continuity style" which elides the constructed nature of film as a medium, thus allowing the spectator to escape completely into the film's fantasy world … This contrasts with what are often viewed as the more "difficult," esoteric aesthetics and complex open-ended narratives associated with films produced in other parts of the world. … Hollywood has begun to corner this niche market too, with films like Ang Lee's gay Western romance *Brokeback Mountain* (2006)—produced by Universal's subsidiary "independent" company Focus Features—filling screens that would have been showing the latest Godard or Tarkovsky 20 years earlier.
>
> *World Cinema's "Dialogues"*, 2–3

As in the case of Scorsese's *Hugo*, a closer and more attentive look at Stephen Daldry's *The Hours* may reveal a very different story.

From the very beginning, *The Hours* is just the opposite of what Cooke describes. Centered on Virginia Woolf, a writer who was anything but a central and dominant figure in the literary field in her time, the film began with Michael Cunningham's novel, which returned to Woolf's working title for what would become *Mrs. Dalloway* (1925). Like a genuine postmodernist, Cunningham reinterpreted Woolf's masterpiece from the viewpoint of the present, answering questions *Mrs. Dalloway* left open, continuing or inventing narrative threads that Woolf only hinted at. He constructed a narrative on three temporal layers, each focused on a character that is a mirrored figure of Woolf. As Michael Wood notes, Cunningham's novel "is haunted by *Mrs. Dalloway*—appropriately, because its theme is the haunting of present lives by memories and books, by distant pasts and missed futures, by novels and poems to be read and written" ("Parallel Lives").

Woolf's novel tells the story of a single day in the life of Clarissa Dalloway, a middle-aged woman married to an important politician, Richard, and who is giving a party. During the day, Clarissa meets with a number of thoughts and people from her past, regretting opportunities she missed—marrying her early admirer Peter Walsh, having a love relationship with her friend Sally Seton, reading more and better—before the novel concludes with her party, during which she hears the news of the suicide of Septimus Warren Smith, a survivor of the Great War who is constructed as Clarissa's double. Cunningham's novel retains Woolf's time span—a single day in a woman's life—but multiplies it in three interrelated temporal periods: a day in Virginia Woolf's life as she's working on *Mrs. Dalloway* away from London, in Richmond, where Leonard had taken her to improve her health and prevent her from making another suicide attempt; a day in the life of Laura Brown, a housewife from Los Angeles in the late 1940s, who reads *Mrs. Dalloway* and identifies with Clarissa's regrets over not changing her life, but also identifies with the suicidal thoughts in the novel; and finally, a day in the life of Clarissa Vaughan, an editor in New York in the early 2000s. Like Clarissa Dalloway, Clarissa Vaughan is giving a party, in this case for her former lover Richard, a poet who has AIDS and who throws himself out of a window, as Septimus had done in Woolf's novel.

When David Hare agreed to write the script, he knew from the beginning that Cunningham's novel had to be changed radically to be brought on screen. As he said in a number of interviews, the main problem was that the book had a great deal of interior monologue, and while stream of consciousness is the hallmark of Woolf's modernist novel, translating it directly on screen would have meant using voiceovers, which Hare rejected outright: "That's the whole challenge of it. You know what Meryl was going through by the way she walked through the streets. Or you put in scenes of the party planning and so forth. Those are all my scenes—not Michael's scenes—but if you forego the right to go into somebody's head, then you've got to write new events" (David Cohen, "From Script to Screen"). Daldry and Hare kept the plot lines from Cunningham's book but completely rethought the way the three narratives would intertwine and interact. By choosing a temporal construction so different from the chronologically and semantically transparent standard Hollywood film, they were returning to Woolf more than adapting Cunningham's novel.

Endowed with a poet's imagination and a literary understanding of Woolf and Cunningham, Daldry wasn't making a Hollywood film at all. As he told the film critic David Denby, "people ask me what it was like making a Hollywood film, and I never know what to say, exactly, because we made it in Pinewood Studios, outside London, and the only time we went to Hollywood was to deliver the film to Paramount, and they said, 'Thank you'" (Denby interview). Daldry told another interviewer that London's West End theater district

THE DARK HOLLOW AT THE BACK OF THE HEAD

feels like home. I'm a theatre person, that's who I am. I'm happy to make sojourns into the world of movies but I'm basically a theatre director that potters off and does a couple of movies. I've never been to Hollywood. I can count the number of times I've been to Los Angeles on my hands. I've never made a movie there and I've never been there for working reasons. The only reason to go there is for silly awards shows.

LEWIS interview

Daldry's conception of cinema resonates with André Bazin's notion of mixed or hybrid cinema. As Bazin said, "It is no chance matter that some of the best filmmakers are also the best stage directors" ("Theatre and Cinema II," 123).

Daldry loved David Hare's script because it was an entirely fresh take: "It felt unique and 'out-of-genre'. Every other script reminded me of another film—this one didn't and I thought it was incredibly powerful" (Billington interview). Daldry thinks simultaneously like a reader, a writer, and a stage and film director, working with a notion of collective authorship that's akin to the surrealists'. Asked about his work on *The Hours*, Daldry tellingly emphasized "This is something that Virginia Woolf, Michael Cunningham, David Hare and I just made up" (Billington interview). *The Hours* is a film meant to take us back to Woolf's books—not only to *Mrs. Dalloway*—and also to remind us that great art, no matter the medium it manifests in, can affect and change people's lives. Not only a dialogue with the theatre and with film history, *The Hours* is for Daldry a way to bring back books that can have an impact on our lives:

> I do find it thrilling when you go onto Amazon and see that *Mrs. Dalloway* is back in at number four on the international bestseller list. That's amazing, it still makes me go 'wow'. Michael Cunningham is back in at number one, but Virginia Woolf is at number nine! To be honest, anything that makes people read books is a great thing. I just remember a time when people would talk about the fact that books could and would change your life. I think this has gone out of fashion, but anything that brings those books back to the fore is great.
>
> BRETT interview

In his essay "In Defense of Mixed Cinema," Bazin spoke similarly about the effect of film on literature: "As for those who are unacquainted with the original, one of two things may happen; either they will be satisfied with the film which is as good as most, or they will want to know the original, with the resulting gain for literature" (65). More than adapting a book to a new medium, art cinema like Daldry's gives back something to literature, enriching what had been our accepted knowledge of Virginia Woolf.

The Chiastic Architecture of *The Hours*

By opening and closing the film with a symmetrical scene—Woolf's suicide in the River Ouse in 1941—Daldry and Hare present us with a creative reading of Woolf's notion of time, one that is grounded not only in *Mrs. Dalloway* but in a poetic reading of her works, treating them as pieces of a giant puzzle that taken together configure her vision of time and the self.

The film opens with the sound and then a closeup of a running river, before we switch to another closeup of a woman's hands quickly tying her overcoat. We can tell that she's married, because we see a wedding ring. Leaving her house, she walks quickly through a garden, then the camera cuts to another closeup of a woman's hand dipping a pen into an inkwell, and we hear Nicole Kidman's voiceover, reading what's known as the suicide note that Virginia Woolf left for her husband, Leonard. As she writes her farewell letter to the man who loved and supported her through her repeated suicide attempts, Daldry periodically cuts to the film's present, accompanying Virginia on her last journey. This means that we are hearing her thoughts as she walks to the river; she is thinking of the letter she has written to Leonard. We are in her head. The pauses in her thoughts mark what Daldry calls the emotional arch of the film, for as a theatre director, he knows that a pause is sometimes more meaningful than words.

Such pauses follow Virginia's thoughts on what will become the film's nodal points: her suicide ("Dearest, I feel certain that I am going mad again. I feel we can't go through another of those terrible times. And I [pause] shan't recover this time"), together with the poet's multiple self, capable of leading several lives in the same second ("I begin to hear voices [pause] and I can't concentrate"). As we hear "So I'm doing what seems the best thing to do," we see Virginia on the riverbank, and at that moment Philip Glass's music breaks in. But this isn't an ending; on the contrary, it's a beginning, just like Proust's novel that begins where its creator's life ends and the novel appears like a poetic vision seen on his deathbed. This is exactly how Glass conceived of the music, in the rhythm and breath of Woolf's writing, translating her style into a musical composition: "When you first hear it, it seems to start and to stop. And the next time you hear it, it keeps going" (Glass interview). What seems to be an end—Virginia Woolf's life—is in in fact a beginning. But a beginning of what?

Daldry's musical conception of the editing mirrors Philip Glass's music, which features a central piano theme echoed in patterns of repetition by a string orchestra, in musical phrases that seem to begin and to stop, and to begin again. Death never ends anything, it's only a beginning. As Daldry remarked, this film was designed in terms of its rhythm: "It was very much about rhythm, context, cutting patterns and where you need to release certain information to make the tension work" (Billington interview). The tension is

THE DARK HOLLOW AT THE BACK OF THE HEAD 123

FIGURE 4.1 *Stills shown in consecutive order from Stephen Daldry's* The Hours *(2002)*.

released through Daldry's musical editing. As Woolf's letter to Leonard ends and we hear the last word she ever wrote to him—"Virginia"—Daldry shows us in closeup her hand softly resting on the paper, immediately followed by her head sinking under the river's surface and then her suicide note falling to the floor when Leonard drops her letter and runs outside in hopes of saving her (Figure 4.1). The rough cut translates on screen Woolf's stream of consciousness that mixes up all sorts of apparently random images, broken thoughts, and scattered ideas, but at the same time Daldry subtly suggests a logical continuity and organic coherence of these three images. Woolf's last word materializes on the screen as the actual Virginia, while the writer's hand softly rests on a blue sheet of paper that Daldry shows in a low angle looking like the thin surface of a river; now, she seems to be pushed underwater by the godlike narrator's hand. And as she goes underwater, Virginia undergoes a sea change: she becomes a paper being, as Daldry shows her letter slowly falling to the floor while Woolf's body reaches the riverbed.

But the way Daldry films her body seems to tell us that she's not dead but only floating. The camera follows her gliding through the unknown universe in the same rhythm as Philip Glass's music, and slowly the screen becomes black, just as Tarkovsky's closing of *The Mirror* suggested entering a mysterious black tunnel of the poet's camera eye. But the darkness that Daldry captured underwater isn't just a metaphor of Virginia's death, as an untrained eye might assume. It echoes as well the poetics that Woolf had expressed in the ending of *Orlando*, the apparently impossible biography of a man who turns into a woman and lives for three and a half centuries while reaching only age thirty-six. As she wrote in her diary, "it sprung upon me how I could revolutionise biography in a night" (*Diary*, October 9, 1927). Near the end of the novel, as Orlando walks through her ancestors' portrait gallery, she has a revelation about the source of all knowledge:

> She now looked down into the pool or sea in which everything is reflected—and indeed, some say that all our most violent passions, and art and religion are the reflections which we see in the dark hollow at the back of the head when the visible world is obscured for the time. She looked there now, long, deeply, profoundly, and immediately the ferny path up the hill along which she was walking became not entirely a path, but partly the Serpentine, the hawthorn bushes were partly ladies and gentlemen sitting with card cases and gold-mounted canes, the sheep were partly tall Mayfair houses; everything was partly something else, and each gained an odd moving power from this union of itself and something not itself so that with this mixture of truth and falsehood her mind became like a forest in which things moved, lights and shadows changed, and one thing became another.

Orlando, 237

As the screen goes black in Daldry's film, following Virginia's body underwater, we see in white letters the title "The Hours," and we know that the film that now begins is what Virginia sees in the dark hollow at the back of the head when the visible world is obscured in the seconds that precede death. As Daldry perceptively noted of Woolf's notion of creativity: "It's hard to define what Woolf's mental illness was and what the role of the self is in creativity—Virginia Woolf said, 'Unless I go into those dark moments, I can't actually do anything'" (Billington interview).

The film's temporal construction is reinforced by its closing scene, when Daldry shows Virginia at the end of the day when she has started writing *Mrs. Dalloway*, lying down on her bed, in the dark. The screen goes black again and immediately we return to the beginning of the movie. Like Philip Glass's music, the film begins and it stops; and then it begins again and it keeps on going, like the flowing river. This time, Daldry's camera shows Virginia entering the river but not going underwater. Her head remains at the surface, as she contemplates the river running endlessly, like Glass's music that accompanies us while the credits start running.

Through this chiastic construction, Daldry suggests that everything we've seen in between—the day in three women's lives in different time periods, confronted with existential choices: to live, to die—is but a revelation that Virginia sees in the seconds before she drowns. It isn't her life but her afterlives that flash before her eyes. So the three characters we see on screen interacting in almost surrealist ways through coincidences of situation and patterns of behavior and language—Virginia Woolf, Laura Brown and Clarissa Vaughan—are more than illustrations of the act of reading, as some critics have argued. Daldry tells us a more complex story about time that goes beyond the obvious meeting between a writer—Woolf—a reader—Laura Brown—and the book's heroine, Clarissa, in a different time.

This transgression of the borders of individuals and of eras was a point of view that Woolf had creatively reached for her own fiction by learning from Dostoevsky, Tolstoy, and Proust. "There's not a single living writer (English) I respect; so you see, I have to read the Russians," she wrote to her Greek teacher, Janet Case (Letter 1250, in *Letters*, v.2). As she wrote in an essay she worked on simultaneously with *Mrs. Dalloway*:

> The novels of Dostoevsky are seething whirlpools, gyrating sandstorms, waterspouts which hiss and boil and suck us in. They are composed purely and wholly of the stuff of the soul. Against our wills we are drawn in, whirled round, blinded, suffocated, and at the same time filled with a giddy rapture. . . . But, as we listen, our confusion slowly settles. A rope is flung to us; we catch hold of a soliloquy; holding on by the skin of our teeth, we are rushed through the water; feverishly, wildly, we rush on and on, now submerged, now in a moment of vision understanding more than

we have ever understood before, and receiving such revelations as we are wont to get only from the press of life at its fullest.

"The Russian Point of View"

Like Dostoevsky's characters, and like Woolf herself, Clarissa Dalloway lives so intensely that time multiplies or collapses. Even to live a single day becomes dangerous: "She felt young; at the same time, unspeakably aged . . . She had a perpetual sense, as she watched the taxicabs, of being out, out, far out to sea and alone; she always had the feeling that it was very, very dangerous to live even one day" (*Mrs. Dalloway*, 7). This becomes Daldry's poetics of *The Hours*: in the blink of an eye, the simple story of Virginia Woolf's suicide expands back into her former self writing *Mrs. Dalloway* sixteen years earlier but also forward into the life of the depressed housewife Laura Brown, who will "choose life," as she resolutely declares at the end, leaving behind a husband and two children after having contemplated suicide. And from there, it spreads even farther, into the life of Laura Brown's son the poet Richard, now grown up, who has a Mrs. Dalloway of his own in the form of Clarissa Vaughan. Clarissa in turn is now in a relationship with Sally, who has resurfaced from her previous existence as Sally Seton in the pages of *Mrs. Dalloway*.

Whereas Dostoevsky taught Woolf about accelerating the narrative speed when going into "dark moments," Proust showed her the reverse: how to make time linger, to analyze experience thoroughly down to its last thread. Both methods—compression and expansion—are put to work by Daldry in the three-layered narrative of *The Hours*. The narrative time is at once a few seconds and twelve hours of three lives told over the course of a two-hour film. This multiple representation of time is intimately related to Woolf's notion of the self. In her 1925 essay "The Russian Point of View," Woolf writes that "it is the soul that is the chief character in Russian fiction. Delicate and subtle in Tchekov, subject to an infinite number of humours and distempers, it is of greater depth and volume in Dostoevsky; it is liable to violent diseases and raging fevers, but still the predominant concern."

Both in Dostoevsky and in Tolstoy, Woolf was drawn to scenes in which a character's life passes before their eyes at the moment of facing death. She read *Anna Karenina* three times (1909–11, 1926, 1929), and as she wrote to Vita Sackville-West, "Practically every scene in *Anna Karenina* is branded on me" (Letter 1980, in *Letters*, v.4). Surely no scene moved her more than Anna's suicide, when she plunges onto the train tracks as though she's diving into a pool: "A feeling seized her, similar to what she experienced when preparing to go into the water for a swim, and she crossed herself. The habitual gesture of making the sign of the cross called up in her soul a whole series of memories from childhood and girlhood, and suddenly the darkness that covered everything for her broke and life rose up before her momentarily with all its bright past joys" (*Anna Karenina*, 768). In *The Idiot*, Dostoevsky gives perhaps the most famous of his many fictional versions of his own near-death experience, when he was reprieved moments before he was to be executed for his involvement in the Petrashevsky Circle, a progressive literary group. As his Prince Myshkin recalls, there was a man once who

> had once been led to a scaffold, along with others, and a sentence of death by firing squad was read out to him, for a political crime. After about twenty minutes a pardon was read out to him, and he was given a lesser degree of punishment; nevertheless, for the space between the two sentences, for twenty minutes, or a quarter of an hour at the least, he lived under the certain conviction that in a few minutes he would suddenly die.... It seemed to him that in those five minutes he would live so many lives that there was no point yet in thinking about his last moment.... now he exists and lives, and in three minutes there would be *something*, some person or thing—but who? and where? ... yet he said that nothing was more oppressive for him at that moment than the constant thought: "What if I were not to die! What if life were given back to me—what infinity! And it would all be mine! Then I'd turn each minute into a whole age, I'd lose nothing, I'd reckon up every minute separately, I'd let nothing be wasted!"
>
> *The Idiot*, author's emphasis

To live several lives in your last minutes; to see them as clearly as possible; to know that you're soon becoming *something*, some person or thing—this is the poetics of Daldry's *The Hours*. As the screen turns black and "The Hours" is shown in the dark, Virginia Woolf becomes both some *person*—in fact, a triad of people—and some *thing*: the film *The Hours* itself. As Daldry told David Denby, "the whole sweep in the end is a very complicated mathematical combination between three characters. Which, in the end, would be one, if you like" (Denby, "How *The Hours* Happened"). Daldry's Woolf will see not only herself writing *Mrs. Dalloway*, but also her own future. In Laura Brown and Clarissa Vaughan, Virginia returns to life from the pages of the book she turned into when she went under the river's surface in the opening of the film.

Hare and Daldry bring Proust on screen in the character of Richard, the poet dying of AIDS, for whom Clarissa is throwing a party. In addition to his prize-winning poetry, Richard has also written a lengthy novel, *The Goodness of Time*. Daldry shows this Proustian novel on a shelf, right next to Woolf's own writings, in reverse chronological order, left to right: *The Years*, *The Waves*, *Mrs. Dalloway* and finally *The Goodness of Time*, telling us subtly that the goodness of time is to come back in the future. Like Proust's *Recherche*, Richard's work is a long, autobiographical novel that people find difficult to read. One of his former lovers confesses in an annoyed tone to Clarissa: "I read the book." "Oh, Goooood," replies Clarissa, lengthening the phrase. "Exactly," he says. "A whole chapter on should [the hero's mother] buy nail polish? And then guess what, after fifty pages, she doesn't. The whole thing seems to go on for eternity, nothing happens, and then wham! For no reason, she kills herself." This caustic summary plays on the famous complaint by an early critic that Proust's novel begins with fifty pages describing how a gentleman turns over in bed. When Clarissa goes to buy flowers in the morning, the florist confesses to her: "I actually tried to read Richard's novel." "Oh, you did," replies Clarissa embarrassedly. "It's not easy, I know. It did take him ten years to write." "Maybe it just takes another ten to read," the florist concludes. Toward the end of the film, Clarissa finally meets Laura Brown, Richard's mother. She asks Laura: "Have you read the poems?" "Oh, yes," comes Laura's quick answer. "I also read the novel. You see, people say the novel's difficult."

Richard combines Proust with Clarissa Dalloway's mirrored double, Septimus Warren Smith, with whom she identifies in death: "He had killed himself—but how? Always her body went through it, when she was told, first, suddenly, of an accident; her dress flamed; her body burst. He had thrown himself from a window" (156). She speculates about the reasons for his suicide: "there were the poets and the thinkers. Suppose he had had that passion . . . there was in the depths of her heart an awful fear. . . . She had escaped. But that young man had killed himself" (157). In a compliment to Proust's structure, which closes as if the entire novel is what our narrator writes on his deathbed, Hare and Daldry chose to open and close the film with Virginia entering the river. The final frame shows Virginia's head above the water, looking down the stream while the flowing river's movement is doubled by Philip Glass's piano music echoed in the string orchestra (like the creator's single voice is echoed by a chorus of voices, all her own creation) and by Virginia's voiceover: "Leonard, always the years between us. Always the years. Always the love. Always the hours."

Daldry masterfully synchronizes the rhythm and flow of the river with the rhythm of David Hare's poetic coda, written to mirror the opening with the reading in voiceover of Virginia Woolf's actual suicide letter to Leonard, and finally with Philip Glass's central compositional theme. The river that constantly flows without stopping is made of the same repetitive wavelike movements— "always the years between us. Always the years. Always the love. Always the hours." While Virginia's suicide note to Leonard was real, the actual words we hear in Virginia's were written by David Hare: "I wrote it. I wanted to restate the spirit of the suicide note, but I didn't want to use exactly the same words. So I was faced with what I regarded as a moral problem: could I write a piece of Virginia Woolf that's not by Virginia Woolf?" He admitted that he wasn't "wholly at peace" with his decision: "I'd be a bit pissed off at having lines attributed to me that I didn't write. Particularly if I were Virginia Woolf, who struggled so hard to write exactly what she wanted to write and nothing else. I apologize to her ghost" (Cohen, "From Script to Screen").

Unlike in the opening of *The Hours*, where Daldry's camera follows Woolf's body underwater—the waters standing for the poet's brain—the film closes with a shot showing Virginia's head above the surface, her head

THE DARK HOLLOW AT THE BACK OF THE HEAD   129

not turned to the camera, in a timeless look at the river's flow. He closes his film symmetrically to its opening, but with a difference, because the closing turns back time to a few seconds before the opening left off, and thereby suggests that Virginia has resurfaced after her underwater vision of the film we've just seen. Her eyes that watch the river's flow are now "fished from the bottom of the sea" (*Orlando*, 28). Virginia resurfaces from death at the end, just as Laura Brown, her future reader, resurfaces with a terrified gasp from a daydream vision of drowning herself.

Asked in August 1922 by the newspaper *L'Intransigeant* to respond to the question "What would you do if you knew the world were about to end?" Proust sent an unwittingly ominous reply three months before his sudden death of pneumonia:

> I think that life would suddenly seem wonderful to us if we were threatened to die . . . Just think of how many projects, travels, love affairs, studies, it—our life—hides from us, made invisible by our laziness which, certain of a future, delays them incessantly. But let all this threaten to become impossible for ever, how beautiful it would become again! Ah! If only the cataclysm doesn't happen this time, we won't miss visiting the new galleries of the Louvre, throwing ourselves at the feet of Miss X, making a trip to India. The cataclysm doesn't happen, we don't do any of it, because we find ourselves back in the heart of normal life, where negligence deadens desire. And yet we shouldn't have needed the cataclysm to love life today. It would have been enough to think that we are humans, and that death may come this evening.
>
> "Et si le monde," 2

Woolf's Novel as Poetry: Revolutionizing the Self and Time

When Daldry came to David Hare's script, he loved it for challenging him to rethink one of his favorite writers: "Having done an English Literature degree at university, I was deeply aware of Virginia Woolf and somehow she'd always stayed with me. The great thing about her, one of the reasons she is so current in our consciousness is that she can be reinvented by each generation. She feels like a contemporary rather than a literary figure from the past. She was a central figure in the 1970s women's movement with *A Room of One's Own*, so she has huge social as well as a literary and cultural importance" (Johnston interview). As he told another interviewer:

> The great thing, I think, about Virginia Woolf is that she is reinvented for each new generation. She still seems to me to be radical, and the producer and I were keen to get a contemporary voice, somebody who could be

our Virginia Woolf, someone who spoke directly and vibrantly to us now. I thought Nicole Kidman was a phenomenal character actress in *The Blue Room* at the Donmar. She was sexy, difficult, dark, animal and witty and so it felt like this aspect of Nicole would be a fantastic element to have as Virginia Woolf. The danger is you get some fusty old version of Virginia Woolf that was lost in the midst of time, so it felt more appropriate to have her as dynamic as the writing still is today.

BILLINGTON interview

Daldry chose Kidman—after seeing her on stage at London's innovative Donmar Warehouse—in order to break from the traditional representation of Woolf, who on the British stage has famously been played by Eileen Atkins, and many expected her to play the part in *The Hours*, too. But Daldry had a very different role in mind for her. "I asked Eileen to do it because she is such an authority on Virginia Woolf, and it seemed wrong to have the film without her in it. I think it's a great honour that she agreed to be in it" (Billington interview). Yet he cast Atkins not as Woolf but as the florist with whom Clarissa Vaughan has a conversation that reveals how much Clarissa is stuck in the past, voicing her resentment over Richard leaving her. The florist scrutinizes Clarissa as if seeing through her, in a nod to Atkins playing Woolf on the stage. She asks Clarissa some uncomfortable questions about Richard's autobiographical novel, in which Clarissa appears as a main character, and she also suggests what Clarissa refuses to admit: that she's very unhappy with his having left her for his male lover, Louis. The entire conversation is a tracking scene in which Daldry alternates the florist's silent expressions and few words with Clarissa's. As they pace through the shop, separated by a row of flowers, they seem to be a visual metaphor of two temporal lines that meet in Daldry's film: the past representation of Woolf and her present apparition in *The Hours* as Clarissa Vaughan.

It isn't a matter of chance that Daldry mentions *A Room of One's Own* in relation to what he calls Woolf's "huge social as well as a literary and cultural importance." *A Room of One's Own* is a key link in the complex story that Daldry tells us through his film. Woolf's 1928 essay became one of the most powerful feminist manifestoes not only because it raised questions of gender, sexuality, and identity in relation to literature but also because it put forward the notion of an androgynous self manifested in all great artists. Her examples are her own mentors: Shakespeare, Proust, Tolstoy (*A Room*, 75). Literature is no longer tied to a single gender or genre ("women's writing"), but rather presented the transgression of genders as well as genres as the source of creativity. Like Proust before her and Tarkovsky later, Woolf believed that poetry must be at the heart of any artistic endeavor, so her writings can't be described accurately as mere "novels." Daldry and Hare thought in similar terms about *The Hours*, describing it as being "out of genre" (Daldry) and "not any particular kind" of movie (Hare).

THE DARK HOLLOW AT THE BACK OF THE HEAD   131

Like André Breton, Woolf rejected the novel as such. In the *First Manifesto of Surrealism*, Breton wrote that the only excuse for writing a novel would be if it integrated the marvelous, which for Breton is synonymous with poetry: "In the realm of literature, only the marvelous is capable of fecundating works which belong to an inferior category such as the novel, and generally speaking, anything that involves storytelling" (*Manifestoes*, 14). In a letter to E.M. Forster in 1927, Woolf wrote that "Nothing induces me to read a novel except when I have to make money by writing about it. I detest them. They seem to me wrong from start to finish—my own included" (Letter 1835, in *Letters*, v.3). A few days later, she wrote to her nephew Julian Bell that he should write anything but a novel: "I rather hope it won't be a novel. Anything is better than a novel. Try an autobiography" (Letter 1836, in *Letters*, v.3).

But in 1928 Woolf herself published *Orlando*, a novel in the form of a biography, which she wrote off in her diary as a mere joke and fantasy, and many critics took her at her word.[1] *Orlando* has often been seen as an oddity, and at odds with the rest of her poetic novels, yet it is of a piece with *A Room of One's Own*, written at the same time and widely understood as a fundamental feminist text. *A Room of One's Own* is structured around a story Woolf made up in order to introduce her notion of the true artist's androgynous mind. She imagines the life of Judith Shakespeare, a sister just as gifted as her brother, endowed like him with a poet's androgynous mind, who disappeared from history and has finally resurfaced, we can infer, as Woolf herself—a man who becomes a woman and who crosses three and a half centuries from the Elizabethan period all the way to the present moment, October 11, 1928. This was also Orlando's story. His name recalls Orlando from Shakespeare's *As You Like It*, the man who declares his love to Rosalind, his lover whom he doesn't recognize as she's costumed herself as a young man named Ganymede, in a nod to Zeus's cupbearer and lover. Woolf's work simultaneously on *A Room of One's Own* and *Orlando* is telling for the conception of time and the self behind her uncanny poetic novel, and the essay elaborates the theory behind the strange "biography" of *Orlando* that crosses three and a half centuries and that has puzzled Woolf critics for decades.

Woolf had stayed with Daldry for a number of reasons, one of them being very much that they shared a common understanding of life and the self, and their biographies overlapped to some extent. Just as Proust hid his

---

[1]This reading remained prominent from 1928 onward. Desmond MacCarthy described it as "a wonderful phantasmagoria" (Review of *Orlando*, *Sunday Times*, October 2, 1928, in *Virginia Woolf: The Critical Heritage*, 225). Maria DiBattista writes that "*Orlando* may seem a major detour in Woolf's quest for an expressive form that will capture 'the essence of reality'" ("Introduction," *Orlando*, xxxvii). Elizabeth Bowen remembers that "We regarded this book as a setback.... The book was, we gathered, in the nature of a prank, or a private joke; worse still, its genesis was personal" ("*Orlando* by Virginia Woolf," 131). "The book is a novelist's holiday, not a novel" (133).

own homosexuality behind nearly every character in the *Recherche* except for the narrator and his double, Charles Swann, Woolf hid her own behind the androgynous principle of creativity as well as Orlando's story. To be a gay woman writer in 1928 one needed more than a room of one's own, and what one could do was either project one's desires and tastes as someone else's, as did Proust, or frame them as a fantasy as Woolf did.

Woolf found the perfect metaphor for this project in Shakespeare: "one goes back to Shakespeare's mind as the type of the androgynous, of the man-womanly mind" (*A Room*, 71–2). Woolf also found the self defined as androgynous in Proust's writings. In *Sodom and Gomorrah*, Proust goes even farther than Woolf to say that not only the authentic creative mind, but the human being itself is androgynous: "the race of inverts, who readily link themselves with the ancient East or the golden age of Greece, might be traced back further still, to those experimental epochs in which there existed neither dioecious plants nor monosexual animals to that initial hermaphroditism of which certain rudiments of male organs in the anatomy of women and of female organs in that of men seem still to preserve the trace" (40). Human beings recuperate this identity in the land of dreams: "The race that inhabits them, like that of our first human ancestors, is androgynous. A man in it appears a moment later in the form of a woman" (516). We have here *Orlando*'s poetics in a nutshell.

Daldry finds his own life reflected in Woolf's. Her relationship with Vita Sackville-West lasted over a period of three years (1925–8) that formed Woolf's most prolific period, when she wrote *Mrs. Dalloway* (1925), *To the Lighthouse* (1927), and *Orlando* (1928), while Daldry is an openly gay theatre director who married his best friend, the American performance artist Lucy Sexton, with whom he has a child. If in the 1920s a gay woman writer married to her best friend, Leonard Woolf, couldn't speak openly about her sexuality, and projected herself in countless male doubles from Septimus Warren Smith to Orlando, in the 2000s a gay male theatre director married to his best friend could speak about his personal life with a directness that Woolf could only dream of:

> There is no hedging with Daldry. He recently explained that yes, he does have sex with his wife, but if anyone asks, he always says he's gay because it's easier and people prefer it.
>
> "They don't like the confusion," he shrugs.
>
> How does his wife feel about being married to a gay man? I ask.
>
> "You'd have to ask her," he says. "But do you know what I honestly think? I think one of the great things about our marriage is, we're never going to get a divorce, and we don't have to worry about infidelity. To marry your best friend is one of the great gifts of life, and to have kids with your best friend is fantastic."

WOOD interview

THE DARK HOLLOW AT THE BACK OF THE HEAD   133

This was the world the author of *A Room of One's Own* dreamed of when she spoke of Shakespeare's sister resurfacing in better times. Shakespeare appears twice in *Orlando*'s apparently chronological narrative, in another chiastic construction. Rather than being at odds with Woolf's more realistic novels, *Orlando* is the logical development of the project begun with *Mrs. Dalloway*, as we find out when we reach the present moment, after 350 years during which Orlando turns into a woman. The final thirty pages tell a story very similar to the one in *Mrs. Dalloway*. Like Clarissa, Orlando goes out shopping early in the morning and plunges into all sorts of memories from her past. In a department store she sees an elderly, heavy woman, dressed in furs who reminds her of somebody: this is Sasha, the mysterious Russian with whom Orlando fell in love as a boy during Shakespeare's time. But we recognize in her also a version of Sally Seton, with whom Clarissa Dalloway was in love as a young girl and whose kiss she never forgets. She reappears at Clarissa's party in *Mrs. Dalloway* as a plump, elderly mother of numerous children. Orlando continues her plunge into the past—but whose past?—while she drives through London in 1928, when another memory breaks in: "'He sat at Twitchett's table,' she mused, 'with a dirty ruff on . . . Was it old Mr. Baker come to measure the timber? Or was it Sh—p—re?' . . . 'Haunted!' she cried, suddenly pressing the accelerator. 'Haunted ever since I was a child'" (*Orlando*, 229). Woolf herself is haunted both by Shakespeare and also by her metaphorical self, Orlando. In this respect, Orlando is more metatextual than any other character Woolf created, for s/he is the literary analog of her concept of the artist's androgynous self. Like Septimus haunted by his dead comrade Evans, Woolf is haunted by the literary past she looks up to, and her gallery of ghosts includes Tolstoy, Dostoevsky, Proust, and towering over them all, Shakespeare.

Daldry's construction of *The Hours*, framed by Virginia in the waters of the river, takes on a different meaning when we look back at *Orlando*'s own chiastic construction. For this wasn't the first time Shakespeare's ghost haunted the pages of *Orlando*. In the beginning, when Orlando was a boy and was waiting to meet Queen Elizabeth, he stumbled upon a man whose name we're not told:

> But there, sitting at the servant's dinner table with a tankard beside him and paper in front of him, sat a rather fat, rather shabby man, whose ruff was a thought dirty, and whose clothes were of hodden brown. He held a pen in his hand, but he was not writing. He seemed in the act of rolling some thought up and down, to and fro in his mind till it gathered shape or momentum to his liking. His eyes, globed and clouded like some green stone of curious texture, were fixed. For all his hurry, Orlando stopped dead. Was this a poet? Was he writing poetry? . . . but how speak to a man who does not see you? who sees ogres, satyrs, perhaps the depths of the sea instead?
>
> *Orlando*, 17

Even though the young Orlando fails to recognize him, the reader recognizes Shakespeare himself. What passed for a time-transgressing fantasy is revealed in the last pages of *Orlando* as Woolf's realism pushed to the limits. If Clarissa thought how dangerous it is to live even a single day, Orlando goes even farther: imagine what it means to live even a few minutes—or a few centuries. A trapdoor opening on a beautiful sunny morning can take Orlando back three and a half centuries, to when she met Shakespeare. Because Shakespeare lies hidden within her, it's no longer implausible to live three and a half centuries while always being in the same present moment.

Similarly, Daldry shows Virginia mulling over the opening of *Mrs. Dalloway* in a scene that echoes Shakespeare's first apparition in *Orlando*. One morning, Virginia tells Leonard: "I think I may have a first sentence." As she enters her room, a closeup of her hand shows her hesitating over a jar filled with pens as if she's a painter choosing the right brush, and she sits down with a writing board on her lap. She smokes absent-mindedly looking into the unknown, and comes back with her opening sentence: "Mrs. Dalloway said she would buy the flowers herself." The minute she writes this down, Daldry cuts to Laura Brown voicing it three decades later, and eight decades later Clarissa acts it out: "Sally, I think I will buy the flowers myself." Daldry's rough cut, fast-paced editing, and the chronologically arranged montage bring Orlando, Shakespeare, and Woolf herself to life together on screen.

Woolf knew from Proust that our memory extends both before our individual life and after our death. As the critic Jean-Jacques Mayoux has observed:

> *Orlando* in one sense is a *Time Regained*, with a radical difference, a difference in tone. The painful tension in Proust's work comes from the anguish which passing time causes him and the importance he attaches to regaining it. The total lack of dramatic pressure, of emotive tonality in *Orlando* comes from the absence of the flow of life and of the peril of death. *Orlando* is the happy solution to a problem which is not posed . . .
>
> "Le roman de l'espace et du temps," 249

Clarissa could plunge back into the past when she was young and unmarried, with every option still ahead, all choices yet to be made. Orlando can plunge back even farther, while staying like Clarissa always in the present moment, October 11, 1928. We are in a mode of hyperrealism exploded to encompass a revolutionary poetic understanding of the notion of time and of the self. If earlier versions of Clarissa inhabit the middle-aged Clarissa, how many versions of the poets whom Orlando loves inhabit her as well? "So she was now darkened, stilled, and become, with the addition of this Orlando, what is called, rightly or wrongly, a single self, a real self" (229–30).

THE DARK HOLLOW AT THE BACK OF THE HEAD   135

As Winifred Holtby has observed, Woolf "had, in all her books, played with the notion of time and its importance. In *Mrs. Dalloway* the whole significance of fifty years had been gathered into twenty-four hours; it was only going one step further, in *Orlando,* to spread the experience of some forty years out over three centuries" (*Virginia Woolf*, 162).

Read as a continuation of *Mrs. Dalloway* and a pushing to the limits of the dimensions of the temporal plunge, the last thirty pages of *Orlando* tell a very realistic story. Every morning, Orlando takes a walk through her ancestors' gallery of portraits that date back to the Elizabethan period. As she looks down the gallery, she can travel in time through this tunnel in the blink of an eye, and everything we've seen in the book, including Orlando's multiple identities, her travels, and her change of sex, are the musing of a poet's mind over her ancestors' portraits. Every episode, every country, every age is Orlando's poetic answer to the question: who would I have been had I lived in such a period and such a space?

The human self is not individual, but plural, and not limited to his own chronology: "If I can have in me and round me so many memories which I do not remember, this oblivion . . . may extend over a life which I have lived in the body of another man, even on another planet. . . . The being that I shall be after death has no more reason to remember than the man I have been since my birth than the latter to remember what I was before it" (*Sodom and Gomorrah*, 522–3). In *The Hours*, Woolf's ghost is resurrected in a myriad of other selves, connected through mysterious links like the infinite selves that inhabit Orlando: Laura Brown, Clarissa, Richard, Louis, even the florist. Time opened simultaneously toward the past and future creates the double rhythm of Woolf's poetic prose, expressed in metaphors and recurrent phrases. They create the two tempos that will materialize in Daldry's cutting patterns and leitmotifs, and also in the two tempos of Philip Glass's music. In a masterly stroke, Daldry synchronizes three types of rhythm: the rhythm of Woolf's writing, the rhythm of his editing and pacing, and the rhythm of Glass's music. All fall on the same beat in a film that does justice—as no literary study has managed to do to this day—to Woolf's revolution of time and the poetic mind.

Daldry's principle of bringing together a linguistic rhythm with a visual and a musical rhythm can already be found in *Orlando*:

For if there are (at a venture) seventy-six different times all ticking in the mind at once, how many different people are there not—Heaven help us—all having lodgment at one time or another in the human spirit? Some say two thousand and fifty-two. . . . These selves of which we are built up, one on top of another, as plates are piled on a waiter's hand, have attachments elsewhere . . . so that one will come if it is raining, another in a room with green curtains, another when Mrs. Jones is not there, another if you can promise it a glass of wine—and so on; for everybody can multiply from his own experience the different terms which his different selves have made with him.

Orlando, 225–6

In a diary entry from 1927, while she was working on *Orlando*, Woolf wrote that a friend told her at dinner that "I have no logical power and live and write in an opium dream. And the dream is too often about myself" (*The Diary*, v.3, December 22, 1927). As she walks through her ancestral house, Orlando is struck by a thought:

Ah, but she knew where the heart of the house still beat ... Gently opening a door, she stood on the threshold so that (as she fancied) the room could not see her and watched the tapestry rising and falling on the eternal faint breeze which never failed to move it. Still the hunter rode; still Daphne flew. The heart still beat, she thought, however faint, however far withdrawn; the frail indomitable heart of the immense building.

232

The house, a ghostly object-being like the haunted house in André Breton's *Mad Love*, is a metaphor for the actual space where we hear the heartbeat and which is the space of Woolf's book: the brain of the poet, the blood pulsating in her temples as she pursues her dreams, just as Apollo pursues Daphne in the tapestry. This is the room of her own that she sought in 1928 in the mirror text of *Orlando*. Discussing the temporal arch in *To the Lighthouse*, Jorge Luis Borges described Woolf's treatment of time and objects as showing "a few hours in several peoples' lives, so that in those hours we see their past and future," adding: "The preoccupation with time is present, as well, in *Orlando* (1928). The hero of this extremely original novel— undoubtedly Virginia Woolf's most intense and one of the most singular and maddening of our era—lives for three hundred years and is, at times, a symbol of England and of its poetry in particular" ("Virginia Woolf," 174).

Mrs. Dalloway creates a double temporal rhythm in two ways: first, by intertwining the objective time marked by the beating of Big Ben's chime with the inner, subjective time lived differently by each character; and second, by the use of shared metaphors and imagery to construct the interiority of apparently unrelated characters. Both devices are employed on the opening page, when Clarissa plunges in the waters of memory as she opens a window on the morning of her party:

And then, thought Clarissa Dalloway, what a morning—fresh as if issued to children on a beach.... What a lark! What a plunge! For so it had always seemed to her when, with a little squeak of the hinges, which she could hear now, she had burst open the French windows and plunged at

Bourton into the open air. How fresh, how calm, stiller than this of course, the air was in the early morning; like the flap of a wave; the kiss of a wave; chill, and sharp and yet (for a girl of eighteen as she then was), solemn, feeling as she did, standing there at the open window, that something awful was about to happen; looking at the flowers, at the trees with the smoke winding off them and the rooks rising, falling; standing and looking.

Mrs. Dalloway, 3

While the alternation between inner and outer time is punctuated by "then" and "now," it's in the "then" that most of the sentence takes place as we listen to Clarissa's thoughts and Woolf's poetics of rhythm comes out. It is mostly based on repetitions of words, but also of symmetrical structures— "What a lark! What a plunge!" and "How fresh, how calm"—related to the sea imagery: "fresh as if issued to children on a beach," "like the flap of a wave; the kiss of a wave." When considered together, these enumerations and repetitions create the feeling of waves breaking on the shore, sometimes calmly, other times violently. Like the waves, they come one after another, in succession: "What a lark! What a plunge!"

But the most elaborate construction is found when the very rhythm of the sentence is reproduced both at the level of sound and of meaning: "rising, falling; standing and looking." It is from such passages that Daldry learned the synchronizing of sound, image, and word that structures his editing. So too Philip Glass learned that to translate Woolf's style into music is to create patterns of repetition and to play them at a distance, to create an effect of echoing: "How fresh, how calm, stiller than this of course, the air was in the early morning; like the flap of a wave; the kiss of a wave; chill, and sharp and yet (for a girl of eighteen as she then was), solemn, feeling as she did, standing there at the open window, that something awful was about to happen." The sentence begins with Woolf's poetics of the wave that makes grammatical, syntactic, and semantic patterns recur at a distance. Glass's musical phrases are composed only of few notes, played over and over again. But each instrument is made to echo the central theme played on the piano, creating the rhythm of a breathing body, a beating heart that accelerates as if "something awful was about to happen," for "it was very, very dangerous to live even one day," as Clarissa feels (7). As Borges already observed, *Orlando* "is also a musical work, not only in the euphonious virtues of its prose but in the structure of its composition, which consists of a limited number of themes that return and combine. We also hear a kind of music in *A Room of One's Own* (1930), in which dream and reality alternate and reach an equilibrium" ("Virginia Woolf," 174).

And indeed, the rhythm Clarissa hears "rising and falling" is that of her own blood pulsating; the waves are the movements of blood in this body through which Woolf perceives the world, interrupted by the deathlike beat of irreversible time: "one feels in the midst of traffic, or waking at night, Clarissa was positive, a particular hush, or solemnity; an indescribable pause; a suspense (but that might be her heart, affected, they said, by influenza) before Big Ben strikes. There! Out it boomed. First, a warning, musical; then the hour, irrevocable" (4). Similarly, in *The Hours*, the moments that narrate the interior flow of thoughts of Virginia, Laura, or Clarissa, punctuated by Philip Glass's soft piano, rising and falling, stopping and beginning again, are interrupted or concluded irrevocably by the sound of a clock ticking in the background.

In *Mrs. Dalloway* the comparisons with the sea imagery, or the repetition of wave-shaped phrases like "rising and falling," don't belong only to Clarissa's interiority. They return a few pages into the novel with Septimus Warren Smith, Clarissa's double who feels the same temptation or danger every day that he might cease to exist: "Septimus heard her say 'Kay Arr' close to his ear, deeply, softly, like a mellow organ . . . which rasped his spine deliciously and sent running up into his brain waves of sound . . . the excitement of the elm trees rising and falling, rising and falling . . . so proudly they rose and fell, so superbly" (19). And then similar repetitions appear even with the anonymous third-person narration: "It was a splendid morning, too. Like the pulse of a perfect heart, life struck straight through the streets. There was no fumbling—no hesitation. Sweeping and swerving, accurately, punctually, noiselessly" (46–7). If characters who have never met are expressing their intimate interiority through the same imagery and even identical phrases, it means that they are controlled by a single authorial voice that brings them together. This poetics traverses all Woolf's mature writings and reaches a climax with *The Waves*.

While *Mrs. Dalloway* only anticipated *Orlando*'s multiple selves that inhabit characters and come back from their past to haunt them, *The Waves* actually begins with a poetic exploration of the underwater universe that the poet saw at the end of *Orlando* as the dark pool where all art is born. This sea is a living, dormant being; "the grey cloth became barred with thick strokes moving, one after another, beneath the surface, following each other, pursuing each other, perpetually. As they neared the shore each bar rose, heaped itself, broke and swept a thin veil of white water across the sand. The wave paused, and then drew out again, sighing like a sleeper whose breath comes and goes unconsciously" (*The Waves*, 337).

Woolf opens the poetic novel-experiment written in six voices—three male (Bernard, Louis, and Neville) and three female (Rhoda, Susan, and Jinny)—with the image of a dormant woman waking up: "the sky cleared as if the white sediment there had sunk, or as if the arm of a woman couched beneath the horizon had raised a lamp and flat bars of white, green and yellow spread across the sky like the blades of a fan" (337). No longer as transparent as the repeated "rising and falling" from *Mrs. Dalloway*, Woolf's phrases create the rhythm of waves following one another, and soon they will materialize in her narrators' six voices: "thick strokes moving, one after another, beneath the surface, following each other, pursuing each other, perpetually." Now the waves configure a musical structure, and it's only natural that this music comes from birds. In her diary, Woolf constantly spoke of hearing voices like birds speaking in Greek, a recurrent sound in her dreams: "One bird chirped high up; there was a pause; another chirped lower down" (337). Rising and falling, high sounds counterbalanced by lower sounds, musical alternation in six voices—the first six lines spoken by each of the six characters open with a symmetry of verbs and genders: *see* (Bernard), *see* (Susan), *hear* (Rhoda), *see* (Neville), *see* (Jinny), *hear* (Louis)— we have here Philip Glass's compositional principle for *The Hours*.

The Fourth Character in *The Hours*: Philip Glass's Music

Woolf scholars who have generally seen in Daldry's *The Hours* only an adaptation of Michael Cunningham's novel are missing Hare and Daldry's complex and organic reading of Woolf's writings as a whole. Bert Cardullo bemoaned the loss of the "literary effect" in the cinematic medium, regretting that the film complicates Cunningham's more straightforward temporal structure: "For Cunningham tells the stories of Woolf, Brown, and Vaughan in discrete, alternating chapters, whereas Daldry and Hare do a fair amount of skipping around in time, moving freely among the three strands through the use of match cuts that, sometimes banally, sometimes ponderously, draw parallels between Woolf and her 'descendants'" ("Art and Matter," 672). The best reply to this criticism comes from David Hare himself: "the great mystery of adaptation is that true fidelity can only be achieved through lavish promiscuity" (*The Hours: A Screenplay*, ix).

As Paul Cooke writes, a typical Hollywood movie would emphasize exterior events in a chronological flow leading to a clear ending, but Daldry's *The Hours* does just the opposite. It intertwines four narrative threads—not just three as critics usually think, forgetting the first narrative thread, of Woolf's suicide, that frames the film. These four narratives communicate less through the dialog than through the paraverbal and the nonverbal, through what Daldry called "layered subtextual emotions" ("Three Women"). Emotional arcs, dilemmas rather than clear-cut answers, interior time, disrupted chronology, symphonic music translating Woolf's poetic rhythm, and a subtle reading of Woolf's writings—all this is worlds apart from a typical "Hollywood" production. As Daldry remarked, "In the global market it's obviously hard to be clear cut. But sometimes it confuses us that *The Hours* is perceived as an American film rather than a British one" (qtd. in Sheila Johnston, "A Day in the Life," 27).

We can understand the film's artistry by looking closely at Philip Glass's music and its role in the overall structure of the film. As Daldry says in an interview included in the DVD version of the film, "The process of the score was a long and lengthy one. We were putting on a whole variety of different test scores onto the film and just to see what the film itself would speak to and would yield to. And the film was rejecting everything. Traditional film score seemed to reduce or simplify or sentimentalize what were layered subtextual emotions." David Hare elaborates: "We all knew from the very start that this was a fantastically difficult film to score because it is not in a genre. A composer takes his cue from the idea of what kind of film this is. But this film isn't any particular kind. What we're really talking about is someone who rather than writing score program music is a composer in his own right. I would say there only are two or three in the world, and I think obviously Philip is the preeminent example among them" ("The Music of *The Hours*"). When he saw the film, Glass didn't feel at all that the emphasis on death and insanity painted a melodramatic, sentimental portrait of Virginia Woolf:

> For her, committing suicide wasn't a tragic event, it was an act of volition which would complete her life in a way. It's an idea that comes up in Japanese literature more than in Western literature: that taking a life can be a fulfillment of a life, can be the completion of a life. So it wasn't done as an act of desperate unhappiness or insanity, it was done in a very different way. So that the music doesn't have to echo a conventional idea of death. It's more an existential idea of choice.
>
> "The Music of *The Hours*"

Glass knew that the emotional point of view was key to Woolf's style: "There's no question that the emotional point of view is conveyed by the music. Images are surprisingly neutral. Not that they don't have an emotional content of their own, but they can be easily manipulated, depending on the music. So that the direction the music takes it's the arrow that you shoot in the air; everything follows that." ("The Music of *The Hours*"). Rather than a readily consumable product, Daldry pointed out,

> I suppose with this film we tried to make something that you could watch again, find different connections, find different emotional resonances . . . It always strikes me that the emotional hit, the emotional power of the film comes in very different moments for me . . . we worked very hard on this film to give it a complexity that is truthful to how actually people live their lives, to the very acute and profound choices that people make and the cost of those choices in the search for happiness.
>
> "Three Women"

The success of *The Hours* comes from a shared understanding of Woolf's style by Daldry, Hare, and Glass, each in his own medium. As Hare confesses,

THE DARK HOLLOW AT THE BACK OF THE HEAD 141

I've made Virginia Woolf the substitute author, which was something that was not in Michael's book. I invented that. When you read Michael's book, his prose makes you aware that Michael is the author of the book. But I was very exercised by the problem of, if you are telling three stories, who is the author? And so I sort of made Virginia Woolf the substitute author of the whole thing. And that's how it tied together, but for each one of them, as Stephen says, they're a dab of color that only makes sense in juxtaposition to the other color, and I think that's very hard for actors to accept, because normally they're used to owning the central strategy of the film.

DENBY interview

Philip Glass, too, knew that what appears in Woolf's poetic writings as the anonymous narrator's voice would become his music that functions as a voiceover, tying the different temporal layers together: "it looked to me as I saw it even the very first time that what the music had to do was to somehow convey the structure of the film. The story's very complicated and the music could take on a very important role in the film as I saw. To make it viewable, to make it comprehensible, so the stories didn't seem separate, so that the stories were tied together." He went on to discuss his architectural conception of the music: "You might have thought you could have a different music for each of the periods, but I said no, I wouldn't do it that way. I wrote the same music to go through all three. As these characters reappear, variations of these themes appear so you had the feeling that the music of the beating really is the music that you hear all through the film" ("The Music of *The Hours*").

This is the beating of the heart that Orlando spies on as she walks through her house every morning, the beating that Clarissa and Peter hear throughout the book but whose source they can't locate, and finally, the beating of the heart of the dormant sea in the opening of *The Waves*: "The wave paused, and then drew out again, sighing like a sleeper whose breath comes and goes unconsciously" (337). Glass translated *The Waves*'s beating heart of the dormant sea waking up to a new day into the rhythm of a person waking up, and ultimately, into the tempo and rhythm of his music: "When you first hear it, it seems to start and to stop. And then the next time you hear it, it just keeps going. It's that feeling you get in the morning when you're not quite sure you're awake yet. And the music does that too; it kind of starts and stops, it goes on and it stops, it goes on and it stops, and then it keeps going" ("The Music of *The Hours*"). The repetitive wavelike phrases in Woolf's style and in Glass's score have a precedent in Proust. As his narrator is listening to Vinteuil's septet at a soirée, "again and again one phrase or another from the sonata recurred, but altered each time, its rhythm and harmony different, the same and yet something else, as things recur in life. . . . Then the phrases withdrew, save one, which I saw reappear five times or six without being able to distinguish its features, but so caressing. . . .

142   TIME REGAINED

Then this phrase broke up, was transformed, like the little phrase in the sonata, and became the mysterious call of the start" (*The Captive*, 345–6).

In an article on Glass's score, Deborah Crisp and Roger Hillman have noted that Cunningham's novel wouldn't have suggested that music would play a major role in the film: "Simply in terms of adaptation issues from novel into film, nothing in the sources prepares for the prominence of Glass's score in the film" ("Chiming the Hours," 30). Yet music works so beautifully in the film because both Glass and Daldry understand Woolf's writings in the same manner as her mentor Proust understood Vinteuil's music, and particularly its temporal complexity. Glass chose a combination of instruments that would translate this interpretation into music: "I chose the piano because I wanted an instrument that was very personal, that could cross the periods very easily. The piano can do that, and I combined it with a large string orchestra to give it a kind of density and weight of sound. In the same way that we're looking back through time, we're looking back and forward at the same time" ("The Music of *The Hours*"). Orlando's tunnel in time now reaches the medium of music. As Daldry perceptively notes: "What's fantastic is that Philip's work is incredibly complex. It works as another stream of consciousness within the film, almost as another character that links, complicates and expands any particular scene that we're in. And there is some sort of a gap sometimes between the image and the music, so that there is a counterpoint between the two. And I think he's written one of the great scores" ("The Music of *The Hours*").

The Musical Rhythm of Editing

Closely synchronized with Glass's music and with Woolf's rhythmical style, Daldry develops a complex form of editing. He knew that when it comes to editing, "in the end, it's about rhythm" (Billington interview). His editing makes the individual voices into variations of a single authorial voice, grounded on Woolf's cutting between the "then" and the "now," as in the opening of *Mrs. Dalloway*. Without a knowledge of Woolf's rhythm and style, Daldry's rough cuts can be written off as "strained and simplistic," as by a reviewer who regretted that the film doesn't follow the more straightforward chapter-by-chapter temporal alternation found in Cunningham's novel:

> The book of *The Hours* does this, but the film, almost giddy with the opportunities, over-eggs the pudding. In the novel, a disturbed and unravelling Virginia Woolf lowers her head into a washbasin, then pauses, afraid to look up again to face herself in the mirror. In the film, when Nicole Kidman as Woolf does this, director Daldry cuts to Meryl Streep lifting her head. This is getting carried away. Such editing links between

THE DARK HOLLOW AT THE BACK OF THE HEAD   143

the women happen frequently at the beginning of the film, before we have had time to get to know the characters. The effect is strained and simplistic.

MARK COUSINS, "Throwing the Book at Film"

In *Mrs. Dalloway*, as Virginia feels the morning air and hears the squeak of the hinges, Proust's involuntary memory enters the stage and a window onto the past opens. Woolf employed a series of leitmotifs that create repetitive patterns throughout time. Glass translates these leitmotifs into music, and Daldry brings them into setting and action as well, a lesson he learned from his work as a theatre director:

> it's to do with a series of leitmotifs. Hopefully it's more fun on the second or third viewings because you get to see more of the connections—my favourite is wallpaper—between the different strands. Apart from the emotional language you're working on, you're working with a behavioural language and trying to find behavioural rhythms and language. The book deals with internal monologues, what could be termed 'voiceover,' which David very rightly rejected early on. It's about actions, really. When we come down to it, Michael, it's about actions. Which is basically late Stanislavsky rather than early Stanislavsky.
>
> BILLINGTON interview

Daldry's subtle reading of Woolf's cinematic imagination coincides with recent approaches on Woolf in literary studies. "As several critics of her work have noted, a number of her narrative techniques are analogous to the film techniques of montage, multiple points of view, and simultaneity of events" (Rubenstein, *Virginia Woolf*, 118). As examples, Rubenstein cites Elaine Showalter's highlighting of Woolf's "cinematic techniques" in *Mrs. Dalloway*, including "montage, close-ups, flashbacks, tracking shots, and rapid cuts," and she notes that "Laura Marcus points out that attention to the cinematic aspect of Woolf 's writing has been present virtually from the earliest critical commentary on her work, beginning with Winifred Holtby's 1932 analysis of her 'cinematographic technique'" (238). In Woolf's essay "The Cinema," written the year after she published *Mrs. Dalloway*, she herself anticipates the young medium's future development, and she foregrounds the very techniques that Daldry uses so prominently in *The Hours*, including the compression of time, the clash of emotions through juxtapositions, and the strategic use of repetitions. Interestingly, she sees the cinema as able to solve narrative problems that confronted Tolstoy:

> We should see these emotions mingling together and affecting each other. We should see violent changes of emotion produced by their collision. The most fantastic contrasts could be flashed before us with a speed

which the writer can only toil after in vain; the dream architecture of arches and battlements, of cascades falling and fountains rising, which sometimes visits us in sleep or shapes itself in half-darkened rooms, could be realised before our waking eyes. No fantasy could be too far-fetched or insubstantial. The past could be unrolled, distances annihilated, and the gulfs which dislocate novels (when, for instance, Tolstoy has to pass from Levin to Anna and in doing so jars his story and wrenches and arrests our sympathies) could by the sameness of the background, by the repetition of some scene, be smoothed away.

Daldry has fulfilled Woolf's prophecy to the very last word. He shows how Virginia, Laura, and Clarissa's emotions are mingled together and literally affect each other. When Virginia tells her niece that she was thinking of killing her heroine but changed her mind, Daldry cuts to Laura sitting up on her hotel bed with a horrified gasp, having just dreamed of drowning herself. Fantastic contrasts of the sort that Woolf would soon go on to explore in *Orlando* are flashed before us when Clarissa Vaughan and Richard's mother, Laura, meet at the end of the film. Whereas Clarissa has been stuck in a moment in the past when she lived with Richard, like Mrs. Dalloway in her twenties when she was in love with Peter Walsh, Laura has left her family whom she outlives in the end: her husband dies of cancer, her daughter dies, and her son Richard commits suicide. In sharp contrast to Clarissa, whom she's facing, she confesses that she regrets nothing. "It was death," she says. "I chose life."

Woolf's essay on cinema also anticipates Daldry's editing principle for *The Hours*: the dream architecture of arches, which sometimes visits us in sleep or shapes itself in half-darkened rooms, can now be realized before our waking eyes. Woolf's prophetic conception of cinema inscribes Daldry in a tradition that goes from Georges Méliès to Andrei Tarkovsky and to Raúl Ruiz. For we can see over a two-hour film the vision Virginia Woolf has in the final seconds before she drowns in the River Ouse. And as we watch Clarissa Vaughan leaving her house to buy flowers for her party, we hear Woolf's voiceover utter a prophecy: "A woman's whole life in a single day. And in that day, a lifetime."

Windows in the Fabric of Time

Woolf had struggled to organically unite her disparate characters, who could easily have drifted apart. Daldry and Hare obtained this organicity through theatrical means. As Daldry explained:

> The thing about the theatre is that the most important thing you can do as a director is to make sure that everybody is in the same world—you have to create the world and make sure everyone buys into it. I have seen pieces

of theatre where individual actors are astonishing, but they're astonishing in totally different productions and they just happen to be sharing the same stage. I've seen it in the cinema as well. So that was my main task in this film, which was a challenge given the fact that we were out of sequence, that there were three stories and that there had to be one emotional arc and the themes and narrative and emotional strands had to tie in together.

BILLINGTON interview

Two types of scenes are illustrative of Hare and Daldry's artistry in tying together the strands of the film: the scenes that show Virginia's god-like authorial control over Laura and Clarissa and the scenes that translate onto the screen the disparity between the characters' inner time and outer time, which Erich Auerbach argued in the final chapter of *Mimesis* was Woolf and Proust's major revolution in the concept of reality.

Early in the morning, three women wake up at what seems to be pretty much the same time. A closeup shows Virginia lying in bed on her side, looking into the void, not yet willing to get up. As she closes her eyes, a rough cut takes us to a metro station in New York, seen through a train that enters the station. It is the year 2001 and Clarissa Vaughan's partner Sally is returning home from work. Daldry thus materializes Virginia's train of thought on screen as she closes her eyes and sees herself in the future.[2] Daldry films this scene from the opposite platform, focusing on the darkness of the tracks that separate us from the platform that's lit. With the pillars between the two platforms surrounded by the same darkness, it looks like someone is watching the scene from behind prison bars. Virginia feels trapped. Later in the film she asks her sister Vanessa desperately: "Do you think one day I can escape?" She will years later, when she commits suicide.

Like Septimus in *Mrs. Dalloway*, the poet Richard is constructed as a mirror of Clarissa, and implicitly of Woolf herself. On the morning of the party, while she chooses flowers, Clarissa talks to the florist about Richard's autobiographical novel, *The Goodness of Time*. When the florist asks "It's you, isn't it? In the novel, isn't it meant to be you?" an embarrassed Clarissa replies, "Ah, yes, I see. Yeah, sort of. I mean, in a way. Richard's a writer, that's what he is. He uses things, which actually happened. Many years ago we were students, that's true, but then he changes things." But the florist knows better, and when she interrupts with "Oh, sure," Clarissa's reply discloses the deeper meaning of the act of writing: "I don't mean in a bad way." The florist looks at her silently, but like a mirror of truth, and then Clarissa's reply "It's more like . . . he makes them his own" is punctuated

---

[2]Michael LeBlanc aptly finds a dream logic in this scene's editing: "There is a musicality in the rhythmic intercutting of the characters in this waking-up sequence, a lyricism that intermediates across historical periods through a sort of dream logic" ("Melancholic Arrangements," 115).

146   TIME REGAINED

emotionally with Glass's piano rhythm that suggests a crescendo, a tension
that flows into the next shot while the music keeps playing.

Daldry's quick-paced editing then cuts to a closeup of Virginia's hand,
writing *Mrs. Dalloway*. But the music keeps going, like the waves, and
another wave of sound breaks into Woolf's mind as we hear her inner voice
revealing the poetic core of her book: "A woman's whole life . . ." As she
continues to look somewhere beyond the camera, her voice flows together
with Glass's music into the next shot, which shows Clarissa leaving the
florist's carrying an immense bouquet of flowers, while Virginia's mind
continues ". . . in a single day . . . Just one day." Daldry's camera zooms into
Virginia's absent-minded look as she pursues her thought, ". . . and in that
day . . .," and we cut to Laura Brown sitting pensively at her kitchen table as
Virginia concludes her thought ". . . a whole life." Virginia has just made her
own future existences by writing them into her book: first Clarissa, then
Laura. Later on, she will make Richard's destiny her own as well by writing
it up to his last breath.

In the afternoon, Vanessa and the children visit Virginia, and as they're
sitting down for tea Virginia is absorbed in thought. Her characters are
speaking to her; she hears their voices. Vanessa asks her: "Virginia, what
are you thinking about?" and Daldry gives us the answer through the rough
cut to Laura's reading Virginia Woolf's thoughts in the book. To excuse
her sister's unresponsiveness, Vanessa tells her daughter: "Your aunt's a very
lucky woman, Angelica, for she has two lives. She has the life she's leading,
and also the book she's writing." Indeed, she has two lives, but not
those Vanessa has in mind. These are the future Laura and Clarissa. As
Maria Leavenworth asks, "Is Mrs. Brown a figment of Woolf's imagination,
is this the story that Woolf is writing? ... The editing in these
scenes reinforces how one story affects another in a way that is beyond
the novel's capacity and emphasizes Virginia's agency in the events" ("A
Life," 518).

Like Woolf, who wrote in her diary and in her suicide note about the
voices she heard, Richard too is haunted. When Clarissa goes to visit him on
the morning of the party in honor of his poetry prize, she begins by asking
"Any visitors?" "Yes," he replies. "Are they still here?" "No, they're gone."
"Hm. How did they look?" "Today? Sort of like black fire. I mean sort of
dark and light at the same time . . . they were singing. May have been Greek."
Michael Cunningham borrowed this detail from Woolf's diary, because in
the ancient Greek literature that Woolf learned to read in the original, the
language of birds is synonymous with the language of prophets. It's not
surprising that Rhoda, Woolf's double in *The Waves* and the female
counterpart of the poet Bernard, hears the mysterious song of birds in which
she reads her own future, for she will drown herself as will Woolf a decade
later. Richard concludes that "I seem to have fallen out of time." Once again,
Richard resembles Proust's narrator. On waking,

PLATE 1 *Piero della Francesca's fresco* Madonna del Parto *(1457), Museo della Madonna del Parto of Monterchi, Tuscany.*

PLATE 2 *Van Gogh*, Wheatfield with Crows *(1890) and Drawing by Akira Kurosawa for* Dreams: "Crows" *(1990)*.

PLATE 3 *Van Gogh*, Girl in the Woods *(1882) and still from Akira Kurosawa's* Dreams: "Sunshine through the Rain" *(1990)*.

PLATE 4 *Stills from Andrei Tarkovsky,* Solaris *(1972) and Akira Kurosawa, final shot in* Dreams *(1990).*

PLATE 5 *Van Gogh*, Starry Night over the Rhone *(1888).*

PLATE 6 *The red book hidden in the riverbed. Still from the opening credits to Raúl Ruiz's* Time Regained *(1999).*

PLATE 7 *Little Marcel (Georges du Fresne) meets with his oldest self (André Engel). Still from Raúl Ruiz's* Time Regained *(1999).*

PLATE 8 *The hole into which Chow Mo-wan whispered his secret at the temple at Angkor Wat. Still from Wong Kar-wai,* In the Mood for Love *(2000).*

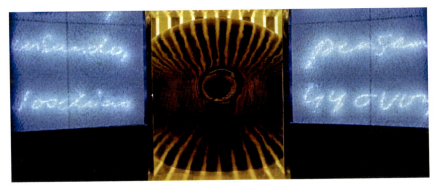

PLATE 9 *The opening shot of Wong Kar-wai's* 2046 *(2004).*

PLATE 10 *The mummies of two lovers holding each other, from whose bodies a plant grows in the room where all wishes come true. Still from Andrei Tarkovsky,* Stalker *(1979).*

PLATE 11 *Jep Gambardella posing as Proust in an iconic photo from 1896. Still from Paolo Sorrentino's* La Grande Bellezza *(2013).*

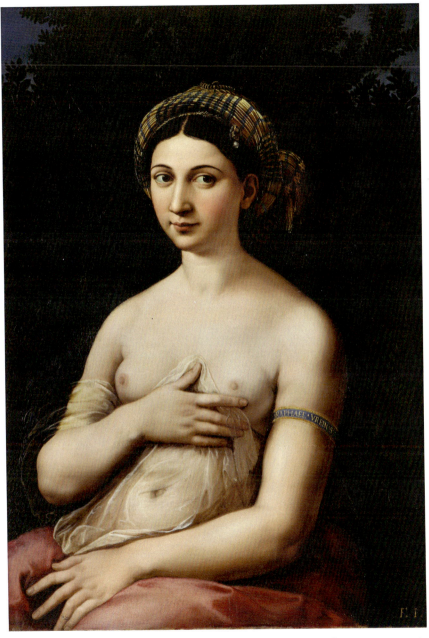

PLATE 12 *Raphael's* La Fornarina *(1520) seen by Jep at night in a museum in Paolo Sorrentino's* La Grande Bellezza *(2013)*.

PLATE 13a and b *Final scene from Paolo Sorrentino's* La Grande Bellezza *(2013) showing Jep's recuperating the lost memory of his dead lover, Elisa De Santis.*

from the black storm through which we seem to have passed (but we do not even say *we*), we emerge prostrate, without a thought, a *we* that is void of content.... when sleep bore him so far away from the world inhabited by memory and thought, through an ether in which he was alone, more than alone, without even the companionship of self-perception, he was outside the range of time and its measurements.

Sodom and Gomorrah, 517–19

The film's characters have a prophetic sense without knowing it. During her conversation with Richard's former lover Louis, Clarissa breaks into tears and confesses what's on her mind: "I don't know, maybe it's just nerves from the party. Bad hostess. It's like a presentiment." Little does she know what she'll witness later that day, when she returns to Richard's apartment just in time to see him throwing himself out the window. On the day Laura decides to commit suicide but changes her mind and returns home to give birth to her second child and then leave her family, she picks up her little son Richard and, in the car, a strange conversation happens between the lines. Richard looks at her intensely as if knowing what she was about to do and also what she will do. He is, after all, the future poet Richard, Virginia Woolf's male self in the year 2001, and he too can hear voices. Laura asks him "What is it, honey? ... What's wrong? What?" He doesn't answer, and Daldry cuts to the grown-up Richard, in whose stream of consciousness we've been without knowing it. Opening such windows in the fabric of time, Daldry follows in the footsteps of Tarkovsky, whose mirror shows the past and future at the same time. Even as he dies, Richard, like Virginia, continues to hear voices. A few moments before the fatal moment, Clarissa asks him "Are they here?" "Who?" says Richard. "The voices," Clarissa says. "Oh, the voices are always here."

As the film approaches the end, Virginia talks to Leonard after dinner about her day, and tells him, "Only one more thing. Mrs. Dalloway's destiny must be resolved." Daldry cuts to Clarissa receiving the late visit of Richard's mother, Laura, whom she had called after Richard threw himself from the window. Following the conversation that explains Laura's choice to leave the past behind her and start afresh, Clarissa seems more resolved to continue with her life with Sally.

The second type of scene that Daldry constructs in a translation of Woolf's style is the one juxtaposing and contrasting inner and outer time. As Glass's music breaks in with the theme that marks interior time, we see Louis leaving Clarissa's house and sighing with relief; from the window on the upper floor of the house, it's not Clarissa watching him leave, but Virginia. Inside, Clarissa is trying to calm down, and as the music pauses we hear her sigh, not with relief but exhaustion. Her sigh flows into Virginia's breathing out with her cigarette smoke, as she sits back in her armchair, pensive. The music softly breaks in again, as if it were Virginia's own soul.

But the music disappears when the clock strikes, waking Virginia from her reverie. "Out it boomed. First a warning, musical; then the hour, irrevocable" (*Mrs. Dalloway*, 4).

A second occurrence of irrevocable time is when Clarissa talks to her daughter about one morning when she was young and time seemed endless: "I remember one morning, getting up at dawn. There was such a sense of possibility. You know that feeling? And I remember thinking to myself: so, this is the beginning of happiness. This is where it starts. And of course, there will always be more. Never occurred to me that it wasn't the beginning. It was happiness. It was the moment. Right then." Daldry punctuates the moment by a pause in which we hear the ticking of a clock. Then the doorbell abruptly rings, bringing Clarissa back to the present moment. In such moments we hear a hand controlling the life of our characters, and the most moving scene of all in *The Hours* is the one in which Leonard and Virginia talk about the decisions she's made that day about the lives of her characters. "In your book, you said someone had to die. Why?" asks Leonard. Virginia explains that "Someone has to die in order that the rest should value life more. It's contrast." "And who will die?" Leonard wants to know. Virginia pauses, looks intently at Leonard, and finally discloses: "The poet will die. The visionary." Daldry cuts to little Richard sleeping in his room, while the ticking of the pendulum clock in Leonard and Virginia's house becomes the ticking of the small clock on Richard's bedtable. That was the hour when Richard's destiny was decided; a terrible hour; irrevocable.

Characters who have presentiments of what the future will bring, who sense *the* moment as Clarissa does in *The Hours*, and who express the terrible bursting of the future into the present moment through music—of birds or musical instruments—had all appeared before in Proust. A chiastic relationship connects *The Hours* back to Proust's *The Captive*—a perfect resonance for a film in which Woolf's three selves (Virginia, Laura, and Clarissa) feel trapped in their lives and want to escape, as Albertine wishes to escape her relationship with Marcel. This relationship is framed by music: from Vinteuil's sonata to Woolf's rhythm of waves that becomes her poetics, all the way to Philip Glass's music that undergirds the architecture of Daldry's film.

One night, close to the moment when Albertine will escape from the emotional prison Marcel has locked her in, and shortly before her death in a riding accident, they sit together and she's about to kiss him goodnight as usual, when Marcel has a presentiment of the same kind Clarissa experiences in *The Hours* and that Virginia has of the future poet Richard, himself a mirrored Proust. Marcel kisses Albertine, who is wearing an elaborately embroidered Fortuny gown:

> I kissed her a second time, pressing to my heart the shimmering golden azure of the Grand Canal and the mating birds, symbols of death and resurrection. But for the second time, instead of returning to my kiss, she

drew away with the sort of instinctive and baleful obstinacy of animals that feel the hand of death. This presentiment which she seemed to be expressing overcame me too, and filled me with such anxious dread that when she had reached the door I could not bear to let her go, and called her back.

The Captive, 538

He wants her to undress: "there are those fateful birds between us. Undress, my darling" (539). But she refuses to do so, and the cooing of pigeons outside Marcel's apartment turns into the crow of death and the song of the owl, the bird of the eternal night, the same voices that sing like birds to Woolf, and that haunt Richard, beckoning him to commit suicide.

The resemblance between their cooing and the crow of the cock was as profound and as obscure as, in Vinteuil's septet, the resemblance between the theme of the adagio and that of the opening and closing passages, it being built on the same key-theme, but so transformed by differences of tonality, tempo, etc. that the lay listener who opens a book on Vinteuil is astonished to find that they are all three based on the same four notes . . . Likewise, this melancholy refrain performed by the pigeons was a sort of cockcrow in the minor key.

The Captive, 539–40

To hear the word "death" like a threat pulsating in the very heart of life opens events beyond the present moment. They are gateways to the past and future. Daldry's Virginia decides that "the poet will die. The visionary," and we see little Richard sleeping peacefully, not knowing that his fate has just been decided. Septimus's suicide also becomes Woolf's and later on, Richard's. Woolf shares with Proust this conception of time as a net whose knots are trapdoors into the future that the poet's mind opens through presentiments:

I know that I then uttered the word "death," as though Albertine were about to die. It seems that events are larger than the moment in which they occur and cannot be entirely contained in it. Certainly they overflow into the future through the memory that we retain of them, but they demand a place also in the time that precedes them. One may say that we do not see them as they are to be, but in memory are they not modified, too?

The Captive, 540

It isn't only Orlando who is "haunted ever since I was a child" (229), but Clarissa as well. Windows become trapdoors through which we glimpse the fabric of time:

For so it had always seemed to her when, with a little squeak of the hinges, which she could hear now, she had burst open the French windows and plunged at Bourton into the open air. How fresh, how calm, stiller than this of course, the air was in the early morning; like the flap of a wave; the kiss of a wave; chill, and sharp and yet (for a girl of eighteen as she then was), solemn, feeling as she did, standing there at the open window, that something awful was about to happen.

Mrs. Dalloway, 3

Suddenly, in the silence of the night, I was startled by a noise which, though apparently insignificant, filled me with terror, the noise of Albertine's window violently opened . . . the noise had been violent, almost rude, as though she had flung the window open, crimson with rage, saying to herself: "This life is stifling me. I don't care, I must have air!" . . . I continued to think as of an omen more mysterious and more funereal than the hoot of an owl, of that sound of the window which Albertine had opened.

The Captive, 541–2

Albertine, Septimus, Richard, Virginia, Laura, Clarissa—they all need air, they're all suffocating in the life they're living. Some choose death and throw themselves out of the window; others throw themselves into the heart of life. But they all find a gateway to something else. Next time the trapdoor opens, Raúl Ruiz will resurrect Proust in the form of a surrealist poet and filmmaker. And as the sound of a giant stone gate opening is heard at the end of Ruiz's *Le Temps retrouvé*, we are greeted by death masks on blocks of stone that move by themselves, and we know this is Proust's tomb we've entered. As Proust knew well, a book "is a huge cemetery in which on the majority of the tombs the names are effaced and can no longer be read" (*Time Regained*, 310). Sometimes filmmakers of genius, like Raúl Ruiz, can make visible the letters effaced by the passage of time.

5

In the Paradise of Trapdoors

Proust, André Breton, and Raúl Ruiz

In 2009, two years before his death, the Chilean surrealist filmmaker Raúl Ruiz had still so many stories to tell, and one of these that he hoped to bring to screen was *Hamlet*, but a *Hamlet* like no one had seen before. He told an interviewer that he was "working on a *Hamlet*, to return to the Viking traditions" (Bovier et al. interview, 86) and he summarized the germ of the story as follows: "A man finds a bone, a femur with holes in it; and he realizes it isn't a bone at all, but a flute. So he starts playing this flute, and from the flute a voice is heard that orders him: 'Go find the rest of my body.' This Viking legend is one of the first versions of *Hamlet*" (80–1). Andrei Tarkovsky, one of Ruiz's own heroes, had also thought of Hamlet at the end of his life. Three decades after Tarkovsky's death, Ruiz would reflect back on his life but also on his future projects through a similar take on *Hamlet* that understands objects as ghosts imprisoned in apparently immobile objects. "Perhaps the immobility of the things that surround us is forced upon them by our conviction that they are themselves and not anything else" (*Swann's Way*, 5). But what else could they be? If a flute is a fragment of what was once a living being, what André Breton would call the object-being or the phantom-object, what part of what being is Ruiz's film *Time Regained*? If we'd play it as the first Hamlet does the bone flute in the Viking legend, what story would it tell us?

For Ruiz, to make Proust's final volume into a film was an organic development of his long career, during which he made over a hundred films. Not only did Ruiz find in Proust a virtual filmmaker, he also discovered in him something that literary studies had not seen: a protosurrealist. Amid the eclectic theories and cultural references that abound in Ruiz's theoretical texts and films, which have made scholars think of him as a baroque

152 TIME REGAINED

filmmaker,[1] two elements are developed through all his films: Proust's camera perspective and the surrealists' future-oriented object, itself an organic development of Proust's apparently inanimate object with a life of its own. It wasn't a matter of chance that André Breton and Philippe Soupault tried to enlist Proust as a collaborator on their magazine *Littérature*. When Breton worked on the proofs for *The Guermantes Way* and found magical treasures in it, this wasn't just a passing fancy. As Ruiz shows us through his film, it was the passing of the baton from one visionary poet to another.

Ruiz read and reread Proust all his life:

> I first read him in Spanish while I was still living in Chile. No doubt it's easier for a stranger to attempt to adapt such a literary monument. And the translations of *À la Recherche*—which I also read afterwards in French, of course, but also in Italian and Portuguese—are just as fascinating enterprises. I wanted to adapt Proust's work ever since I first read it, but as financially speaking this project was out of the question, I had to content myself with including Proust in all my other films.
>
> FRODON interview

One of the reasons why Proust is to be found in all Ruiz's films is that "Proust thinks immensely in cinematographic terms . . . he uses cinematographic techniques" (Bouquet and Burdeau interview, 47).

Ruiz knew that due to the immense time Proust requires from his reader, he is one of the most cited yet least read world writers. But this didn't seem to be a problem for Ruiz, as even a devoted reader like himself can never hold the entire book in mind. Interviewed by *Cahiers du cinéma*, he put it bluntly: "No one has really read Proust. There's a strange effect of amnesia to it. Every time I read *Time Regained*—I must have read it twenty times—it's a different book. It's like a book of sand" (Bouquet and Burdeau interview, 46). Alluding to the constantly changing Book of Sand in Borges' short story of that name, Ruiz underscores the open-ended aspect of Proust's poetic novel, which he embodied in his film. Later in the interview he goes farther: "One must assume that no one has read Proust, that those who have, forgot him and that everyone, even though they may not have read

---

[1]"Le cinéma de Raoul Ruiz s'accommode fort bien du qualificatif de « baroque ». Récits labyrinthiques aux accents borgésiens et à la mise en scène caravagesque, les films de cet exilé chilien empruntent tant au style qu'à la sensibilité de l'art et de la littérature baroques" (Richard Bégin, "L'écran baroque," 25). Even an article entitled "Surrealist Proust" doesn't really speak about Proust as a protosurrealist as one might expect, but discusses Ruiz and Proust's eclecticism: "Ruiz's collating of a multiplicity of styles, from the magic (Méliès) or Gothic darkness (Feuillade) or early cinema, to realist and academic painting, impressionism, expressionism, surrealism and even cubism, combines the retrospective process with the modernist vision" (Beugnet, 140).

him, remembers something else" (Bouquet and Burdeau interview, 53). Unlike adaptation studies that postulate our knowledge of the text that's being adapted for screen, Ruiz's adoption requires no such pre-reading: "we can very well watch the film without having read Proust and perhaps it's even better to do so" (Barde interview, 1).

Though he was a constant reader, Raúl Ruiz distanced himself from scholarship: "I read in buses, elevators, airplanes, but I'm not a library reader" (Nicaise interview, 111). It's perhaps this freshness of nonacademic reading that enables Ruiz to show us through his *Time Regained* that ideas circulate creatively across media, often far from the originals. His film becomes a work that no longer fits within the frame of adaptation studies, and it challenges our very notion of what cinema presents on screen. Ruiz found in Proust's perspective a way of looking at reality, focused on emotions rather than actions, that runs counter to the usual association of cinema with movement. This led him to a notion of film as *tableau vivant*, which he opposed to action-driven Hollywood films: "The contemplative aspect of cinema is very important and is beginning to disappear ... Hollywood's theoretical bias, and by extension that of the majority of those involved in the industry, is based on a false idea of the perception of cinema" (Nicaise interview, 109). Like Stephen Daldry in *The Hours*, Ruiz found art cinema's specificity in its treatment of time that privileges inner duration with its mixing up of different temporal layers and different selves.

Back in Chile, when Ruiz started making movies, he was a supporter of the socialists and communists. His short film *La Maleta* (1963) was criticized for ignoring Chilean reality, but the Dutch documentary filmmaker Joris Ivens defended Ruiz: "Your criticism is out of line, all these young people are surrealists: they viscerally distrust what passes for reality" (Bovier et al. interview, 78). Ruiz's poetics resonates with Bazin's notion of mixed cinema: "I am always trying to make this connection between different ways of producing: film, theater, installations, and videos" (Klonarides interview). Ruiz shares with Bazin an understanding of reality that builds on surrealism's championing of automatism, objective hazard, and chance encounters: "One of the reasons that brought me to cinema was that I didn't know what it was. It's not a narrative, it's not poetry, it's something else: it's a mix of accidents and automatisms" (Leroux interview, 18).

Adoption, not Adaptation

"My film is an adoption, not an adaptation of Proust's novel," Ruiz declared in the interview "Dans le laboratoire de *La Recherche*" (Bouquet and Burdeau, 53). "A Proust aficionado could be offended by this approach," the interviewer interjects. "Oh, don't worry," Ruiz ironically replies, "they already were. In the selection committee for Cannes there were a few 'Proust aficionados.' To suddenly see incarnated the characters of a book you love comes as a shock. But the entire problem of cinema is there. We must accept this literarisation it imposes" (48).

French scholars of adaptation have tended to see Ruiz's film as only confirming our accepted knowledge of Proust—"The filmmaker manages to transcribe the beauty and the originality of the text" (Amandine Cyprès, "Dis(ap)paritions"). Yet if Ruiz did nothing more than translate in the sense of staying faithful to Proust, the result wouldn't be much of a gain either for literary or cinema studies. Here we can recall André Bazin's lesson that mixed cinema is called to betray the original. To adopt, rather than adapt, means to make something your own. It's what Harold Bloom meant by internalizing the predecessor's model and moving beyond it. Anthony Lane, writing for *The New Yorker*, warns that "one should be wary of presuming that Ruiz has simply—or, indeed, intricately—adapted [Proust] for the screen" ("Telling Time," 187). In turn, Jonathan Romney reminds us that fidelity "may be an especially misleading value in dealing with a book in which a key preoccupation of the jealous narrator is the very impossibility of establishing fidelity" ("Masque of the Living Dead" 30). He concludes that "this isn't simply an adaptation, but a dialogue with the novel" (33).

But how does Ruiz's notion of adoption differ from adaptation? Thinking through the problem of the special perception that cinema asks of the audience, Ruiz found in Proust not only a cinematic mode of thinking but a form of understanding the very process of human memory, synonymous with *dreaming*, *imagining* and *inventing*: "Proust discovers that memory is an act of imagination" (Bouquet and Burdeau interview, 53). For it was Proust who first wrote: "What an abyss of uncertainty, whenever the mind feels overtaken by itself: when it, the seeker, is at the same time the dark region through which it must go seeking . . . Seek? More than that: create" (*Swann's Way*, 61). Yet the majority of essays written on Ruiz's *Time Regained* resemble those dedicated to Tarkovsky's *Nostalghia* and *The Mirror*. Both literary and film scholars mostly engage with the specific passages that Ruiz brings to screen in direct citations from Proust, leaving out all those passages that Ruiz alludes to yet doesn't reference directly. Nor do they consider any literary sources other than Proust, even though Ruiz's understanding of Proust as a protosurrealist comes from re-reading Proust through André Breton's *Nadja* and *Mad Love*. If we look only at how faithful or unfaithful Ruiz is to Proust's final volume, we miss out on the larger network of ideas that Ruiz's reading creates. Gilles Taurand, with whom Ruiz co-wrote the script for *Time Regained*, hinted at the film's surrealist temporality: Ruiz, he says, "believed that Proust's use of metaphor is truly cinematographic and he tried to bring it into the spectacle . . . he tried to represent the surreal time" (Grassin interview). What's true of Proust—that one must continually reread him, as Ruiz himself did—is true of Ruiz as well: his films, he has said, "would have to be seen many times, like objects in a house, like a painting" (Klonarides interview).

Ruiz claimed that "Everything has been said on Proust" (Bouquet and Burdeau interview, 47), yet his *Time Regained* proves just the opposite. Just as Kurosawa's Van Gogh became a character who epitomized the world circulation of ideas, so does Ruiz make Proust's *Recherche* into a true world product: "*Time Regained* may be a French production of the greatest of French novels, but somehow the Frenchness doesn't swamp you; the ludic Ruiz is a Chilean, his Proust is an Italian, and his Charlus is an American, John Malkovich" (Lane, "Telling Time," 189). For all those who deplore what's lost from the original, or who claim that cinema and literature are incompatible arts, Anthony Lane has an answer: Proust "was not fond of the cinema, but if he, and not merely his work, were alive today, he might well change his mind" (189).

Opening and Closing: The Stone Book

In planning a film, Ruiz has said, "You must see in your mind's eye the first and final scene, the first and final plane. And this is true of all the temporal arts (cinema, but also music), all arts connected to duration" (Leroux interview, 19). Working with Gilles Taurand, "I wrote sequences of events, most importantly some prologues and epilogues, and then he worked from there alone and presented me with the scenes. With Gilles, it was a little magical" (Barde interview, 2).

Ruiz assembled an exceptional cast that makes the film very much an example of world art cinema. The Italian Marcello Mazzarella plays the adult narrator next to four other versions of Proust: Georges du Fresne is the child, Pierre Mignard is the adolescent at Balbec, André Engel is the aged, dying Proust, and Patrice Chéreau is the Proustian narrator who does voiceovers off screen. In addition, the cast features Catherine Deneuve as Odette, John Malkovich as the Baron de Charlus, Emmanuelle Béart as Gilberte, Chiara Mastroianni as Albertine, Pascal Greggory as Saint-Loup, and Vincent Perez as Morel. Ruiz's *Time Regained* plays on the autobiographical aspect of the film in a way that is reminiscent of Andrei Tarkovsky's cast for *The Mirror*. He mixes up real actors' names with those of their characters, and he also casts family members to create doubles, mirror effects, and symmetries, pointing toward Proust's insistence that everything must return in time. The adolescent Gilberte is played by Camille du Fresne, twin sister of Georges du Fresne who plays the young Proust. Along with Catherine Deneuve we find her own children: Bloch is played by Christian Vadim, her son with the director Roger Vadim, while Albertine is Chiara Mastroianni, her daughter by the aptly named actor Marcello Mastroianni. And towering above the rest is another Marcel(lo), the Italian actor Marcello Mazzarella. Proust couldn't have done better himself.

The secret of Ruiz's innovative reading of Proust lies in the film's chiastic construction, which Ruiz speaks of when he says that he always sees in his mind's eye the ending and the beginning, the prologue and the epilogue. The final volume of Proust's monumental work, *Le Temps retrouvé* tells the story of how the narrator has the revelation of the passage of time at a party thrown by the decayed aristocratic Guermantes family, and half of the volume is taken up by occurrences of involuntary memory that offer our would-be writer the structure of his still future book. The narrator is constantly preoccupied with writing a book, yet like Swann with his essay on Vermeer, he continually procrastinates, wasting his time on social gatherings or solitary musings. So no book is actually written within the frame of the book itself, but once we see on the last page the last word—*le Temps*—we realize that the book the narrator intends to write is the very one we've just read. In this sense, Proust's ending takes us back to the beginning. Ruiz's film does the same, only this time it's a film that is constantly promised yet never actually accomplished, until at the end we realize we've just seen it. It's the film of a dying man's mixed-up memories, based in a dream vision of a future work of art: the very film we're watching. And the ending must take us all the way back to the beginning.

Ruiz opens his film with a shot of the River Vivonne, with the church in Illiers-Combray in the background. The church bells ring three times: twice on a higher and then lower note, and a third time only once, followed by the central theme in Jorge Arriagada's score. As Ruiz remarked, "Jorge Arriagada has completely invented and composed [Vinteuil's] sonata starting from the musical references in Proust: Saint-Saëns, Wagner . . . He worked on the film structures I shared with him before we started filming" (Barde interview, 2). As Arriagada's string crescendo breaks in, Ruiz cuts to a closeup of the Vivonne, and as we watch it flowing incessantly, the credits run on screen. It's not clear if Ruiz's camera moves together with the Vivonne or not. Though this is apparently a straightforward shot, a closer look reveals Ruiz's temporal architecture and the answer to the much discussed question: whose is the camera eye in this film?

Scholars have put forth all sorts of suppositions for reading the opening credits; some saw a metaphor of irreversible time, whereas others swore that the camera moves along the river in a tracking shot to mirror time's passage. But the secret lies in Ruiz's use of an optical illusion, a lens that deforms the image. In reality, the camera doesn't move; what we see is indeed the same part of the river through a distorting lens that Ruiz often uses in the film when he wants us to see what Proust sees. Most notably, this deformation of the image appears in the crowd scenes at lavish parties, when Ruiz superimposes several images deformed in opposite directions, as we hear Patrice Chéreau's voiceover citing Proust that he was "X-raying" the people around him.

Through this optical illusion, which little Marcel enjoys so much, Ruiz tells us that the perspective from which we see the film is the child's, and this

IN THE PARADISE OF TRAPDOORS 157

is why it is only the youngest of Ruiz's five versions of Proust who plays with optical instruments like the magic lantern, the peep box, or deforming lenses—all ancestors of the film camera.[2] Little Marcel crosses temporalities carrying a magic lantern that he uses both as projection device but also as a film camera. Through this twist, Ruiz shares with us his idea that the origin of cinema lies in the magic of young Marcel's eye, in the child's perspective seeing the magic underneath the habitually perceived reality. André Breton first gave preeminence to children's logic as the poetic logic that will help us reveal the surreality around us (*First Manifesto of Surrealism*), and Ruiz's surrealist intuition found a successor in Martin Scorsese's *Hugo*, which as we saw in chapter 1 shows how Georges Méliès—himself one of Ruiz's heroes—could be brought back to life as a surrealist filmmaker through the child Hugo who is in him and who fixes the broken automaton he had turned into.

In addition to the deforming lens, there is another element Ruiz has hidden in his second opening shot that indicates the fixed position of the camera, something that no one has seen so far: something lies in the riverbed as the waters run over it. On a closer look, it proves to be a book with a red cover (Color Plate 6). The book is the one that Marcel picks up in the Guermantes' library toward the end of the novel and the end of Ruiz's film: George Sand's *François le Champi*, the book that his mother read to him at bedtime in the opening of the novel. Marcel says in *Time Regained* that if,

> even in thought, I pick from the bookshelf *François le Champi*, immediately there rises within me a child who takes my place, who alone has the right to spell out the title *François le Champi*, and who reads it as he read it once before, with the same impression of what the weather was like then in the garden, the same dreams that were then shaping themselves in his mind about the different countries and about life, the same anguish about the next day. Or if I see something which dates from another period, it is a young man who comes to life.
>
> 285

At the end of Ruiz's film, the aged narrator played by André Engel picks up this very book from the floor of his bedchamber where he will soon die. As he opens it, he turns to the mirror in which we see his empty bed retaining

---

[2]Mieke Bal's *The Mottled Screen: Reading Proust Visually* (1997) treats optical devices in Proust as metaphors for literary devices, and she argues that "the technological represented by various optical instruments . . . is used mainly to add relief in a strictly figurative sense" (71). More recently, Patrick ffrench has taken the analysis of Proust's magic lantern as metaphor for psychoanalytical projection: "The magic lantern operates . . . as a metaphorical device," representing "the projection of a luminous world, and an interpretative structure determined by sexual desire and aggression" (*Thinking Cinema with Proust*, 78–9).

the shape of the sleeper as a ghostly presence. At that moment children's laughter, clear as a crystal bell, is heard from the book's pages, and we know that little Marcel has come to life again. And then, Ruiz gives a clear nod to Tarkovsky's scene in *The Mirror* that rewrites Proust, when little Ignat reads from his father's book from the doorframe and as if by magic his aged mother appears at the door as his grandmother whom he doesn't recognize: Ruiz switches from the oval mirror back into little Marcel's bedroom, where we find Marcel reading from a similarly red-bound book. In this case Marcel reads from Victor Hugo's poem *À Villequier* in his book *Les Contemplations*, an autobiographical poem Hugo wrote when his pregnant nineteen-year-old daughter Léopoldine drowned together with her husband, who tried to save her, in the Seine at Villequier, where their boat capsized: "Il faut que l'herbe pousse et que les enfants meurent" ("For grass must grow and children die"). Little Marcel stands up to talk to the aged Marcel, whom Ruiz shows only in the mirror of time, carrying his own red book (Color Plate 7).

By having the oldest and the youngest versions of Proust appear on screen at the same time, yet in different frames, Ruiz brings the ending back to the beginning. But not yet. Little by little, time starts running back, the Vivonne runs to its source, and the narrator becomes younger all the time. From André Engel's image in the mirror, we switch to seeing only his shadow shown in profile, on the wall, like a projection of little Marcel's magic lantern (Figure 5.1a), as he says "I have died several times. I loved Albertine more than myself, but then I stopped loving her. It was the same for Gilberte, I stopped loving her a long time ago. Each time I became someone else. And this is how you grow indifferent to death." "Are you saying this to reassure yourself?" asks perceptive little Marcel. "It's not for me that I fear," the shadow replies, "but for my book. I only need a little more time." The boy asks: "Will you read it to me?" The dying narrator nods silently as the front door is heard closing; an excited little Marcel knows that Swann has finally left, and tells his oldest self: "It's mamma." Voicing little Marcel's excitement, Jose Arriagada's sonata breaks in, this time only with the melancholic voice of one violin amid children's laughter. But a miracle happens. The dying narrator (played by André Engel) steps out of the mirror and out of the shadow, and lo and behold, he becomes younger, now in the prime of life (Figure 5.1b). The ageless Proust (Marcello Mazzarella) joins the child, waiting for his mother to come up and kiss him goodnight.

A closeup of little Marcel smiling happily cuts to the next to last scene of Ruiz's film: a ruined cathedral which we enter as we hear the sound of an immense tombstone being opened, with three death masks on it (Figure 5.2). It's a ruined Greek temple, damp and decayed, with broken statues, like Tarkovsky's house in the dream from *The Mirror* when the house falls slowly to pieces, destroyed by water that pervades everything. Ruiz's camera moves behind walls, as if spying on the three versions of Proust we encounter here like another, invisible self: the adult remains seated on a bench in the

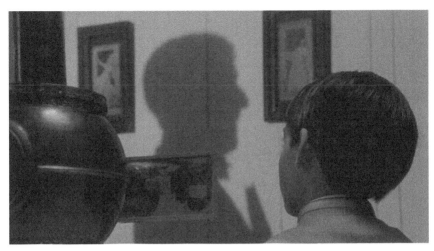

FIGURE 5.1 a, b *The dying Marcel steps out of the mirror and out of the shadow as his younger self to join little Marcel. Stills from Ruiz's* Time Regained.

ruined space of memory that is Venice, signaled by striped red and white poles, while the oldest Proust slowly walks in the footsteps of the child as if not to disturb him. The boy is the only one who seems never to have been in this place, and he explores it curiously.

We then exit the temple onto the beach at Balbec. The ageless Marcel leaves behind his oldest and the youngest selves, and goes to a waiter to ask him to find out a detail on the lacework of a woman's blouse. And finally, Ruiz's camera follows the three Marcels as they walk toward the beach and the sea, looking at them only from behind, in a nod to the surrealist René Magritte's paintings showing men in melon hats from behind. The adult

FIGURE 5.2 *Funerary masks on Marcel's tombstone that opens onto the ruins of memory. Still from Ruiz's* Time Regained.

Proust (Marcello Mazzarella) remains at the top of the stairs, while the dying narrator, like a caring father, follows the child who's already happily running on the beach. These are the dreamers, and the landscape in front of them is their dream that we're spying on together with the ageless Marcello Mazzarella, from whose perspective the entire film is filmed to point at Proust's own position: *hors du temps,* outside time.

As Ruiz's camera follows the gaze of this ageless Proust, we follow the child on the seashore and finally we see only the agitated, foamy sea that Ruiz films in an echo of Tarkovsky's final shot of *Solaris* that showed the ocean that dreams the entire universe, the mirror that could bring the past once again into the future. We are back at the beginning in a mirrored construction not only of scenes symmetrically depicting water—the Vivonne and the sea at Balbec—but also of another pair of symmetrically constructed scenes that turn the water scenes into much more than a mere metaphor for time. Looking back at the beginning where the ending takes us, we realize that the book hidden in the riverbed during the credits is not only little Marcel's volume by Victor Hugo. It's also the dying Proust's own book.

Just after the opening shot of the Vivonne, the red book in the riverbed is transformed into manuscript pages, which Proust's maid Céleste is writing as Proust dictates to her from bed. Tired and needing to rest, he interrupts the dictation and asks her to bring him a set of old photographs and a magnifying glass. Together with him, through the distorting lens of the magnifying glass we see the characters in the film, as first Marcel's voice and then someone else's calls their names in a faint voiceover, like a butler calling out the names of the guests at a dinner party. We are entering the dying Proust's theatre of

IN THE PARADISE OF TRAPDOORS 161

the mind, where he sees his entire oeuvre, latent, unwritten, only dreamed. As in an old peepshow, the characters enter on the stage of his mind's eye. As Marcel had noted of the climactic party at the Guermantes', "it offered me all the successive images—which I had never seen—which separated the past from the present, better still it showed me the relationship that existed between the present and the past; it was like an old-fashion peepshow, but a peepshow of the years, the visions not of a moment, but of a person situated in the distorting perspective of Time" (*Time Regained*, 344). The person situated in the distorting perspective of time is both little Marcel and dying Marcel.

When Ruiz first read Proust back in Chile, he began with *Time Regained* and worked his way backwards. As Jonathan Romney observes, "Bringing us into Proust by the exit, Ruiz invites us to read backwards, to follow the river back to its source" ("Masque," 31). Ruiz's architecture of the film, constructed around a few visionary seconds in which the dying narrator creates his entire book, anticipates Daldry's take on Woolf three years later. As Anthony Lane wrote in his review of *Time Regained*, it develops

> a careful inquiry into what it might be like—what it might wring out of a man, especially a weakening one—to write such a book. . . . Watching the movie again, I wondered whether all of it unfolds within the cranium of the expiring Proust, whether his bedroom is as much a greenhouse of memory as Charles Foster Kane's, and whether Gilberte, like the other young girls in flower, is just one of his innumerable Rosebuds.
>
> "Telling Time," 187–9

Though he doesn't pursue this insight further, Lane rightly senses where the heart of the matter lies in Ruiz's reading of Proust.

Ruiz himself has said of the inception of his film: "I adopted a principle that helped me a lot from the very beginning: I imagined a family photo floating in a river. These are the kind of images that stimulate me to film" (Bouquet and Burdeau interview, 50). If the structure of the film as a zooming into family photographs may suggest only a past-oriented object, the very beginning of the film turns to the future, as the same distorting lens prophetically sees a still indistinct future book. In the end it becomes visible to the dying poet, who could not only resurrect a lost past from photographs, but could also see the not yet born future in the waters of memory.

In his *Poetics of Cinema*, Ruiz asserts that "Films are like human beings: you look at them and they look back at you" (II, 106). To illustrate this theme he describes a story he knew as a child, about the sea as a living being:

> On more than one occasion in the islands of southern Chile I have heard sailors, who frequent the turbulent waters of the misleadingly named Pacific Ocean, say that from the depths of sea—especially on certain days of immaculate skies and peaceful waters—there emerge faces with

malevolent stares; which, as if in a vertiginous dissolve, look at the sailors while pulling menacing faces and diabolical grimaces, saying to them: "Be careful, be very careful." Do these faces look at whoever looks at them? Or at someone who projects their intimate and metaphorical image of the sea (an image that is formed since childhood)?

Poetics of Cinema II, 107

Throughout the film, Ruiz reminds us in key scenes that this is an underwater universe seen by a dying man, reflected in the dark pool at the back of the head we can glimpse only in dreams, as Virginia Woolf writes in *Orlando*. But what he sees in those waters is what Aleksei sees in the oval mirror in Tarkovsky's *The Mirror*: his past and future selves together.

This phenomenon of seeing oneself from the outside, as a projection, is encountered many times in Proust's giant novel, but it is only the narrator and his double, Charles Swann, who actually encounter themselves. First, Swann sees himself in a dream, as a wretched man crying on a platform station, beckoning him to follow him. Secondly, it's when Swann hears Vinteuil's sonata and remembers his wounded love for Odette: "And Swann could distinguish, standing motionless before that scene of remembered happiness, a wretched figure who filled him with such pity, because he did not at first recognize who it was, that he had to lower his eyes lest anyone should observe that they were filled with tears. It was himself" (*Swann's Way*, 493). Proust's mirrors, like Ruiz's, await us at the beginning and at the end, and in *Time Regained* it's the narrator's turn to recognize himself in a book,

this extraordinary *François le Champi*. This was a very deeply buried impression that I had just encountered, one in which memories of childhood and family were tenderly intermingled and which I had not immediately recognized. My first reaction had been to ask myself, angrily, who this stranger was who was coming to trouble me. The stranger was none other than myself, the child I had been at that time, brought to life within me by the book.

Time Regained, 283

From this passage Ruiz gets his intuition to turn the dying Proust into a book, one that is a past book—*François le Champi*—but also a future book: his own. The book in the waters of the Vivonne is looking at us, and we are looking at it, projecting our own childhood memories. This is why Ruiz insisted that one needn't have read Proust to understand the film, just as Tarkovsky insisted that his film *The Mirror* wasn't incomprehensible at all: both of them are presenting us with the very mechanisms of our own memories and dreams.

IN THE PARADISE OF TRAPDOORS

On his deathbed, Ruiz's Proust has a dream vision of Gilberte cutting roses in a garden. Waking up, Proust calls Céleste into his room and asks anxiously if there are roses in the house; there aren't, but an oversized rose appears in closeup on a screen on which Ruiz shows raindrops that glide down what looks like a window, and the entire scene, including Proust's room, looks like an underwater scene. In a parallel scene, the dying Proust picks up a photo of young Gilberte, on which she'd written him a few affectionate lines. As he turns over the photo to read the text, the screen is blurred again by heavy raindrops that seem to efface the handwriting, just as time effaces the names on the tombstones in the cemetery that becomes the stone-book hidden in the riverbed of the Vivonne. In the film's next to last scene, from photographs examined under a magnifying glass, as from a small cup of tea, there rises what Proust called the vast structure of recollection:

> But when from a long-distant past nothing subsists, after the people are dead, after the things are broken and scattered, taste and smell alone, more fragile but more enduring, more immaterial, more persistent, more faithful, remain poised a long time, like souls, remembering, waiting, hoping, amid the ruins of all the rest; and bear unflinchingly, in the tiny and almost impalpable drop of their essence, the vast structure of recollection.
>
> *Swann's Way*, 63–4

But isn't photography significantly different from the medium of cinema that Proust dismissed? "Some critics now liked to regard the novel as a sort of procession of things upon the screen of a cinematograph. This comparison was absurd," he writes. "Nothing is further from what we have really perceived than the vision that the cinematograph presents" (*Time Regained*, 279). Critics often argue that Proust's interest in photography is paired with his dismissal of cinema,[3] but what many forget is Proust's own paradoxical

---

[3]The majority of studies dedicated to Proust and photography stem from Roland Barthes' *Camera lucida: Reflections on Photography* and tend to privilege the actual appearance of photographs in Proust's work and/or the way they function as metaphors for Proust's "visual writing" along with other optical devices (lenses, magnifying glass, magic lantern). This is the case of Mieke Bal's *The Mottled Screen: Reading Proust Visually* (1997): "Rather than adventuring into cinematographic writing, Proust explores photography's productivity to the point of absurdity" (222). Surrealist photographer Brassaï's posthumous work *Proust in the Power of Photography* (1997) argues that photography structures Proust's narrative, which is anything but cinematic. Julia Kristeva's *Time and Sense: Proust and the Experience of Literature* (1996) analyzes Proust's devices as "kinetoscopic." More recently, Áine Larkin's *Proust Writing Photography* (2011) speaks about "the photographic poetology detectable in the novel's narratological and temporal structure" (5). Mary Bergstein's *In Looking Back, One Learns to See: Marcel Proust and Photography* (2014) explores the cultural history of photography.

and contradictory understanding of photography as well. As Michael Wood argues, "Proust . . . is both for and against photography, and by extension for and against the cinema," for "neither makes sense without the other" ("Other Eyes," 101, 109). On the one hand, Proust dismisses the technological medium of photography as a poor instrument for capturing lost time. As Sara Danius has remarked: "In Proust, photography comes to represent everything that genuine memory is not" (*The Senses of Modernism*, 118). In *Thinking Cinema with Proust*, on the other hand, Patrick ffrench considers the metaphoric use of the magic latern and aims to "rethink cinema with Proust" by showing how film theory, philosophy, and Proust's novel "may mutually illuminate each other" (68). In his view, "the screen is not a window onto the world, but a structured and duplicitous surface. . . . Both the *Recherche* and the cinema inaugurate a screened world, a projected world, and thus suspend and relativize the conditions of objective knowledge" (70).

For Proust, photography too results from a process of re-creation: "Pleasure in this respect is like photography. What we take, in the presence of the beloved object, is merely a negative, which we develop later, when we are back at home, and have once again found at our disposal that inner darkroom the entrance to which is barred to us so long as we are with other people" (*Within a Budding Grove*, 616–17). Simply taking a photograph is not the way to recapture lost time, which is subject to our chance encounter with the object that forms its prison, and usually this object is irrationally connected to the lost past:

> already at Combray I used to fix before my mind for its attention some image . . . a cloud, a triangle, a church spire, a flower, a stone, because I had the feeling that perhaps beneath these signs there lay something of a quite different kind which I was to discover . . . For the truths which the intellect apprehends directly in the world of full and unimpeded light have something less profound, less necessary than those which life communicates to us against our will in an impression which is material because it enters us through the senses but yet has a spiritual meaning.
>
> *Time Regained*, 273

The past returns through involuntary memory, and that's not something we can rationally control. When we look at a photograph, we seek to recover something of which the photograph is only a poor representation. The only way to capture the essence of a loved one is through movement, something that cinema, unlike photography, can do:

> Perhaps, also, that activity of all the senses at once which yet endeavours to discover with the eyes alone what lies beyond them is over-indulgent to the myriad forms, to the different savours, to the movements of the living person whom as a rule, when we are not in love, we immobilize.

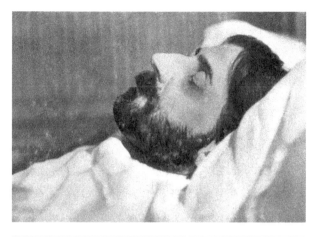

FIGURE 5.3 *Man Ray,* Marcel Proust on his deathbed *(1922) and still from Ruiz's* Time Regained *showing the dying Marcel dictating his novel to Céleste.*

> Whereas the beloved model does not stay still; and our mental photographs of it are always blurred [*des photographies manquées*].
>
> Within a Budding Grove, 84

If photographic fixity is the domain of the dead, movement is that of the living. In Ruiz's film, photography is only the first part in the story that brings the past back to life; the second is film, which can animate a life that is about to be stilled in death. This transformation is suggested through Ruiz's choice to model the dying Proust on the photograph taken by Man Ray, on November 19, 1922, a day after Proust died (Figure 5.3). Six days later, on the front page of *Les Nouvelles littéraires*, Jean Cocteau wrote of Man Ray's photograph: "Those who have seen this profile of calm, of order, of plenitude, will never forget the spectacle of an unbelievable recording device come to a stop, becoming an art object: a masterpiece of repose next to a heap of notebooks where our friend's genius continues to live on like the wristwatch of a dead soldier." Cocteau's stunning vision of Proust continuing to live like a dead soldier's wristwatch is echoed in Ruiz's film through the bells of Combray that we hear throughout, including at the funeral of Marcel's great friend Robert de Saint-Loup, like Big Ben in *Mrs. Dalloway* or the ticking of the clock in Daldry's *The Hours*. The bells turn the film into a giant tomb, as Proust described a book as a cemetery from which the names have been effaced. In this sense, Ruiz's film is also a requiem for Proust, underscoring that everything we see in the film is what passes on the theatre of memory in the last seconds of a dying visionary's life.

The Miracle and Demon of Analogy

When Ruiz chose to represent Proust's book—and ultimately his body—as a surrealist object in the shape of a stone-book prophesying its future, he was revisiting Proust's "miracle of analogy" that takes us outside time. Proust knew that his future self lay nested within his past self, and that both lived "in the one and only medium in which it could exist and enjoy the essence of things, that is to say: outside time [*en dehors de temps*] . . . on those rare occasions when the miracle of an analogy had made me escape from the present" (*Time Regained*, 262–3).

In surrealism's cult book *Nadja*, André Breton rewrites Proust's *miracle d'une analogie* as the "demon of analogy" that lays bare the hidden pattern of reality that can help us escape time's irreversibility: "By what latitude could we, abandoned thus to the fury of symbols, be occasionally a prey to the demon of analogy, seeing ourselves the object of extreme overtures, of singular, special attentions?" (*Nadja*, 111). Breton theorized the analogy as the manifestation par excellence of poetic genius: "Only on the level of analogy have I ever experienced intellectual pleasure. For me the only manifest truth in the world is governed by the spontaneous, clairvoyant, insolent connection established under certain conditions between two things whose conjunction would not be permitted by common sense" ("Ascendant Sign," 134). Ruiz's turning a stone into a book wasn't something that common sense would permit. But it was clairvoyant beyond a shadow of doubt. This Proustian/Bretonian analogy becomes the poetical principle behind Ruiz's treatment of objects as trapdoors toward lost paradises that can be relived in the future.

When an aging but still beautiful Odette opens the double doors to a salon early in Ruiz's film, a blinding light like a flashbulb of Proust's photographic involuntary memory bursts through the doors, and all of a sudden we find ourselves in little Marcel's childhood room, where he plays at night with his magic lantern. Later, Gilberte angrily rings a bell to summon a servant when Marcel has broken a teacup, because she indirectly confessed to him her interest in women; this bell becomes the bell at Combray that causes Marcel to fall all the way back into childhood. Later in the film, Marcel finds at Gilberte's the broken cup glued back together, hidden in a mahogany box. The second he lifts the lid, children's laughter is heard, and we know that the child in him who was in love with Gilberte is there, alive as ever.

Thinking of his films as *tableaux vivants*—in Proust's understanding of objects around us as only apparently inanimate—Ruiz constructs his film as a landscape that opens and closes with the flowing waters of the Vivonne and of the sea. "Phenomena of nature," Ruiz writes, are not only "living beings, but also thinking beings" (*Poetics of Cinema* II, 106). If living objects and miraculous analogies enable Proust to recover lost time, Ruiz follows Breton in taking a step outside time altogether. Of the five actors playing Proust in his film, it is the apparently ageless adult played by Marcello Mazzarella who mostly travels throughout all the temporal layers that are mixed up in the mind of the dying Proust, as if to bring the different selves together. Ruiz turns his perspective into his camera eye. Most notably in the *bal de têtes* scene where everyone is aged, crippled, turned into caricatures of what they once were, the narrator is Marcello Mazzarella. A visibly aged, dim-sighted Oriane de Guermantes played by Edith Scob remarks with a touch of envy, "But you, my friend, you haven't changed a bit. Not a single white hair. You look ageless."

The Film, a Surrealist Object-being Made of Multiple Selves

As in the case of Scorsese's *Hugo*, scholars have mostly seen in *Time Regained* a nostalgic reflection on the history of cinema, the "lost time" of art cinema, the era of Deneuve, Mastroianni and Pisier, "a film that is a ceremony of re-animating and celebrating the mummies of Paris, of literature, and of cinema itself" (Romney, "Masque," 33). "The faces of Deneuve [Odette] and Pisier [Madame Verdurin], then, become the icons—much like Proust's infamous madeleine—which evoke our own cinematic memories" (Melissa Anderson, "Time Regained," 43); this is a "retrospective of cinema" at the end of the twentieth century (Martine Beugnet, "Surrealist Proust," 139). Jean-Loup Bourget writes of Proust's objects in Ruiz's film as "gateways that open magically onto the past" ("*Le Temps retrouvé*," 134). Ruiz himself certainly saw his film as a reflection on cinema's history, but continuing to the present, not caught in a lost golden age: "The fact that Proust reflects back on the 19th century literature encourages one to reflect back on cinema from Méliès to our present day" (Bouquet and Burdeau interview, 52).

Ruiz turns the journey from the past into the present toward the future. In *Time Regained*, he doesn't bring Proust's multiple selves to life in order to point toward the fragmentary nature of the modernist self, but rather to

FIGURE 5.4 *Marcel sees Robert de Saint-Loup for the first time at Balbec in Ruiz's Time Regained.*

suggest the organic development of the metamorphoses through which a soul or an idea passes in time. When the dying Proust's thoughts drift to Saint-Loup's funeral, he glides down even deeper through another trapdoor, as he remembers the first time he met Saint-Loup in Balbec. Suddenly Marcello Mazzarella's place is taken on screen by his adolescent self (Pierre Mignard) in a restaurant in Balbec, looking out through a window at Saint-Loup, while we can still hear in voiceover the funeral service and the bells from the opening of the film (Figure 5.4). A dark omen lurks in the background behind Saint-Loup: an anonymous funeral. The scene shows Marcel looking at Saint-Loup as if he has a presentiment of his future death, which Ruiz shows through an optical illusion generated by Marcel's position in the frame that makes two different objects seem one: the coffin behind and Saint-Loup's mounting into a carriage. It looks like a hearse.

A carriage or an omnibus that turns into a hearse. Here Ruiz is paying tribute to Georges Méliès, whose major discovery was the disappearing and the transformation act or what he called "vues fantastiques" ("Les Vues Cinématographiques," 369). One day as he was filming the Place de l'Opéra, the camera stopped working for a minute: "During that minute, the passers-by, the omnibus, the cars had changed their place ... I instantly saw a Madeleine-Bastille omnibus changed into a hearse and men changed into women" (385). As Méliès concluded, it was this trick that made "the surreal [*le surnaturel*], the imaginary, even the impossible itself visible" (387). Ruiz's optical illusion that shows the carriage-hearse drawn by an ominous headless horse is also a creative response to Méliès's *The Merry Frolics of Satan* (1906), where we travel through the cosmos on a carriage drawn by a horse's skeleton. Ruiz's Robert de Saint-Loup embarks unwittingly on the one-way trip our life is.

But the dying Proust's free association doesn't rest there, and we glide even further down to the moment when Marcel and his new friend talk about Saint-Loup's descent from the house of Guermantes. As a child at Combray, little Marcel had turned "the Guermantes" into an object of desire, an invisible city on the map of his dreamland. As they walk on the Balbec beach, Robert tells Marcel that the old war cry of the Guermantes was "Combraysis," and a fresher layer of time wells up. Three men in black who look like funeral attendants raise their top hats to greet him as he passes by. One can't but feel the shudder of death in this ominous salute, and the bells from Robert's own funeral service come through again from what was then the future, yet is now past time for the dying Proust.

But instead of returning to Robert's funeral service, Proust's dreaming memory next returns to an even earlier moment. Walking on the beach with his grandmother, the adolescent Proust has the impression that he sees Robert, wearing his military uniform, though his death in the war is still years ahead. Riding a horse on the beach and crying "Combraysiiiiiiiiis!," Saint-Loup passes by a funeral: four pallbearers carry the coffin while behind them walk four others, who raise their hats again when Saint-Loup passes by them. He has just unwittingly witnessed his own funeral. But Proust's pragmatic grandmother interjects promptly: "But I see absolutely nothing there! Let's go." These funeral attendants, dressed in black, are shadows and doubles of Saint-Loup, himself a double of Marcel. As Ruiz has commented:

> Is there some sort of general ban that forbids our seeing in this second shot, a double of the character we saw in the close shot? Thus every time we see the character in the film sequence (moments B, C, and D), we are really seeing the multiple doubles of the first character. And perhaps they are all but the imagined doubles of each spectator? These doubles, which Scandinavians refer to as *hamr*, are the splitting up of an original image (I am still imagining).

> *Poetics of Cinema* II, 39

Showing Marcel, Saint-Loup, and the pallbearers by the sea as an ominous prophecy, Ruiz is reimagining Proust through André Breton's description in the opening of *Mad Love* of the "seven or so" women in his past:

> I find them wandering speechless by the sea, in single file, winding lightly around the waves. . . . We must try to glide, not too quickly, between the two impossible tribunals facing each other: the first, of the lovers I shall have been, for example; the other, of these women I see, all in pale clothes. So the same river swirls, snatches, sheds its veils, and runs by, under the spell of the sweetness of the stones, the shadows and the grasses. . . . To

glide like water into pure sparkle—for that we would have to have lost the notion of time. But what defense is there against it; who will teach us to decant the joy of memory?

5–6

Proust and Ruiz can both teach us. "Time is not linear," explains Ruiz. "Proust could have written in no matter what period, that would have been different, but his gaze would have been the same: that of another dimension he perceives" (Barde interview, 1). Breton was right: to glide like water into pure sparkle—for that we would have to have lost the notion of time. Proust's ark that becomes Ruiz's camera glides on the waters of memory and can make time go back or move forward at will.

The Theatre of Memory

Ruiz's viewers have been fascinated by *Time Regained*'s treatment of objects: a statuette or a piece of furniture, even an entire set can move by itself. Objects appear and disappear or they move around, yet no one seems to notice. Most importantly, the set often moves, changing before our eyes as if on a theatre stage. In the beginning, in dying Proust's room, the furniture is on rails and it moves around, left to right or right to left, sometimes enlarged, other times downsized. When the camera's eye moves from the writer's bed toward the window and we hear him remembering Combray, the trees outside are pulled out of the window frame like a theatre curtain or a set changing during a play. Closer to the end of the film, during a concert, the rows of seats move by themselves, with spectators on them, left to right and right to left, like props on the large theatre stage of life.

Encouraged by Ruiz's own explanations, scholars have read in this changeability Proust's denouncing of life's falsity and theatricality, backed by Proust's *Time Regained* that often describes society as a puppet show, a peepshow, a theatre were nothing is authentic and real. In 1986, Ruiz had turned Calderón de la Barca's *La vida es sueño* into a film, *Memoria de apariencias: la vida es sueño*, and as he said in 1999, "The genre 'theatre of the world' goes all the way back to the 16th century. Calderón's comedies are in that genre. The world is a theatre, and in the world there are all the artificial elements of theatre. . . . In Proust's room, all the furniture is set on tracks and it moves in the opposite direction from the camera. The statues move too" (Bouquet and Burdeau interview, 48–9). This is true as far as it goes, but scholars have failed to see the complex poetics of the object that Ruiz brings on screen. Anthony Lane writes off the moving set and objects as mere devices intended to point to the theatricality and emptiness of the puppet characters in a costume drama:

why else would his arrangements of furniture and foliage glide and shove so weirdly within the frame, if not to puncture the settled plush of the genre, and to hint that the beau monde, like its favorite possessions, is little more than an elegant prop to be dragged in and out of the wings? Far from being inveigled into the hauteur of that world, we are encouraged to view its noble protagonists as poor players who strut and fret their hours—their whole lifetimes—upon the stage.

"Telling Time," 189

Similarly, Martine Beugnet sees the film as "a comment on cinema itself, as the art and language of illusion and lie" ("Surrealist Proust," 149). Though all this is true, it's again only half the story, as things always are both with Ruiz and with Proust, who delights in arguing one side of the matter for pages and pages—in this case, the falsity of society and of art—only to argue just the opposite later. Amid all his criticisms of society and art, they offer Proust his own universe, enabling for true artists "the discovery of our true life, of reality as we have felt it to be ... In this conclusion I was confirmed by the thought of the falseness of the so-called realist art, which would not be so untruthful if we had not in life acquired the habit of giving to what we feel a form of expression which differs so much from, and which we nevertheless after a little time take to be, reality itself" (*Time Regained*, 277).

On a closer look, we realize that Ruiz's shifting objects and sets create a version of the toy theatre little Marcel plays with. Whenever things appear oversized it's because the dying Marcel is inspecting them with a magnifying glass. Less than the baroque theatre of life, closer to Proust's surrealist world is the theatre of the mind, which is the perfect metaphor to sustain a film that's seen by a dying man in his mind's eye in the final minutes before his death. That everything we see takes places on the theatre of the mind is supported by the film's editing, which connects scenes using free association to jump between very different temporal levels, as voluntary memory (looking at photos) is slowly replaced by involuntary memory. The film itself has an involuntary memory. One scene shows in closeup only Proust's shoes as he walks on the sidewalk, just after he's returned to Paris from his sanitarium. The film switches to a similarly filmed scene of an earlier Proust, walking in the same shoes to the Guermantes' party, when he trips on an uneven paving stone and plunges down into a memory of Venice. In this case, it's no longer the dying Proust's free association of memories that's responsible for the juxtaposition of scenes and different times; it's the film's memory, because for Ruiz, film is "a mirror granted memory" (*Poetics of Cinema* II, 107), a *res cogitans* (106).

Less obvious than the unexpected horizontal movements of objects are the vertical movements through time that Ruiz creates. These affect only

Marcel, as he is the one who can travel up and down through the watery universe of his memory. The vertical movements are optical illusions that Ruiz achieves through camera movements that we will also encounter in Ruiz's most creative follower, Paolo Sorrentino. Ruiz makes the camera create the illusion of moving up and down between temporal layers, and the most brilliant example comes quite early in the film.

Little Marcel is in a salon with top hats and white gloves on the floor where he encounters Robert de Saint-Loup, who is looking through a stereoscope. He offers it to Marcel, who sees something that a kinetoscope rather than a stereoscope would show: a short film of a dying horse. Marcel rubs his eyes as if waking from a dream, and we now see him alone, with no trace of Saint-Loup or the optical instrument. The boy looks out the window, and the camera shows him from the outside, but time has passed because Marcel is now dressed differently. As in Tarkovsky's *Mirror*, the window frame is also a mirror and a corridor in time. Ruiz's camera switches again to show Marcel's head from the back, looking down at the garden outside, and the camera glides down onto a childhood scene where a younger little boy—most likely Marcel himself from an even earlier time—is running around on a hobby horse. Switching again to show us Marcel from the front, the camera shows him coming down from the window as if he is taking an elevator, while the building behind him seems to be pulled up like the backdrop in a theater when a scene is being changed.

For Proust and Ruiz as for the surrealists, theatricality isn't opposed to reality. Ruiz's world offers us the reality hidden underneath the everyday reality that maintains that objects are themselves and nothing else. It's what happens when trapdoors open as if by accident or when an objective hazard makes us see that there is so much the untrained eye misses in *this* reality. As André Breton memorably wrote in *Nadja*:

> Perhaps life needs to be deciphered like a cryptogram. Secret staircases, frames from which the paintings quickly slip aside and vanish (giving way to an archangel bearing a sword) or to those who must forever advance), buttons which must be indirectly pressed to make an entire room move sideways or vertically, or immediately change all its furnishings; we may imagine the mind's greatest adventure as a journey of this sort to the paradise of trapdoors.

112

Breton's paradise of trapdoors becomes Ruiz's commonplaces that hide treasures if we know how to make them come to life:

> A commonplace is some sort of vacant lot that no one frequents and that all have forgotten, until one day someone finds a corpse or oil. Now, cinema

IN THE PARADISE OF TRAPDOORS 173

is also the art of organising commonplaces around one or many stories. I suspect that if in each vacant lot (that is, in each one of the film's shots) we place a corpse over here, and a treasure over there, and an amusement park elsewhere, by the end of it, we will have a greater urge to stay in the vacant lots. Even they are all linked by some motorway. I mean to say, a story.

Poetics of Cinema II, 106

As Proust well knows, "it depends on chance whether or not we come upon this object before we ourselves must die" (*Swann's Way*, 60). Four times in Ruiz's film, a surrealist chance encounter reveals the future nested in objects: in the apparition of an oversized rose in Proust's bedchamber, in the superimposition of the lovers' names and identities when little Marcel mistakes Albertine's signature for Gilberte's, in the repeated scene with the ghostly top hats, and finally, when Proust the adult receives Gilberte's letter during the war. Each time, another trapdoor opens onto a paradise that André Breton called, in the footsteps of Proust, *l'or du temps*.

What's in a Name? That which We Call a Rose

The scene into which little Marcel descends from the window after looking into Saint-Loup's stereoscope is one of the most important scenes in the love story between Marcel and Gilberte when they are both young, at Combray. We're in a garden on a bright summer day and young Marcel, played by Georges du Fresne, encounters twelve-year-old Gilberte, played by Georges's twin sister, Camille, who is wearing a hat with hawthorn flowers on it. Courteously, Marcel takes his hat off to greet her, but she looks at him seductively, making a sexual gesture that confuses and embarrasses him (Figure 5.5). Already a Lolita, Gilberte makes a circle with her right thumb and index finger, an inviting opening—another trapdoor, Breton would say—while slowly moving her left index finger up and down. Marcel lifts his hat a second time, but suddenly it's to an older Gilberte, who is in a similar garden, cutting roses. Now his adult self, he confesses that he thought many times of her gesture that day, but she dismisses the sexual interpretation: "I was only twelve, so it was a very innocent gesture [*un geste plein d'innocence*]." "Oh, yes, you mean a very indecent one [*plein d'indécence*]."

In the background, a group of people is about to have their photograph taken. Saint-Loup is among them and calls Marcel and Gilberte to join in. Little Marcel is there again, a step behind the photographer, witnessing the moment when his memory takes this photograph of a future self. But instead of posing with the group, Proust the adult is playing like a child, raising his arms in a gesture that suggests flying—time's flight, as well as

FIGURE 5.5 *Gilberte's inviting erotic gesture to little Marcel in Ruiz's* Time Regained.

the flight of the dying man's memory—while Marcel the child doubles his gesture, with his eyes shut and arms stretched out, flying over the sea of time. And in a second, the photograph is taken, the three-dimensional scene flattens, and we are back in Proust's bedroom, looking at this very photograph under the magnifying glass. The photograph was only a trapdoor to paradise.

"Céleste," the dreamer calls out, "are you here? Please tell me the truth: are there roses in the house?" "Roses?! Absolutely not, sir. It hurts me that you say this." "I believe you, Céleste, I do. But when Monsieur de Charlus was here earlier..." "No one was here, sir. I swear to you," Céleste assures him, even though an immense pink rose with dewdrops or raindrops on its petals materializes for a brief second in closeup as Marcel says the name "Charlus" (Figure 5.6a). "Why this unlikely apparition?" asks Amandine Cyprès. "Where does the scent that so disturbs the writer come from? It would appear that it comes from the rose we've seen in the previous scene. In the end, our character is looking at photographs and his memories resurface, all mixed up" ("Dis(ap)paritions"). Martine Beugnet believes that "like other images of flowers and nature later in the film ... this apparition, monstrous in its proportions and artificial perfection, has the unreal aspect of those colored details from retouched postcards that were fashionable early in the century" ("Surrealist Proust," 152). Yet rather than mere artificiality or the nostalgic kitsch of early postcards, Ruiz is actually invoking a very specific, and surrealist, image: Salvador Dalí's 1958 painting *Meditative Rose* (Figure 5.6b). On a barren, desert-like landscape that looks vaguely in the far background like Tuscany or the countryside in Spain, two

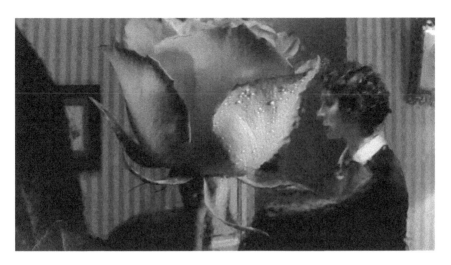

FIGURE 5.6 a, b *The surreal rose in Marcel's bedroom in Ruiz's* Time Regained; *Salvador Dalí's* Meditative Rose.

minuscule silhouettes throw their shadows. But above them, magically, an immense red rose with a dewdrop or tear on its petal occupies the center of Dalí's painting against an azure sky. This meditative rose that hovers over the shadows of what once were two lovers becomes the magic rose that Ruiz shows us in closeup.

Even the azure sky makes it into Ruiz's cinematography from Dalí's painting; when Marcel says his maid's name—"I believe you, Céleste, I do"—Ruiz, like Proust himself, materializes her name on screen by showing the door behind her opening, not onto the dark corridor in Marcel's house, but onto a perfect azure sky, *céleste*. Scholars have noted a similar clear sky in Magritte's paintings, without identifying one in particular. Yet no Magritte painting has that azure sky with an immense rose floating in it. Ruiz was anything but vague in his cinematographic construction, and meticulous in choosing the perfect painting to find in Proust the very heart of surrealism's project, carefully keeping even the dewdrop from Dalí's rose petals.

Gilberte, Albertine, Albertinage, Libertinage

A name contains the prophecy of its own future. Ruiz's Proust glides again into the paradise of the *or du temps* through the trapdoor of a name when he picks up an old photo of Gilberte at age twelve that she had inscribed for him. Seen through a water screen that has the effect of a magnifying glass on which rain drops heavily, the photo takes us back into Marcel's childhood bedroom. The water that comes down is projected onto the wall in the dark room lit only by candles, and we hear Françoise's voice saying: "This isn't Gilberte's signature, I know it well." "But of course it is Gilberte's," the boy insists. "Look," she replies, "this is an 'A,' not a 'G'." "No, Françoise, you say this to tease me." "I call it as I see it. This is an 'A' and the other one an 'l'." Ruiz cuts to a closeup of a piece of paper on which we see a series of words dissolving into one another: "Gilberte" turns into "A lberte," then "A lbertine," "A lbertinage," and finally, "Libertinage" before we see it in the scene that opens with a photo of Robert's lover Rachel, former prostitute turned actress, whose dress and makeup Gilberte imitates one evening.

This metamorphosis is Ruiz's entire creation, one that rereads Proust through a surrealist poetics borrowed from Breton's *Nadja* and Georges Méliès's disappearing act. Ruiz's poetics of film as *tableaux vivants* is here brought about through a revisiting of Breton's concept of *tableaux changeants*. Describing a textual optical illusion of the kind that Ruiz recreates on screen, Breton remembers in *Nadja* how the word "rouge" in a sign reading "Maison ROUGE" appeared to say "POLICE" when read from a different angle:

IN THE PARADISE OF TRAPDOORS

This optical illusion would have no importance if on the same day, one or two hours later, the lady we shall call the *lady of the glove* had not taken me to see a *tableau changeant* which I had never heard of before and which was part of the furnishings in the house she had just rented. This object was an old engraving which, seen straight on, represents a tiger, but which regarded perpendicularly to its surface of tiny vertical bands when you stand several feet to the left, represents a vase, and, from several feet to the right, an angel.

59

The scene that Ruiz recreates exists nowhere in Proust, but it brings together and rewrites two scenes that appear in *The Fugitive*. After Albertine dies in a riding accident, the narrator goes to Venice and while there receives a telegram that had been misdirected at first. It reads: "My dear friend, you think me dead, forgive me, I am quite alive, I long to see you, talk about marriage, when do you return? Affectionately, Albertine" (869). But how could Albertine, who has left him and died, send him a telegram, and talk about marriage? The answer is revealed twenty pages later, when he reads a letter he has received from Gilberte:

> Gilberte wrote to inform me that she was marrying Robert de Saint-Loup. She told me that she had sent me a telegram about it to Venice but she had had no reply ... The telegram that I had received a few days earlier, and had supposed to be from Albertine, was from Gilberte. As the somewhat labored originality of Gilberte's handwriting consisted chiefly, when she wrote a line, in introducing into the line above it the strokes of her *t*'s, which appeared to be underlining the words, or the dots over her *i*'s ... it was quite natural that the clerk who dispatched the telegram should have read the loops of the *s*'s or *y*'s in the line above as an "-ine" attached to the word "Gilberte." The dot over the *i* of Gilberte had climbed up to make a suspension point. As for her capital *G*, it resembled a Gothic *A*.

879

By rewriting this episode as a much earlier scene that shows little Marcel misreading "Gilberte" for "Albertine," whom he would meet only years later, Ruiz makes Gilberte's name into a surrealist object that contains its reader's destiny. For the act of reading, as Proust goes on to tell us, is both a creation and a projection of the reader's desire:

> How many letters are actually read into a word by a careless person who knows what to expect, who sets out with the idea that the message is from a certain person? How many words into the sentence? We guess as

we read, we create; everything starts from an initial error; those that follow (and this applies not only to the reading of letters and telegrams, not only to all reading), extraordinary as they may appear to a person who has begun at the same place, are all quite natural.

890

Ruiz goes even further than Proust in reading in Gilberte a future Albertine who loves women, and in her the idea of "libertinage" that he materializes on screen, first into a photo of Rachel, and then into Gilberte herself dressing up as Rachel playing the lead in a play entitled *La Profanation*.

While critics have noted the similarity that Ruiz points at by showing Gilberte's and Rachel's faces dissolving into each other, no one has observed that Ruiz does so through what became Georges Méliès' most renowned cinematic trick: the disappearing act. Gilberte dresses up in Rachel's costume to go down to dinner with Robert and Marcel. But as Ruiz's camera shows her exiting her room and coming through the frame of the corridor, something magical happens that we realize only a moment later. We are downstairs with an impatient Robert, who's checking his watch, his back turned to us, looking at a staircase from which Gilberte should come down any minute. "Gilberte?" he cries out. "But what is she doing?" Gilberte seems to appear at the top of the stairs; but on a closer look, we realize it's Rachel. The staircase is framed by the entrance to the salon, with curtains like a theatre stage, where Robert is standing. But as Rachel/Gilberte comes down the spiral staircase, she briefly exits the frame and disappears, though we can still hear her footsteps. Confused, Robert turns to the camera, looking somewhere above the frame, as if the ghost has passed by him. He turns back to the staircase, and this time Gilberte, dressed identically to Rachel, descends the same stairs and we're back in the film's immediate reality.

Ruiz's disappearing act looks back not only at Méliès but also at Tarkovsky's treatment of the disappearing act in *Nostalghia*. In Domenico's ruined house, a pensive Andrei stands next to a mirror that doubles his identity on screen. And as he turns his head, Tarkovsky's camera tracks his gaze, until we stumble upon the object that caught his eye: himself with his head turned to his right, but shown from the back, looking back at Andrei looking at him. What Tarkovsky creates through the tracking shot, Ruiz creates without moving the camera. If for Méliès the static camera was a technical necessity, for Ruiz his film is a living tableau on which we can read the characters' future written in letters of desire.

The Trapdoor of a Word

Ruiz's transformation of Proust's words into the camera's movements yields one of the most powerful scenes in *Time Regained*. We are at a dinner party during World War I, and Marcel (Marcello Mazzarella) has just received a letter from Gilberte, who claims to prefer to stay at her country estate to protect her deceased father's art collection. At the dinner party, newsreel-style images of the war are projected onto a large screen, but no one bothers to watch. Absenting himself from the noisy crowd, Marcel finds a seat and reads Gilberte's letter, and we hear Emmanuelle Béart's voice offscreen:

> You have no idea what this war is like, my dear friend, or of the importance that a road, a bridge, a height can assume. How often have I thought of you, of those walks of ours together which you made so delightful through all this now ravaged countryside ... As for the shortcut up the hill which you were so fond of and which we used to call the hawthorn path, where you claim that as a child you fell in love with me ... I cannot tell you how important it has become.
>
> *Time Regained*, 95

But the second we hear Béart's voice uttering the word *route* (path, road), Ruiz transforms the word into a channel in time that sucks Marcel in. He continues to read the letter as if nothing has happened, but his chair is pulled back and lifted up on the projection screen. Next to him appears young Marcel (Georges du Fresne) with a projection camera, playing with it as if it were a film camera, filming people's indifference toward the war and death shown in the newsreel projected on the screen behind him (Figure 5.7). Writer and filmmaker share the frame, for it is in the visionary power of literature and a child's eye that the future of cinema quietly waits, like the ghosts in Proust's world, for the day when a filmmaker like Ruiz can break the spell

FIGURE 5.7 *Adult Marcel reading, young Marcel filming, in Ruiz's* Time Regained.

that keeps them prisoners. For Ruiz, the word *route* behaves like Tarkovsky's oval mirror from *Zerkalo*: it is a trapdoor that opens onto other worlds. This is what a simple word like *route* can do on screen in Ruiz's hands.

Top Hats as Phantom-objects

Ruiz thought of his films as mirrored structures,

> linking ideas, sequences and situations, which, though placed in different parts of the film, and despite what the distances between them may be (or rather, and I would be willing to say, the greater the distance the better), connect with each other, one reinvigorating the other.... Five or six shots remind us of another five or six shots from another film and they feed each other by means of an effect that I call "mirrors of duration."
>
> *Poetics of Cinema* II, 40

Three scenes situated at a distance in Ruiz's *Time Regained* construct the larger poetic arc of the film. Like Proust's Vinteuil's sonata, based on the varied repetition of the "petite phrase," these scenes are linked both visually and auditorily. Two of them are in an almost perfect mirror construction, showing the same salon with top hats and white gloves spread on the floor; these are placed close to the beginning and ending of the film, while the third is the film's next to last scene.

The first time, young Marcel stands up after playing with his magic lantern. We are in his bedroom, and he walks towards the camera, but suddenly he is in front of an immense double door that opens by itself onto the salon with the top hats, which appear to have been left there by gentlemen going in to a soirée. Marcel enters, jumps over the hats as if he's playing hopscotch, and approaches an adult Saint-Loup dressed in military uniform, who is looking into a stereoscope (Figure 5.8a). A second later, Saint-Loup is gone, and so are the hats. The second time, close to the end of the film, just after the pianist Morel has finished playing at the Guermantes' party, we are standing behind the adult Marcel facing the same double doors. The applause for Morel can still be heard, and Marcel adjusts his bowtie as if he is preparing to go on stage. And in that second, with the same strange sound as if we're entering a crypt, the double doors open by themselves onto the salon with the top hats. But this time, instead of Saint-Loup holding an optical device, we see the Guermantes' butler holding a red book (Figure 5.8b). This is the book from which little Marcel will rise in the penultimate scene, to open the crypt-like door for the third and last time. Now it reveals a ruined cathedral, a giant tomb with death masks on it.

FIGURE 5.8 a, b *Symmetrical scenes from the beginning and closing of Ruiz's* Time Regained *showing little Marcel (Georges du Fresne) and older Marcel (Marcello Mazzarella).*

Much discussed by scholars, the top hat scenes have been interpreted as a metaphor of death, or as yet another example of the artificiality and theatricality of social life. According to Amandine Cyprès, "The empty hats perhaps have a resonance like a mise en scène of the inconstancy of people, of worldliness" ("Dis(ap)paritions"). More specifically, Martine Beugnet has noted the surrealist force of the scene: "The enigmatic-looking surrounding space recalls the world of Magritte, summoning an ill-defined feeling of threat and the presence of death throughout its mysterious layout

182　　　　TIME REGAINED

and lines of hats like tombstones" ("Surrealist Proust," 147).[4] Yet the scenes suggest more than social artificiality and ephemerality. Ruiz places these scenes in the beginning and ending of his film. In between, an entire world is summoned to life, ghosts come to share our life again. And ultimately, the room with the top hats opens onto a giant tomb whose crypt, when opened, lets in Ruiz's camera that reads, in the death masks sculpted on the walls, future existences inscribed on the stone in the riverbed of the Vivonne.

Proust anticipates Breton's object of desire in which we read our own inner thoughts. This secret pattern is configured by Ruiz in turn, in his geometric placement of the top hats on the floor. Or as Proust put it: "Just as a geometer, stripping things of their sensible qualities, sees only the linear substratum beneath them, so the stories that people told me escaped me. . . . The result was that, when all the observations I had succeeded in making about the guests during the party were linked together, the pattern of the lines I had traced took the form of a collection of psychological laws" (*Time Regained*, 39–40). This pattern hidden underneath reality's skin in Proust is resurrected in all its magnificence in Breton's *Mad Love*:

> A person will know how to proceed when, like the painter, he consents to reproduce, without any change, what an appropriate grid tells him in advance of his own acts. This grid exists. Every life contains these homogenous patterns of facts whose surface is cracked or cloudy. Each person has only to stare at them fixedly in order to read his own future . . . Everything humans might want to know is written upon this grid in phosphorescent letters, in letters of *desire*.
>
> 86–7, Breton's emphasis

When he mentions the cloudy surface of the patterns of facts, Breton has in mind what he calls in *Mad Love* the logic of Hamlet, who reads in the clouds—now a whale, now a camel—his own desire. And it was the same Hamlet who reads his father's face in the map of the sky: "And then, of course, there is the human physiognomy of a starry night (recall that the archaic Hamlet recognised his father's face, Orveld, as a constellation)" (Ruiz, *Poetics* II, 107). Whose face should we read in the map of trapdoors opened by Ruiz's top hats?

Ruiz himself offers one possible answer: "When Proust speaks of his work as a cathedral, I can say that just like with a cathedral, my work is never finished, we can always add something to it" (Barde interview, 1). The

---

[4]Ruiz's top hats may also evoke the surrealists' predecessor Méliès, from whose magic hat an entire world rises, as in Méliès's film *The Hat with Many Surprises* (1901). There a magician takes out from his hat an entire dinner party, complete with guests, and then makes them all disappear.

ruined Greek temple at the end of *Time Regained* is just such an open structure that Ruiz invites us to explore through several versions of Proust: "*Swann's Way* is the first volume of *À la recherche* and I wanted to oppose it to *Time Regained*, which is the last one . . . I wanted to see the Tenebrae at the end through the bright magic lantern of childhood" (1).[5] The camera's pacing in the ruined cathedral tells us something about whose eye it is that sees all this. We walk slowly, spying on the other Prousts who explore the ruins. "Sometimes we don't know if Proust is inside or outside the camera frame, but he's always there" (Barde interview, 1–2).

The Self, an Abandoned Quarry

Statues are everywhere in Ruiz's film, sometimes more prevalent than humans, who themselves appear in several cases posing as statues. In all shapes and sizes, statues structure the film, but one statue appears more than any other: Callipygian Venus or Venus with beautiful buttocks. We see her in an elevator at Balbec in a memory Marcel accesses before she follows him into the present as he has lunch with Saint-Loup. In the Guermantes' library, as he muses on the nature of art and how to defeat the passage of time, he plunges again back onto the beach at Balbec, and six boys—his doubles, no doubt—carry the Venus from the seashore and outside the frame, bringing her into the "present" moment where she materializes out of nowhere on the tea table next to Marcel. And finally, we see her for a last time in the ruined Greek temple in the penultimate scene.

But there is one scene where the Callipygian Venus is the main character. During the concert at the Guermantes' party, Marcel falls back into a memory from the time when Albertine was alive and they lived together. She is playing a phrase from Vinteuil's music on the piano, but she stops, declaring that the music is so monotonous that it puts her to sleep. As she puts away the score, Marcel starts lecturing her: "If it weren't so late, my little Albertine, I'd show you that these recurrent phrases that you yourself have started to recognize . . . this little phrase that keeps coming back, insisting, and which you write off unwittingly as monotonous . . . well, in literature, good literature that is, it's like a hidden reality, revealed through a material phrase." But all the time while a bored Albertine isn't listening to his speech, ten statues materialize on our screen in closeup, as the rose did earlier. In a

---

[5]As Dominique Jullien writes, "The scenes at Combray allow for different behaviors that point back at different moments in time to manifest simultaneously" (*Proust et ses modèles*, 45). Through his film, Ruiz shows us that not just at Combray, but in every moment, the self is inhabited by several other selves coming from different times.

tracking shot that supposedly follows Marcel pacing around the room, the statues seem to move by themselves, in the opposite direction from the camera, but at a higher speed than we'd expect. When we return, looking left to right with the camera, the statues come back too, but their angle has changed. As in other scenes, words become trapdoors, and when Marcel says that the little phrase returns "insisting," we see the recurrent Venus in the second position; then she appears again in the fifth position when Marcel says "hidden reality," and finally we see her in the ninth position (Figure 5.9).

Almost everyone who discusses Ruiz's film tries to explain the use of recurrent statues, especially the Callipygian Venus. Patrick Bray argues that her repeated presence "calls attention to a material trace in the figural image. This very materiality serves to provoke an awareness of the filmic experience of time, necessarily inciting different memories in different viewers" ("The 'Debris of Experience'," 479). Guy Scarpetta proposes that the Venus is

> a rare motif that is as symbolic as it is functional, for it combines the allusion to the world of Sodom (the image of the naked, exposed buttocks), [and] the conflict between appearance and hidden truth (viewed from the front, Callipygian Venus is a 'modest' figure who covers up her breasts; inversely, viewed from behind, she completely indecently displays her buttocks).... To put it differently, here there is a kind of *index* of Proustian narrative art as such.
>
> "Réflexions," 70

But why this image in particular? In his interview for *Cahiers du cinéma*, Ruiz says that he chose it by chance: "I chose it because it's an *imago*. An

FIGURE 5.9 *Callipygian Venus, the recurrent statue in Ruiz's* Time Regained.

IN THE PARADISE OF TRAPDOORS

image chosen arbitrarily. . . . the scene with stealing the statue from the beach isn't in the book, but it gives a special force to the idea of reminiscence" (Bouquet and Burdeau interview, 53). But a follower of the surrealists like Ruiz knows that a chance encounter is never just an accident. Re-inscribed in the correct context, it becomes part of the cryptogram of reality.

Preoccupied with tracing everything in the film back to Proust, Patrick Bray is surprised that "while the rest of the sequence strictly adheres to the passage in the text, reference to the statue is to be found nowhere in Proust's novel" ("The 'Debris of Experience,'" 480). More interesting is Amandine Cyprès's observation that "this scene connects explicitly, through the pattern of recurrent statues, Ruiz's aesthetics to Vinteuil's and therefore to . . . Proust's. There is some sort of metaphorization of the novel itself through this apparently insignificant motif" ("Dis(ap)paritions"). But a subtle artist like Ruiz doesn't need to be so explicit, or so faithful. More than a motif, a metaphorization, or a simple invention by Ruiz, the Venus statue embodies the very architecture of the film's vision, and it is Ruiz's creative transformation of the core poetic principle of Proust's work. For it is the poet's self that is an abandoned quarry: "So that my personality of today may be compared to an abandoned quarry, which supposes everything it contains to be uniform and monotonous, but from which memory . . . can, like some sculptor of genius, extract innumerable different statues" (*Time Regained*, 285). Proust always conceived of the arts as different facets of the same principle, and whenever he speaks of painting, sculpture, music, or literature he speaks of one and the same thing, through a poetics of modulating repetition that anticipates Virginia Woolf's poetics of the wave.

The secret to understanding the architecture of this abandoned quarry lies in the mirroring of the cornerstones of the novel's arch, *Swann's Way* and *Time Regained*. Constructed as a double of the narrator through his intertwined love for art, music, and Odette, Charles Swann glimpses the principles hidden underneath the surface of things that the narrator will fully understand in *Time Regained*. In *Un amour de Swann*, it's not Odette that Swann loves, but first the engravings she reminds him of and then Vinteuil's "petite phrase," which he projects onto her through a series of associations of ideas that makes him a victim of the mechanisms of memory. Hearing the phrase, "he was like a man into whose life a woman he has seen for a moment passing by has brought the image of a new beauty . . . although he does not even know her name or whether he will ever see her again" (*Swann's Way*, 296). But he will see her again, a few pages later, when he hears Odette play the phrase on the piano. A second apparition of this structure of thought appears years later, when the narrator meditates on Vinteuil's music:

The concert began . . . I should have liked to be a character in those *Arabian Nights* which I never tired of reading and in which, in moments of uncertainty, there appears a genie, or a maiden of a ravishing beauty, invisible to everyone else but not to the perplexed hero to whom she reveals exactly what he wishes to learn. And indeed at that very moment I was favoured with just such a magical apparition. . . . I found myself . . . right in the heart of Vinteuil's sonata; and, more marvelous than any girl, the little phrase . . . came to me recognisable in this new guise.

The Captive, 331–2

Ruiz's choice of Venus has nothing to do with reenacting a dead past; quite the contrary. She is the embodiment of the moments that allow us to escape time, a version of Proust's genie or ravishingly beautiful maiden. The statue's varied repetition is a proof that this sur-reality exists, like Venteuil's modulated phrases, which offer "incalculable colourings of an unsuspected world, fragmented by the gaps between the different occasions of hearing his work performed. . . . again and again one phrase or another from the sonata recurred, but altered each time . . . [they] appear constantly in his work, of which they are the spirits, the dryads, the familiar deities" (*The Captive*, 339–45).

This hidden reality is written in "phosphorescent letters of desire," as Breton says in *Mad Love*. In a corresponding vein, Ruiz shows a phosphorescent light in the scenes that signal the *or du temps*, as with the lamplight on the table where Marcel starts reading Gilberte's letter before his chair is pulled back and raised on the screen. The Venus statue itself is phosphorescent when she appears next to him at dinner with Robert. Nothing in the book or film is unreal, artificial, or merely theatrical; these numinous objects are as real as the book we are reading:

In Vinteuil's music, there were thus some of those visions which it is impossible to express . . . . It seemed to me, when I abandoned myself to this hypothesis that art might be real. . . . It is inconceivable that a piece of sculpture or a piece of music which gives us an emotion that we feel to be more exalted, more pure, more true, does not correspond to some definite spiritual reality, or life would be meaningless.

The Captive, 504

Ruiz's recurrent Callipygian Venus comes from interpreting Proust through the surrealists' poetics. In *Nadja* Breton had developed Proust's theme that memory is a rock quarry from which we extract innumerable different statues. Breton's narrator dreams of encountering a mysterious woman who appears out of nowhere and is "dead white" like a perfect statue. She will haunt him all his life through the ghostly objects of desire whom he loves: Simone, Nadja, Suzanne, Jacqueline, Elisa.

Almost simultaneously with *Nadja*, in 1929 René Magritte created a collage entitled *Je ne vois pas la (femme) cachée dans la forêt* (Figure 5.10). The collage shows a statuesque naked woman who half covers her breasts, though not her sex, with her eyes shut, as if she is dreaming, just like the surrealists whose

FIGURE 5.10 *René Magritte,* Je ne vois pas la (femme) cachée dans la forêt *(1929)*.

188   TIME REGAINED

photos surround her. Magritte created his collage to accompany Breton's survey "Enquête sur l'amour" (*La Révolution surréaliste*, December, 12/15 1929). In his own response to the survey, Breton wrote: "How can we move from the idea of loving to love itself? It is about discovering an object, the only one which I think is indispensable. This object is hidden: we act as if we are children, we are born 'in water,' we 'burn.' *Discovering* it is a great mystery" (71).

*

So what are films for Raul Ruiz? "Films are like human beings: you look at them and they look back at you," he writes in *Poetics of Cinema* (II, 106). Throughout the film, little Marcel is playing with his magic lantern, projecting the world around him, including us as the film's audience. When Odette magically opens a set of double doors at the Guermantes' soirée, a blinding light breaks in and we find ourselves in Marcel's bedroom. He is looking, amused, into the camera's eye—into our eyes—and asks: "Am I disturbing you? Should I stop?"

Hidden in the dark, he projects the world of the film we see; but behind him, other projections appear. They are from our own magic lantern, the film we see in our dreams. As Ruiz says in *Poetics of Cinema*: "the projection of a film in a dark room, and at no more than 24 frames per second, partially reproduces the delirious state of dreaming." He says that a friend

> recently saw a film that had left an impression on him when he was eight years old, and he tells me that the film *recognised him* as an old relative. The film *recognised him,* they looked at one another and greeted each other. Without a doubt, a metaphor. I asked the person telling me the story whether it had been the actors that had recognised him. His reply was that it hadn't been the actors, but somebody in the film. Someone circulating from actor to actor.
>
> II, 109–10

For Ruiz, to see a film is to project our own film onto it, to watch and be watched: "in the waking dream that is our receiving the film, there is a counterpart; we start projecting another film on the film. I have said 'to project,' and that seems apt. Images that leave me and are superimposed on the film itself, such that the double film—as in the double vision of Breton traditions—becomes protean, filled with palpitations, as if breathing" (II, 110).

But the most ominous breath that makes the film palpitate with another layer of time superimposed on the film we're watching is that of Proust as he is dying. Following a soirée at the Verdurins, we see Marcel (Marcello Mazzarella) in a train compartment, wearing summer clothes, reading the Gouncourts' diary. His attention is drawn to the window as the train pulls into a station and sees children running on the platform, looking at him and laughing a crystal laugh, as if inviting him to come out and play. But when

FIGURE 5.11 *Still from Ruiz's* Time Regained *showing little Marcel (Georges du Fresne) and older Marcel (Marcello Mazzarella).*

Ruiz's camera returns from the window frame, Marcel's clothes have changed. He is now wearing a winter coat and a bowler hat, and as he looks outside, yet within himself, lo and behold, the train window frames a young boy in a blinding winter landscape looking back at him (Figure 5.11).

It is the young Marcel, and what we're seeing is not an actual living image, but a photograph that dying Proust sees through his magnifying glass from his bed, as Ruiz's editing reveals. But inside the train compartment, the eternally young Marcel seems to look into the distance, not at himself young, but rather "within me, as though from a height, which was my own height, of many leagues, at the long series of the years" (*Time Regained*, 531). Ruiz's choice of a shadowy lighting for the train compartment (including Marcel's own shadow) contrasts with the glowing light of the winter scene in the photograph framed by the train window. This makes the compartment into a camera obscura of the mind that projects childhood's golden days into the darkness of our train of thought when the world outside is obscured from view. Divided by the crimson train curtain that visually separates the temporal layers but also frames the photograph, the adult and the child echo Swann's dream in which he sees himself crying on a train platform, begging his other self to follow him and turn back time. Bringing together the effect of the camera obscura, the magic lantern, the shadow theatre and the theatre of the mind in one single image, Ruiz epitomizes the secret of time regained: "I wanted to see the Tenebrae at the end through the bright magic lantern of childhood" (Barde interview, 1).

As Proust insisted, the reality hidden beyond our visible realm is one that no voluntary memory can access. Like a midwife, the artist can only help this reality be born; he never creates it, he's only responding to a call that comes to him from somewhere else: "those truths written with the aid of shapes for whose meaning I searched in my brain . . . they composed a magic scrawl, complex and elaborate . . . . I was not free to choose them, that such as they were they were given to me" (*Time Regained*, 274).

This magic scrawl hasn't yet been fully deciphered, nor will it ever be. When Ruiz constructed his film as a narrative inscribed on a stone book hidden in the riverbed of the Vivonne, he couldn't know that only a year later, Proust would resurface in Hong Kong in the form of yet another secret story inscribed on another ruined temple, in Wong Kar-wai's *In the Mood for Love* (2000). Or that the stone would turn into a trapdoor taking us to the paradise of the future in Wong's *2046*. When Ruiz decided to cast Marcello Mazzarella as Proust he couldn't know that he was setting in motion an ongoing pattern of varied repetition, continued in 2013 when Paolo Sorrentino brought Marcel/Marcello back to Italy, turning him into the writer Jep Gambardella, whose chef d'oeuvre will be the film *La Grande Bellezza*.

> How many great cathedrals remain unfinished! The writer feeds his book, he strengthens the parts of it which are weak, he protects it, but afterwards it is the book that grows . . . For it seemed to me that they would not be "my" readers but the readers of their own selves, my book being merely a sort of magnifying glass like those which the optician at Combray used to offer to his customers—it would be my book, but with its help I would furnish them with the means of reading what lay inside themselves.
>
> *Time Regained*, 508

6

Dream of the Red Chamber 2046

Cao Xueqin and Wong Kar-wai

In an interview for *Cahiers du cinéma* in 1999, a month before *Time Regained* was shown at the Cannes Film Festival, Raúl Ruiz noted that "Proust discovers that memory is an act of imagination," and he quoted a remark by Einstein: "I know that time is a dimension, yet how come I can see its three dimensions, but not time itself?" (Bouquet and Burdeau interview, 53). "This is a central problem of cinema," he continued, adding that few directors shared his preoccupation. "One of the few filmmakers today who constructs his works on the problem of time is Wong Kar-wai," the interviewers interject. "I haven't seen his films yet," admits Ruiz, "I've been told over and over again that I should, and I soon will" (53). Ruiz would soon have the occasion to see them, as Wong's companion films *In the Mood for Love* and *2046* would be in the Cannes competition in 2000 and 2004 respectively. Both Wong and Ruiz have also been present in Cannes as part of the jury: in 2002, we find Ruiz in the jury presided over by David Lynch and in 2006, Wong Kar-wai is president of the jury. Standing out as Wong's most poetic films, *In the Mood for Love* and *2046* should be seen as a single film, based on their simultaneous production, their organic architectural construction, and the two sides of a single story they tell: how to escape time's irreversibility, how to change events, and how to recapture a lost past in the future.

Set in Hong Kong over a period of four years, 1962–6, *In the Mood for Love* tells the story of two Shanghai émigrés, Chow Mo-wan (Tony Leung) and Su Li-zhen (Maggie Cheung), who rent rooms in the same building and soon discover that their spouses are involved in an adulterous relationship. Mo-wan and Li-zhen fall in love themselves while writing martial arts novels together in a hotel room whose number is 2046. When Mo-wan asks

Li-zhen to run away with him to Singapore, she decides that she can't leave her husband, and the couple never meets again. Or do they? *In the Mood for Love* closes with Mo-wan visiting the Buddhist temple complex at Angkor Wat in Cambodia, where he reenacts what Wong says is "an old legend": when someone had a secret to hide, they would go off to a mountain, carve a hole in a tree, whisper their secret into it, and cover the hole with earth so that no one could find it out.

2046 is haunted by the same mysterious legend, as Mo-wan goes first to Singapore, then back to Hong Kong. Now a journalist who supplements his income by writing more martial arts novels, he has many one-night stands yet is very much alone, living in a room at the Orient Hotel, where he has taken the room next to his and Li-zhen's old room 2046. Over a period of three years, from 1966 to 1969, we follow him as he writes two "futuristic" stories called *2046* and *2047*. He interacts with a number of potential love interests, Bai Ling, Mimi/Lulu, and Jing-wen, while he secretly looks for his lost love from *In the Mood for Love*, Su Li-zhen. Her absent presence haunts Mo-wan through every woman he meets in *2046*, in each of whom he finds his lost beloved's traits only partly embodied. She then returns as a second Su Li-zhen, this time a gambler in Singapore, now played by Gong Li. While *In the Mood for Love* envisions happiness in a potential future that Mo-wan dreams of, in *2046* happiness is only to be found in the past, toward which the future is oriented, including in Mo-wan's futuristic sci-fi stories *2046* and its sequel, *2047*.

Wong presented these films as the second and third parts of the so-called Hong Kong trilogy that began with *Days of Being Wild* (1990), which had featured a sad love story between Li-zhen (played by Maggie Cheung, as in *In the Mood for Love*) and a playboy (Leslie Cheung). Yet *In the Mood for Love* and *2046* are more like a single hinged mirror. Wong filmed *In the Mood for Love* and *2046* concurrently, mostly with the same actors, and as he said in an interview in 2004, "I remember I had in mind a certain rapport between the two films and I found the connecting point when filming a scene for *In the Mood for Love* in a hotel, I noticed a room number beginning with 20 . . . So I thought to myself I could call the other film *2046*, and *In the Mood for Love* and *2046* would be like two chapters of the same film" (Ciment and Niogret interview, 90).

In the Mood for Love and *2046* are usually described by critics as "nostalgia films" (Ackbar Abbas, *Hong Kong*, 40) about Hong Kong in the 1960s. According to Vivian Lee, "As metatext, nostalgia in Wong's films follows a structure of regression, as the characters, usually melancholic subjects, fall into repetitive loops of obsessive memories. This understanding of nostalgia draws attention to metatextuality and inter-referentiality as two key aspects of the cinematic imagination of the past, which is most vividly demonstrated in the 1960s trilogy" ("Infidelity," 379). But the way Wong approaches the problem of time is much more complicated than that: "I don't think [my films] are nostalgic, only that I will miss things after they disappear. I think now I only want to preserve, to stop time, to fix things on the reel. Later when the audience sees this film, they may not like the story, but they learn something about events that happened in the past" (*Interviews*). Asked whether he was giving a portrait of the 1960s, Wong replied: "I think these things could happen in any time period; they have no relation to the end of the century. In fact every day is the end of the century." To preserve old things so that others can learn something about events in the past was also at the heart of Andrei Tarkovsky's cinema, which brought together the Japanese concept of *sabi* ("rust," "patina") and Proust's notion of time as sculptor that leaves its imprint on objects. But to learn from one's past by making a memory of the events is also a Buddhist idea that we find preserved in both Japanese and Chinese culture.

Critics tend to describe *2046* as a sequel to *In the Mood for Love*. But this isn't how Wong conceived it:

> I didn't want *2046* to be only a sequel to *In the Mood for Love* because I believe that the latter told a story that closed upon itself. Apart from that I was very attached to the character of Chow, the writer. Then I wanted to have all characters pass through this room 2046. But two years later I thought it would be too difficult, so I decided to have the characters distance themselves from room 2046: the story would be centered on the writer and it would also speak of us. I came to feel that, unwittingly, *2046* epitomizes all my films in a way. . . . In the end, the film had a strange structure, resembling a book with different chapters, which I like very much.
>
> CIMENT and NIOGRET interview, 90

Far from a pure sequel, *2046* became the base from which, Wong argues, we should look back to *In the Mood for Love*: "At a certain point, these two films are a mirror of each other. And if the audience hasn't seen *In the Mood for Love*, they should watch *2046* first. If they want to know what happened between Maggie and Tony, they should watch *In the Mood for Love*—it's like the missing chapter of this novel" (*Interviews*).

To understand Wong's construction of the two films as a mirrored experience at the intersection of film and literature, one needs to look back at Wong's upbringing and education. In Stephen Teo's view, *2046* "is easily the most literary of Wong's films" (*Wong Kar-wai*, 152). Silver Wai-ming Lee and Micky Lee have argued that "Modern Chinese literature inspires Wong to make films" (Introduction to *Wong Kar-wai: Interviews*), and they reference novels by Louis Cha and Shi Zhecun as well as Liu Yichang as the basis for various of Wong's films. Yet his upbringing included classic as well as modern works, both Chinese and Western:

I was born in Shanghai, and I came to Hong Kong with my parents when I was five years old, in 1963. We spent a lot of time in cinemas. And my father always wanted me to learn all the literature, the classic Chinese literature. So I had big books when I was thirteen. My brother and sister—they are much older than me, and they stayed in Shanghai—always spoke in letters about things I didn't know at the time, like Balzac and Tolstoy and Gorky . . . because I wanted to communicate with them, I tried to read that kind of book. Big books. But I like Balzac. And after that, I got interested in Japanese literature, because it is easy to find Chinese translations. After that, all kinds of books. South American, American.

BRUNETTE interview [1995], 114

In many interviews Wong has cited his father's desire for him to read Chinese as well as Western "big books," and as we'll see, *In the Mood for Love* and *2046* are indebted to classical as well as modern Chinese and world literature.

Critics prefer to think of Wong as embedded in contemporary Hong Kong culture, even as "*the* Hong Kong World Cinema director" (Ingham and Fung, "In the Mood," 296). Hence, for Stephen Teo, "*2046* is a historical epic about Hong Kong's sense of loss" (*Wong Kar-wai*, 139), providing a way to "harness Hong Kong and its channels of global capitalism to underwrite his exploration of time and emotion" (152). As closely as Wong's films are tied to Hong Kong, he has never wanted his films to be pigeonholed in terms of their local setting and its history as a former British colony that was returned to China in 1997: "some asked me if *Ashes of Time* could be about '97. If so, then the judges [at film festivals] would be very interested. But I feel, 'So what?' How much do westerners understand Hong Kong? They only see it as a topic, a common language" (*Interviews*). The same could be said about *2046*, which has mostly been seen as a political film, because of Wong's own declarations that it concerns how things change over time, something to be tested against China's promise that nothing would change in Hong Kong for fifty years: "I don't deny that the inspiration of *2046* comes from a political language, but I put the language into another context: not politics, but love" (*Interviews*). The film begins with footage of the 1967 riots that spelled the beginning of the end of British rule, and 2046 will be the final year of the fifty-year transitional period, yet dates are never a diarist's preoccupation in Wong's twin films. *2046* features events that take place on a series of Christmas Eves, from 1966 to 1969. Even if time seems to be running chronologically, carefully marked by white characters on a black screen, we have a feeling of being stuck in limbo, where it's always the same day: December 24.

But why would the Christian holiday structure a film based on a clearly marked Buddhist theme, in both *In the Mood* and *2046*—that reality is only a dream, an illusion, a fiction? Looking more closely into Wong's complex intertextual dialogues both with classical Chinese literature and with world art cinema may reveal some unsuspected answers.

The Secret Story of *In the Mood for Love* and *2046*

The main connecting point between the twin films is the theme of a never revealed secret. "The secret will be the main point of the story," as Wong decided for *In the Mood for Love* (*Interviews*), and there has been a lot of speculation over what this secret could be. In the first film's final scene, Mo-wan whispers it into a hole in a wall of a temple at Angkor Wat. The entire scene is non-verbal, filmed in the haunting rhythm of Michael Galasso's string music, composed in the spirit of Shigeru Umebayashi's waltz that Wong uses throughout the film whenever he shows the missed or almost missed encounters between Mo-wan and Li-zhen.

We never know what Mo-wan whispers into the hole, but in the slow movement, sometimes tracking forward, other times backward, we do see what else is on these walls dating back to the twelfth century during the Khmer Empire: scenes from the two major Hindu epics, *Rāmāyana* and *Mahābhārata*, together with the thirty-two hells and thirty-seven heavens of Hinduism. Vishnu is at the center of these representations, as the deity to whom the temple was initially dedicated. But Wong's camera shows us in closeup what Proust would call the imprints of time or Tarkovsky would evoke as *sabi*: faded colors, almost indistinguishable figures in bas-relief portraying loves, wars, births, deaths and rebirths, heaven and hell. In a word, the world. As Wong explained in an interview, "We can look at the whole thing from a distance to provide another dimension. So we looked for all these things in Thailand because we were shooting in Bangkok. We were trying to find some temples. . . . Years ago I saw a documentary on Angkor Wat, and I'm impressed by the place. It's like a museum of jealousy, passion, love, so I think we should end the story there" (*Interviews*).

Wong's choice to end his film in the ruins at Angkor Wat is also a nod to Tarkovsky's closing *Nostalghia* in the ruins of the Romanesque cathedral at San Galgano in Italy. In the closing scene at Angkor Wat, we see Mo-wan's head, filmed from behind, gently whispering his secret into a hole that he covers with his cupped hand; with his eyes closed and lips moving slowly, it's an erotic but also a very sad scene, as the temple's walls bear the traces of time and human suffering, while Mo-wan whispers into the wall his suffering over losing his beloved, Li-zhen. We seem to be spying on a very intimate moment, but then something incredible happens: Wong cuts to a high-angle perspective and we see another closeup of someone's head from behind, now

FIGURE 6.1 *A monk watches Mo-wan whispering his secret, in* In the Mood for Love.

the shaved head of a Buddhist monk looking at Mo-wan down below as he whispers his secret (Figure 6.1). But who could this monk be? Where has he come from, and what does this tell us about the perspective from which *In the Mood for Love* is filmed? Why has Wong included this very brief shot at this climactic moment?

A few moments later, after a slow tracking shot shows us the temple and the imprints of time on its walls, Wong cuts to another closeup of the hole into which Mo-wan has whispered his secret: this time, we see a few leaves of green grass growing out of the hole, as if the barren stone wall has come to life (Color Plate 8). But how could this be, and what does this tell us about the secret that's been whispered into it?

One possible explanation is that the green grass is like Proust's ghosts imprisoned in stones that are called back to life by our realization that they were once human. In this reading, the grass is a metaphor for the secret love story between Li-zhen and Mo-wan that has evidently resulted in their having a child. This is suggested just before the Angkor Wat scene, when Li-zhen and Mo-wan return to the building where they once lived, and where Li-zhen returns to live on her own with her son.[1] Though *In the Mood for*

---

[1] Many critics read this differently. Ackbar Abbas writes that Mo-wan and Li-zhen meet "in a hotel room, where all that takes place is discourse, not intercourse" ("Wong Kar-wai's Cinema of Repetition," 125).

Love doesn't include any sex scenes between the two lovers, Wong did include one in the initial filming, but then dropped it to keep the child's identity a mystery: "That's in the script. I'd like to have some ambiguity. That's perhaps his son . . . the age matches; but that proves nothing. One never knows" (*Interviews*). So the secret whispered into the stone could indeed be a new life.

The story of deciphering the secret lies in the "old legend" that Wong mentions in several interviews and which he repeatedly stated was the connecting point between the two films. *In the Mood for Love* closes with a tracking shot of Angkor Wat from what appears to be a path among ruined walls. Following the shot of the Buddhist monk watching Mo-wan from a distance, the camera's pacing suggests the monk slowly walking and contemplating these ancient stories of love, lust, death, and rebirth written on the stones of the temple. But from a distance in time. The last image we see on the screen before it turns black is a double image of the hole. In the distance, we see what appears to be a chapel of the temple, with a mysterious entrance into a black void; in the foreground stands a smaller block of stone with a perfectly round black hole (Figure 6.2). They both anticipate the void we enter as the film closes with a black screen and a citation from the novelist Liu Yichang in white characters: "He remembers those vanished years. As though looking through a dusty windowpane, the past is something he could see, but not touch. And everything he sees is blurred and indistinct."

The distance from which this secret story is told is the Buddhist monk's distance, both literal and religious, in that the monk knows that the reality

FIGURE 6.2 *The final shot of Angkor Wat.*

around us is but a dream, an illusion from which we will be awakened into the void we all came from.

Closing *In the Mood for Love* with the juxtaposition of two entrances into the void—the door to the temple chapel and the round hole in the man-sized block of stone standing in the foreground—Wong echoes the juxtaposition of the time-bound Mo-wan and the monk, to tell us that Mo-wan, doubled with the Buddhist monk, becomes the stone with a hole in it. Significantly, *2046* opens where *In the Mood for Love* left off—the round hole in the block of stone is now turned into a black tunnel opening in the wall of a room in a futuristic hotel, warped and enlarged, with the distorted neon-yellow vertical stripes on the room's panes looking like the dreamer's dilated iris, with the black void as the pupil. *2046* then closes with the same image: a black hole from which we had slowly moved backwards in the opening of the film, and then at the very end we slowly move toward it again. A tunnel in time that unites both films, past and future, a bridge of dreams through which lovers communicate, the black camera's eye that knows the entire story from the very beginning.

So what is the "old legend" Wong has drawn on? A stone that bears a secret that tells of a lustful life full of love and suffering; a stone-man that becomes a writer and a Buddhist monk at the very end. Asked by Michel Ciment and Hubert Niogret "What is the legend that you talk about, the one that tells the rocks a secret?" Wong gives a rather vague answer: "It's a legend from an old book. I will use this legend in *2046* and *In the Mood for Love* at the same time" (Wong Kar-wai, *Interviews*). What Wong is drawing on is a Buddhist myth, part of the Chinese "stone lore" that Jing Wang discusses in her book *The Story of Stone*. This lore was given its classic literary expression in Cao Xueqin's novel *The Story of the Stone* (1763, also known as *The Dream of the Red Chamber*), one of the four major classical Chinese novels. When Wong spoke of "an old book," he was referring both to a book written long ago—Cao died in 1763, leaving his story unfinished—and also to a book he read long ago as a child: "My first book was *Romance of the Three Kingdoms*, then *Water Margin*, and *Dream of the Red Chamber*" (*Interviews*). As we will soon see, Cao's masterpiece left a major trace on Wong's notion of time and the means to visualize it in space, in ways comparable to Raúl Ruiz's dream about the future of cinema, which he tried to accomplish in *Time Regained*. Appropriately, the translator David Hawkes refers to Cao as the Proust of China ("Introduction," 22), while Stephen Teo has named Wong the Proust of Hong Kong. Wong's twin films, in fact, draw on Proust as well as Cao Xueqin in their representations of time and the self.[2]

---

[2]Wong never clearly stated that he read Proust, but he never denied having read him either, and he had the chance several times to do so when in interviews his films were compared to Proust's *Recherche*. As is often the case with Wong, he leaves this question open.

Scholars who have looked for Wong's literary sources haven't gone back beyond modern writers such as Liu Yichang, and no one has analyzed the films in relation to Cao Xueqin. In "We Can't Go On Meeting Like This," Martha Nochimson has noted that *The Dream of the Red Chamber* is "the work most significant for non-Chinese to acquaint themselves with as a context for Wong's heritage films" (456), but beyond giving a one-sentence synopsis, she doesn't pursue this context. A single sentence, however, can't begin to give an idea of Cao Xueqin's masterpiece, or its relevance for Wong's twin films. Cao's immense novel presents a complicated story of how the book we read today as *The Dream of the Red Chamber* came into being, telling the still more complicated story of its hero, Jia Bao-yu, who desperately loves his sickly yet beautiful and intelligent cousin Lin Dai-yu. He is tricked by his family into marrying another cousin, the equally beautiful, wise, and down-to-earth Bao-chai, who adores him. Discovering during the marriage ceremony that under the veil is Bao-chai instead of Dai-yu, Bao-yu is mortally pained, and he soon ends up leaving his pregnant wife. The last time he is seen before the story closes, he is a Buddhist monk who leaves our world. He is only twenty years old.

Cao frames his story with a complex set of stories within stories. The book's 120 chapters explain the tragic love triangle Bao-yu—Dai-yu—Bao-chai through another story, which tells of a stone thrown away by the goddess Nüwa when she was repairing the sky. It is later found by a Buddhist monk in the form of a magic jade, on which the monk carves the story of a stone that loves a flower, Crimson Pearl, which he waters every day with sweet dew. To repay this debt, Crimson Pearl and the jade stone are brought into the Land of Illusion so that the flower, now in the form of Dai-yu, can repay Bao-yu with her tears over the course of a lifetime. Their love story ends with Dai-yu's death and Bao-yu's becoming a monk; he returns to the Void as he entered the world, accompanied by a Buddhist monk and a Taoist sage. Eons later, yet another monk, Kongkong dauren ("reverend Void," translated by David Hawkes as "Vanitas"), finds the inscribed stone and decides to copy the text before taking it to Cao Xueqin, who will work on it for ten years in his "Nostalgia Studio" (*The Story*, 1:51). *The Story of the Stone* is the story of Bao-yu, a celestial stone turned into jade turned into a story written on a block of stone by a Buddhist monk, who will be none other than Bao-yu himself at the end of his story. A story told years later by someone who understands that earthly life and love are mere illusions and faded dreams. That's why everything looks "blurred and indistinct," as Wong's narrator tells us at the end of *In the Mood for Love*.

Just before Bao-yu exits the story, his father sadly prepares to write to his family the news that his son is leaving them to become a monk instead of doing his filial duty. But then Bao-yu materializes before him:

When he came to write about Bao-yu, he paused for a moment and looked up. There, up on deck, standing in the very entrance to his cabin and silhouetted dimly against the snow, was the figure of a man with shaven head and bare feet, wrapped in a large cape made of crimson felt. The figure knelt down and bowed to Jia Zheng, who did not recognize the features and hurried out on deck, intending to raise him up and ask him his name . . . he looked into the man's eyes and with a sudden shock recognized him as Bao-yu. "Are you not my son?" he asked.

The Story 5: The Dreamer Wakes

Here Bao-yu looks like Wong's Buddhist monk who's looking down from the walls of Angkor Wat at Mo-wan, who is whispering his secret story. But why would Wong mention a legend about a hole in a tree, yet end up using a stone for inscribing Mo-wan's secret story? An answer can be provided by Jing Wang, in *The Story of Stone*:

The association of stone and enlightenment abounds in Buddhist legends. Bodhidharma is known to have spent nine years facing a rock in meditation. In the Shao-lin temple of Ho-nan Province today, one can view the legendary rock that bears the vague impression of the meditating saint. The portrayal of eccentric arhats seated on rock platforms lost in meditation can also be seen in paintings. In the hand scroll *The Sixteen Arhats*, dated 1591, one finds a figure "absorbed in a tree trunk that is transmuted into a rock grotto."

85

The tree and the stone function in free variation in the Buddhist stone lore. But if this were all that Wong used creatively from *The Story of the Stone*, it wouldn't be enough to explain the complicated temporal construction of *2046*, where time with its three dimensions—past, present, and future—is represented as space. *2046* is a year in the future but it is also a space in the past: the room in which Li-zhen and Mo-wan fell in love while writing literature in *In the Mood for Love*. It's significant that the two future-oriented episodes in *2046* are in fact two books written by Mo-wan, *2046* and *2047*, which tell of a man who returns from another time and space in 2046. These tales look prophetic of Mo-wan's future, as if he already knows what the future will bring.[3] Like Cao's Buddhist meta-narrative of the story

---

[3] As Ewa Mazierska and Laura Rascaroli note, in Wong's films "the future is typically revealed to us at the very beginning, either in voiceover or visually" ("Trapped in the Present: Time in the Films of Wong Kar-wai," 16).

of the stone, Wong's Angkor Wat scene circumscribes the apparently chrono-logical story of Mo-wan and Su Li-zhen within what he calls the timeless space of the temple:

> To me, Angkor Wat is timeless. This film can be understood on three levels. The first one is the fictional story: a love story between the male and female protagonists. During that period of time, we could see the events happen in history. It is like a documentary. In the film, we put the fictional drama and the real documentary together. The last level is the sense of timeless space. To Angkor Wat that has experienced ages of change, a tourist passing by is just a second, or one of many chapters.

> *Interviews*

This timeless space will be the red room 2046 in the film *2046*.

The construction of a prophetic narrative nested within the larger narrative is something to be found in the fifth chapter of Cao's novel, which tells of a dream Bao-yu had as an adolescent in a red room belonging to a lustful woman, Qin-shi. In this dream, Bao-yu returns to his previous existence when he was a jade stone in love with the flower Crimson Pearl in the Land of Illusion where the fairy Disenchantment dwells. There he sees without understanding the registers that include lists of the most important women in his land and also in our novel. The dream is prophetic of the tragedy that will follow, and we can see chapter five as a magic mirror that brings together Bao-yu's past, present, and future—a *mise en abyme* for Cao's entire novel. In a similar way, Wong's red room 2046 will become a vision of time itself but also the secret space from which the entire story emanates, as it brings together all the women in Mo-wan's life and is the point toward which we move in the final shot of *2046*. It is a visual synonym for the hole in the wall at Angkor Wat from which both Wong's films radiate outward.

The first published edition of Cao's novel dates from 1791–2, three decades after the author's death in 1763; the book had circulated in manuscript in different variants on which several commentators left their thoughts. Cao definitely wrote the first eighty chapters, but there is an entire branch of the discipline of "Redology" dedicated to debating whether the last forty chapters belong to Cao or not. They are generally attributed to the editor of the 1791–2 edition, Gao E, who was apparently invited by Cao's family to soften the criticism directed against the Emperor and the attack on Confucian values like filial duty in favor of a Buddhist detachment from illusory human existence. Whatever the book's compositional history, Wong's films reflect the full 120-chapter version.

Wong's idea that "The secret will be the main point of the story" isn't new. Cao described his own novel as a secret, in the frame tale that tells of a

202   TIME REGAINED

Buddhist monk who writes it on the stone before another monk copies it. Just before the transcription of the "transcription" of the story begins, Cao includes an oracular quatrain:

Pages full of idle words
Penned with hot and bitter tears:
All men call the author fool;
None his secret message hears.[4]

1:51

In 1927, a manuscript was found that includes a commentary on these verses by one Red Inkstone, thought to be the pen name of Cao Tianyou, a cousin of Cao Xueqin. In his introduction, David Hawkes quotes Red Inkstone's comment on the quatrain: "Xueqin, having run out of tears, departed this life . . . leaving his book unfinished . . . If only the Creator would produce another Xueqin and another Red Inkstone to complete this book, how happy the two of us would be, down there together in the World of Shades" (1:35).

It would take another 230 years for the Creator to produce another Cao Xueqin in the person of the filmmaker Wong Kar-wai, and another Red Inkstone in the person of Wong's fictional persona, the writer Chow Mo-wan, to complete this book. The heart of the two mirrored corridors that are *In the Mood for Love* and *2046* is the hole in the stone seen in closeup at the end of *In the Mood for Love*, the emptiness from which all creation appears. As Cao writes of the inception of his tale, "starting off in the Void (which is Truth)," the monk who copied out the story "came to the contemplation of Form (which is Illusion); and from Form engendered passion; and by communicating Passion, entered again into Form; and from Form awoke to the Void (which is Truth)" (*The Story* 1:51). As Wong noted of the Angkor Wat scene: "this documentary . . . is not only about the events, but it also has an effect like waking up somebody" (*Interviews*).

"At any era, at any place, Angkor Wat is an absolute thing. I think everyone's heart has an Angkor Wat, an eternal sacred place. After living a luxurious or frustrated life, when you go back to your eternal sacred place, it is like a cleansing, a confession, or a consolation" (Wong Kar-wai, *Interviews*). In *2046*, the red chamber in the Orient Hotel takes the place of Angkor Wat, as the place to which Mo-wan returns to find the consolation he needs after losing his beloved Li-zhen in *In the Mood for Love*. This is the architectural principle of construction for Wong's mirrored films: from Void through Form and Passion and back to the Void. His creative transformation of one of the major masterpieces of world literature unto the medium of film

---

[4]A more literal translation of this line would be: "Who can understand the story's flavor?" I am grateful to my good friend Zhang Yanping, Assistant Professor at Fudan University, for this clarification.

fulfills the wish of Red Inkstone, revealing the secret at the heart of Cao's novel. But to make the secret legible, we need to tell a more complex story.

The Chiastic Construction of *2046* and the Memory of Time

2046 tells the story of Mo-wan's return to Hong Kong from Singapore, where *In the Mood for Love* left him. He is now a journalist, and in addition to the martial arts novels he co-wrote with Li-zhen in the past, he starts writing erotic and futuristic novels. In the film we're told of two such stories: one called *2046*, the other *2047*. Mo-wan writes these from his room in the Orient Hotel, where he decides to move because of the room number—2046—that he happens to see one evening, as he's dropping off an old friend—and maybe lover in a former life—Mimi/Lulu, played by the actress Carina Lau. Later on, Mo-wan returns to rent this very room, but he learns that Mimi/Lulu has meanwhile been stabbed to death there by her boyfriend, so Mo-wan moves into the room next door. From room 2047 he will spy through a hole in the wall on the women who pass through room 2046 and with whom he will be connected sexually or emotionally.

First, he spies on Jing-wen (Faye Wong), the hotel owner's oldest daughter, who is in love with a Japanese man, a relationship her father disapproves of. They break up several times over the course of the film before getting married in Japan at the end. As she is intelligent, delicate, and quiet, she reminds Mo-wan of Li-zhen, and he falls for her, but his love isn't reciprocated. Jing-wen moves out and is replaced by Bai Ling, a beautiful courtesan. Mo-wan develops a sexual relationship with her. She falls desperately in love with him, but the relationship goes nowhere, as this time it is Mo-wan who isn't in love. The last emotional layer involves a third woman whom he meets on a visit to Singapore, a gambler (played by Gong Li) who shares the name of his lost love Su Li-zhen. Mo-wan wants her to return with him to Hong Kong, hoping to retrace with her his love story with the first Su Li-zhen. In *In the Mood for Love*, on the eve of his departure for Singapore Mo-wan had confessed to Li-zhen that he loved her and asked her to join him. Now, as if in a recurring dream, on the very same street Mo-wan asks the second Li-zhen to go with him, but back to Hong Kong. Like the first Li-zhen, but for a different reason, she says no: she knows that he doesn't love her but only the ghost of the first Li-zhen.

These four love stories are apparently told in chronological order over four Christmases, with the dates announced in white characters on a black screen. But the film's construction isn't as chronological as it may seem, as the perspective from which everything is narrated is the Buddhist monk's from the end of Angkor Wat. For him there's no difference between past, present, and future, and he knows that the hidden cryptogram of reality only becomes legible in retrospect, once we've awoken from the dream that reality is. This puzzle principle is Wong's editing principle for *2046*: "I believe a great deal in chance. In fact, my films are made up of the addition of small parts. At the end, I discover the whole. It seems to me to be a very Chinese way of thinking . . . In other words, it's like a puzzle whose order I wouldn't know, but whose pieces would assemble themselves little by little. In my view, every film has its own bit of luck" (*Interviews*).

This explains why the apparently chronological story of Mo-wan from 1966 to 1969 is intertwined with the futuristic stories into which he puts his own life. Despite their androids, time-travelling trains, and manga-like characters, *2046* and *2047* are autobiographical stories of missed encounters or unrequited love. Mo-wan's *2046* is described as an erotic book that he writes just after he moves into the adjacent room 2047 following Mimi/Lulu's tragic death. As we enter his fictional universe, we hear Mo-wan in voiceover say that the story is "all about men and women looking for love, risking everything to get to a place called 2046. I made it as erotic and as enjoyable as possible. The story was popular. Some were curious about why I had written a futuristic story. But to me, 2046 was just a hotel room number. I made up the whole thing, but some of my own experiences found their way into it." But as we hear Mo-wan's voiceover saying this, we see onscreen, stretching erotically, the first Su Li-zhen from *In the Mood for Love*, still played by Maggie Cheung, in one of the few shots in which she appears in *2046*. This supposedly futuristic sci-fi novel is a story about Mo-wan's past, in an attempt to change the course of the future.

Later in the film Mo-wan writes a second story, *2047*, after he realizes that Jing-wen is devoted to her Japanese lover and that she'll never choose him. Because Jing-wen's father still disapproves of the relationship with her lover and prevents them from getting together, Mo-wan decides to make her happy by writing her a story. As we hear him say in voiceover:

> I promised to write a story, based on my observations, to show her what her boyfriend was thinking. As a joke, we thought the story should be called *2047*. Maybe I was getting too involved. I started to feel that it wasn't about her boyfriend at all. Rather it was more about me. I began imagining myself as a Japanese man on a train leaving 2046, falling for an android with delayed reactions. If someone wants to leave 2046, how long will it take? No one knows.

On the train, his Japanese avatar talks to a bartender, who warns him against falling in love with the cabin attendants, as they are only mechanical constructions that always break down in the end: "They will serve you devotedly, like an intimate friend. But you must never fall in love with them. . . . Events can creep up on you without you even noticing," the bartender warns, using a sentence from a key scene in *In the Mood for Love*, where this was what Mo-wan said to Li-zhen when confessing his love for her. "Do you know the Buddhist canon?" the bartender continues. "The Decay of Celestial Beings? Even the immortals experience this process. Our cabin attendants are superbly designed, but there's one problem. When they've served on so many long journeys fatigue begins to set in . . . This one is failing fast. I think you'd better give up." Mo-wan's protagonist is in love with an android that looks at times like Jing-wen and other times like Mimi/Lulu, and he hears Mo-wan's own words from *In the Mood for Love*, now spoken by the android Mimi/Lulu: "Do you know what people did in the old days when they had secrets? They'd climb a mountain and find a tree." And the story of the secret is told all over again.

Wong's puzzle-like editing of these different temporal layers—past, present, and future—takes the shape of a chiasmus with two concentric ring structures that open and close *2046*. This double ring structure is a mirror of *The Dream of the Red Chamber*'s own symmetrical construction that opens and closes with the story of the inscribed stone, which frames the story of the stone turned into Bao-yu. *2046* opens and closes with the image of a giant black hole—the very same one from Angkor Wat, as multiplied in the juxtaposed image of two voids, the one seen in close up and the one in the distance, in the last shot of *In the Mood for Love*. In the opening, we move slowly away from it. In the end, we move slowly toward it as the camera's eye closes while we return, like Bao-yu, now again Brother Stone entering into the Void where we all came from. Symmetrically, the second ring structure of the chiasmus nested inside this frame is composed of two parts that turn out to be both from the film-book of *2047* written by Mo-wan. They both show Mo-wan as the Japanese lover of Jing-wen in a futuristic train, sadly returning from a place—or time—called 2046.

In *Chiasmus in Antiquity*, John Welch has called the trope a triptych construction with two symmetrical wings developed around a center. As Welch shows, the chiasmus is a figure of memory used in ancient religious texts to organize an orally transmitted narrative. Significantly, for Wong the mirrored structure he used in *2046* is "a very Chinese way of thinking. For us, time is a circle that begins where it ends and the other way around" (Ciment and Niogret interview, 91–2). In a film like *2046* concerned with the construction of a timeless memory, chiasmus is an indispensable architectural principle—all the more so in a film whose preface is Liu Yichang's "All memories are traces of tears," which we see written on the black screen after the first two parts of the two concentric ring structures have unfolded. The map these tears draw includes major irradiating centers like Cao's *Dream of the Red Chamber* and Andrei Tarkovsky's films.

As we enter *2046* we move away from the black hole that looks simultaneously like a wound, a hole in a tree, and a black tunnel into the void. As the camera slowly moves backwards, the hole begins to look like the mouth of a giant brass instrument that appears flanked by surreal walls inscribed with blue luminescent letters. We can barely make out the words written there, for as we're told at the end of *In the Mood for Love* about Mo-wan's perspective on his story, "everything he sees is blurred and indistinct." In *2046* the camera's eye resumes the distanced perspective of the Buddhist monk at Angkor Wat at the end of *In the Mood for Love*. We see things in *2046* simultaneously from a maximum and minimum distance, as in the voyeuristic scenes where Mo-wan looks from his room 2047 at Bai Ling as she gets dressed in 2046, at Jing-wen and Bai Ling smoking on the hotel rooftop, at his characters in the novel *2046*, where a Japanese man spies on Mimi/Lulu making love to the man who will murder her in her red room 2046. This shifting distance is like the doubled narrative perspective in Cao's *Dream of the Red Chamber*, where the Buddhist monk (whom Bao-yu will eventually become) is the one who inscribes the story on the stone, a story lived in turn through Bao-yu, whom we follow step by step in his love for Dai-yu before he becomes a monk at the very end. Anthony Yu has noted that this double perspective makes *The Story of the Stone* stand out in the world of fiction: "I believe that the 'flavor' or 'secret message' of the work lies in the differentiation between the Buddhist 'reading' of the world and our reading of literary fiction. . . . Whereas Buddhism draws from its 'reading' the conclusion that detachment is the ultimate wisdom, the experience of reading fiction, at least according to our author, is nothing if not the deepest engagement" (*Rereading the Stone*, 149).

In *2046*, this shifting between minimal and maximum distance is suggested through the film's editing. Thus in one of the voyeuristic scenes when Mo-wan spies through a small crack in the panel that separates the rooms, instead of cutting to what is in the next room, we next see Mo-wan at a restaurant with Bai Ling, enjoying dinner with friends and playing cards. To look at himself, from a distance, through a small crack in the fabric of time: this is the Buddhist perspective on the whole story, both that of the monk at Angkor Wat and that of the monk who writes Bao-yu's love story on the magic stone in Cao's novel. And last but not least, Wong turns this perspective into his camera's eye, to suggest that everything we see in the companion films is what Mo-wan sees in his mind's eye as he looks back from the distance granted him by the Buddhist awakening from the illusion that life is.

With this in mind, we can now enter into the world of *2046*. As the camera pulls back from the black hole at the beginning, we see luminescent blue letters framing the void (Color Plate 9). But here something strange happens: while the camera moves slowly backward, we can barely make out the letters, not only because they're blurred and indistinct, but because the camera quickly moves away from them, using a cut to the title "2046." The title is followed by the names of the lead characters, shown slowly this time, in the rhythm of Shigeru Umebayashi's haunting music. The only way to read what's written to the right and the left of the black void/hole/wound/eye is to pause the film. And if we do this, we also read the film as well as watch it—a double perception that is suggested by Wong himself, as both the film and Mo-wan's book are called *2046*—and we are handsomely rewarded. It turns out that the blue letters inscribed on the symmetrical panes are a fragmentary citation from Nat King Cole's recording of *Quizás, quizás, quizás*—a song we'd repeatedly heard in *In the Mood for Love*. On the left wing we see: "[pe]nsando / los días," and on the right wing: "pensa[ndo]" and below it some indistinct characters, whose meaning and even language are uncertain (Color Plate 9).

Broken words that tell of thinking, meditating, contemplating—*pensando*—and of the passage of time, *los días*, framing our story and the void at its heart. Framing is a key feature of Wong's films, and this becomes particularly prominent for *2046*, where the framing is repeatedly shown on screen, whether through writing, or through red curtains, or the window-like frame of train cabins. Whenever the camera moves away from something, slowly zooming out, we see Mo-wan's attempt to arrest the passage of time, as he looks back into the black void of his love for his lost Li-zhen. Whenever the camera zooms quickly in, as in the scenes showing us the train to the mysterious destination 2046 in Mo-wan's futuristic stories, it means that he is throwing himself into the future, hoping to recapture his lost past with Li-zhen. He sees her in every woman he meets, and also tries to forget her in all sorts of relationships, mostly one-night stands, which makes him seem to be a philanderer to those who don't go beyond the surface of his story. But if we zoom slowly in, as in the last frame of *2046*, moving back toward the void, we return to the past that Mo-wan tries to recapture: the moment when he was happiest, in *In the Mood for Love*, in the magic red room 2046 when he was with Li-zhen.

Observing that *2046* opens where *In the Mood for Love* left off, Stephen Teo argues that Wong uses the black hole "as a time tunnel that sucks in travelers. He leads us into the fantasy world of science-fiction, cutting directly from the hole to a shot of a futuristic mystery train as it plunged through the hole" (*Wong Kar-wai*, 138). No doubt the hole becomes a tunnel that sucks travelers in, but it also becomes Wong's camera's eye. Dudley Andrew remarks that *In the Mood for Love*

> became a fetish film when it elaborately concealed the void at its center. The spectator does not identify with the couple whose love is continually deferred so much as with the camera which searches for marks, then for traces, of feeling ... All this, perhaps all cinema, is condensed in the epilogue at Angkor Wat, where the hero whispers his longing into a crevice, the film's (and the lovers') holy tabernacle ... Angkor Wat is like

a movie theater in which, above which, and behind which hovers deferred romance. If the camera, for all its incessant tracking, could only burrow into that crevice in the ancient wall, exposing desire once and for all! . . . Is this not the structure of nostalgia, the emotion proper to cinephilia?

What Cinema Is!, 90

But the camera *does* burrow into the crevice, and it's not desire but a secret that's meant to be exposed. It's no secret that the two have loved each other. But the fact that they had a sexual relationship is a secret kept from the viewer—and that this relationship produced a child is a secret that is likely hidden even from Mo-wan himself. The structure of nostalgia that Andrew notes is only half of the story. For the perspective from which both films are told is the Buddhist monk's. He not only faces toward the past; he also knows the future, for he has already lived the story we're reading/watching.

A void that comes into the world through a gateway inscribed with riddling words was no invention of Wong's at all, but a creative transformation of the story of the stone's entry into the world of men in Cao's novel. When the jade stone is found by the monk Vanitas, passing by on a search for immortality, he reads its long inscription (in effect, the novel itself), and finds a quatrain on the back:

Found unfit to repair the azure sky
Long years a foolish mortal man was I.
My life in both worlds on this stone is writ:
Pray who will copy out and publish it?

1:48–9

He then brings the stone, our future Bao-yu, into "The Land of Illusion"—our world—through a stone archway. A couplet is inscribed on either side of the arch:

Truth becomes fiction when the fiction's true;
Real becomes non-real when the unreal's real.

1:55

The opening of *2046* is a futuristic visual replica of the opening of Cao's *Story of the Stone*, as the luminous broken words taken from Nat King Cole's song *Quizás* from *In the Mood for Love* enter a dialogue, beyond time and space, with this Buddhist couplet that warns that the real and the unreal are disguised as each other.

In *The Story of the Stone,* Bao-yu prefers to read the Taoist teachings of Chuang Tzu instead of the Confucian writings recommended by his family.

The dream of the butterfly is perhaps the most quoted passage from *The Book of Chuang Tzu*:

> Once upon a time, I, Chuang Tzu, dreamt that I was a butterfly, flitting around and enjoying myself. I had no idea I was Chuang Tzu. Then suddenly I woke up and was Chuang Tzu again. But I could not tell, had I been Chuang Tzu dreaming I was a butterfly, or a butterfly dreaming I was now Chuang Tzu? However, there must be some sort of difference between Chuang Tzu and a butterfly. We call this the transformation of things.

20

Wong at first thought of structuring *2046* through two stories told by two mirrored writers: "I thought I'd have two writers in the film: the first, who lives in the 1960s, writes a futuristic fiction; in the future, a second writer writes a novel on the 1960s. And at the end we don't know which part is the reality and which is the fiction" (Ciment and Niogret interview, 91). Wong described the Angkor Wat scene in similar terms: "The whole thing is like a fiction, it's like a dream, but there's a certain element which is true, which is factual. . . . It is like the remains of these things and we can see all these rocks. We see there's thousands of stories like this over the years, and these form a history" (*Interviews*).

Cao's novel too is structured through a mix of fiction and reality, combining Chinese stone lore with a realistic story based on his own family and its decay from the Emperor's favor, and conveying Buddhist and Taoist teachings opposed to the officially accepted Confucian principles of his time. Modern "Redology" has usually focused on the autobiographical aspect, but recent approaches are starting to emphasize the fictional aspect and Cao's aesthetics. Anthony Yu describes the book as "a grand parable of Buddhist quest and enlightenment" (*Rereading the Stone*, 136), but he adds: "the Buddhist view of reality is but one side of *Hongloumeng*. To perceive only that affirmation is to miss a more profound aspect of Cao Xueqin's art, namely, how the author has succeeded in turning the concept of world and life as dream into a subtle but powerful theory of fiction that he uses constantly to confound his reader's sense of reality" (141).

Wong's triptych of fiction [*jia*]—dream [*meng*]—truth [*zhen*] is an epitome of Cao's novel: commonly known under the title *Hongloumeng* (*The Dream of the Red Chamber*), it mixes fiction and truth, with the two major families in the novel called Jia and Zhen. Bao-yu retraces his steps at the end of the story, as he becomes a monk and then once more a stone. Again we find an oracular couplet, mirroring the one from the beginning on the archway to the Land of Illusion. The end of the novel sees the jade stone returned to the peak in the Great Fable Mountains where it was found, and a final couplet closes the story on itself:

An otherworldly tome recounts an otherworldly tale,
As Man and Stone become once more a single whole.

The Story 5: *The Dreamer Wakes*

Cao returns to the archway with oracular couplets several times in key scenes. In chapter 5, when Bao-yu has the prophetic dream in the red room of the lustful Qin-shi he returns to his origins—the Land of Illusion framed by the real-fiction couplet where he encounters his lost love, Dai-yu, again a fairy Crimson Pearl flower as in their previous existence when he was a stone. But at the same time, he also sees (without understanding) his future story, losing Dai-yu, marrying Bao-chai, and leaving her. Closer to the ending of the novel, before becoming a monk, Bao-yu has another dream, as his soul temporarily departs from his body in a state close to death. In this dream, symmetrical to the one in chapter 5, he enters through a gate to "The Paradise of Truth, with a couplet framing its archway":

When Fiction departs and Truth appears, Truth prevails;
Though Not-real was once Real, the Real is never unreal.

The Story 5: *The Dreamer Wakes*

What has changed in Wong's *2046* is that the riddle framing the entrance into the film's world no longer reveals karma or the divine will, but it does reveal a hidden pattern in the fabric of events that only a retrospective, extratemporal view allows us to perceive. It brings us back into Wong's previous film, *In the Mood for Love*, where Nat King Cole's song was associated with Mo-wan's emotions, just as Shigeru Umebayashi's wordless waltz was associated with Li-zhen's. Mo-wan confesses his love in *In the Mood for Love*, whereas Li-zhen remains silent, even though she loves him too. He is the one who is constantly hoping, like his Japanese character in his future book *2047*, that he will regain his lost past: *quizás*, perhaps. Li-zhen is quiet and pensive, deep and haunting like Shigeru Umebayashi's waltz.

The electric blue words on the archway to the Land of Illusion in *2046* echo a pair of mirrored scenes in *In the Mood for Love*, when the two lovers meet in mirrors or in dreams, much as mirror and dream become synonyms in *Hongloumeng*, as Anthony Yu has shown. And significantly, these two scenes frame the void in the middle: the magic red chamber 2046 where time stops and where lovers meet. These scenes take place in the hotel's red-curtained corridor. In the first part of *In the Mood for Love*, we see Li-zhen, on her first visit to the hotel, leaving room 2046 after telling Mo-wan that "we won't be like them," i.e. their cheating spouses. But as she moves down the corridor that opens in front of the camera, reality freezes and she stops in her tracks. Everything is frozen, except for Shigeru Umebayashi's music that breaks in and flows into the next scene, which shows Li-zhen in room

2046 later on with Mo-wan; they are writing and laughing. The camera shows us their faces only in a mirror, never simultaneously but only successively. Because the music flows from the corridor scene into the one back in the room, Wong subtly suggests that the frame freezes to give her time to reconsider and come back. But does she really come back to the room? *Quizás*.

So too, toward the end of *In the Mood for Love*, Mo-wan is waiting in vain for Li-zhen to come back to room 2046 and go with him to Singapore. As he leaves the room, we again see the corridor from the same angle as before. Now it's Mo-wan who freezes in his tracks, as the camera slowly pulls back, and Nat King Cole's *Quizás* breaks in. Perhaps he returns to the room. Perhaps she would come back, if not now then maybe at some point in the future of *2046*, in the women he encounters: the second Li-zhen, Jing-wen, Bai Ling, Mimi/Lulu. Li-Zhen's and Mo-wan's freezing in their tracks in the hotel's red corridor is a means to turn back time and make a different choice: the world of the "perhaps," or what will be the world of the futuristic fiction he will write in *2046*.

The same effect is obtained in *2046* through the second concentric ring of the structure of the film. As we enter through the gateway to the land of illusion, we cut to a futuristic scene that will later be revealed as part of Mo-wan's book *2047*. We see him as Jing-wen's Japanese lover whispering, as Mo-wan had done at Angkor Wat, into the void, now the eye-like hole in the wall. Symmetrically, at the other end of the film, we see the android he loves, Jing-wen, whispering back, with tears in her eyes. Wong turns the void/stone/wound/eye into a bridge of dreams through which lovers communicate beyond time and space.

From Cao Xueqin to Andrei Tarkovsky

Before Wong, it was Andrei Tarkovsky who used his camera's eye in *Nostalghia* to allow Andrei, in Italy to communicate with his wife in Russia through dreams and memories. The dreamer's eye has turned into the camera's eye and the camera has become Andrei's bridge of dreams crossing time and space. Similarly, Wong not only shows the lovers in Mo-wan's novel *2046* secretly communicating through the hole or tunnel, which is both an attentive ear and a wound in their hearts; he also suggests that everything in the film is seen through Mo-wan's eye. Repeated framings show one partner of a dialogue obscuring the other through screens, openings in walls, panes through which characters spy on each other; these are visual extensions of the camera's or the writer's eye, looking onto his world (Figure 6.3a and b). They are all replicas of the framing of the hole covered with green grass at the end of *In the Mood for Love* at Angkor Wat, where the right side of the image shows the vertical carvings in the stone

FIGURE 6.3 a, b, c *Jing-wen as the android spying on her Japanese lover; Mowan spying on Bai Ling in the adjacent room, 2046; Jing-wen as the android seen through the train window, in Wong Kar-wai, 2046.*

wall. In *2046*, the hole's framing carvings become the red curtains, the walls, and screens, obscuring and revealing a presence at the same time.

The most complex construction of the camera's eye comes in a beautiful shot of the *2047* story showing Jing-wen as the android in the train that has left the magical region called 2046. Wong brings together his two tempos and double movements: the high speed of the train and the very slow motion of the android, the zoom in and zoom out of the world we see; maximum and minimum distance at the same time. The android is looking out through an oval window at a world that rushes past; this is our fleeting, irreversible time. But we are inside this train-hotel that freezes time and that shows everything, Jing-wen included, in slow motion. The oval window is framed through a second rectangular frame with round edges that looks like the train's window. But then something incredible happens: the handrail that Jing-wen sits on as she gazes at the world outside is doubled by an identical handrail, but it is outside the rectangular train window, where no one could sit. Or maybe the ghost of Mo-wan sits there, looking at his character like an author who hides himself inside the narrative. A third oval frame complicates what we see even more, and this is the largest frame we see on the screen. Mirroring the second oval frame, this third frame is revealed to be an extension of the camera's/director's eye: the oval frame is a giant eye because we can see clearly the striations of the iris on screen. And finally, an invisible rectangle frames it all: the projection screen of the film we're watching (Figure 34c).

This complicated set of four symmetrical frames recalls Cao's multiple framings of Bao-yu's and Dai-yu's love story and also Tarkovsky's visual extensions of Andrei's memory's camera eye. These framings in Mo-wan's futuristic story create the impression of two parallel trains—the first one with the android looking out through the window, the second with the invisible writer-director looking onto the world he creates and with which he falls in love—like the lovers who are forever separated though they are always together, like Li-zhen/Dai-yu and Mo-wan/Bao-yu. This complex framing cites not only Tarkovsky's *Nostalghia* but also *The Mirror*, which features an oval mirror in which Aleksei, Tarkovsky's authorial self, simultaneously sees his past and his future.

In the story *2047*, Jing-wen is an android from the future, but she is only an avatar of Li-zhen, the lost woman from Mo-wan's past who haunts the movie *2046*. This is why the train's bartender explains her through the Buddhist canon of celestial Beings who are subject to decay and mortality. In Cao's novel, the Buddhist monk and Taoist sage who bring the story into the world of men are superior beings, but they will die too, and the monk Vanitas is in search of immortality when he chances upon the story on the stone. These superior beings aren't granted immortality, but they are given long life, and they give us one of the world's longest novels, to illuminate mankind about the ephemeral condition of all things.

Like Cao's multiple projections of the shape-shifting stone throughout his novel, Wong projects the shifting oval/square framing throughout his film, in scenes that open other dimensions of what the stone-void actually is. First, the void returns in the futuristic *2047* tale when the android offers to become the wounded Japanese traveler's tree so that he can share his secret.

FIGURE 6.4 *Jing-wen as android inviting the Japanese traveler to whisper his secret in* 2046.

Bringing her thumb and index finger into a circle, she tempts our hero to whisper his secret into the hole. But her erotic gesture isn't just a reference to the hole at Angkor Wat; it is also an intertextual one to Raúl Ruiz's *Time Regained*, which had been shown in the Cannes Festival competition five years before *2046*. Ruiz recreated on screen the secret erotic gesture with which the seductive young Gilberte invites little Marcel to sexual play in the bushes at Combray (Figure 5.5): it's the very gesture that Wong's android makes, inviting Mo-wan's Japanese avatar to whisper his secret into the hole formed by her fingers (Figure 6.4).

In chapter 116 of Cao's novel, Bao-yu has a dream symmetrical to the one in Chapter 5, in which he returns to the immortal world. Now an adult, Bao-yu returns to the room that holds the manuscript of the very book we're reading. He has always sought to return, because the red chamber is where he was happiest. He sees the book we're reading in the form of the "Main Register of the Twelve Beauties"—one of multiple titles listed in chapter 1 for Cao's novel is *The Twelve Beauties of Jinling*—and he has a revelation: "I know I've been somewhere like this before. I remember it now. I was in a dream. What a blessing this is, to return to the scene of my childhood dream!" (*The Story 5: The Dreamer Wakes*). So too in Wong's *2046*, Mo-wan seeks to return to the red room 2046 where he once was happy. But in the further narrative layer of his story *2047* he does come back from *2046*, and everybody wants to know why he'd leave a place that grants one's deepest desires. A timeless space.

Behind this dimension of Wong's film lies a further doubling of classical fiction and modern film, specifically again the films of Andrei Tarkovsky. When Wong included two apparent sci-fi stories—*2046* and *2047*—in his film, he was building on two cult films by Tarkovsky: *Solaris* (1971) and *Stalker* (1979). Both films confront us with entities outside ordinary space and time: *Solaris* features a giant sentient ocean that dreams the world of the film we're seeing, and *Stalker* portrays a quest to reach a secret room in a mysterious space called the Zone, where everyone's deepest wish can supposedly be granted. Solaris's giant ocean-mirror reflects the characters' memories, bringing back people from the dead and multiplying them infinitely. The psychologist hero, Chris Kelvin, is sent on the spaceship that studies Solaris after several scientists and astronauts have mysteriously disappeared; while on the spaceship he dreams of his dead wife, Hari, and keeps trying to recover her in mannequins embodying his desire that his memory brings back from the past in his dreams. Like Mo-wan's android Jing-wen, Hari falls apart several times, but each time a new Hari is projected back by the magic mirror of Solaris. In Wong's *2046*, the magic mirror is the room 2046 that reflects back multiple images of the lost Li-zhen—the second Li-zhen, the android Jing-wen, Mimi/Lulu, and Bai Ling—but they all fall apart, and none survives.

Like Wong's *2046*, Tarkovsky's *Stalker* grows organically from his previous films but also develops in a religious direction. This direction is Buddhist for Wong and Christian for Tarkovsky, but Wong's reading of *Stalker* finds points of intersection between the two takes on reality. Tarkovsky's *Stalker* is a minimalist, almost allegorical story—a dimension emphasized through the common nouns used as proper names for the characters: the Stalker, the Professor, and the Writer. The Stalker is guiding his two companions into the Zone, a space guarded by police and sealed off from the common world because it has been the site of some disaster, possibly a nuclear accident or a toxic chemical event or some otherworldly visitation. According to the Stalker, the Zone contains a room in a ruined house that grants the deepest wish of whoever enters it.

The Stalker insists that the Zone doesn't allow anyone to go directly to the house, and the bulk of the movie consists of the three men's tortuous struggle through the Zone's post-apocalyptic landscape until they finally reach their goal. The Zone features the same relativity of space and time that structures Mo-wan's story *2047*: some take longer to arrive to 2046, and no one returns, except for Mo-wan's Japanese hero, his authorial mask. In Tarkovsky's film, it's the Stalker who returns from the Zone to bring people to the place where their secret wishes are granted. Tarkovsky constructs his Stalker as a Jesus-like, but also Judas-like figure with a bandaged neck as if he tried to hang himself, trying to bring mankind to faith. In Wong's *2046*, the only one who returns from 2046 is Mo-wan himself, in a vain attempt to run away from pain and to recover happiness at some point in the future.

Significantly, in *Stalker* the entrance into the promised but perhaps illusory paradise looks like the entrance into a black void. The Stalker leads his clients through a hellish landscape—shades of Bosch or of Dante's Inferno—culminating in a long, winding tunnel that leads to an Edenic landscape of woods and grass. There stands the ruined house with a hollow black entrance. When the men finally enter the paradise of the promised land, all they see is emptiness, ruin, and decay. Or at least this is what is found by those who cannot *see*. Like the Buddhist monk who takes Bao-yu beyond the gateway to the Land of Illusion, Tarkovsky's Stalker tells the professor and the writer when they're in the room: "Your innermost wishes will be made real here. Your most sincere wish! Born of suffering! ... No need to say anything. You just have to concentrate and try to recall your whole life. When a man thinks of the past, he becomes kinder. But most important: you have to believe!" In a corner of the room, Tarkovsky's camera eye catches a strange sight: a very slow zoom-in closeup, of the kind Wong will develop at length in *2046*, shows us the shadowy mummies of two lovers, frozen forever in an eternal embrace. Their skeletal bodies seem to melt into the ruined room, bearing the traces of time's decay and human suffering. Ashes to ashes, dust to dust. But in a ray of light we see love's magic: from the bodies of the embraced lovers, a green plant is growing, just below a hole in what is either a stone or a petrified tree trunk (Color Plate 10).

We have here another secret path that leads from Tarkovsky's universe into Wong's. The magic room in the Zone finds its replica in the final image from *In the Mood for Love*, which shows the strange entrance into the chapel at Angkor Wat; we will enter there together with Mo-wan, when he returns to 2046 in the next film. Tarkovsky's superb metaphor of love's transformation, beyond death, into a new life—the young plant growing from the lovers' bodies—is behind Wong's closeup, also filmed in a very slow zoom-in closeup, of the hole in the temple wall from which green grass grows. Ultimately, Wong's image looks back both to Tarkovsky's *Stalker* and also to Cao's novel, in which Bao-yu and Dai-yu loved each other in a previous existence when he was just a stone and she was just a flower. As Anthony Yu has remarked, "The excellence of *Hongloumeng* is thus to be found in its masterful translation of the mythic and religious into the realistic, so that this particular instance of sympathy between a plant and a stone is told in the most unforgettable human terms" (*Rereading the Stone*, 136). The same can be said of Tarkovsky's *Stalker* and Wong's pair of films.

Drawing equally on a Chinese novel and a Russian filmmaker, Wong is also finding common ground between two apparently opposed religious views, Buddhism and Christianity. As developed by Wong, both religions argue for leaving behind the suffering caused by our passions in favor of a form of awakening, a cleansing, a healing distancing from these passions. "Let everything that's been planned come true. Let them believe. And let them have a laugh at their passions," says Stalker. "Because what they call passion actually is not some emotional energy, but just the friction between their souls and the outside world." This last sentence could equally have been said by Cao's Bao-yu turned a Buddhist monk at the end of his earthly travails.

From the Zone to the Hotel-train

More than a gateway to the void, in *2046* the black hole becomes a tunnel and a train to the time-space destination 2046. The train that appears in Mo-wan's stories *2046* and *2047* is a transformation of the magic corridor from *In the Mood for Love* where we alternately see Mo-wan and Li-zhen freezing in their tracks and returning to the red room. This secret corridor lit by a red light takes us to Wong's hidden sources: Cao's novel and Tarkovsky's *Stalker*. In the red chamber in chapter five of *The Story of the Stone*, Bao-yu sees the records of both the past and the future, arranged in neatly stacked chronological volumes for each province. He only looks into the one where he is from—*The Twelve Beauties from Jinling*—but as with Wong's hotel as a spatialization of time itself, we know that there is also a room 2045, and also a room 2048. There is a past before Mo-wan's past and there is a future after his futuristic stories.

Wong's entire film is structured like a train that travels in time. The train is echoed in the corridor of the Orient Hotel, and in the repeated framing of some of the most important women in *2046*, through the hotel's rooftop sign, as when Bai Ling smokes pensively (Figure 6.5). Showing them next to the empty shape of the red "O" in "Orient Hotel," Wong signals one of the multiple transformations of the black void or the tunnel in time, the train that takes us back to the place where we've been happiest. By emphasizing the red "O," Wong alludes both to the red corridor in the magic hotel from *In the Mood for Love* but also to the cylindrical spaceship corridor in *Solaris* and the long tunnel in *Stalker* that takes us to our heart's most secret desire. In *Solaris*, the spaceship's corridor, constructed in a series of red O-shaped arches, becomes a tunnel that sucks Chris Kelvin back into the past when his wife Hari was alive, and brings her back to him.

FIGURE 6.5 *Bai Ling on the rooftop of the Orient Hotel, in Wong Kar-wai's 2046.*

Wong's Orient Hotel is also a nod to Agatha Christie's *Murder on the Orient Express* (1934), turned into a major film in 1974 by Sidney Lumet. In the novel and film, someone murders an American businessman on this train running from Istanbul to Paris, and Hercule Poirot has to investigate the murdered man's fellow passengers in the first-class compartment, several of whom try to deflect suspicion from themselves by mentioning a mysterious woman wearing a red kimono. Wong opens *2046* with the murder of Mimi/Lulu, a passenger who inhabits room 2046 in the Orient Hotel and who is stabbed by a jealous boyfriend. In *Murder on the Orient Express*, Poirot discovers that all the passengers in the compartment had joined together and stabbed the businessman, to avenge the death of three-year-old Daisy Armstrong, whom he had kidnapped and then killed. Wong uses this literary-cinematic past in his trainlike hotel to configure his own narrative of death and desire. He keeps the red kimono of the ghostly presence in the Orient Express in the red dresses worn by the women in *2046*: Mimi/Lulu is wearing red in Mo-wan's story *2046* and so is Li-zhen when she appears briefly as an android in room 2046 in a red latex dress. The mysterious woman in a red kimono who doesn't actually exist on the Orient Express is brought to the fore by Wong and turned into the ghost of the beloved Li-zhen.

Mo-wan exits the film through the same gateway he entered by, slowly returning to the black void of his wound, but also to the space of happy memories. A final conversation with Bai Ling marks his awakening. "Why can't it be like it was before?" she asks sadly, in a final attempt to resume their relationship. On a black screen, in white characters, we read: "He didn't turn back. It was as if he'd boarded a very long train heading for a drowsy future through the unfathomable night." When the image returns, we see Mo-wan alone in a cab that we've seen before, first in *In the Mood for Love*, and now again in *2046*. This cab had appeared in the earlier film in two scenes, repeated with a difference: in the first scene, Mo-Wan and Li-zhen are pretending to enact their spouses' affair, but the second time they actually live it. After they've rehearsed breaking up on the street, we see them again in a cab, from behind, and we see her gently resting her head on his shoulder: "I don't want to go home tonight," she says, and we know they will go to their secret room 2046. In *2046*, the same set of double scenes appears, but in the black and white of memory, and at first it is Bai Ling sitting next to Mo-wan, not Li-zhen. But in the doubled scene Mo-wan is alone in the cab, resting his head on the shoulder of Li-zhen's ghost, as his voiceover breaks in: "Everyone goes to 2046 with the same intention. They want to recapture lost memories. Because in 2046, nothing ever changes."

To *see* time means to rise above the three-dimensional structure of past, present, and future. This was Raúl Ruiz's dream for the cinema of the future, able to show this vision simultaneously rather than tell it successively. Sharing this goal with Ruiz, Wong could find a similar approach to the problem of time and being in Cao's novel. "*The Dream* eventually reorganizes the temporal-spatial paradigm. . . . By suppressing the progressive concept of time, it foregrounds a profoundly spatial view of existence" (Wang, *The Story of Stone*, 188).

In the end, showing this vision of time is a question of showing the memory of a place. This is a very Proustian notion, as Ruiz tells us in the interview that concluded with his expressed intention to watch Wong's films, recommended to him as akin to Proust's temporal construction: "In the system of classical memory, we need a palace of memory, a familiar place, like your house, Paris, it doesn't matter, and an arbitrary image in that place. We imagine a journey that's always the same, which allows us to read in all directions, straight ahead, backwards, only selections" (Bouquet and Burdeau interview, 53). To read backwards and forwards is to be outside time, to look at it from a distance, like Proust's telescope and microscope at the same time. It's appropriate that David Hawkes introduced Cao to the Western world as the Proust of China. Like Cao before him, and Ruiz and Wong after him, Proust believed that "our memory presents things to us, as a rule, not in their chronological sequence but as it were by a reflection in which the order of the parts is reversed" (*Within a Budding Grove*, 208).

The Dream of Chamber 2046

The color red that brings together all the feminine characters in *2046* has a complex meaning. "In old China," David Hawkes has observed in his Introduction, "storeyed buildings with red-plastered outer walls—this is the literal meaning of '*hong lou*'—were a sign of opulence and grandeur . . . But '*hong lou*' early acquired another, more specialized meaning. It came to be used specifically of the dwellings of rich men's daughters, or, by extension, of the daughters themselves" (1:19–20). The red that embellishes almost every scene in *2046* is a sign of opulence and grandeur, even though these women aren't at all the daughters of rich men. These flower-women—their sumptuous cheongsams often have flowery patterns—will come to life in *2046* when Mo-wan brings to this room all the women with whom he has some sort of relationship. Almost every shot in the Orient Hotel has a subtle frame: a red curtain, separating the space and the interlocutors, sometimes occupying half of the screen, otherwise discreetly marking a thin frame to the left or right side of the image.

In a scene from Mo-wan's story *2046*, we see his Japanese self looking down from a crack in the ceiling of room 2046 to see Mimi/Lulu making love with the boyfriend who will later stab her. A closeup of the voyeur's eye shows a tear slowly forming and dropping down through the crack. But here Wong creates a subtle and moving effect by showing a quick shot of the red-hued tear falling through the black void, like a comet traversing the night sky. If "all memories are traces of tears," Wong has subtly materialized on screen the oracular quatrain that frames Bao-yu's story:

Pages full of idle words
Penned with hot and bitter tears:
All men call the author fool;
None his secret message hears.

Wong's two temporalities in *2046*, the chronological one and the timeless retrospective one, have a precedent in Cao's novel. As David Hawkes remarks, "A Dream of Red Mansions" can mean both a vision of beautiful women living in luxury *and* a dream of vanquished splendor, and Cao's reason for writing creates a precedent for Mo-wan. He wrote to his brother: "Having made an utter failure of my life, I found myself one day, in the midst of my poverty and wretchedness, thinking about the female companions of my youth. . . . Then and there I resolved to make a record of all the recollections of those days I could muster—those golden days when I dressed in silk and ate delicately" ("Introduction," 20).

Initially, Cao intended to compose a drama rather than a novel (Hawkes, "Introduction," 43). It's significant that the "Twelve Young Ladies of Jinling" is performed as a play during chapter 5 when thirteen-year-old Bao-yu has his dream, epitomizing the entire story to follow. Seeking to rest, he has come into the red room of Qin-shi, who's involved with her father-in-law. Her room is decorated with paintings and objects that had belonged to famous courtesans. "'I like it here,' said Bao-yu happily. 'My room,' said Qin-shi with a proud smile, 'is fit for an immortal to sleep in'" (1:127). As he falls asleep, he returns to the paradise of his previous life, when he was a Stone in Waiting, in love with Crimson Pearl Flower, the future Dai-yu: "Bao-yu's dreaming self rejoiced. 'What a delightful place!' he thought. If only I could spend all my life here'" (1:108). Like Mo-wan at the end of *2046*, boarding the train of thought to the one place where he'd been happy, Bao-yu will return to this very place in a symmetrical dream he has later, before deciding to leave his wife Bao-chai and become a monk: "I *know* I've been somewhere like this before. I remember it now. It was in a dream. What a blessing this is, to return to the scene of my childhood dream!" (*The Story 5: The Dreamer Wakes*).

As he returns in chapter 5 to the Land of Illusion from chapter 1, Bao-yu sees the inscription on the gate about reality and fiction, and then a second one about "love's debts" that are "hard to pay," but he doesn't know what to make of it. Wong puts us in the same position in the opening of *2046*, when he cuts so quickly from the blurred letters of the half-written words flanking the black void that we can't avoid being uncomprehending like Bao-yu, unless we replay the film and return to the opening scene. Even then we need to stop the time of the film (online or on DVD) so as to read and make sense of the fleeting words, blurred as if literally written in tears.

Contemplating the second inscription he sees in his dream, "I see," said Bao-yu to himself. "I wonder what the meaning of 'passion that outlasts all time' can be. And what are love's debts?" (1:130–1). So too at the beginning of *2046*, we can't know the meaning of the blue letters framing the black void unless we've watched *In the Mood for Love*—unless we know of Bao-yu/Mo-wan's previous existence—and unless we remember Nat King Cole's song *Quizás*, unless we know Spanish, unless we identify the origin of the quote. So many contingencies that Wong asks us to overcome in order to decipher the secret of the complex story in *2046*.

Mo-wan's renewed connection to his past occurs one night in Hong Kong when he takes a drunken Mimi/Lulu back to the hotel where she lives. As he leaves the room, he sees the number on her door: 2046. A mere room number gets Mo-wan to move into the hotel, opening onto a past he thought he'd left behind, a memorial of all the women he'd met in his life and who remind him of his lost lover, Li-zhen. She is the very soul of the room and of Wong's film. The way Wong invests this magic room with a soul that returns in different guises is reminiscent of Proust, who speaks of spaces that become places of memory and the ghost of those whom we have lost: "We construct our house of life to suit another person, and when at length it is ready to receive her that person does not come; presently she is dead to us, and we live on, prisoners within the walls which were intended only for her" (*Within a Budding Grove*, 287). Mo-wan is indeed a prisoner of 2046, the space he has built and rebuilt in his literary world, waiting for Li-zhen to return.

The Book of Tears

The shifting cast of women in Mo-wan's life can be compared to those in Cao's novel. Among the twelve women of whom Bao-yu dreams prophetically in chapter 5, three stand out as playing major roles in his life: Dai-yu, the only woman he really loves, but whom he's not allowed to marry; Bao-chai, Dai-yu's mirror image and opposite—down to earth and practical—whom Bao-yu doesn't love but is nonetheless connected to, and whom he marries to obey his family; and Qin-shi, the lustful woman involved in an adulterous relationship with her father-in-law. In the dream world Bao-yu enters, she marries him under the name Ke-qing, which means "two-in-one" because she is Dai-yu and Bao-chai put together. Ke-qing and Bao-yu make love in the dream, but next day, as they walk through the Land of Illusion, they reach a place "where only thorn-trees grew and wolves and tigers prowled around in pairs" (1:147). This is the Ford of Error, and suddenly "there was a rumbling like thunder from inside the abyss and a multitude of demons and water monsters reached up and clutched at Bao-yu to drag him down into its depths" (1:147). But as Bao-yu wakes up calling out "Ke-qing! Save me!" (1;147), he finds his maid Aroma next to him. Qin-shi, in whose red room he had the prophetic dream, is startled to hear Bao-yu calling out her real name: "'Ke-qing' was the name they called me at home when I was a little girl. Nobody here knows it. I wonder how he could have found it out?" (148).

As the red room 2046 will overlap and mix up the figures of the women Mo-wan encounters there, so does Bao-yu's dream. Dai-yu and Bao-chai, the two women closest to Bao-yu, don't appear as themselves in his dream, but they do exist secretly nested in his own name. It is made up of one syllable of each of their names in a chiastic fashion: "Bao-yu" means *precious jade*, the first syllable taken from Bao-chai (*precious hairpin*), the second from Dai-yu (*jade belt*). Together, they become his "two-in-one," manifested in the dream of the red chamber as Ke-qing, the childhood self of the room's current occupant, Qin-shi. But the mixing up of women's identities doesn't end here: Ke-qing transforms herself from the dreamworld into the first woman he sees on waking, his chief maid Aroma, who initiates him sexually just after he wakes up from this dream.

The three major feminine presences in chapter 5 are signaled through symbolic signs coming from their names: the jade and the greenwood (*lin*) are always a sign of Bao-yu and Dai-yu, whereas the gold and snow (*xue*) point to Xue Bao-chai. The color red signals all three. Each woman has both her sign and her song. The prologue to the twelve songs belongs to Cao's authorial mask, as what we're about to hear are several love stories in which Bao-yu is involved, even though only one is the real one: "And so perform / This *Dream of Golden Days*, / And all my grief for my lost loves disclose" (1:140). The first two songs seem to concern the love triangle Bao-yu—Dai-yu—Bao-chai, but in fact they both speak of the sad love story between the jade and the crimson pearl flower, whose destinies are inextricably tied with that of Bao-chai, who is Bao-yu's destined wife and Dai-yu's mirrored double. Like a ghost, Dai-yu vanishes the minute Bao-yu marries Bao-chai. She dies of a broken heart, but with her debt of tears repaid.

Wong's creative transformation of Cao's chiastic ring structure, together with the *mise en abyme* of the entire novel through a play with dancing and singing, gives the architecture of *2046* and the complex relationships between the characters. Whereas Cao contemplated writing his story as a drama, Wong initially intended to structure *2046* through the music of three operas. As he remarked at Cannes in 2001, "we wanted to make it as an opera because in opera there's always the structure, a stage work, act one, act two. And the theme of opera, most of the time, is promise and betrayal" (Brunette interview [2001], 132). He added further details in 2004: "The original story of *2046* was not as complicated as the final cut of the film. I wanted to use the number 2046 to tell three stories—each with an opera music theme. They are *Norma*, *Tosca*, and *Madama Butterfly*. . . . During the film development, only *Norma* remains. The reason is that the story of this opera is quite similar to the plot involving Faye Wang" (*Interviews*).

Even though Wong renounced the idea of using three operas, he did associate each woman with a song or musical theme. Thus, Shigeru Umebayashi's waltz remains the expression of the lost beloved Li-zhen, as this music breaks in when the frame freezes on the red-curtained corridor in *In the Mood for Love*. Composed for a couple's dance, the wordless waltz translates the love between Li-zhen and Mo-wan, while also reflecting the woman it stands for: Li-zhen doesn't express herself as much through words as through the way she looks at Mo-wan, her gestures, even her cheongsams. Wong asked Shigeru Umebayashi to echo the same musical theme for the principal women in Mo-wan's life in *2046*. It's as if Li-zhen from *In the Mood for Love* has decomposed into signs that partially materialize in the second Li-zhen, Jing-wen, Bai Ling, and Mimi/Lulu.

Umebayashi's music connects these women in *2046* but also differentiates between them; they sometimes receive their own music. Jing-wen is associated with Bellini's aria "Casta Diva," from the first act of *Norma*. "Casta Diva" is sung by the Druid priestess Norma, who falls in love with the proconsul Pollione during the Roman conquest of Gaul. Her love is forbidden because he is the enemy, and though she bears him two children, he leaves her for the younger priestess Analgisa. "Casta Diva" (chaste goddess) is Norma's prayer to the Moon to bring peace on earth, while she hopes to regain her lover's affection. It is played in *2046* while we watch Jing-wen pensively smoking and thinking of her Japanese lover; she remains cold and chaste to Mo-wan's half-expressed affection, because she wants her lover, whom she marries in the end.

The beautiful Bai-Ling is associated with the Cuban songwriter Ernesto Lecuona's *Siboney*, sung by Connie Francis, about a woman pining for her lover: "Ven a mi que te quiero y que todo tesoro eres tu para mi." Bai-Ling lives for a while in room 2046 where Mimi/Lulu was murdered; she is a ghost both of Mimi/Lulu, but also of Ke qing, Bao yu's dream bride. Though Mo-wan wants to emphasize her courtesan-like behavior—he insists on paying her for having sex with him to keep her at a distance—she resembles Li-zhen as much as Ke-qing, as she genuinely loves him. She is also very fragile, like Jing-wen, and like Mimi has bad relationships with treacherous men.

Almost as absent as Li-zhen is the second Li-zhen in *2046*, whose two apparitions form the third concentric ring structure of the film. Her presence is associated with the "Long Journey" part of the music composed by Shigeru Umebayashi, music just as haunting as the waltz associated with the real Li-zhen from *In the Mood for Love*. The second Li-zhen is a gambler whom Mo-wan meets in Singapore. Of all the women in 2046, it is she who most resembles Li-zhen, in appearance and in her elegant yet erotic walk. Wong makes this point when filming her second apparition toward the end of *2046*, from the same angle and in slow motion as he had used to film the original Li-zhen (Maggie Cheung) in *In the Mood for Love*.

But alas, Mo-wan was only happy when he was together with Li-zhen in the room 2046 in *In the Mood for Love*. Like Bao-yu before him, he didn't know how to stay in that dreamed fairyland, and he strayed into the cursed place that Cao calls the "Ford of Error" and couldn't find the way back to the room where, as in Tarkovsky's *Stalker*, all wishes are granted. "The Zone is a very complicated system of traps and they're deadly," the Stalker warns his clients. "It lets pass all those who have lost hope. Not good or bad but wretched people." The Professor wants to know: "Why did they come here? What did they want?" "Happiness, I guess." "Yes, but what kind of happiness?" insists the Professor. "People don't like to speak about their innermost feelings" replies the Stalker. "They return from the room, and I lead them back, and we never see each other again."

Indeed, the people who come to 2046 don't like to speak about their innermost feelings. As in Cao's novel, in *2046* people express themselves above all through tears. In Stephen Teo's view, the actresses' ability to shed "tears beautifully at key moments to reinforce the notion of delayed emotion" is "the single most wondrous achievement of Wong Kar-wai's direction of *2046*" (*Wong Kar-wai*, 144). In Cao's novel, tears similarly become ghostly signs of Dai-yu, whose presence is manifested through the tea and wine Bao-yu is served in the dream in Chapter 5.

Near the end of *In the Mood for Love,* we see Li-zhen alone in room 2046 waiting for Mo-wan in the hope of leaving with him to Singapore. She is sitting quietly next to the triple mirror where we previously saw them together happily writing their novels. The camera is still for a while and no sound is heard. A tear slowly runs down her face, expressing all the love and hope that are now lost, as they've missed their moment again. This scene is multiplied through all the women Mo-wan interacts with in *2046*. The second Li-zhen cries desperately when Mo-wan leaves after kissing her passionately; one of the most moving slow-motion scenes in the train shows a closeup of the android Jing-wen, as a tear slowly forms in her eye for what seems an eternity; and one evening at dinner, when Bai Ling's lover has abandoned her after promising to take her to Singapore, she asks Mo-wan to tell her about the city; slowly, a tear runs down her cheek as she meditates on her wretched fate.

Meditating on women in their prime, "à l'ombre des jeunes filles en fleurs," Proust was the first to construct a hotel—the Balbec Hotel—as a location that brings some of these women together across time. But Marcel knows, like Mo-wan after him, that they are only ghosts of the one lover: "Our intuitive radiography pierces them, and the images which it brings back, far from being those of a particular face, present rather the joyless universality of a skeleton" (*Within a Budding Grove*, 648). For the book of our memory, as he later remarks of his novel itself, is an immense cemetery on whose tombstones the letters are almost completely effaced, as are the blue panes in *2046* written in broken words, half effaced by the traces of tears. *The Story of the Stone* is a book of tears, too, and closes with a quatrain that mirrors Cao's opening quatrain that spoke of a book written "in hot and bitter tears," hiding a "secret message," as well as the couplet about the reversals between reality and fiction. A later reader of the manuscript added a quatrain to expand a little on the author's original envoi:

When grief for fiction's idle words
More real than human life appears,
Reflect that life itself's a dream
And do not mock the reader's tears.

The Story 5: The Dreamer Wakes

This in a nutshell is the story of *In the Mood for Love* and *2046*, a two-in-one film and a mirror for Cao's Ke-qing, "Two-in-one," the woman encountered in the land of dreams made of the two women who are one: Dai-yu and Bao-chai. In Wong's films, these will be the two Su Li-zhens. Mo-wan himself is apparently very different from one film to another–kind, loving, and devoted in *In the Mood*, but a philanderer in *2046*—but he too has a precedent in Cao's *Story of the Stone*. For there were two Bao-yus: our character in the story, Jia ("fictional, unreal") Bao-yu, and a second one belonging to the other family in the novel, Zhen ("true") Bao-yu, whose story we do not know. As we're shown on the gateway to the Land of Illusion, "Truth becomes fiction when the fiction's true; / Real becomes non-real when the unreal's real."

In *2046*, we see the story of the unreal Mo-wan, the philanderer and the womanizer, seeking not only his lost love but his lost past self from *In the Mood for Love*. In *The Story of the Stone* it is only in a dream that the fictional Bao-yu encounters his "true" self. As he tries to get hold of his other self, he wakes up:

"Come back, Bao-yu! Come back, Bao-yu!" Aroma heard him calling his own name in his sleep and shook him awake. "Where's Bao-yu?" she asked him jokingly.

Though awake, Bao-yu had not yet regained consciousness of his surroundings. He pointed to the doorway: "He's only just left. He can't have got very far." "You're still dreaming," Aroma said, amused. "Rub your eyes and have another look. That's the mirror. You're looking at your own reflection in the mirror." Bao-yu leaned forward and looked. The doorway he had pointed to was his dressing-mirror.

The Story 3: The Warning Voice

As Anthony Yu concludes, "The epic peregrination of the narrative . . . asserts the paradox that only time can proffer to us a sense of the brevity and insubstantiality of our world. In this way *Hongloumeng* participates in certain elemental traits of dream literature from China and elsewhere" (*Rereading the Stone*, 138). Asked about his poetics of repetition, Wong replied: "I want to show the changes through not having changes" (*Interviews*). Or as Proust wrote decades earlier:

> a certain similarity exists, although the type evolves, between all the women we successively love, a similarity that is due to the fixity of our own temperament, which chooses them, eliminating all those who would not be at once our opposite and our complement, apt, that is to say to gratify our senses and to wring our hearts. They are, these women, a product of our temperament, an image, an inverted projection, a negative of our sensibility. So that a novelist might, in relating the life of his hero, describe his successive love-affairs in almost exactly similar terms, and thereby give the impression not that he was repeating himself but that he was creating, since an artificial novelty is never so effective as a repetition that manages to suggest a fresh truth.
>
> *Within a Budding Grove, 647–8*

7

Let This Novel Begin

Sorrentino and Proust

. . . for everything must return in time, says Proust, the phrase that serves as the epigraph to this book. I opened my account with Martin Scorsese's *Hugo*, both a tribute to Georges Méliès as a protosurrealist filmmaker and a revolutionary reading of Proust's cinematic imagination. I now close with a follower of Scorsese and of Proust: Paolo Sorrentino, who is both a writer and a filmmaker. In the two years before he released his Academy Award-winning *La Grande Bellezza*, he published a novel, *Everybody's Right* (*Hanno tutti ragione*, 2011) and a collection of short stories, *Tony Pagoda and His Friends* (*Toni Pagoda e i suoi amici*, 2012). Too often seen largely or even exclusively through the lens of Italian cinema, this highly literary artist is deeply engaged with French literature, and with European and American film. When he accepted the Oscar for *La Grande Bellezza* as the best foreign film of 2013, Sorrentino credited the inspiration of the rock band Talking Heads, the Argentinian football player Maradona, and two filmmakers: Federico Fellini and Martin Scorsese.

Film critics have regularly compared him to Fellini, but his films are closer to Scorsese's epic themes, technique, and style. From *One Man Up* (2001), to *The Consequences of Love* (2004), *The Family Friend* (2006), *Il Divo* (2008), and *This Must Be the Place* (2011), to *The Great Beauty* (*La Grande Bellezza*, 2013), *Youth* (2015) and *Loro* (2018), as well as the television series *The Young Pope* (2016) and *The New Pope* (2019), Sorrentino has dealt with problems of power, politics, and faith, and with the passage of time, aging, and death. Most of his films are set in Italy, but they draw on a range of European and American sources, and they speak to a world audience through problems that are common to human beings regardless of their nationality, language, culture, or race.

La Grande Bellezza tells the story of Jep Gambardella, who lives in Rome and works as a journalist for a cultural magazine. Jep is the "re dei mondani," the king of socialites, and leads a frenetic nightlife in a decadent Roman society that includes all sorts of artists and intellectuals, priests and nuns, businessmen, mafiosi, and TV stars. Once a promising author of an acclaimed novel called *L'Apparato umano* (*The Human Apparatus*), Jep hasn't managed to write any fiction in forty years since then. On the morning following a party for his sixty-fifth birthday, he receives a visit from a man he's never seen before: the husband of Elisa De Santis, Jep's first and only love when he was eighteen years old. Her husband has come to tell him that Elisa has died, leaving a diary in which she confessed that Jep was the only man she ever loved. Thus begins Jep's inner journey, prefaced with the opening words of Louis-Ferdinand Céline's novel *Journey to the End of the Night*, which we see on screen at the beginning of the film in Italian. In the French original, they read: "*Voyager, c'est bien utile, ça fait travailler l'imagination . . .*". The journey of Jep's imagination will be not so much through Rome as through his own past. Gradually, Jep recaptures the lost memory of his love story, following a series of scenes involving aging, the passage of time, and the death of people younger than himself. As the film ends, an involuntary memory of the start of his love affair with Elisa finally breaks in, and Jep exits the screen as we hear his voiceover saying "Let this novel begin."

But why would Paolo Sorrentino decide to make a film about a writer who hasn't published anything serious in many years? A writer who contents himself with journalism, who wastes his time observing the strangeness of human nature from an ironic yet intimately engaged distance during dinner parties and long, solitary walks at night through the city. A writer who dreams of writing a novel, yet never gets around to it. A writer who only wants to make time return and be young again. Before becoming Jep Gambardella in Rome, this writer lived in Paris. His name was Marcel Proust.

*

To delve into *La Grande Bellezza*'s creative reinvention of Proust's *Recherche*, we need to look into the role played by writing in Sorrentino's life and its relation to his conception of cinema. His first obsession, carried over into film, has always been writing: "I was studying economy and commerce, but I had a mania for writing. I wrote everything: short stories, poetry. It was a real obsession. The minute I finished studying for an exam I started writing. Cinema I actually discovered around 18 or 19 and since then I started working on it systematically. So I thought it could be interesting to bring my writing to the cinema" (Zonta interview, 212). Like his model Martin Scorsese, Sorrentino comes from a family that didn't have many books: "My father worked in a bank and my mother was a housewife. I come from a house with no books. There were only a dozen bestsellers" (220). All the more reason to become an avid reader, and then a writer. As he told an interviewer for *La Stampa*,

> I am more a writer than a filmmaker, in my twenties I only wrote scripts. I like cinema, it's wonderful work, but when I have time I also write

books. The book allows me an unbridled freedom. Everything I see unfolding is on the page. Whereas when you work for cinema you know that what you write will depend on other realities and other people. Writing for the screen poses many barriers and obstacles. The novel ends when the publisher publishes it, the script is only the first step.

ELKANN interview

Asked if he'd like "to also become a great novelist," the ironic Sorrentino replied: "I haven't yet become a great filmmaker, I feel that I've only begun learning the craft. Others are great filmmakers: Fellini, Scorsese, Bergman. But I'm young, and I'm happy because I think I've yet to make my major film. This is a condition that stimulates me for the future."

Another interviewer remarked that in *La Grande Bellezza*, "One of your characters makes us laugh by saying 'I love Proust and Ammaniti.' Jep's life comes out of [Niccolò] Ammaniti's novels, whereas the film moves toward Proust. Are you unsure whether you're a writer or a filmmaker?" Sorrentino replied: "My film owes a lot to my passion for literature, its influence, its digressions, the reflections it allows for. I'm also citing Flaubert, another writer with whom we could compare Jep—of course, much greater than him" (Codelli interview, 30). Asked by Adrian Wootton what he most likes in film production, Sorrentino replies with words that could be very well Jep's, as well as Proust's: "Ah, writing is the most beautiful moment. It's when I'm completely alone and I can allow myself a sort of liberty, even a physical one. I don't have to account for this to anyone, I'm home alone, I can fantasize about being omnipotent without anyone around to judge me. I can do anything" (Wootton interview).

Asked about his artistic models, Sorrentino says that "wanting to become a filmmaker in Italy, I did learn from Fellini's films" (Codelli interview, 30), but he puts greater emphasis on American film. As he told another interviewer, "American cinema fascinates me and influences me a lot." Beyond technique and the *mise en scène*, he admires American cinema's epic themes such as the decadence of a people, a theme that film critics usually connect only to Fellini's *Rome* and *La dolce vita*.[1] "So," the interviewer asks, "we can say that your films ... aren't consciously heirs of Italian cinema?" "Totally. From the point of view of the choice of themes and the directing I'm very close to the US" (Zonta interview, 215). Asked for the hundredth time if *La Grande Bellezza* is a reworking of *La dolce vita*, Sorrentino smiled ironically: "I prefer to leave Fellini in his empire. I am very far down as compared to him" (DP/30 interview).

---

[1]For Anton Giulio Mancino, any metafilm about Rome can only be Fellinian: in Sorrentino's film, we see "a Rome openly metacinematic, hence Fellinian" ("Roma," 7). "Each sequence establishes a Roman route, once again in Fellini's manner from *Roma*," writes Bernard Nave ("La grande bellezza," 353).

While it's American cinema that Sorrentino feels most influences his films, when it comes to writing, he speaks of Europe: "But when I write, I am heavily influenced by European literary references. For instance, while I liberated myself from Wenders, I'm not really liberated from some of the writers I loved in my youth, like Sartre's *The Wall*, or Camus and Céline. . . . Therefore, when I write, my literary references, especially French, abound" (Zonta interview). Sorrentino says that making a film is a process of research: "When I was young, before I discovered the cinema, if I was asked what I wanted to do when I grew up, I used to say: university professor or researcher. And this has stayed because before making a film, I first analyze and research the theme like a researcher, in order to satisfy my curiosity. I say to myself: how wonderful that now I can set myself to study . . . That's my greatest curiosity: a world that I can study and discover" (Zonta interview, 219). As with many of the filmmakers included in this book, for Sorrentino filmmaking means first of all the freedom to bring literary ideas to screen, conjugated with the power of painting and music.

Music is always organically woven into the fabric of Sorrentino's films. Like Stephen Daldry, Sorrentino uses musical concepts to discuss his work as a filmmaker: "A director is like a drummer, he's responsible for the rhythm" (Wootton interview). "We can create using music" ("Come funziono," TEDx talk). "I always choose the music beforehand, because I then shoot some sequences based on the music I have already chosen" (Crowdus interview, 13). For Sorrentino, music turns the disharmony of life into harmony. In *La Grande Bellezza*, the common denominator of the several contemporary composers selected by Sorrentino—David Lang, Arvo Pärt, Vladimir Martynov, Zbigniew Preisner, and John Tavener—is a commitment to minimalist composition that goes back to liturgical music and Gregorian chant, giving Jep's inner journey a religious sense. As Sorrentino told another interviewer,

Arvo Pärt discovered the force of his sacred minimalist music when he heard in a shop a Gregorian chant without harmony, meter, timbre or orchestration, basically without anything. I see the life of those around me exactly like this: without harmony, timbre and orchestration. Cinema can bring all this back. It can orchestrate a biography. It can give it a timbre and meter. It can find hidden threads between the interstices that bring to light the beauty of our disharmony. In this sense, *La Grande Bellezza* isn't a *j'accuse*, as some believe. It's the very opposite: it's a tender recognition of the enchantment that lies buried under the emptiness, the disharmony and the vulgarity of certain characters that live in Rome and in Italy.

MEREGHETTI interview

Along with music, poetry is defining for Sorrentino's cinema, as it was for Tarkovsky before him: "If I feel alone and abandoned, I start to function, I start to accumulate material. And then I do the hardest thing in this work: I start making rhymes. I don't know how to explain what are rhymes in cinema, but I think it's to combine, to juxtapose things. Here it helps to know what kind of game you can play, all the things that a game can do to make you associate things; that's what makes possible this kind of work I do" ("Come funziono" TEDx talk).

Not every reviewer has appreciated—or indeed understood—the complex games that Sorrentino plays in *La Grande Bellezza* with combinations and juxtapositions of times, memories, works of literature, art, and music. Thus Vincent Malausa is completely dismissive in a review published in 2013 by *Cahiers du cinéma*, the major film journal ironically established by André Bazin, who had a far deeper understanding of cinema as a meeting place of the arts:

> The pompous title of his sixth film, *La Grande Bellezza*, invites us ironically to pose the question: is there anything uglier than a Sorrentino film? They all have in common an obscenity brought by a petty detail . . . he's running after the virtuosity of the Coen brothers but produces only flashy vignettes, he's searching for Paul Thomas Anderson's overelaborate strangeness (weird music, acrobatic plans, oneiric intrusions) and borrows the rigid pose of the one who's teaching lessons to others . . . The temptation of the grotesque is evident—hence the sad confusion with Fellini . . . The opening scene of *La Grande Bellezza* announces a cross between 8½ and the total cynicism and dry irony of Ulrich Seidl.
>
> "PAOLO SORRENTINO," 23

To this kind of approach, Sorrentino himself gives the best reply:

> A fault I find in certain critics is that they live mostly in the films they watch, and this makes me dubious. But if I find a critic with an avid understanding of life and who hasn't buried himself for decades in a cinema theatre, I'd listen to what he has to say, I'd even let him in more into my work. Instead I sometimes read what aspiring young critics write on the internet, even though the abstruse writing of the 19-year-olds pisses me off. But they're young and full of vitality, even when they're off the mark and they stick to their obsessions.
>
> SPILA and TORRI interview

To describe Sorrentino as aping the Fellinian carnivalesque evokes precisely the aspect of Fellini that Sorrentino rejects: "In Fellini, I love everything minus his passion for the circus" (Minoli interview). To speak sarcastically of "weird music" and "oneiric intrusions" is to miss the very elements that subtly bind the film's scenes together, building on the innovations of Proust and the surrealists and the filmmakers who have followed in their wake.

For Michael Sicinski, *La Grande Bellezza*'s cultural references "are very stodgy, literary manoeuvres, the overweening symbolic Biblethumps of the novelist-turned-filmmaker" ("Paolo Sorrentino: A Medium Talent," 20). Brendan Hennessey finds that *La Grande Bellezza* simply has *too many* references:

> Cinematic gestures towards Fellini's *La dolce vita* (1960), 8½ (1961) and *Roma* (1972), Pasolini's *Accattone* (1960), Antonioni's *La notte* (1961), and Scola's *La terrazza* (1980) combine with a complex set of literary recalls. Céline, Proust, Ammaniti, Pirandello, Moravia, D'Annunzio, Dostoyevsky, Flaubert, and Breton are all cited outright in the film, amassing a heavy textual burden to a crowded field of allusion.
>
> "Reel simulations," 452

We seem to be back in Milos Forman's *Amadeus* (1989), when the Italian composers at the Viennese court dismiss Mozart's *Abduction from the Seraglio* for having "too many notes."

Sorrentino's take on cinema is bound to upset cinematic purists. Asked whether he often goes to the movies, he replied: "No, I don't go often. I prefer to watch again the films I love and that taught me something rather than watch new films. It must be that I'm getting old . . . I like to call to mind what Fellini used to say: 'every time I decide to go to the cinema I find something more interesting on the street.' . . . I think cinephilia is sterile. And I prefer literature to cinema" (Spila and Torri interview). Even more frustrating for the supporters of a "pure" cinema is Sorrentino's insistence on the problem of language:

> In general, there's a lack of preoccupation about language and its style, which should be essential . . . My preoccupation with language comes from obsessive research into the other arts. For instance, I try to keep up to speed with what happens in the world of photography or music. But I realize I'm pretty alone in this; rarely do we find a good interlocutor on photography. Others are stuck when it comes to painting, but it's not even contemporary painting, as they say "Caravaggio invented everything." Fine, but we can't go on saying this for thirty years. We should try to see what others have done as well.
>
> ZONTA interview, 222–3

Even when Sorrentino's literary references are acknowledged, they are rarely accorded more than a passing mention. Thus Gary Crowdus evokes Proust in the title of his interview with Sorrentino, "In Search of *The Great Beauty*," and in the only monograph so far written on Sorrentino, *La maschera, il potere, la solitudine: Il cinema di Paolo Sorrentino*, Franco Vigni titles his chapter on *La grande bellezza* "Alla ricerca del tempo perduto," and yet neither critic discusses Proust at all. Though the ghost of Proust calls them, they don't respond to his voice.

*

Modeled on Proust, Sorrentino's Jep Gambardella is an authorial mask: "I share quite a few things with Jep, especially a sort of disenchanted way of looking at life and searching for emotions. I think that the search for beauty and emotions triggers my desire to make movies" (Jahn interview). Asked why his protagonists are all aging men who look back on their past, Sorrentino confessed that "I've been afraid of getting old since I was 20, or even before then. When I was little—I must have been 6 or 7 years old—I asked my mother, 'When do you die?' She said, 'When you are 100 years old', and I started to cry because I thought there was so little time in between" (Jahn interview). Critics are surprised that Sorrentino was only forty-three when *La Grande Bellezza* came out. But they forget that time, as Proust never tired of reminding us, isn't an objective category: "If I can pretend to be a 65-year-old it's a good thing, it's a compliment for me," says Sorrentino (Hébert interview).

Proust via Céline: The Imaginary Character of Life

Sorretino has said that he read Céline's *Voyage au bout de la nuit* "when I was 22 and it marked me forever" (Elkann interview), and he displays its opening lines in Italian at the start of his film. In the French original, they read:

> Voyager, c'est bien utile, ça fait travailler l'imagination. Tout le reste n'est que déceptions et fatigues. Notre voyage à nous est entièrement imaginaire. Voilà sa force.
>
> Il va de la vie à la mort. Hommes, bêtes, villes et choses, tout est imaginé. C'est un roman, rien qu'une histoire fictive. Littré le dit, qui ne se trompe jamais.
>
> Et puis d'abord tout le monde peut en faire autant. Il suffit de fermer les yeux.
>
> C'est de l'autre côté de la vie.

Voyage, 7

[Travel is useful, it exercises the imagination. All the rest is disappointment and fatigue. Our journey is entirely imaginary. That is its strength. It goes from life to death. People, animals, cities, things, all are imagined. It's a novel, just a fictitious narrative. Littré says so, and he's never wrong. And besides, in the first place, anyone can do as much. You just have to close your eyes. It's on the other side of life.]

As Sorrentino's leading man Toni Servillo has remarked, "The story of this film is also that of a journey in one's memory and mind. This is a movie that takes place very much in the main character's head" (Gruber interview).

As Proust emphasized before Céline, "reality does not exist for us so long as it has not been recreated by our thought . . . we acquire a true knowledge only of things that we are obliged to re-create by thought, things that are hidden from us in everyday life" (*Sodom and Gomorrah*, 221, 229). In *Céline et Proust*, Pascal Ifri notes that as early as 1932 a journalist described Céline as "a strange Proust of the plebeians" (2), and Ifri devotes his book to studying Proust's influence on Céline and the intertextual relationship of the *Recherche* and the *Voyage au bout de la nuit*. What Sorrentino loves in Céline could equally describe Proust's work: "his morbid obsession with getting to know human beings. His tools are disenchantment and irony, tools with which I am very familiar and which I navigate with very well, better than other approaches" (Crowdus interview, 11).

Interestingly, Céline's opening to his novel combines the title of Proust's opening volume, *Du côté de chez Swann*, with the powerful ending of André Breton's first manifesto of surrealism, which was published eight years before Céline's novel and was the talk of Paris in the late 1920s: "*L'existence est ailleurs*," concludes Breton. "*C'est de l'autre côté de la vie*," rewrites Céline. Breton's opening question from *Nadja* is directly quoted by Jep in a conversation after it makes a first appeareance in a key scene of *La Grande Bellezza*, when a mysterious, invisible girl asks Jep: "Who are you?" In *Nadja*, Breton describes himself as haunted and as haunting people and places. The self that haunts different selves traverses from Proust to *Nadja* to the multiple Prousts in Raúl Ruiz's *Le Temps retrouvé*. A further link in this signifying chain is Jep Gambardella, who haunts the streets of Rome and is haunted by phantoms from the past, as Sorrentino is haunted both by his literary past and his cinematic forebears.

The only occurrence of Proust's name in Céline's *Voyage au bout de la nuit* presents him as a haunting and haunted presence: "Proust, who himself was half ghost, immersed himself with extraordinary tenacity in the infinitely watery futility of the rites and procedures that entwine the members of high society, those denizens of the void, those phantoms of desire, those irresolute daisy-chainers still waiting for their Watteau, those listless seekers after implausible Cytheras" (61). Céline's description of Proust—almost a phantom, losing himself in the rites and rituals of high society, these cardboard people, ghosts of desire, who engage in orgies while waiting in vain for elusive Cytheras—gives us Jep in a nutshell.

The Museum of Memory

Proust and Jep Gambardella, those listless seekers of implausible Cytheras. Kythira or Cythera is the island of Aphrodite in the version of the Greek myth that gives her as Uranus's daughter, born from sea foam mixed with the blood spilled when Chronos castrated his father. Sorrentino alludes to this version of the myth when he constructs the mysterious lost lover from Jep's youth. The Island of Cythera became part of the Roman Empire, and a Saint Elisa tried to convert it to Christianity before being killed by her father because she refused to marry the man he'd chosen for her. With his passion for researching his subject, Sorrentino makes Saint Elisa into Jep's lost lover, Elisa De Santis. Jep recalls her on the island where he'd fallen in love with her, with the Greek Kythira transposed to an Italian island of modern loss, Isola del Giglio (lily island), where the Costa Concordia cruise ship foundered in 2012, an incident we see briefly replicated in the movie. An Italian Aphrodite, in the film's climactic flashback Elisa bares her breasts, inviting Jep to become her lover, though we've learned at the beginning of the film that she later went on to make the choice that her namesake Saint Elisa had rejected, marrying a man she didn't love.

A scene placed at the heart of *La Grande Bellezza* is a *mise en abyme* for the entire film, and is a nodal point where Sorrentino's art cinema intersects with Proust, Tarkovsky's *Nostalghia*, and Alexander Sokurov's *Russian Ark* (2002)—two films that engage with Proust's notion of time and the idea of saving the world through a work of art as a spiritual journey. In this central scene, Jep goes to a dinner party where Rome's high life is on full display. He is accompanied by Ramona, a beautiful stripper who is rather past her prime; she is a mirror of Proust's demimondaine Odette de Crécy, who manages to work her way into high society. This party corresponds to the soirée given by the Princesse de Guermantes in *Time Regained*, where Marcel has the revelation of the passage of time and the collapse of the old aristocratic order, as the recently married Princesse de Guermantes is none other than the vulgar former Madame Verdurin, whose marriage has finally bought her a place in the high society she always longed to join. Bored with the party's luxuriant display of debauchery and fake art, Jep steps outside the theatrical lights of the party, where people crowd together to see a seven-year-old girl pressured by her parents to create paintings by throwing her paint-covered body at a huge canvas, like an unsettling cross between Jackson Pollock and Lolita.

Jep approaches a man who is carrying a drink and an elegant cane: "Hi, Stefano!" he says. "Do you have the case with you?" "I always do," Stefano replies. We shift to a closeup of Ramona's eye looking through the round keyhole of an old wooden door in the Piazza dei Cavalieri di Malta, known as "the hole of Rome": through this substitute camera's eye she sees the beautifully lit cupola of Saint Peter's Basilica—appropriately, as Saint Peter holds the keys to heaven. Stefano's case is a briefcase divided into sixteen compartments, each holding a key that opens doors to museum collections that Jep loves to visit at night when there are no tourists. A friend of Rome's princesses, Stefano is the figure of the connoisseur par excellence, modeled on Proust's Charles Swann, the collector of art and men: "As for Swann himself, he still often called on some of his former acquaintances, who, of course, belonged to the very highest society. And yet when he spoke to us of the people whom he had just been to see I noticed that, among those whom he had known in the old days, the choice that he made was dictated by the same kind of taste, partly artistic, partly historic, that inspired him as a collector" (*Within a Budding Grove*, 127). Whereas Stefano collects keys that lead to Rome's artistic treasures, Jep is a collector of beauties, whether men, women, or moments in time. If Swann is a double of Marcel, Jep is a double of both of them.

In the museum scene, as in Jep's nighttime walks and in a final shot of the Tiber during the credits, Sorrentino's long, flowing shots turn the camera into a gliding boat, an ark that travels in time collecting the world's beauties. This camera's gliding movement comes to Sorrentino from another filmed museum, in Alexander Sokurov's stunning *Russian Ark* (2002). Filmed in Saint Petersburg's Hermitage Museum in a single ninety-six-minute gliding shot, *Russian Ark* tells the history of modern Russia from the founding of Saint Petersburg by Peter the Great, a secularized Saint Peter, the patron of Rome, to the Russian Revolution of 1917. *Russian Ark* is told by two narrators: an anonymous, invisible one, who directs the camera but whose voice we hear constantly, and a visible one, the Marquis de Custine, author of a travel book, *La Russie en 1839*. With its focus on Russian artists' imitation of Raphael and the Italian masters, Sokurov's *Russian Ark* is the perfect precedent for Sorrentino's own practice of the ark-camera in a film that collects Rome's and life's beauties in the form of a museum of memory.

In Sokurov's film, many paintings in the Hermitage are seen as if through a dark lantern, while at other times they glow with a chiaroscuro light, inspired by the museum's impressive Rembrandt collection. In the opening scene we hear a voice, evidently of the director, transported back to 1839: "I open my eyes and I see nothing. I only remember there was some accident. Everyone ran for safety as best they could. . . . As for what happened to me, I just can't remember." Gliding through a group of Russian officers dressed for a dinner party, the voice continues: "Can it be that I'm invisible? Or do they just not notice me? Interesting . . . Has all this been staged for me? Am I expected to play a role? What kind of play is this? Let's hope it's not a tragedy." We are in a grand theatre of the mind of the contemporary filmmaker who decides to make a film about Russia's past and its beauties, which echo those of Rome. As the Marquis remarks to his unseen companion: "Truly, it's like we're in the Vatican. . . . Weren't those decorations inspired by sketches of Raphael?" (The Vatican Galleries in the Hermitage were indeed commissioned by Catherine the Great in the style of Raphael.)

"Better than the Vatican," replies the off-camera voice. "This is Saint Petersburg." "So they're copies?" muses the Marquis with a voice that comes directly from Dostoevsky's pages. "Russians are so talented at copying."

As they walk through the Hermitage's Vatican Galleries, they marvel at the beauties on the walls and the ceilings. "The czars were mainly Russophiles," the unseen companion explains. "But they dreamed of Italy. Wasn't the Hermitage created to satisfy those dreams?" "Raphael isn't for you," the Marquis remarks: "He's for Italy." In *La Grande Bellezza* the artworks Jep sees configure his personal history, whereas in Sokurov's film they configured Russia's. But Jep *is* Rome. At his birthday party, a drug addict and former TV star, well past her prime, pops out of a giant birthday cake wearing the number 65—Jep's age—on her breasts, shouting: "Happy birthday, Jep! Happy birthday, Rome!"

In the Hermitage, the earthly beauty of Massimo Stanzione's "Cleopatra" hangs next to Saint Cecilia and a Christ on the cross. The Marquis disapproves: "Right next to Saint Cecilia? Can you imagine! By Carlo Dolci. And next to an Eastern still life. As a Catholic, that shocks me." But the Catholic Sorrentino is no longer shocked, as we see in the juxtapositions of sacred and sexual love that he creates in Jep's museum tour. As Stefano leads Jep and the stripper Ramona into the darkened museum, Sorrentino presents us with a display of statues and paintings that in reality are housed in the Capitoline Museums and the Pallazzo Barberini, and Jep shows Ramona the colossal statue of a reclining river god that is actually located in the courtyard of the Capitoline Museums. This is the statue that appears on the film's poster behind Jep, who is nonchalantly sitting on a marble bench, looking into the camera with the ironic smile and posture drawn from one of the most iconic photos of Proust (Figure 7.1).

In the film, Jep appears in this posture on the same marble bench in a high-end couture shop where he teaches Ramona about the right way to perform one's role in the most theatrical social ritual: a funeral. Shown in a theatrical light on the stage of life, Jep/Sorrentino is a contemporary Swann/ Proust who has switched centuries and is now performing on the stage of Rome's social theatre (Color Plate 11).

As he shows the statue of the river god to Ramona, Jep explains to her that "Stefano has the keys to Rome's most beautiful buildings." "Is he a doorman?" the naïve stripper inquires, sounding like Odette, the former prostitute who lacked any artistic sense. "No, he's not a doorman," comes Jep's indulgent reply, accompanied by his ironic smile. "He's friends with the princesses." A further parallel to Swann, friends with princesses while some take him for a mere Jewish tradesman: "No doubt there were still a few people in the room—the Duchesse de Guermantes was one—who would have smiled at this assertion (which, in its denial of Swann's position as a man of fashion, seemed to me monstrous, although I myself, long ago at Combray, had shared my great-aunt's belief that Swann could not be

FIGURE 7.1 *Photo of Marcel Proust (1896).*

acquainted with 'princesses')" (*Time Regained*, 392). Opening the museum doors with his cane like a master of ceremonies, Stefano resembles not only Swann but another mirror of Marcel, the Baron de Charlus, whom Proust modeled on Robert, Comte de Montesquieu-Fézensac, down to the elegant cane featured in a well-known portrait of the count.

The camera glides through the empty corridors, and the light carried by Stefano casts a mysterious aura on a few resonant statues: the river god, the Capitoline Venus or *Venus pudica* who covers her body, which looks ahead toward Jep's own Venus, Elisa De Santis; and finally the *Dying Gaul*, himself a mirror of Jep, who exits the film by closing his eyes and saying into the camera that every journey always ends with death. The climax of this nocturnal stroll is filmed in an atmosphere that could pass for a dream. In a chiaroscuro room, we can only see a closeup of Jep smiling blissfully. But what has brought that smile that Jep so rarely wears? His lantern casts a gradually increasing light—a round light in a dark room, like Proust's magic lantern—that reveals the painting that embodies the great beauty hidden at the heart of Sorrentino's film, which Jep tries to recuperate throughout his entire journey: Raphael's *La Fornarina* (Color Plate 12).

As the website of the Barberini Galerie Corsini Nazionali states:

> The subject of this portrait, according to tradition, was Raphael's inspirational muse and mistress: Margherita Luti, the daughter of a baker in Trastevere, hence known as "Fornarina." . . . The pose of her hands, one placed on her lap and the other on her breast, follows the classic statuary model of the "Venus Pudica": a gesture of modesty which yet directs the viewer's gaze to what she actually seeks to conceal. Other symbols of the goddess of love are the bracelet inscribed with the words "*Raphael Urbinas*," the painter's signature as well as a token and pledge of love.
>
> https://www.barberinicorsini.org/en/opera/la-fornarina

In a recent article, Giuliano Pisani writes that the term *fornarina* had sexual connotations: "'forno' ('oven') and its cognate 'fornaia' ('woman baker') etc. metaphorically indicate the female sexual organ and the woman prostitute." He believes that Raphael "portrays in the 'Fornarina' the celestial Venus, namely the type of love that raises the soul toward the search for truth by means of the 'celestial' beauty. This Venus differs from the other Venus, the 'terrestrial' Venus, namely the generating power of nature, who is connected with the terrestrial beauty and has procreation as her goal"("Le Veneri di Raffaello," 122).

In his use of Raphael, Sorrentino echoes Tarkovsky's use of Piero della Francesca's *Madonna del Parto* in *Nostalghia* to depict the two beauties who haunt Andrei—his wife Maria and the seductive Italian Eugenia. Superimposing the sacred and profane versions of Aphrodite/Venus on the portrait of his lover, Raphael follows in the tradition of Praxiteles, who had depicted his own lover, the great courtesan Phryne, as Venus of Knidos or Venus Pudica. His sculpture survived through its Roman copies, the most famous being the one housed in the Capitoline Museums that Jep sees seconds before he encounters Raphael's *Fornarina*.

By signing his name "Raphael Urbinas" on his lover's bracelet next to her breast, Raphael engages visually with one of the most beautiful of all erotic poems, the Song of Songs, which was traditionally read as an allegory of the love of God and Israel or the Church. In the poem's climax, the Shulamite maiden tells King Solomon: "Set me as a seal upon your heart, as a seal upon your arm; for love is as strong as death" (8:6). Raphael places himself as a seal on his beloved's arm, turning his "profane" lover into a sacred one, so that she can live forever. Jep recovers his love for Elisa in the great beauty of Raphael's eternal art, echoed in the late flashback in which Jep sees Elisa

240

TIME REGAINED

baring her breasts (Color Plate 13). The title "La Grande Bellezza" appears for a second time in the film in the last scene, just before the credits, following a closeup of the beautiful Elisa, who looks pensively over her shoulder at the camera. The screen turns black and the title is gradually lit by the lantern of memory for the last time; and we know that she is Jep's *grande bellezza*, she is his Fornarina, on whose arm he places his seal: the title of the novel he will now write, or the film we've just seen.

A connoisseur of the intersections between literature, painting, and music that his sources trigger, Sorrentino chooses David Lang's choral composition *I Lie* in the opening scene of *La Grande Bellezza*. Lang's text, by a Yiddish poet, Joseph Rolnick, is in dialogue with the Song of Songs as it tells the story of a woman waiting at night for her lover to return. Sung in Yiddish, the song is doubly mysterious; if translated, it would be: "I lie down in bed / And put out the flame; / He will come to me today, / The one who is dear to me. / . . . The night has a great many hours: / Each drearier than the last./ One only is a cheerful one: / When my beloved comes." By creating a composition that has the tone of Gregorian chant, Lang superimposes profane and sacred love, thus musically introducing the central problem of Sorrentino's film: turning what is beautiful in our past, the moments when we felt closer to understanding the deeper meaning of our existence, into a work of art that outlasts the passage of time.

When Jep walks through the museum corridors at night, accompanied by Stefano and Ramona and by the slow movement of Bizet's First Symphony, the last work of art he contemplates is *La Fornarina*. As she gradually emerges from the darkness, a strange sound is superimposed on Bizet's music: the sound of waves breaking on the seashore. We are now in Jep's mind as he has an involuntary memory of his island idyll with Elisa, and Jep in turn is in the footsteps of Proust's Marcel, whose memory of Albertine is always associated with the sound of the sea at Balbec. Sorrentino is also building on Raúl Ruiz's *Time Regained*, where wailing seagulls and the sound of waves always take us back to Marcel's adolescence and the beach at Balbec.

Nor is this the only intertext, as Sorrentino's museum echoes a strikingly similar passage from André Breton's *Nadja*: "How much I admire those men who decide to be shut up at night in a museum in order to examine at their own discretion, at an illicit time, some portrait of a woman they illuminate by a dark lantern [*une lampe sourde*]. Inevitably, afterwards, they must know much more about such a woman than we do. Perhaps life needs to be deciphered like a cryptogram" (*Nadja*, 112). *Nadja* comes to life, and literature returns through film. Ultimately, Sorrentino turns his film into the manifestation of *la grande bellezza*, as the "lampe sourde" or dark lantern of cinema allows the bearer to hide in the darkness while illuminating the object of his desire.

This lantern lights Sorrentino's entire film—the haggard flashes of the beauties of memory, as Jep calls them in the last scene of the film. Jep's memory is this dark lantern that casts light on his past to bring his museum of memories

LET THIS NOVEL BEGIN   241

to life. This is why so many scenes are filmed at night, with a strong contrast, a chiaroscuro, between flashes of light and perfect darkness. Ultimately, these flashes of light come from Jep's mind's eye, corresponding to the lighthouse whose beams traverse the Isola del Giglio. And the moonlight camera light that shows the beauties of the city comes from Proust's pages, where it cast its light on the beauties of Paris: "The moonlight was like a soft and steady magnesium flare, by the light of which some camera might, for the last time, have been recording nocturnal images" (*Time Regained*, 164).

Sorrentino's film begins like Proust's book when Jep is confronted with an involuntary memory of his lost love Elisa, and like Marcel, Jep searches throughout the film to fully recover this memory, to come to terms with time's passing and to renew his vocation as a writer. In the opening, at Jep's birthday party, in the middle of a carefully choreographed dance to El Gato DJ's *Mueve la colita* (*Move your ass*), Jep steps in the middle of two rows of dancers facing each other, while he is facing us. The music grows dim, as we're entering Jep's mind and hear him in voiceover, recalling an old question, "What do you like most really in life?" He continues: "To this question, as kids, my friends always gave the same answer: pussy. Whereas I answered: 'the smell of old people's houses.' I was destined for sensibility. I was destined to become a writer. I was destined to become Jep Gambardella." And as Jep says this in voiceover looking into the camera, the title of the film appears looming on the night sky of Rome.

In Breton's *Nadja*, the narrator similarly feels destined to be a visionary who bears a unique message:

> the affinities I feel, the attractions I succumb to, the events which occur to me and me alone—over and above a sum of movements I am conscious of making, of emotions I alone experience—I strive, in relation to other men, to discover the nature, if not the necessity, of my difference from them. Is it not precisely to the degree I become conscious of this difference that I shall recognize what I alone have been put on this earth to do, what unique message I alone may bear, so that I alone can answer for its fate?
>
> *Nadja*, 13

Sorrentino's intertextual dialogue goes back through Breton and Proust to Proust's direct predecessor, Flaubert, who appears on at least three occasions in *La Grande Bellezza*: twice cited for his never accomplished project of writing a novel about nothing, and a third time as an ironic authorial mask for both Jep and Sorrentino. Talking one night at a dinner party to Stefania, a self-important political novelist whose books were published only because she was sleeping with the leader of the Communist Party, Jep cuts her short as she is stating that Roman life is "pure collectivism": "Do you know that Flaubert wanted to write a book about nothing? If he'd met you, we'd have had a masterpiece, what a shame!" When he finds Elisa De Santis's husband waiting for him in the hallway outside his apartment, the man asks: "Gambardella?" Jep responds ironically, in French, "C'est moi." Flaubert is present not only through these more or less direct citations,[2] but especially through a mode of seeing the world, at the same time from a maximum and a minimum of distance, which is the revolutionary technique of *Madame Bovary*. Counterpoint, anticlimax, and irony are Sorrentino's favorite devices, learned from Flaubert, but also from Flaubert's follower Proust. They structure the narrative and are the major principles for Sorrentino's editing.

The anticlimax as editing principle appears in the scene when Jep receives the news of Elisa De Santis' death. We see Jep and her husband from a distance, standing outside Jep's apartment, two aged men who've never met before, crying over the woman they both loved. A Flaubertian anticlimax breaks in to counteract the gravity of the scene with the irony of life that continues unmoved by anyone's death. As they part outside Jep's building in the rain, Sorrentino edits in a closeup of a nun passing by, as she breaks into a raucous laugh before she runs away as two other nuns approach. This scene, which creates a bitterly ironic counterpoint to the death of a central character, is modeled on the death of Emma Bovary, the last romantic character in the first realist novel:

> As the death rattle grew more pronounced, the priest's prayers grew more urgent, mingling with Bovary's muffled sobs; at times, every sound seemed to be overlaid by the muted drone of the Latin syllables, which resonated like a tolling bell.
>
> Suddenly, they heard the sound of heavy clogs on the pavement, and the soft rapping of a stick; then a voice rose from below, a raucous voice, singing:
>
> *Souvent la chaleur d'un beau jour,*
> *Fait rêver fillette à l'amour.*
>
> Emma reared up like a galvanized corpse, her hair hanging down her back, her wide-open eyes staring fixedly. "The blind man!" she cried.
>
> And Emma began to laugh, a ghastly, frenzied, despairing laugh, believing she could see the wretch's hideous face, like a symbol of ultimate terror, looming through the dark shadows of eternity.
>
> *Il souffla bien fort ce jour-là,*
> *Et le jupon court s'envola!*
>
> A spasm cast her back onto the mattress. They all drew close. She no longer existed.
>
> *Madame Bovary*, 290

---

[2]Sorentino may also be indirectly citing Flaubert's *Dictionnaire des idées reçues* in his use of Raphael's *La Fornarina*: "Fornarina*. She was a beautiful woman. This is all you need to know" (*Dictionnaire*, 37).

The despairing, crazy laugh and the vulgar song sung by the anonymous voice underscore the absurdity of existence in the face of death—a bitter truth that Proust and Jep share with Flaubert.

"Whom I haunt:" Marcel Proust

While Sorrentino's style is indebted to Sokurov and his editing principles come in part from Flaubert's practice of the anticlimax, his character Jep is closely modeled on Proust's Marcel, down to his deep interest in fashion. As Breton writes in *Nadja*, "who I am" is "whom I haunt" (11). Early in the film, we see Jep extremely interested in a wealthy neighbor's suit: "Catellani? The best, of course. Did Catellani the tailor make your suit?" he asks one morning in the elevator with his mysterious neighbor, who remains silent. Toward the end of the film, Jep discovers that his well-dressed neighbor is a mafioso, who finally answers the question as he is led away into custody: "To be honest, Catellani hasn't had many brushed fabrics in recent years. In my opinion, Rebecchi's still the best tailor in Rome." As in Proust's world where fashion is a form of art for connoisseurs, such apparently trivial details still matter. Sorrentino picks up here on the final scene in Ruiz's *Time Regained*, which reunites three different Prousts—the child, the one on his death bed and the adult one—on the beach at Balbec, and the adult Proust approaches a waiter to ask him to find out a specific detail about the needlepoint on a woman's blouse.

The adult Proust in Ruiz's *Time Regained* who is interested in fashion is played by the Italian Marcello Mazzarella, paving the way for Sorrentino's Jep, played by the equally charming and expressive Toni Servillo. In Proust's world, Marcel (who discourses at length on Albertine's Fortuny gowns) shares the passion for fashion as art with another great collector and aesthete, the Baron de Charlus: "M. de Charlus 'possessed'—and this made him the exact opposite, the antithesis of me—the gift of observing minutely and distinguishing the details of a woman's clothes as much as of a painting" (*The Captive*, 291). Like Jep, Charlus could have been a great writer if not for his passion for gossip and the night life of both high and low society: "I believe that if M. de Charlus had tried his hand at prose . . . he would have become a master of the pen. I often told him so, but he never wished to try his hand, perhaps simply from laziness, or because his time was taken up with dazzling entertainments and sordid diversions or from a Guermantes need to go on gossiping indefinitely" (292). Laziness—*pigrizzia* in Italian—is a word that often comes up in Sorrentino's interviews when he wants to describe what prevents filmmakers, writers, and artists from truly making a difference in history. The same laziness keeps Swann from writing his eternally promised essay on Vermeer; the same laziness and ennui keep Marcel from setting himself to write, until the very end of the *Recherche*.

Like Marcel, who only publishes occasional journalistic articles even though his friends praise his literary talent, Jep hasn't written a book in forty years. Talking to Dadina, the editor of the magazine he writes for, about why he hasn't written anything substantial since his bestselling and award-winning *L'Apparato umano*, she chides him: "You're lazy. You never leave Rome. Go to Giglio to do that report on the Concordia I asked you to do 50 times." Unwittingly, she is sending him to the island where he will recover his long-submerged memory of Elisa. Later in the film, Ramona, the forty-two-year-old stripper whose father is an old friend of Jep's, becomes his occasional companion. One evening, as they sit on Jep's terrace, she asks him bluntly: "Why didn't you write another book?" The answer is Proust's own answer—and Charles Swann's, too: "Because I went out too much at night. Rome makes you waste a lot of time. It's distracting. Writing requires focus and peace." Like Marcel in *Time Regained*, Jep feels that time is passing, and he can no longer waste it leading a shallow life devoid of meaning.

An important Proustian element in the film is Jep's relationship with his maid—a direct equivalent of Proust's Françoise. Just after his birthday party, Jep is sitting in the kitchen, after another sleepless night. His maid asks: "You want infusion? [tisana]." He replies: "Urge, chérie" ("I need it, chérie"). Significantly, the maid offers him the Proustian tea (*tisane* in French, *tisana* in Italian) which Jep accepts in French. A second scene with the maid takes place at an unlikely time for both Jep and Marcel: early morning. The maid assumes that Jep will be going to bed after a typical night out, but he says: "Last night I went to bed at 22:30. Now I don't know what to do. Morning is an unknown object to me. Unknown." She then teasingly says: "Sir can help me clean the house then," to which Jep replies, "Sir can't, sir feels strange." The maid gets the last word: "Sir's a rascal." She appears in a third scene, at a party at Jep's apartment overlooking the Colosseum, after Andrea and Ramona have died and his friend Romano has left Rome. Jep talks again to his Françoise: "They've been asking me for years why I don't write another novel. But look at these people. This wildlife! This is my life, and it's nothing. Flaubert wanted to write a book about nothing, but he failed, so could I do it?" He then remarks on the coffee that the maid has served him, his version of the café au lait on which Proust subsisted in the final weeks of his life: "It's nice. Thanks, rascal."

Not sleeping at night, drinking too much, procrastinating about writing and producing a book about nothing—all this points not so much to Flaubert, who worked hard every day to find *le mot juste*, but to Flaubert's most brilliant follower, Proust, and his fictional self: "If only I had been able to start writing! . . . what always emerged in the end from all my efforts was a virgin page, undefiled by any writing . . . I slept for a few hours after all towards morning, I read a little, I did not over-exert myself" (*The Guermantes Way*, 196–7). Marcel's maid, Françoise, doesn't understand much of the business of writing, but she is willing to help her master in the most practical way she can: "These 'paperies,' as Françoise called the pages of my writing, it was my habit to stick together with paste, and sometimes in this process they became torn. But Françoise then could be able to come to my help, by consolidating them just as she stitched patches on the worn parts of her dresses ... so that I should be making my book in the same way that Françoise made that *boeuf à la mode*" (*Time Regained*, 510–11).

The Sea Inside

A recurrent scene, closely modeled on Proust, structures Jep's descent into his past. At Balbec, Proust's Marcel saw the reflections of the sea projected on his wall while lying on his bed, daydreaming. So too Jep, after he's returned from one of his incessant dinner parties, often contemplates his bedroom's ceiling, where he sees in a dream vision the endless sea from the Isola del Giglio when he was eighteen and in love with Elisa. This is why Jep has kept refusing Dadina's request to do the article on the Costa Concordia that went aground at the island: he doesn't want to return to that lost scene of his past.

Sorrentino changes the music every time Jep contemplates the sea on his ceiling. As in Ruiz's *Time Regained,* children's laughter and seagulls' cries accompany Jep's plunging into the past, as he mourns the loss of Elisa, the girl who will remain for him the goddess of the sea. When the children's laughter surfaces from the past, Jep is a boy again, running around a monastery's garden with another little girl and a nun; when the seagull's wailing is heard, it's the eighteen-year-old that rises inside him and takes his place, bringing Elisa back to life, as young and as beautiful as ever. Twice such scenes are accompanied by Arvo Pärt's *My Heart's in the Highlands*, even though the highlands are ironically hidden deep inside him, underneath what Jep calls "the blah blah blah" of everyday existence. Set to Pärt's moving liturgical music, Robert Burns's lyrics of love and longing become sacred, while Jep's first love becomes the only thing he ever believed in.

The first scene shows Jep going to bed after his birthday party. Slowly, his eyes turn dark blue, like the sea, and with him we plunge into a different scene, showing Jep outside on his terrace at dusk, having a drink and lying in a hammock. As he stands up, he looks down from his terrace, and the camera softly glides down, following children running and playing with a nun in a beautiful garden—a space of memory, not the actual view from his terrace (Figure 7.2). As Marcel says near the end of the *Recherche*, "A feeling of vertigo seized me as I looked down beneath me, yet within me, as though from a height, which was my own height, of many leagues, at the long series of the years" (*Time Regained*, 531). This is a version of Ruiz's scene showing

FIGURE 7.2 a, b, c *Jep looking down from his terrace into the memory garden of his childhood. Stills in consecutive order from* La Grande Bellezza.

Proust on his deathbed looking at photographs and descending as if on an invisible elevator from the salon where, a child again, he strangely meets an adult Robert de Saint-Loup. In front of Ruiz's camera, now placed outside and moving on the vertical all the way down, we see little Marcel coming down into the garden. Children are laughing and playing happily and a young Gilberte invites him with her sexual gesture. In Sorrentino's memory scene, Jep—hidden behind the gliding camera—runs after a little girl in the garden; perhaps she is herself the future Elisa De Santis.

The second scene when Jep plunges into the sea above his bed takes place just after he returns from making a visit to Elisa's husband, hoping to learn more about Elisa's feelings, only to find that her husband has destroyed her diary. This time it's nighttime, and Jep smokes pensively in the dark. As he contemplates the sea on his ceiling, David Lang's *World to Come* begins, with a soprano solo followed by a wailing cello. A tear forms in the corner of Jep's eye, and he starts dreaming again of his past. He's swimming offshore at the Isola del Giglio, still his sixty-five-year-old self, while the young Elisa looks at him from the shore, where she's sunbathing. A speedboat rushes toward him, almost killing him. But he dives down at the last second, then lo and behold, he resurfaces a young man. "For man," Proust writes, "is that ageless creature who has the faculty of becoming many years younger in a few seconds, and who, surrounded by the walls of the time through which he has lived floats within them as in a pool the surface-level of which is constantly changing so as to bring him within range now of one epoch, now of another" (*The Fugitive*, 830).

In October 1891, a twenty-year-old Proust published in a cultural magazine, *Le Mensuel*, a short piece entitled "Souvenir" (Memory), which would become one of the nodal stories in the *Recherche*. It is a first-person narrative telling of an older man returning to the house of his beloved, named Odette, with whom he had lived a passionate love story when they were young. Her house was by the sea, and as he returns there years later, his words could pass for Jep's: "Was I right, after so many years had passed, to come to this house, where I had perhaps long been forgotten? This house that had once been so welcoming, where I had spent profoundly sweet hours, the happiest of my life?" ("Souvenir," 7). But Odette is now near death, forced by a terrible illness to lie in bed. Her only consolation is watching the sea: "I plunge my gaze into that blue sea, whose grandeur, which is apparently infinite, holds so much charm for me. The waves that come to break ashore are so many sad thoughts that cross my mind, so many hopes I must abandon" (8).

Though Proust's "Souvenir" is only a sketch, it's surreal how much of it can be seen to prophesy *La Grande Bellezza*. Even though the old man is heartbroken to see his beloved aged and sick, hearing her talk about the poetry of the waves makes her seem young again: "While she was talking to me, her gaze had become animated; the cadaverous color of her complexion had disappeared. She had recovered her formerly gentle expression. She was once again pretty. My God, she was beautiful! I would have liked to take her in my arms; I would have liked to tell her I loved her" (9). He then leaves and walks toward the sea, with the feeling that this is the last time: "I crossed the long entrance hall, the delightful garden on whose paths the gravel would, alas, never again grate under my footsteps. I went down to the beach; it was deserted. I strolled pensively, thinking of Odette, along the sea that was pulling out, indifferent and calm. The sun had disappeared behind the horizon; but it was still splashing the sky with its purple rays" (9). Proust signed this short piece "Pierre de Touche," a pun meaning *touchstone*, but also, if read literally, the stone destined to be touched, anticipating the stone that Proust will describe in the *Recherche* that houses the ghost of those whom we have lost and who call out to us to bring them back to life.

One evening, Jep is sitting on his terrace with Ramona, sharing confessions about their first sexual experiences. After Ramona tells him her story, it's Jep's turn, but he seems reluctant. As he sits silently, the first chords of Arvo Pärt's "My Heart's in the Highlands" are heard suggestively. When Jep faces the camera, we shift briefly to a scene on an island. It's night and two lovers face each other under the moonlight, with the sea behind. As if talking to himself, Jep says: "On an island, one summer. I was 18, she was 20. At the lighthouse, at night. I went to kiss her, she turned away. I was disappointed. But then she turned to look at me. She brushed me with her lips. She smelled of flowers. I didn't move, I wasn't able to move. Then she took a step back and said . . . She took a step back. And said . . ." But Jep can't utter another word, and Ramona, embarrassed, stands up and bids him goodnight. Instead of learning what Elisa had said to him, we hear the haunting chorus in Arvo Pärt's liturgical setting of Robert Burns' lyrics:

> My heart's in the Highlands, my heart is not here,
> My heart's in the Highlands, a-chasing the deer;
> Chasing the wild-deer, and following the roe,
> My heart's in the Highlands, wherever I go.

The wild deer that Jep's heart chases is the transcendent moment of perfect beauty, the moment when time stood still on an island, under the moonlight, when he was 18. It's the moment of unspeakable beauty and splendor, a sacred moment that will never come back.

In the Paradise of Phantoms

Jep is doomed to retrace his steps every night as he walks on the empty streets of Rome, trying to learn what he should have simply recognized, a mere fraction of what he forgot: his young self, his love for Elisa, eternal youth and time that stands still. "Eternal people," as Sokurov's Russian Marquis muses on one of the Flemish paintings in the Hermitage. But Jep wasn't the first to walk at night in a world of phantoms, shadows of the *mondanité* where the socialites seem like automata or frozen statues. In two draft passages that never made it into the published version of *Swann in Love*, Proust speaks of the god called *Mondanité*. As J.M. Cocking notes, "Proust's aim is to convey an idea of la Mondanité, personified as the god which rules the lives of aristocrats who, though quite devoid of any snobbish regard for their own aristocracy, obediently go through the motions it dictates" (*Proust*, 139). Like Jep (and like Sorrentino himself), "Swann is able to abstract this notion of mondanité because his observation is sharpened by detachment" (139). Jep describes himself as the "re dei mondani," the king of socialites, who's so well versed in the codified rituals of society that he can instruct Ramona in its rules of behavior and of dress, including the socially prescribed lines to recite at Andrea's funeral—the ultimate ritual over which the god Mondanité presides.

La Grande Bellezza returns us to the Proust before Proust—the one from the variants and drafts of the *Recherche*, but also from the young Proust's early volume of poetic sketches, *Les Plaisirs et les jours* (1896). Many of the titles in Proust's slender work could be applied to Jep's *mondanità*: "Violante, ou la mondanité," "Mondanité et mélomanie de Bouvard et Pécuchet," and, interestingly, "Fragments de comédie italienne." Jep's early novel, published at the age of twenty-five, followed by the long period in which he publishes nothing substantial, has a direct antecedent in Proust's early book—also published at the age of twenty-five, followed by the decades in which he published almost nothing, leading André Gide, famously, to reject for Gallimard the first volume of the *Recherche*, taking it as the musings of a mere socialite.

At one of the parties he attends, Swann has the impression that the *gens du monde* around him are as immobile as statues. As Cocking remarks:

> We have here, then, a dream-picture, with the merest hint of a nightmare; the nightmare of withdrawn and inhibited emotion which Surrealism and films influenced by Surrealism have often expressed. The detachment which makes it possible for Swann to "observe" is tinged with a morbidity which transforms observation into one kind of dreamlike "vision," and this relationship with reality is associated with pictures and novels.
>
> 140

Jep's life, like Marcel's, is led in the pursuit of phantoms, and he is attracted to everything connected to death.

In *Time Regained* the Baron de Charlus lists for Marcel the many people who have died during the years Marcel has been away from Paris, in a litany

250   TIME REGAINED

that mocks and at the same time praises the blind fate that has spared him so far. Jep, too, is surrounded by death, starting with the death of his beloved Elisa. Ramona, his Odette who keeps him company for a while, dies most likely of cancer, soon after the suicide of his friend Viola's son Andrea. Like Mozart's Don Giovanni, Jep sits down to dinner with Death itself, only he doesn't know it. Dining out with Ramona, of whose deadly illness he has no clue, Jep is taken by surprise by Andrea, who appears out of the blue. Their conversation is Proustian, constructed on the surface through Flaubert's irony and anticlimax: "How are you?" Jep asks Andrea, to which he receives a most unexpected and direct answer: "Not well. Proust says that death may come to us this afternoon. Proust is scary. Not tomorrow, not in a year, but this afternoon." Andrea is quoting from *The Guermantes' Way*:

> We may, indeed, say that the hour of death is uncertain, but when we say this we think of that hour as situated in a vague and remote expanse of time; it does not occur to us that it can have any connection with the day that has already dawned and can mean that death . . . may occur this very afternoon. . . . Perhaps those who are habitually haunted by the fear of the utter strangeness of death will find something reassuring in this kind of death—in this kind of first contact with death—because death thus assumes a known, familiar, everyday guise.
>
>   427

When Andrea quotes Proust that death may come "this afternoon," Jep discounts the gravity of the questions that torment him too: "But it's evening already, so it'd be *tomorrow* afternoon." But Andrea doesn't give up: "Turgenev said: 'Death looked at me, noticing me.'" As he says this, a terrified Ramona looks at him as if Turgenev is speaking directly to her. Death looks at each of them through the other's eyes, noticing them. "Don't take these writers so seriously," Jep advises. "Who should I take seriously then?" asks Andrea. "Nothing, apart from the menu, of course," comes Jep's prompt answer, itself a double-edged irony of Proust's own kind directed ironically at Proust's culinary passion, which receives a lot of attention over the course of his novel.

While Jep and Ramona are out at night in the museum, just after Jep contemplates *La Fornarina* we suddenly see Andrea at the wheel of his automobile, staring into the camera and then closing his eyes. The sound of the engine pushed to the limit while he shuts his eyes tells the viewer that we're witnessing his suicide. This scene Sorrentino recreates from Breton's *Nadja*:

> one evening, when I was driving a car along the road from Versailles to Paris, the woman sitting beside me (who was Nadja, but might have been anyone else, after all, or even *someone else*) pressed her foot down on

mine on the accelerator, tried to cover my eyes with her hands in the oblivion of an interminable kiss, desiring to extinguish us, doubtless forever, save to each other, so that we should collide at full speed with the splendid trees along the road. What a test of life, indeed! . . . I often find myself, eyes blindfolded, back at the wheel of that wild car. . . . as regards love, the only question that exists for me is to resume, under all the requisite conditions, that nocturnal ride.

152–3, footnote

When read through Sorrentino's intertext with Breton's *Nadja*, what may seem just random editing in of Andrea's suicide following Jep's contemplating his Fornarina is revealed as its organic continuation: coming to terms with Elisa's death enables Jep to recuperate his identity as a writer and ultimately write the novel that is the film we're now seeing. At the end, in the last scene, when Jep is finally able to access the long-forgotten memory of her naked beauty under the moonlight, he also reaches the end of his life. With his eyes closed, smiling, he is Andrea himself back at the wheel of the wild car, but now smiling, not despairing. Love is what makes us take that journey to the end of the night that Céline's book speaks of in the opening of the film. And as the ending of the film takes us back to its beginning, the film is truly about to begin when it ends, for Sorrentino's camera ark glides along the waters of the Tiber to the music of Vladimir Martynov's *The Beatitudes*, and the credits run in the rhythm of the music and water. And we are back to Proust, where *Time Regained* is only the beginning of the *Recherche*.

The Disappearing Giraffe

If Jep, like Proust and Breton, leads his life in the pursuit of phantoms, what meeting could be more important than the one with his own phantom from the past? Proust's hero finally begins his *recherche du temps perdu* after he comes to terms with the realization in *Time Regained* that everyone around him is aging or dying. Prompted by his encounter with *La Fornarina*, Jep descends gradually into his museum of memories to find the phantom of himself at age 18. His descent is prefaced by the death of younger people— first Andrea, then Ramona. One of the film's most moving scenes, set to Zbigniew Preisner's *Dies Irae*, shows the oldest men at Andrea's funeral, carrying out his coffin: Jep, Romano, their friend Lello, and Dadina's partner, a silent poet who observes but never speaks. A world where the young are buried by the old can only be a graveyard.

Surrounded by death in its many guises, Jep continues his solitary night strolls on the streets of Rome. One night, after Andrea and Ramona's death, while his friend Romano is giving his last performance—a poetic narrative of his life—on stage in front of a very small audience, Jep arrives at the

Baths of Caracalla. One of the most beautifully preserved ruins of Ancient Rome, the Baths are Sorrentino's version of Tarkovsky's ruined San Galgano cathedral in *Nostalghia*, Ruiz's ruined Greek temple in *Time Regained*, or Wong Kar-wai's temple at Angkor Wat in *In the Mood for Love*. In classical epic, the underworld descent often becomes a place in which the poet revisits his literary forebears—Odysseus meets the ghost of Achilles in *Odyssey* 11, while in the sixth book of the *Aeneid* Aeneas in turn encounters Homer's heroes, together with his own lost love Dido. And last but not least, in the Inferno's limbo Dante meets his predecessors, whose circle he joins: Homer, Horace, Ovid, Lucan, and Virgil. Now Sorrentino chooses the Baths of Caracalla to stage a chance encounter with the cinematic past.

Walking into the Baths, Jep is arrested by a surreal, and in fact surrealist, apparition: a giraffe, theatrically lit, under a dark archway. In awe at this miraculous apparition, Jep silently doffs his hat. Now an old friend, Arturo, appears on this improvised set and tells Jep he's rehearsing the climactic disappearing act for his magic show. Jep asks Arturo: "You can make the giraffe vanish?" "Of course I can make the giraffe vanish!" Arturo replies. "Then make me vanish, too," the exhausted Jep requests. "Jep, do you think that if I could really make people vanish I'd still be here at my age, playing these circus games? It's just a trick," Arturo replies. He exits the stage, with his last words echoing behind him.

But another phantom has appeared behind Jep: his friend Romano, who has come to say goodbye; he has decided to leave Rome after forty years, disappointed that his writing and acting are appreciated only by a handful of people. Romano disappears into the darkness through another archway, but when Jep turns aback to the archway with the giraffe, it's empty. Children's laughter accompanies the giraffe's disappearance, and we remember that when Jep first stepped into the ruins, the wailing of seagulls could be heard. Framing the scene, the bird cries and the children's laughter become the sound of memory. Together, Jep's two earlier selves—the childhood one and the youthful one—appear in the ruins where a magician is performing a disappearing act for the oldest of Jep's selves. It's significant that the giraffe's vanishing frames the disappearance of Romano. His name is hardly random: Jep is now left in a Roma without a Romano. The only one left is Jep himself, and this is why he asks Arturo to make him disappear. Just as Raúl Ruiz brought together all of Proust's past selves in the ruins of the ancient Greek temple, from the childhood one to the narrator on his deathbed, Jep's childhood and adolescent selves are resurrected by the involuntary memory prompted by sounds.

On a number of occasions, when Sorrentino was asked about the surrealist apparitions in *La Grande Bellezza*—the giraffe, a flock of flamingoes that suddenly appear on Jep's terrace—he insisted that they're actually realistic. As he said concerning the giraffe scene: "For me, it's very plausible, because an illusionist I know told me he was able to make an elephant disappear nearby at the Colosseum, so I only changed the place and the animal, but to me, it was plausible" (Wootton interview). As Bazin said: "The realism of the cinema follows directly from its photographic nature. Not only does some marvel or some fantastic thing on the screen not undermine the reality of the image, on the contrary it is its most valid justification. Illusion in the cinema . . . is based on the inalienable realism of that which is shown" (*What Is Cinema?*, 1:108).

Critics have discussed Sorrentino's apparitions without perceiving their surrealist roots. For Alessia Martini, the giraffe episode is "one of the most Fellinian of scenes in *La Grande Bellezza*" ("Concept City," 115). In an essay focused on special effects, Brendan Hennessey finds in this scene a general allusion to circuses and to the powers of CGI:

> Arturo and his giraffe reveal Sorrentino's broad highlighting of illusion: like the flamboyant CGI flamingos later seen perched on Jep's deck, the towering giraffe sustains a mode of presentation common to the circus or the cinema. . . . For the spectator, the viewing of the film is overwhelmed by the consciousness that the film is being viewed, elevating and anointing the filmmaker as a magician, a performer of illusions. . . . this giraffe denotes a tradition of animated special effects in cinema that developed directly from painting.
>
> "Reel simulations," 456–7

Yet Sorrentino's giraffe and flamingos owe more to surrealism than to *Fantasia* or *Who Framed Roger Rabbit?*. Following the recuperation of Georges Méliès as the protosurrealist father of art cinema in Scorsese's *Hugo* and Ruiz's *Time Regained*, Sorrentino's giraffe scene engages with Méliès's films centered on the disappearing act, like *Escamotage d'une dame au Theatre Robert Houdin* [*The Vanishing Lady*] (1896), which shows a woman's repeated disappearance, and *Illusions fantasmagoriques* [*The Famous Box Trick*] (1898), where the magician exits at the end of his act by making himself disappear.

By choosing a giraffe, of all things, for the disappearing act, Sorrentino is taking up a highly charged political and religious reference from one of the seminal surrealist films: Luis Buñuel's *L'Âge d'or* (1930), written by Buñuel and Salvador Dalí. A response to the Rif War (1920–7) between the Moroccan Berbers and their Spanish colonizers, later joined by France in the name of Catholicism, *L'Âge d'or* embodied the surrealists' political stance throughout the 1920s. The surrealists were the only group of intellectuals in France to take a combative stance against France's intervention in the Rif War, in which they saw everything surrealism stood against: imperialism, the Catholic Church, and the puritan bourgeoisie with its repressive morality.

L'Âge d'or tells a surrealist story of how a new imperial Rome was founded in 1930 by the European colonizers on the burial site of four

Catholic bishops who had been killed in the Rif Mountains by the Berber rebels. As Buñuel and Dalí's story goes: "The old mistress of the pagan world has been for centuries now the secular headquarters of the Church. . . . But the very old imperial city has entered too in the whirlwind of modern life." Set in contemporary Rome, *L'Âge d'or* tells the story of a colonial official and an aristocratic woman who are desperately trying to make love in the most public places. Society and the Church always come between them, preventing them from fulfilling their desires. The climax of the film takes place in a garden with beautiful statues at a villa outside Rome. As they are finally about to make love, they are interrupted by a vision the man has in which he sees the woman transformed into the goddess of chastity, Artemis, whose statue is next to them. Suddenly she is kissing an aged conductor, whom her parents had invited to perform music from Wagner's opera *Tristan and Isolde* at a party. As in the medieval romance, Buñuel and Dalí's heroine ends up with old King Mark of Cornwall, while Tristan goes mad with love and returns in the guise of a Christian monk to remind her of their love.

In *L'Âge d'or*, the *Tristan fou* episode becomes what Breton would call *amour fou* in his 1937 volume of that name, and the disillusioned lover, in a moment of rage, goes to her room and throws out of the window a series of surrealist objects: first a burning tree, then a Catholic bishop, followed by . . . a giraffe. While the tree and the bishop simply fall to the ground, the giraffe plunges into what appears to be a sea of burning lava. With its bitter criticism of the Church's corruption and politics, as well as the surrealist apparition of the giraffe—a recurrent apparition in Dalí's paintings, such as *The Burning Giraffe* (1937)—*L'Âge d'or* provided the perfect intertext for Sorrentino's criticism of decayed Rome, in which love from Jep's past—of the pure, not mad kind—can resurrect him through the book he may finally be able to write, as Proust's Marcel could recover Combray in Paris.

In constructing the disappearing giraffe scene using a mirrored pair of archways framing a black void, Sorrentino is preparing for the final scene, when Jep descends for one last time into his past, seeing himself young again, under the moonlight, in front of his lover Elisa. Looking at his young self and at his lost love, Jep is now utterly happy and at peace. He looks into the camera's eye and meditates once more, in Proustian terms, on death as the ending but also the beginning of our journey through the world or through the time of the film:

> This is how it always ends. With death. But first there was life. Hidden beneath the blah, blah, blah. It is all settled beneath the chitter-chatter and the noise. Silence and sentiment. Emotion and fear. The haggard, inconstant flashes of beauty. And then the wretched squalor and miserable humanity. All buried under the cover of the embarrassment of being in the world. Beyond there is what lies beyond. I don't deal with what lies beyond.

André Breton's surrealist concept of reality was that there is no beyond. Jep has the revelation that he can write again, like Marcel, about his recovered past and about the social life he'd always considered too trivial to write about, even though he has devoted much of his life to it. Like Ruiz's Proust on his deathbed seeing his entire life just before dying, Jep, now old and weary at the end of his inner journey, eyes shut, says in voiceover: "And so, let this novel begin." In a closeup showing us only Jep's eyes that now open, we hear his voice: "After all, it's just a trick. Yes, it's just a trick."

Through a subtle echoing of the disappearing giraffe scene, Sorrentino tells us that the film we've just seen is about to vanish from our screens. If Méliès's onstage disappearing act entered film through a trick that Méliès himself discovered, Jep's (and Sorrentino's) takes place outside the camera frame, and more specifically behind it. When Jep turns around, the giraffe has disappeared, the trick being now performed by the camera's eye that turns away from the object at the crucial moment. When Jep tells us that his novel that can now begin is "just a trick," we know that he has become the magician who can make himself disappear, as did Méliès at the end of his film *Illusions fantasmagoriques*, and as did Proust at the end of *Time Regained* in the pages of his just-completed, now-to-be-written novel. Today, Sorrentino reveals to us, Proust's poetic novel would be a film. *His* film.

Meeting Oriane de Guermantes / Fanny Ardant

Jep's filmed disappearing act goes along with unanticipated reappearances, in a new version of surrealist chance encounters that now connect across film history. As he wanders the streets of Rome at night, like Proust's Marcel who arranges his walks for months so that he can run into the Duchesse de Guermantes, Jep runs into Fanny Ardant, the great French actress renowned for having worked with Truffaut, Resnais, Costa-Gavras, Antonioni, Zeffirelli, and Schlöndorff. Here, however, she is playing herself. Jep's face brightens when he sets eyes on her: "Madame Ardant?" he asks, as if he's seen a ghost. She smiles mysteriously and seductively, and at length she replies: "Oui." For the first time in the film, Sorrentino uses the opening chords from Vladimir Martynov's *The Beatitudes*, performed by the aptly named Kronos Quartet, a key composition that will be used in the final scene as well, subtly linking the apparition of Fanny Ardant with Jep's culminating vision of his lost love Elisa.

The casting of Fanny Ardant has received many conflicting interpretations, but no one sees more than a passing nod to one or another filmmaker; without exception, no critic sees an actual connection to the substance of the film.[3] But why would Sorrentino cast a major actress like Fanny Ardant in a walk-on role, keeping her in even after cutting forty minutes from the full three-hour version? The puzzlement was sparked by Sorrentino himself, who always gives rather different answers to this question, yet none seems to be the actual one. A lover of irony, he's not going to do his viewer's work. Asked about her fleeting appearance, Sorrentino replied:

> I worked with Fanny Ardant in previous movies; she was in another movie that I did and in that scene in the script there was the main character that met an important person in Via Venetto, that's a famous street in Rome for *La dolce vita*. In that case, I was happy to do a sort of a homage to *La dolce vita* and Fanny Ardant said to me that she has never done in her life an extra, but only actress. She said that once in life it was nice to do the extra so I thought it was a very good chance for me to have an extra like Fanny Ardant.
>
> AGO interview

Elsewhere, he gives an even more implausible reason: "In big cities you often just bump into famous people, all of a sudden. And mysterious people. Fanny Ardant embodies that combination of being famous and being mysterious" (Titze interview). But so do many other actresses. Why her? Three years later, Sorrentino changes his story again, now putting forth Truffaut rather than Fellini: "I wanted to pay homage to *The Woman Next Door* because Truffaut, next to Fellini and Scorsese, is one of my favorite directors" (D'Amico interview). But Truffaut's movie is an even more unlikely reference than Fellini's, as Ardant plays the role of a strange woman who's committed a crime. No trace of the ghostly, gorgeous appearance as herself in Sorrentino's film, nor any connection to Jep's story. Perhaps the truth lies elsewhere.

Speaking to Jep in French, this fugitive apparition is a ghost from the past. But not just any past: Fanny Ardant famously played Oriane de Guermantes in Volker Schlöndorff's *Un Amour de Swann*, with Jeremy Irons as Swann and Ornella Mutti as Odette. But in Schlöndorff's film, Oriane appeared

---

[3]In a typical comment, Iain Bamforth dismisses Fanny Ardant as a useless apparition, "of no particular relevance to the film's development except perhaps to remind us of a glamorous actress who has aged well" ("Doing the Locomotion," 133). Alessia Martini finds only a nostalgic reference to Fellini, "a ricordare forse che i tempi della dolce vita felliniana sono lontani, e l'unica persona che egli incontra è l'attrice Fanny Ardant che appare come un miraggio, quasi uscita da un'altra epoca" ("Concept City," 113). Or again, Eugenia Paulicelli: "Why Fanny Ardant should appear at this moment of the film is not clear; but maybe she represents the kind of cinema that Sorrentino is aspiring to emulate" ("After *La Dolce Vita: La Grande Bellezza*," 188).

FIGURE 7.3a *Jeremy Irons as Charles Swann and Fanny Ardant as Oriane de Guermantes in Volker Schlöndorff's* Un Amour de Swann *(1984).* **7.3b:** *Jep running into Fanny Ardant on the streets of Rome in* La Grande Bellezza.

with dark hair, even though in Proust's book she's blonde. By giving Oriane de Guermantes back her blonde hair, and by having her cross paths with his contemporary Proust, Sorrentino brings back Proust's character but also the memory of Proust art cinema (Figure 7.3). For Proust's Marcel, Oriane de Guermantes is a desired yet never possessed woman. Dreaming of the Merovingian past associated with the Guermantes' name, Proust's narrator is less interested in the reality before his eyes than in the poetic history nested inside names: "the name Guermantes existed for me in many ways . . . Then once again I began to think of Mme de Guermantes's dwelling as of something that was beyond the bounds of reality, in the same way as I began to think again of the misty Balbec of my early day-dreams . . . [She] was for me the real point of intersection between reality and dream" (*The Fugitive*, 773). Sorrentino takes this perspective to a metatextual level, as the history of art cinema lies nested in the figure of Fanny Ardant.

. . . and the World shall be saved by Beauty

Interwoven with Jep's search for meaning is the figure of Suor Maria, a famous missionary nun (loosely based on Mother Teresa), who has returned from Africa on a pilgrimage to Rome. At the age of 104, her great ambition is to climb on her knees up the Vatican's Scala Sancta, whose twenty-eight steps were said to have been brought to Rome from Jerusalem, where they had supposedly been the staircase that Jesus had ascended on his way to his trial. Jep's editor has pressed him to get a rare interview with her, and when they meet, it turns out that the aged ascetic is a great admirer of his early novel. "Why did you never write another book?" she asks him. "Cercavo la grande bellezza" (I was looking for the great beauty), Jep confesses, "ma non l'ho trovata," which can be translated equally as "I never found it" or "I never found her." Despite Jep's claim that he hasn't found *la grande bellezza*, the final scene shows just the opposite. Juxtaposed with Suor Maria's eager, arduous crawling up the Scala Sancta—quite possibly the last act of her life—Jep's descent into his past is finally completed, as he recuperates the memory of his first lovemaking with Elisa, under the light of the moon and the lighthouse on Isola del Giglio, with the sea behind them. We learn the answer he was seeking to recall to the question asked earlier by Ramona: What did Elisa tell him at that moment? Brushing his face with her lips, Elisa says seductively: "Now there's something I want to show you," and she unbuttons her blouse and exposes her breasts. Looking intently but silently at him, she is Raphael's Fornarina come to life, a memory that leads Jep to hear the sound of the sea as he contemplated Raphael's painting in the museum at night.

The answer Jep was looking for wasn't verbal but visual: Elisa's naked beauty, which is both earthly and spiritual. The moment we see her breasts, we once again hear John Tavener's choral setting of Blake's poem "The Lamb." Instead of finding the words he could use to once again become a novelist, Jep finds the resonant image that makes him a filmmaker. And Sorrentino finds almost word for word in Proust this very transformation of the novelist into a filmmaker, when Marcel contemplates artistic beauty brought to life, thinking in theatrical and cinematic terms. Recalling Albertine in "a series of images fraught with beauty," Marcel says that

> I remembered Albertine first of all on the beach, almost painted upon a background of sea, having for me no more real existence than those theatrical tableaux in which one does not know whether one is looking at the actress herself who is supposed to appear, at an understudy, who for the moment is taking her principal's part, or simply at a projection. Then the real woman had detached herself from the beam of light and had come towards me. . . . Life had obligingly revealed to one in its whole

extent the novel of this little girl's face, had lent one, for the study of her, first one optical instrument, then another. . . . One has seen a woman, a mere image in a decorative setting of life, like Albertine silhouetted against the sea, and then one has been able to take that image, to detach it, to bring it close to oneself, gradually to discern its volume, its colours, as though one had placed it behind the lens of a stereoscope.

The Guermantes Way, 493–6

Jep had experienced Raphael's Fornarina detaching herself from the beam of light in the museum, against a seascape of the sound of waves; now she has become a real woman, Elisa, but also a projection of Jep's stereoscopic memory. Proust's "optical instrument" has become the flesh and bones of Sorrentino's world art cinema.

*

So what, in the end, is *la grande bellezza*? Sorrentino's reading turns Raphael's *Fornarina* into a synonym for beauty, and he is also following in the footsteps of Tarkovsky in *Nostalghia*, where the poet Andrei compares his wife Maria to Piero della Francesca's *Madonna del Parto*, who is both Maria and Eugenia, the temptress who's trying to seduce him. Andrei tells Domenico that Maria looks like the Madonna, "but all dark." Sorrentino reactivates a complex network of books and films he has loved that deal with the concept of beauty. By choosing to decipher Jep's life and the concept of beauty through Raphael's painting, Sorrentino reactivates an entire network of literary and cinematic references that goes from *Nostalghia* and Sokurov's *Russian Ark* back to Dostoevsky, whom Jep's friend the young Andrea has been obsessively reading. In Dostoevsky's most poetic novel, *The Idiot*, the hero Prince Myshkin is caught between his socially approved love for Aglaya Epanchin and an irrational yet pure love for a fallen woman, Nastasya Filippovna, whom he almost marries before she inexplicably deserts him on their wedding day to run off with a former suitor, much as Elisa De Santis will later abandon Jep. Trying to understand Nastasya's effect on him, Prince Myshkin meditates on her unearthly beauty:

He began to look at Nastasya Filippovna's portrait. It was as if he wanted to unriddle something hidden in that face which had also struck him earlier. The earlier impression had scarcely left him, and now it was as if he were hastening to verify something. . . . That dazzling beauty was even unbearable, the beauty of the pale face, the nearly hollow cheeks and burning eyes— strange beauty! The prince gazed for a moment, then suddenly roused himself, looked around, hastily put the portrait to his lips and kissed it.

The Idiot

Later on, seeing the same portrait, Aglaya's sister remarks: "Such beauty has power. You can overturn the world with such beauty." "Beauty will save the world," we hear repeatedly throughout the novel at key moments.

In Tarkovsky's *Nostalghia*, Domenico, the saintly Italian who locks up his family for ten years in the hope of keeping them away from the corrupt world, confesses to Andrei: "I was selfish before. I wanted to save my family. Everyone must be saved, the whole world," and for this purpose he will go to Rome, the center of Catholic faith, in a final attempt to wake up the people of Rome, whose faith is lost. They are only phantoms without life, as Tarkovsky shows Domenico mounted on the equestrian statue of Marcus Aurelius in the piazza of the Capitoline Museums, talking to a crowd of people frozen in their tracks, like lifeless statues. Trying to wake them up and save them, he sets himself on fire, but the Romans remain unmoved, frozen in their daily existences.

Sorrentino returns to the problem of saving a decayed Roman world through beauty, building on Tarkovsky and on Sokurov's filtering of Dostoevsky, combined in a brilliant rereading of Proust's cinematic memory that recovers lost time. The title of Jep's only book, *L'Apparato umano* (also one of the working titles for *La Grande Bellezza*), may have suggested the young Jep's naturalistic or even cynical perspective on "the human apparatus," but in the end, we can see that this human apparatus becomes the movie's own camera. A suggestion that appears phrased in almost identical terms in the opening of Proust's *Recherche*:

> But none of the feelings which the joys or misfortunes of a real person arouse in us can be awakened except through a mental picture of those joys or misfortunes; and the ingenuity of the first novelist lay in his understanding that, as the image was the one essential element in the complicated structure of our emotions [*l'appareil de nos émotions*], so that simplification of it which consisted in the suppression, pure and simple, of real people would be a decided improvement.
>
> *Swann's Way*, 116

But it's not only for the novelist that the image is the one essential element for *l'appareil de nos émotions*; it's also for the filmmaker, and Sorrentino suggests this reading of Proust's metaphor by filming the transformation of Jep the novelist into Jep the filmmaker—the greatest magical act that Sorrentino, follower of Méliès, performs in *La Grande Bellezza*.

"This is how it always ends. With death," says Jep's voiceover in the final scene. "But first there was life . . . The haggard, inconstant flashes of beauty." Before Jep, it was André Breton who spoke of convulsive beauty both in *Nadja* and *Amour fou*: "Beauty is like a train that ceaselessly roars out of the Gare de Lyon and which I know will never leave, which has not left. It consists of jolts and shocks, many of which do not have much importance, but which we know are destined to produce one *Shock*, which does.... Beauty will be CONVULSIVE or will not be at all" (*Nadja*, 159–60, author's emphasis). "Convulsive beauty will be veiled-erotic, fixed-explosive, magic-circumstantial, or it will not be" (*Mad Love*, 19). Jolts, shocks, the haggard, inconstant flashes of beauty. Accompanying the rhythm of our memory or of the heart, like the flashes of the lighthouse, they were dreamed by Proust before Breton and Sorrentino:

> For with the perturbations of memory are linked the intermittences of the heart. It is, no doubt, the existence of our body, which we may compare to a vase enclosing our spiritual nature, that induces us to suppose that all our inner wealth, our past joys, all our sorrows, are perpetually in our possession. Perhaps it is equally inexact to suppose that they escape or return. In any case, if they remain within us, for most of the time it is an unknown region where they are of no use to us ... But if the context of sensations in which they are preserved is recaptured, they acquire in turn the same power of expelling everything that is incompatible with them, of installing alone in us the self that originally lived them.
>
> *Sodom and Gomorrah*, 211–12

In Sorrentino's final scene of remembrance, when Jep has finally recreated the memory of Elisa he thought lost forever, we see his older self replaced in the blink of an eye, as he stands under the moonlight, young again, contemplating his beautiful Fornarina. "The self that I then was, that had disappeared for so long, was once again so close to me that I seemed still to hear the words that had just been spoken, although they were no more than a phantasm" (*Sodom and Gomorrah*, 212).

Rather than a remake of Fellini's *La dolce vita*, Sorrentino's *La Grande Bellezza* is in dialogue with Tarkovsky's *Nostalghia* in this last scene. The juxtaposition of Suor Maria and Jep echoes Tarkovsky's final scene that juxtaposes Domenico and Andrei, the believer and the writer whose faith is lost. "We need bigger ideas," says Domenico. "You need to cross the water with the lighted candle." "Which water?" Andrei wants to know. "The hot water," comes Domenico's response. But as Tarkovsky said in an interview, Andrei dies at the end of *Nostalghia*, so the hot pool over which he carries his lit candle at the end of the film isn't just any water; it's the Phlegethon in the Inferno, the river of fire, and he's crossing beyond. Jep too speaks of the beyond in his next to last scene, and of everything ending with death. Symmetrically, his own film opens with a Japanese tourist who collapses while taking photographs, apparently because of the heat. As Sorrentino remarked in an interview supposedly conducted by his own character Jep Gambardella (probably Toni Servillo in actual fact):

Rome is the best place in the world to live, because it's a dead city. An extraordinary dead city. And the integrity of its body is the great aesthetic and mystical miracle of Rome. It's been dead for two thousand years and still smells nice. In order to feel alive, one needs obsessively to relate to death. And if death has the appearance of a glowing, incredible beauty, doesn't that make you feel even more alive? It's an illusion, no doubt, but what's wrong with going through life living in the bubble of an illusion? Magic is the art of illusion.

SERVILLO interview

*

The world that will be saved by beauty haunts Proust and Dostoyevsky's works, taking the shape of music when filtered through Tarkovsky's long, slow-paced tracking shots in *Nostalghia* and Sokurov's *Russian Ark*, and ultimately it reaches Italy's shores again with *La Grande Bellezza*. Proust's book that started it all is a surrealist camera that records things as if selecting them by chance only to reveal at the very end the invisible pattern hidden underneath the skin of everyday reality: "Traveling lazily upstream from day to day as in a boat, and seeing an endlessly changing succession of enchanted scenes appear before my eyes, scenes which I did not choose, which a moment earlier had been invisible to me, and which my memory presented to me one after another without my being free to choose them, I idly pursued over that smooth expanse my stroll in the sunshine" (*The Captive*, 103).

Jep travels up the Tiber every morning, returning after another night lost to partying, and as the film advances, more and more enchanted scenes appear before his eyes, from his past but also his future, prophesying the film his next novel will be. At the very end, before his final plunge into the museum of memory, when he finally is able to remember—or even better, to relive—the enchanted moment of surreal beauty with Elisa on the Isola del Giglio, we see Jep sitting in the prow of a boat, passing by the island. Then Jep disappears from the screen and becomes the camera, gliding on the water like Proust: "and I set off, trailing my shadow behind me, like a boat gliding across enchanted waters" (*Time Regained*, 1). At the very end, right after he has unearthed Elisa's image buried in his depths, the title "La Grande Bellezza" slowly materializes onscreen—an effect previously used for the scene showing *La Fornarina*—and the credits begin to run. Whereas the title had first materialized against the Roman landscape at the beginning of the film, now it appears against a solid black background, then fades away. The camera now glides on the Tiber, in the rhythm of the water that runs slower and slower until at the very end, as we come to a stop, we pass under the last bridge's dark arcade and the screen slowly becomes black, as if the camera's eye closes and the film ends: the last time Jep closes his eyes, like the dreamer who has dreamed *La Grande Bellezza*.

Jep is a second Marcel, who remarks that "it was my fate to pursue only phantoms, creatures whose reality existed to a great extent in my imagination," and Marcel himself knows that he is a second Charles Swann, "he who had been a connoisseur of phantoms" (*Sodom and Gomorrah*, 559–60). Thinking back to his summers at Balbec, Marcel continues: "When I reflected that their trees—pear-trees, apple-trees, tamarisks—would outlive me, I seemed to be receiving from them a silent counsel to set myself to work at last, before the hour of eternal rest had yet struck" (560). "Beyond there is what lies beyond," Jep meditates in the last scene before he disappears like the phantom he's become. "I don't deal with what lies beyond. And so, let this novel begin."

Sorrentino's insight is that had Proust lived today he would have lived in Rome rather than Paris and would have been a filmmaker. Only a prophet like Proust can dream the cinema of the future, and in its turn, visionary cinema such as Sorrentino's can make us read back from what cinema can do *with* literature, to what this cinema tells us *about* this literature. As André Bazin wrote seventy years ago in his "In Defense of Mixed Cinema": "If we maintain that the cinema influences the novel then we must suppose that it is a question of a potential image, existing exclusively behind the magnifying glass of the critic and seen only from where he sits. We would then be talking about the influence of a nonexistent cinema, an ideal cinema, a cinema that the novelist would produce if he were a filmmaker; of an imaginary art that we are still awaiting" (63). With Sorrentino's Jep Gambardella, as with the other filmmakers with whom we've journeyed through the enchanted realms of literature and art, the waiting has ended. The imaginary art of the future is here. And it's grand, and it's beautiful. It's *La Grande Bellezza*.

Conclusion

The Art of Time Regained: To Be Continued

On what enchanted waters will the camera-ark glide onward from here? *Time Regained* has attempted to navigate the confluence of two apparently different streams—world literature and world cinema—based on the view that their objects of study aren't as separate as scholars usually think. Writers, painters, sculptors, musicians and filmmakers don't think in terms of artistic boundaries when they create, and this is why I propose that we redefine the notion of circulation as it presently exists in the two fields of world literature and world cinema. I have tried to show how literature can gain a new life—a new time—if translated into the medium of film, while film in turn can show what our instruments of literary studies have failed to see, to the gain of both fields.

While I've focused on a particular theme in the work of a set of visionary artists—what Pascale Casanova calls the exceptions that change the stake of the game—there are so many more histories to be told, well beyond the question of time and the interrelations of literature and film. As we've seen with Akira Kurosawa, the history extends to the history of painting; with Stephen Daldry and Philip Glass, it extends to symphonic music and theatre; with Andrei Tarkovsky to poetry, painting, and architecture; with Paolo Sorrentino to the history of both the visual and the verbal arts. I've chosen to emphasize filmmakers with formal literary training and writers who have an active filmic imagination, but all future artists, irrespective of their craft, begin as all of us do in early life: with stories (read or told), with pictures (in books, cartoons, games, films), with music. Even once they've chosen to work in a particular medium, artists maintain the privilege of imagination that takes its cue from a world that knows no borders between the arts.

As a girl growing up in the twilight years of the Romanian communist regime, a time of rationing, pervasive censorship, and closed borders, I nonetheless learned early on that the most fantastic travels can be born in the imagination and in the solitude of the nights when with the aid of only a violet light bulb my father would put on a puppet show for my sister Lavinia and me. And there were filmstrips of magical stories cast on the wall by an old projector, and the shadow theatre we brought to life by playing with our hands in the projector's light in the breaks when he changed the filmstrip and a new story in pictures and words would begin. Time regained has many meanings, but the most personal one for me was revealed by my sister after I had completed the book. She remembered that my favorite filmstrip was called *Little Apple's Trip to the Moon*, based on a story by V. Roschin. It told the story of three friends—Little Apple, Chamomile, and Little Cucumber—who build a rocket to travel to the moon where they celebrate the New Year. This filmstrip was long lost after our parents' death, but my sister found it on YouTube and shared it with me. The first slide shows Little Apple on a chaise longue in his garden reading a book whose title is illegible, but the slide reads: "'Wouldn't it be wonderful if I could travel to the moon?' he said to himself one day." But that wasn't just Little Apple I was looking at: it was myself at age five. And now *Time Regained* opens with Georges Méliès's *Le Voyage dans la lune*. The ghosts of things past remain imprisoned in some inanimate object until one day they come back to share our life once more. So when I read in Ingmar Bergman's *The Magic Lantern* about the cinematograph he used to play with for hours as a child in the darkness of a wardrobe, I felt as if I had met with my double across time.

As the author and filmmaker Alexander Kluge has written, "for tens of thousands of years, there have been films in people's heads: streams of associations, daydreams, experiences, sensuousness, consciousness. The technological invention of cinema merely introduced the added element of reproducible images" ("The Realistic Method and the 'Filmic'"). The natural exchange between the arts happens through translation or adaptation across media, but such crossings aren't easy or automatic. Genuine interanimation across media takes exceptional artistry to create. As André Bazin put it: "For the same reasons that render a word-by-word translation worthless and a too free translation a matter of condemnation, a good adaptation should result in a restoration of the essence of the letter and the spirit. But one knows how intimate a possession of a language and of the genius proper to it is required for a good translation" ("In Defense of Mixed Cinema," 67–8). The results then challenge our accustomed frames of reference and habits of analysis. As Bazin rightly argues, we scholars should make it our business to know the new forms under which our objects of study can reappear, no matter how strange they may seem for our habits of perception of the art they belong to:

When the cinema actually began to follow in the footsteps of theatre, a link was restored, after a century or two of evolution, with dramatic forms that had been virtually abandoned. Did those same learned historians who know everything there is to be known about farce in the sixteenth century ever make it their business to find out what a resurgence of vitality it had between 1910 and 1915 at the Pathé and Gaumont Studios and under the baton of Mack Sennett? ... the same process occurred in the case of the novel. The serial film adopting the popular technique of the feuilleton revived the old forms of the *conte*. . . . Both the author and the spectator were in the same situation, namely, that of the King and Scheherazade; the repeated intervals of darkness in the cinema paralleled the separating off of the *Thousand and One Nights*.

58–9

Conversely, a writer's imagination isn't structured only through other works of literature, but also through films. Norman Manea's prize-winning memoir, *The Hooligan's Return* (2003), structures the painful story of remembering the Holocaust, the deportation and then the experience of exile in the West through the dreams about the past and future from Andrei Tarkovsky's *Ivan's Childhood* (1962). Eugene Vodolazkin's novel *Laurus* (2012) creatively transforms the poetic logic of editing and of montage from Tarkovsky's *Ivan's Childhood*, *The Mirror* and *Nostalghia* into a novel way of understanding time in relation to the invisible reality of the world of spirit.

It's becoming more and more difficult to separate the different worlds through which contemporary stories reach us. Elena Ferrante's *My Brilliant Friend* and Nancy Springer's *The Case of the Missing Marquess* (part of *The Enola Holmes Mysteries* series) quickly turn into an HBO series and a Netflix film respectively. Even before it came out in English, Ferrante's *The Lying Life of Adults* (2019) was announced in May 2020 as a Netflix original series (2023).

It isn't just the translation between the mediums of film and literature that's at stake today. In 2003, Disney finally released the animated short film *Destino* based on Salvador Dalí's paintings and story, a production that started in the 1940s, but remained unfinished until Walt Disney's nephew Roy E. Disney finally took it up again. More recently, Dorota Kobiela and Hugh Welchman's 2017 animated film *Loving Vincent* turns literature, painting, and film on their heads. It's made of 65,000 frames, each an oil painting on canvas, painted by 125 artists from around the world using Van Gogh's techniques, and tries to find the answer for his suicide through his last letter to his brother and through stories about him by those who knew him. There is a lot of work here to be done for scholars of literature and of film, as well as for art historians.

Another promising area includes hybrid works that bring together fiction, images, the graphic novel, and the filmstrip. Such is the case of Posy Simmonds' ironic rewriting of Flaubert's *Madame Bovary* as *Gemma Bovery* (1999) and also of Anne Fontaine's film (2014) based on Simmonds' novel. More than an adaptation of Simmonds' book, Fontaine's film performs a creative post-modern reading of Flaubert's masterpiece through the lenses of Flaubert's own irony and anticlimax. A whole different area is opened by books like Pascal Quignard's *A Terrace in Rome* (2000), *The Sexual Night* (2007), and *Sex and Fear* (1996), which combine the art essay, the poetic novel, fiction and the mezzotint. The forty-seven short chapters of *A Terrace in Rome* function like the mezzotints of Quignard's hero, the seventeenth-century artist Geoffrey Meaume. His mezzotints bring light out of darkness, a similar experience to that of watching films in the darkness of a theatre. No one discipline of study can do justice to such objects.

Not only do filmmakers bring together ideas from different arts to make something new, but they also tell us something we didn't see yet in the literature, theatre, or history they are engaging with. Gregory Doran's 2009 film version of his 2008 stage production of *Hamlet* for the Royal Shakespeare Company teaches us to look back at Shakespeare's play through the eye of the camera that spies on others, and to rethink the language of surveillance and control that pervades the entire play and shapes the relationships between the characters. Hamlet's hand-held camera becomes a very different mirror held up to nature to record the most intimate conversations of the mind with itself. Gale Edwards and Nick Morris's 2000 film version of Andrew Lloyd Webber's *Jesus Christ Superstar*, based on Edwards's 1996 revival in London, rethinks Jesus's story through the 1968 May revolution in France as well as the Holocaust, with Pontius Pilate and the Romans dressed as Nazis. Edwards's unique staging and film move the story farther beyond the canonical one of the gospels, through a historicized political interpretation that originates simultaneously in Tim Rice's lyrics and in the recently discovered gnostic gospel attributed to Judas. To a completely different end, but equally surpassing what a typical film adaptation does, Adrian Shergold's *Persuasion* (2007) invites us to look back at Jane Austen's novel and its power to do things with silence rather than words.

All these developments were already foreseen by André Bazin in the conclusion to his essay "In Defense of Mixed Cinema:"

> The success of filmed theatre helps the theatre just as the adaptation of the novel serves the purpose of literature. *Hamlet* on the screen can only increase Shakespeare's public and a part of this public at least will have the taste to go and hear it on the stage. *Le journal d'un curé de campagne*, as seen by Robert Bresson, increased Bernanos' readers tenfold. The truth is there is here no competition or substitution, rather the adding of a new dimension that the arts had gradually lost from the time of the Reformation on: namely a public. Who will complain of that?

75

CONCLUSION

Indeed, who will?

To be based in only one discipline that maintains the purity of its object doesn't seem substantially different from what Albert Guérard called in 1958 "the nationalistic heresy" in literary studies that the comparatist should fight against ("Comparative Literature?", 4). Perhaps something similar could be said about "the pure object heresy" that underlies our humanistic disciplines. *Time Regained* has tried to find the common root of world literature and world cinema, which remains the relation between the creative mind and the *world*. Bazin, too, spoke of this common source of the arts we should never forget even as we labor for the autonomy of one or another art form: "The concept of pure art—pure poetry, pure painting, and so on—is not entirely without meaning; but it refers to an aesthetic reality as difficult to define as it is to combat" (60).

So is the concept of clearly defined disciplinary boundaries. If their objects of study—be they literature, cinema, painting, sculpture, music or architecture—are far from pure, why should the disciplines that study them be different? To really understand the complex life of art, which entails the circulation of ideas irrespective of their medium, we should look at art as its creators do: with the absolute freedom of the mind in the solitude of our little room at the back of the shop that Montaigne dreamed of, where we can establish "our true liberty, our principal solitude and asylum."

BIBLIOGRAPHY

Video sources

Ago, Alex. "Interview with Paolo Sorrentino." Samuel Goldwyn Theater, November 24, 2013. https://www.youtube.com/watch?v=w38qeRrapvs

Allen, Woody. *Magic in the Moonlight*. Perdido Productions & Gravier Productions, 2014.

Buñuel, Luis, and Salvador Dalí. *L'Âge d'or*. Produced by Vicomte de Noailles, 1930. Corinth Films, 1930.

Daldry, Stephen. "Three Women." Featurette included in the DVD of Stephen Daldry, *The Hours*. Special collector's ed., widescreen version. Hollywood: Paramount Home Entertainment, [2003], 2002.

Daldry, Stephen. *The Hours*. Special collector's ed., widescreen version. Hollywood: Paramount Home Entertainment, [2003], 2002.

Giovanni, Minoli. "Faccia a Faccia." Interview with Paolo Sorrentino. January 12, 2017. https://www.youtube.com/watch?v=isVsb7YRYQU

Glass, Philip, Stephen Daldry, and David Hare. "The Music of *The Hours*." Featurette included in the DVD of Stephen Daldry, *The Hours*.

Gruber, Lilli. "*La Grande Bellezza* di Sorrentino e Servillo." Interview with Paolo Sorrentino and Toni Servillo. June 7, 2013. https://www.youtube.com/watch?v=D2LfyVks6F4

Hébert, Claudia. "Rencontre: Paolo Sorrentino." Cine TFO. January 20, 2014. https://www.youtube.com/watch?v=Ozh0bmTZcrw

Kurosawa, Akira. *Akira Kurosawa's Dreams*. Warner Bros, 1990. United States: Criterion Collection, 2016.

Kurosawa, Akira. *Dodes'kaden*. Toho Studios, 1970.

Kurosawa, Akira. *Ran*. Herald Ace, Nippon Herald Films, Greenwich Film Productions, 1985. Chicago: Home Vision Entertainment; [United States]: Wellspring Media; Chatsworth: Image Entertainment, 2005.

Kurosawa, Akira. *Rashomon*. Daiei Film, 1950. Irvington: Criterion Collection, c2002.

Kurosawa, Akira. *Rhapsody in August*. Kurosawa Productions, 1991.

Kurosawa, Akira. *Throne of Blood*. Toho Studios, 1957. San Francisco: Kanopy Streaming, 2014.

Marker, Chris. *One Day in the Life of Andrei Arsenevich*. New York: First Run/Icarus Films, 1999.

Méliès, Georges. *Arrivée d'un train (Gare de Vincennes)*. Star Film Company, 1896.

Méliès, Georges. *L'Affaire Dreyfus*. Star Film Company, 1899.

Méliès, Georges. *Le Cake-Walk Infernal*. Star Film Company, 1903.

Méliès, Georges. *Le Livre magique*. Star Film Company, 1900. https://www.youtube.com/watch?v=8OmqWrn6EMs

Méliès, Georges. *Le Palais des mille et une nuits*. Star Film Company, 1905. https://www.youtube.com/watch?v=l_-V5HFvj7g

Méliès, Georges. *Le Voyage dans la lune*. Star Film Company, 1902. Los Angeles: Flicker Alley, 2012. https://www.youtube.com/watch?v=ZNAHcMMOHE8\

Méliès, Georges. *Les Moustaches indomptables*. Star Film Company, 1904. https://www.youtube.com/watch?v=oKWymTekryY&t=33s

Méliès, Georges. *Les Quat'cents farces du diable*. Star Film Company, 1906. https://www.youtube.com/watch?v=vlSs36AUb5M

Resnais, Alain. *Van Gogh*. Producers: Pierre Braunberger, Gaston Diehl, and Robert Hessens, 1948.

Ruiz, Raúl. *Le Temps retrouvé*. Gemini Films, France 2 Cinema, Les Films du Lendemain, 1999. New York: Kino on Video, 2001.

Scorsese, Martin. *Hugo*. Paramount Pictures and GK Films, 2011. Hollywood: Paramount Home Entertainment, 2012.

Sokurov, Alexander. *Russian Ark*. Hermitage Bridge Studio and Egoli Tossell Film AG production, 2002. New York: Wellspring Media, 2003.

Sorrentino, Paolo. "Come funziono." TEDx ReggioEmilia. October 20, 2011. https://www.youtube.com/watch?v=mKIJrYKeTcU

Sorrentino, Paolo. "DP/30." Interview. https://www.youtube.com/watch?v=d3d8u4HoZ8E

Sorrentino, Paolo. "Futura Festival Interview," 2013. https://www.youtube.com/watch?v=xWD1ANi9Gnc

Sorrentino, Paolo. *La Grande Bellezza*. Indigo Film & Medusa Film; co-produced with Babe Films, Pathé, France 2 Cinéma, 2013. New York: Criterion Collection, 2014.

Tarkovsky, Andrei. *Andrei Rublev*. Mosfilm Studios, 1966. Irvington, New York: Criterion Collection, 2018.

Tarkovsky, Andrei. *Ivan's Childhood*. Mosfilm Studios, 1962. Irvington, New York: Criterion Collection; Chatsworth, CA: Image Entertainment, 2007.

Tarkovsky, Andrei. *Nostalghia*. Opera Film Produzione, RAI Radiotelevisione italiana, Sovin Film, 1983. New York: Kino Lorber, 2014.

Tarkovsky, Andrei. *Solaris*. Mosfilm Studios, 1972. United States: Criterion Collection, 2002.

Tarkovsky, Andrei. *Stalker*. Mosfilm Studios, 1979. New York: Fox Lorber Home Video, c1993.

Tarkovsky, Andrei, and Tonino Guerra. *Tempo di viaggio*. Radiotelevisione italiana and Facets Video, 1983. Facets Video, 2004.

Tarkovsky, Andrei. *The Mirror*. Mosfilm Studios, 1975. New York: Kino on Video, 2000.

Tarkovsky, Andrei. *The Sacrifice*. Svenska Filminstitutet, 1986. New York: Kino International Corporation: Kino on Video, 2000.

Wong Kar-wai. *In the Mood for Love*. Jet Tone Films Productions, 2000. United States: Criterion Collection, c2002.

Wong Kar-wai. *2046*. Jet Tone Films Productions, 2004. Culver City, CA: Sony Pictures Home Entertainment, 2005.

Worne, Duke. *The Trail of the Octopus*. United States: Hallmark Pictures Corporation, 1919.

Written sources

Abbas, Ackbar. *Hong Kong: Culture and the Politics of Disappearance.* Minneapolis: University of Minnesota Press, 1997.

Abbas, Ackbar. "Wong Kar-wai's Cinema of Repetition." In Nochimson, ed. *A Companion to Wong Kar-wai*, 115–34.

Anderson, Melissa. *"Time Regained." Cineaste* 25.1 (December 1999): 43–4.

Andrew, Dudley. *André Bazin.* Oxford: Oxford University Press, 2013. Ebook.

Andrew, Dudley. "An Atlas of World Cinema." *Framework: The Journal of Cinema and Media.* 45: 2 (Fall 2004), 9–23.

Andrew, Dudley. *Film in the Aura of Art.* Princeton: Princeton University Press, 1984.

Andrew, Dudley. "Foreword to the 2004 edition" of André Bazin, *What Is Cinema?* v.2, xi–xxvi.

Andrew, Dudley, and Hervé Joubert-Laurencin, eds. *Opening Bazin: Postwar Film Theory and Its Afterlife.* Oxford University Press, 2011.

Andrew, Dudley. *What Cinema Is!: Bazin's Quest and Its Charge.* Wiley-Blackwell, 2010.

Annett, Sandra. "The Nostalgic Remediation of Cinema." *Journal of Adaptation in Film & Performance* 7.2 (2014), 169–80.

Apter, Emily. *Against World Literature: On the Politics of Untranslatability.* London, New York: Verso, 2013.

Artemenko, Irena. *The Ethics of Mourning in the Narration of the Self in the Works of Marcel Proust and Andrei Tarkovsky.* Honor thesis, Wadham College, 2017.

Aspesi, Natalia. "That Gentle Emotion that is a Mortal Illness for us Russians." Interview with Andrei Tarkovsky. *La Repubblica*, May 17, 1983. http://www.nostalghia.com/TheTopics/Tarkovsky_Aspesi-1983.html

Auerbach, Erich. *Mimesis: The Representation of Reality in Western Literature.* Tr. Willard R. Trask. Princeton: Princeton University Press, 2003.

Baatsch, Henri-Alexis. *Hokusai: A Life in Drawing.* Tr. Ruth Sharman. London: Thames & Hudson, 2018.

Baker, Aaron, ed. *A Companion to Martin Scorsese.* New York: Wiley Blackwell, 2015.

Bal, Mieke. *The Mottled Screen: Reading Proust Visually.* Stanford: Stanford University Press, 1997.

Bamforth, Iain. "Doing the Locomotion: Paolo Sorrentino's *La Grande Bellezza*." *Quadrant* January-February (2015): 132–4.

Barde, Bruno. "Entretien avec Raoul Ruiz." *L'Avant-scène. Cinéma* 482 (May 1999): 1–3.

Barr, Alfred H, Jr., ed. *Fantastic Art, Dada, Surrealism.* New York: Museum of Modern Art, 1936.

Bazin, André. "Akira Kurosawa's *To Live*." *Cahiers du cinéma*, March 1957. In Bert Cardullo, ed. *Bazin on Global Cinema*, 163–6.

Bazin, André. "An Aesthetic of Reality: Neorealism." In *What Is Cinema?* v.2, 16–40.

Bazin, André. "Bicycle Thief." In *What Is Cinema?* v.2, 47–60.

Bazin, André. "*Cabiria*: The Voyage to the End of Neorealism." In *What Is Cinema?* v.2, 83–92.

Bazin, André. "In Defense of Mixed Cinema." In *What Is Cinema?* v.1, 53–75.

Bazin, André. "Painting and Cinema." In *What Is Cinema?* v.1, 164–72.

Bazin, André. "Theatre and Cinema." Parts I and II in *What Is Cinema?* v.1, 76–94 and 95–124.

Bazin, André. "The Evolution of the Language of Cinema." In *What Is Cinema?* v.1, 23–40.

Bazin, André. "The Grandeur of *Limelight*." In *What Is Cinema?* v.2, 128–39.

Bazin, André. "The Myth of Total Cinema." In *What Is Cinema?* v.1, 17–22.

Bazin, André. "The Ontology of the Photographic Image." In *What Is Cinema?* v.1, 9–16.

Bazin, André. "The Virtues and Limitations of Montage." In *What Is Cinema?* v.1, 41–52.

Bazin, André. "Tout film est un documentaire social." *Les Lettres françaises*, 5:166, July 25, 1947.

Bazin, André. *What Is Cinema?* 2 vols. Ed. and tr. Hugh Gray. Berkeley: University of California Press, 2005.

Bégin, Richard. "L'écran baroque." *Décadrages* 15 (2009): 25–37.

Bergman, Ingmar. *The Magic Lantern: An Autobiography*. Tr. Joan Tate. New York: Penguin, 1989.

Bergstein, Mary. *In Looking Back, One Learns to See: Marcel Proust and Photography*. Amsterdam: Rodopi, 2014.

Beugnet, Martine. "Surrealist Proust: Raoul Ruiz's *Le Temps retrouvé*." In Martine Beugnet and Marion Schmid, *Proust at the Movies*. Burlington, VT: Ashgate, 2006, 132–67.

Billington, Michael. "Nothing is the hardest thing to do." Interview with Stephen Daldry. *The Guardian*. February 12, 2003. http://www.theguardian.com/film/2003/feb/12/oscars2003.oscars

Bird, Robert. *Andrei Tarkovsky: Elements of Cinema*. London: Reaktion Books, 2008.

Borges, Jorge Luis. "Virginia Woolf." In *Selected Non-fictions*. Ed. Eliot Weinberger. Tr. Esther Allen, Suzanne Jill Levine, Eliot Weinberger. New York: Viking Penguin, 1999, 173–4.

Bouquet, Stéphane, and Emmanuel Burdeau. "Dans le laboratoire de *La Recherche*. Entretien avec Raoul Ruiz." *Cahiers du cinéma* 535 (May 1999): 46–53.

Bourget, Jean-Loup. "*Le Temps retrouvé*: Nouvelle esquisse du caractère étrange de Morel." *Positif* 461–2 (July-August 1999): 134–5.

Bovay, Georges Michel, Jean Cocteau et al. *Cinéma, un œil ouvert sur le monde*. Lausanne: Editions Clairefontaine, 1952.

Bovier, François, et al. "Entretien avec Raoul Ruiz." *Décadrages* 15 (2009): 78–86.

Bowe, John. "Martin Scorsese's Magical *Hugo*." *The New York Times Magazine*. November 2, 2011. https://www.nytimes.com/2011/11/06/magazine/martin-scorseses-magical-hugo.html

Bowen, Elizabeth. "*Orlando* by Virginia Woolf." In *The Mulberry Tree: Writings of Elizabeth Bowen*. Ed. Hermione Lee. London: Virago, 1986.

Brassaï. *Proust in the Power of Photography*. Tr. Richard Howard. Chicago: University of Chicago Press, 2001.

BIBLIOGRAPHY

Bray, Patrick M. "The 'Debris of Experience:' The Cinema of Marcel Proust and Raoul Ruiz." *Romanic Review* 101.3 (2010): 467–82.

Breton, André. "Ascendant Sign." In Caws, ed. *Surrealist Painters and Poets*, 134–7.

Breton, André. *Clair de terre*. Paris, November 15, 1923.

Breton, André. "Enquête sur l'amour." *La Révolution surréaliste* 12 (December 15, 1929): 65–76.

Breton, André. "Gradiva." In *La Clé des champs*, 24–8.

Breton, André. "Introduction au discours sur le peu de la réalité." In *Oeuvres complètes*. vol. 2. Eds. Marguerite Bonnet et al., 265–80.

Breton, André. *La Clé des champs*. Paris: Société Nouvelle des Éditions Pauvert, 1979.

Breton, André. "Le message automatique." *Minotaure* 3–4 (December 12, 1933): 55–65.

Breton, André. *Lettres à Simone Kahn 1920–1960*. Ed. Jean-Michel Goutier. Paris: Gallimard, 2016.

Breton, André. *Mad Love*. Tr. Mary Ann Caws. Lincoln: University of Nebraska Press, 1987.

Breton, André. *Manifestoes of Surrealism*. Tr. Richard Seaver and Helen R. Lane. Ann Arbor: University of Michigan Press, 1969.

Breton, André. *Nadja*. Tr. Richard Howard. New York: Grove Press, 1960.

Breton, André. *Oeuvres complètes*. v.2. Ed. Marguerite Bonnet et al. Paris: Gallimard, 1992.

Brett, Anwar. "Stephen Daldry: *The Hours*." Interview. BBC, September 24, 2003. http://www.bbc.co.uk/films/2003/02/03/stephen_daldry_the_hours_interview.shtml

Brunette, Peter. "Interview with Wong Kar-wai (1995)" and "Interview with Wong Kar-wai (2001)." In Brunette, *Wong Kar-wai*, Urbana: University of Illinois Press, 2005, 113–21 and 123–33.

Bullen, Elizabeth, et al. "Cinema and the Book: Intermediality in *The Invention of Hugo Cabret*." *The Lion and the Unicorn* 42 (2018): 73–87.

Cao Xueqin. *The Story of the Stone*. Vol. I: *The Golden Days*. Tr. David Hawkes. London: Penguin, 1973.

Cao Xueqin. *The Story of the Stone*. Tr. David Hawkes and John Minford. London: Penguin, 5 vols., 1973–86. Ebook.

Cardullo, Bert. "Art and Matter." *The Hudson Review* 56.4 (December 1, 2004): 669–76.

Cardullo, Bert, ed. and tr. *Bazin on Global Cinema* (1948–58). Austin: University of Texas Press, 2014.

Casanova, Pascale. *La République mondiale des Lettres*. Paris: Éditions du Seuil, 1999.

Caws, Mary Ann, ed. *Surrealist Painters and Poets: An Anthology*. Cambridge, MA: MIT Press, 2001.

Céline, Louis-Ferdinand. *Journey to the End of the Night*. Tr. Ralph Manheim. New York: New Directions, 1983. Ebook.

Céline, Louis-Ferdinand. *Voyage au bout de la nuit*: suivi de *Mort à credit*. Paris: Gallimard, 1962.

Chapman, Mark A. et al. "Genetic Analysis of Floral Symmetry in Van Gogh's *Sunflowers* Reveals Independent Recruitment of *CYCLOIDEA* Genes in the Asteraceae." *PLOS Genetics* 8.3 (2012): 1–10.

BIBLIOGRAPHY

Chapuis, Alfred and Edouard Gélis. *Le Monde des automates: Étude historique et technique.* Genève: Editions Slatkine, 1984.

Cheah, Pheng. *What Is a World?: On Postcolonial Literature as World Literature.* Durham, NC: Duke University Press, 2016.

Chevrier, Jean-François. "The Reality of Hallucination in André Bazin." In Andrew and Joubert-Laurencin, eds. *Opening Bazin*, 42–56.

Christie, Ian. "Introduction" to Maya Turovskaya, *Tarkovsky: Cinema as Poetry*, ix–xxvii.

Christie, Ian. "The Illusionist." *Sight and Sound* 22.1 (Jan 2012): 36, 38–9, 2.

Ciment, Michel, and Hubert Niogret. "Comme fumer de l'opium." *Positif* 525 (November 2004): 90–4.

Clavesi, Maurizio. *Piero della Francesca.* Milan: Fabbri Editori, 1998.

Cocking, J.M. *Proust: Collected Essays on the Writer and His Art.* Cambridge, England: Cambridge University Press, 1982.

Cocteau, Jean. "Le masque de Proust." *Les Nouvelles littéraires* 1.6 (November 25, 1922): 1.

Codelli, Lorenzo. "Entretien avec Paolo Sorrentino: je cherche un père." *Positif* 628 (June 2013): 27–30.

Cohen, David. "From Script to Screen: *The Hours.*" *Script*, September 24, 2015. https://scriptmag.com/columns/script-screen-the-hours

Cooke, Paul. *World Cinema's 'Dialogues' with Hollywood.* London: Palgrave Macmillan UK, 2007.

Counihan, Francesca, and Bérengère Deprez, eds. *Écriture du Pouvoir, Pouvoir de l'écriture: La Réalité sociale et politique dans l'oeuvre de Marguerite Yourcenar.* Brussels: Peter Lang, 2006.

Cousins, Mark. "Throwing the Book at Film." *Prospect*, March 20, 2003. https://www.prospectmagazine.co.uk/magazine/throwingthebookatfilm

Crisp, Deborah and Roger Hillman. "Chiming the Hours: A Philip Glass Soundtrack." *Music and the Moving Image* 3.2 (Summer 2010): 30–8.

Crowdus, Gary. "In Search of *The Great Beauty.*" Interview with Paolo Sorrentino. *Cineaste* (Spring 2014): 8–13.

Cunningham, Michael. *The Hours.* New York: Farrar, Straus and Giroux, 2000.

Cyprès, Amandine. "Dis(ap)paritions: *Le Temps retrouvé*, de Proust à Ruiz." *Babel* 13 (2006): 287–318. http://journals.openedition.org/babel/986

D'Amico, Valentina. "Una versione estenuante de *La grande bellezza* per raccontare il male di vivere." Interview with Paolo Sorrentino. June 28, 2016. https://movieplayer.it/articoli/la-grande-bellezza-paolo-sorrentino-spiega-le-differenze-della-version_16044/

Damrosch, David. *Comparing the Literatures: Literary Studies in a Global Age".* Princeton: Princeton University Press, 2020.

Damrosch, David. *What Is World Literature?* Princeton: Princeton University Press, 2003.

Danius, Sara. *The Senses of Modernism.* Ithaca: Cornell University Press, 2002.

DeBona, Guerric, "*Hugo* and the (Re-)Invention of Martin Scorsese." In Aaron Baker, ed. *A Companion to Martin Scorsese*, 459–79.

De Medeiros, Ana. "*Les Nouvelles Orientales*: Étude de l'Orient/ Étude de l'Auteur." In Rémy Poignault and Jean-Pierre Castellani, eds. *Marguerite Yourcenar: Écriture, réécriture, traduction*, 189–96.

Denby, David. "How *The Hours* Happened." Interview with Stephen Daldry. *The New Yorker*, March 17, 2003. https://www.newyorker.com/magazine/2003/03/24/how-the-hours-happened

Dennison, Stephanie, and Song Hwee Lim, eds. *Remapping World Cinema: Identity, Culture and Politics in Film*. London, New York: Wallflower Press, 2006.

Dostoevsky, Fyodor. *The Idiot*. Tr. Richard Pevear and Larissa Volokhonsky. New York: Vintage Classics, 2002. Ebook.

Du Blois, Isabelle. *Le double dans les* Nouvelles orientales *de Marguerite Yourcenar*. Dissertation thesis. Département de langue et littérature françaises, Université McGill, Montréal, Québec. March 2001.

Ďurišin, Dionýz. *Čo je svetová literatura?* Bratislava: Obzor, 1992.

Eagan, Daniel. "'A Precise, Beautiful Machine': John Logan on Writing the Screenplay for *Hugo*." *Smithsonian Magazine*, February 24, 2012. https://www.smithsonianmag.com/arts-culture/a-precise-beautiful-machine-john-logan-on-writing-the-screenplay-for-hugo-107504379

Elkann, Alain. "Siamo tutti soli. Il cinema è fatto per consolarci." *La Stampa*, March 5, 2017. https://www.lastampa.it/cultura/2017/03/05/news/paolo-sorrentino-siamo-tutti-soli-il-cinema-e-fatto-per-consolarci-1.34629720

Essai de reconstitution du catalogue français de la Star-Film; suivi d'une analyse catalographique des films de Georges Méliès recensés en France. Bois d'Arcy: Service des archives du film du Centre national de la cinématographie, 1981.

ffrench, Patrick. *Thinking Cinema with Proust*. Cambridge: Legenda, 2018.

Flaubert, Gustave. *Dictionnaire des idées reçues*. Paris: J'ai lu, 1998.

Flaubert, Gustave. *Madame Bovary: Provincial Manners*. Tr. Margaret Mauldon. Oxford World's Classics. Oxford: Oxford University Press, 2004.

Frodon, Jean-Michel. "J'ai pu adapter Proust parce que Victor Hugo était trop cher." Interview with Raúl Ruiz. *Le Monde*, May 18, 1999.

Galt, Rosalind, and Karl Schoonover. *Global Art Cinema: New Theories and Histories*. Oxford: Oxford University Press, 2010.

Gilson, Paul. "Georges Méliès, Inventeur." *La Revue du cinéma* 4 (October 15, 1929): 4–19.

Gorfinkel, Elena, and Tami Williams. *Global Cinema Networks*. New Brunswick: Rutgers University Press, 2018.

Grassin, Sophie. "À la recherche de Raoul Ruiz." Interview with Gilles Taurand. *L'Express*, May 13, 1999. http://www.lexpress.fr/culture/cinema/mort-de-raoul-ruiz-interview-pour-le-temps-retrouve_633625.html#hDdr2P1udfDqMkKJ.99

Green, Peter. *Andrei Tarkovsky: The Winding Quest*. London: Macmillan, 1994.

Guérard, Albert. "Comparative Literature?" *Yearbook of Comparative and General Literature* 7 (1958): 1–6.

Guibert, Hervé. "Le noir coloris de la nostalgie." Interview with Andrei Tarkovsky, *Le Monde*, May 12, 1983. https://www.lemonde.fr/archives/article/1983/05/12/le-noir-coloris-de-la-nostalgie_2834079_1819218.html

Hare, David. *The Hours: A Screenplay*. New York: Miramax Books, 2002.

Harrison, Thomas. "Herodotus' Conception of Foreign Languages." *Histos* 2 (1998): 1–45.

Hawkes, David. "Introduction." Cao Xueqin, *The Story of the Stone*. v.1. *The Golden Days*. Tr. David Hawkes. London: Penguin, 1973.

278   BIBLIOGRAPHY

Hayashi, Osamu. "*Nouvelles Orientales*: Un autre diagnostic de l'Europe?" In Francesca Counihan and Bérengère Deprez, eds. *Écriture du Pouvoir, Pouvoir de l'écriture*, 99–106.

Hennessey, Brendan. "Reel simulations: CGI and special effects in two films by Paolo Sorrentino." *The Italianist* 37:3 (2017): 449–63.

Hiramatsu, Naoko. "Le Dernier Amour de Prince Genghi dans *Nouvelles Orientales* de Marguerite Yourcenar." 慶應義塾大学フランス文学研究室紀要 4 (1999): 87–99.

Holtby, Winifred. *Virginia Woolf: A Critical Memoir*. London: Continuum, 2007.

Hutchinson, Rachel. "Orientalism or Occidentalism? Dynamics of Appropriation in Akira Kurosawa." In Dennison and Lim, eds. *Remapping World Cinema*, 173–87.

Ifri, Pascal A. *Céline et Proust. Correspondences proustiennes dans l'oeuvre de L.-F. Céline*. Birmingham, Alabama: Summa Publications, 1996.

Illg, Jerzy, and Leonard Neuger. "I'm interested in the problem of inner freedom." Interview, March 1985, Stockholm. In *Powiększenie* 1/2 (25/26), Cracow, 1987: 146–76. http://nostalghia.com/TheTopics/interview.html

Ingham, Mike, and Matthew Kwok-kin Fung. "In the Mood for Food: Wong Kar-wai's Culinary Imaginary." In Martha Nochimson, ed. *A Companion to Wong Kar-wai*, 295–318.

Jahn, Pam. "Interview with Paolo Sorrentino." *Electric Sheep*. September 5, 2013. http://www.electricsheepmagazine.co.uk/2013/09/05/the-great-beauty-interview-with-paolo-sorrentino/

Johnson, Vida T., and Graham Petrie. *The Films of Andrei Tarkovsky: A Visual Fugue*. Bloomington: Indiana University Press, 1994.

Johnston, Sheila. "A Day in the Life." *Sight and Sound* 13.2 (February 2003): 24–7.

Johnston, Sheila. "*The Hours*. Stephen Daldry Q&A." Interview with Michael Cunningham, David Hare and Stephen Daldry. http://www.indielondon.co.uk/film/hours_daldry&co.html

Jullien, Dominique. *Proust et ses modèles*. Les Milles et Une Nuits *et les* Mémoires de Saint-Simon. Paris: José Corti, 1989.

Kasel, Jacob. *Poignant Immobility: Temporality in the Works of Barthes, Lispector, Proust and Tarkovsky*. Honors thesis, Wadham College, 2017.

Klonarides, Carole Ann. "Raúl Ruiz." Interview. *Bomb*, January 1, 1991. https://bombmagazine.org/articles/raul-Ruíz

Kluge, Alexander. "The Realistic Method and the 'Filmic'." In *Difference and Orientation: An Alexander Kluge Reader*. Ed. Richard Langston. Ithaca: Cornell University Press, 2019. Ebook.

Kristeva, Julia. *Time and Sense: Proust and the Experience of Literature*. Tr. Ross Guberman. New York: Columbia University Press, 1996.

Kurosawa, Akira. *A Dream is a Genius*. Selected pages. Tr. Sato Kimitoshi. Tokyo: Bungeishunjū Ltd, 1999, 180–2. http://www.nostalghia.com/TheTopics/Kurosawa_on_AT.html

Kurosawa, Akira. "Foreword." *Akira Kurosawa Drawings*. Exhibit catalog. Tr. Noriko Fuku & Associates. Tokyo: Ise Cultural Foundation, 1994.

Kurosawa, Akira. *Something Like an Autobiography*. Tr. Audie E. Bock. New York: Vintage, 1983.

BIBLIOGRAPHY

Kurosawa, Akira. "Tarkovsky and *Solaris*." Tr. Sato Kimitoshi. *Asahi Shinbun*, May 13, 1977. http://www.nostalghia.com/TheTopics/Kurosawa_on_Solaris.html

Lane, Anthony. "Telling Time: The Scandals and Satisfactions of the Proustian Beau Monde." *The New Yorker*, June 19–26, 2000, 187–9.

Larkin, Áine. *Proust Writing Photography: Fixing the Fugitive in* À la recherche du temps perdu. London: Legenda, 2011.

Leavenworth, Maria Lindgren. "'A Life as Potent and Dangerous as Literature Itself': Intermediated Moves from *Mrs. Dalloway* to *The Hours*." *Journal of Popular Culture* 43.3 (2010): 503–23.

LeBlanc, Michael. "Melancholic Arrangements: Music, Queer Melodrama, and the Seeds of Transformation in *The Hours*." *Camera Obscura* 61, 21.1 (2006): 105–45.

Lee, Vivian P.Y. "Infidelity and the Obscure Object of History." In Martha Nochimson, ed. *A Companion to Wong Kar-wai*, 378–96.

Leroux, Gabriel. "Sans désordre préconçu." *L'Etincelle. Journal de la création à l'Ircam*, November 6, 2009, 18–20.

Lewis, Tim. "Stephen Daldry: 'Hollywood? I've never been there'." *The Guardian*. February 10, 2013. https://www.theguardian.com/culture/2013/feb/10/stephen-daldry-mirren-audience-interview

Lowenstein, Adam. *Dreaming of Cinema: Spectatorship, Surrealism, and the Age of Digital Media*. New York: Columbia University Press, 2014.

MacCarthy, Desmond. Review of *Orlando* (1928). In Majumdar and McLaurin, eds. *Virginia Woolf*, 222–6.

MacGillivray, James. "Andrei Tarkovsky's 'Madonna del Parto.'" *Canadian Journal of Film Studies*, 11.2 (2002): 82–100.

Majumdar, Robin, and Allen McLaurin, eds. *Virginia Woolf: The Critical Heritage*. London and New York: Routledge, 2003.

Malausa, Vincent. "Paolo Sorrentino, un invité envahissant." *Cahiers du cinéma*, May 2013: 23.

Mancino, Anton Giulio. "Roma: This must be the (product) place(ment)." *Cineforum* 53.6 (2013): 7–9.

Martini, Alessia. "Concept City: Roma ri-vista e vissuta ne *La dolce vita e La grande bellezza*." *Carte italiane* 2.10 (2015): 107–19.

Mayoux, Jean-Jacques. "Le roman de l'espace et du temps—Virginia Woolf," *Revue Anglo-Americaine*. Paris (April 1930): 312–26. In Robin Majumdar and Allen McLaurin, eds. *Virginia Woolf*, 246–50.

Mazierska, Ewa, and Laura Rascaroli. "Trapped in the Present: Time in the Films of Wong Kar-wai." *Film Criticism* 25.2 (Winter 2000/2001): 1–20.

Méliès, Geo[rges]. "Les Vues Cinématographiques." *Annuaire Général et International de la Photographie*. Paris: Plon, 1907: 362–92.

Mereghetti, Paolo. "'La grande bellezza' integrale Sorrentino." Interview with Paolo Sorrentino. *Corriere della sera*, June 25, 2016. https://www.corriere.it/spettacoli/16_giugno_26/grande-bellezza-integrale-racconto-estenuante-vita-sorrentino-7fcc1e9a-3afb-11e6-a019-901bc4c9f010.shtml?refresh_ce-cp

Montaigne, Michel de. *The Complete Essays*. Tr. M.A. Screech. London: Penguin, 2003.

Moretti, Franco. "Conjectures on World Literature" and "More Conjectures." *New Left Review* n.s. 1 (2000): 54–68, and 20 (2003): 73–81.

Morreale, Emiliano, and Dario Zonta, eds. *Cinema vivo. Quindici registi a confronto*. Rome: Edizioni dell'Asino, 2009.

Nagib Lúcia, and Anne Jerslev, eds. *Impure Cinema: Intermedial and Intercultural Approaches to Film*. I.B. Tauris & Co Ltd: London and New York, 2014.

Nagib, Lúcia, et al. *Theorizing World Cinema*. London: I.B. Tauris, 2012.

Naremore, James, ed. *Film Adaptation*. New Brunswick: Rutgers University Press, 2000.

Nave, Bernard. "La grande bellezza." *Jeune cinéma* 352–3 (Summer, 2013): 130–2.

Nicaise, Pierre-Alexandre and Raúl Ruiz. "Entretien avec Raúl Ruiz." *Cinémas d'Amérique latine* 16 (2008): 108–18.

Nochimson, Martha P., ed. *A Companion to Wong Kar-wai*. Wiley Blackwell, 2016.

Nochimson, Martha P. "We Can't Go On Meeting Like This." In Nochimson, ed. *A Companion to Wong Kar-wai*, 438–61.

Pauchon, Luc. "Voyage dans les *Nouvelles orientales*." *Équinoxe* 2 (Fall 1989): 75–83.

Paulicelli, Eugenia. "After *La Dolce Vita: La Grande Bellezza*." *Italian Style* (2016): 185–94.

Péret, Benjamin. "Au Paradis des Fantômes." *Minotaure* 3–4 (1933): 29–34.

Pisani, Giuliano. "Le Veneri di Raffaello." *Studi di Storia dell'Arte* 26 (2015), 97–122.

Poignault, Rémy, and Jean-Pierre Castellani, eds. *Marguerite Yourcenar: Écriture, réécriture, traduction*. Tours: Société Internationale d'Études Yourcenariennes, 2000.

Posnett, Hutcheson Macaulay. *Comparative Literature*. London: Kegan, Trench, 1886.

Proust, Marcel. *À la recherche du temps perdu*. Eds. Pierre Clarac and André Ferré. Paris: Gallimard, 6 vols. 1954.

Proust, Marcel. *In Search of Lost Time*. Vols. 1–5: *Swann's Way, Within a Budding Grove, The Guermantes Way, Sodom and Gomorrah, The Captive & The Fugitive*. Tr. C. K. Scott-Moncrieff and Terence Kilmartin. Rev. by D.J. Enright. Vol. 6: *Time Regained*. Tr. Andreas Mayor and Terence Kilmartin. Rev. by D.J. Enright. New York: Modern Library, 2003.

Proust, Marcel. "Et si le monde allait finir . . . Que feriez-vous?" *L'Intransigeant* 43.15349 (August 14, 1922): 2.

Proust, Marcel. [Pierre de Touche] "Souvenir." *Le Mensuel* 1.12 (September 1891): 7–9.

Rabelais, François. *Gargantua and Pantagruel*. Tr. M.A. Screech. London: Penguin, 2006.

Reider, Noriko Tsunoda. "Akira Kurosawa's *Dreams*, as seen through the principles of classical Japanese literature and performing art." *Japan Forum* 17(2) 2005: 257–72.

Richie, Donald. *The Films of Akira Kurosawa*. Berkeley: University of California Press, 2d ed. 1970.

Romney, Jonathan. "Masque of the Living Dead." *Sight and Sound* 10.1 (January 1, 2000): 30–3.

Rondi, Gian Luigi. "A Talk with Tarkovsky." April 15, 1980. http://www.nostalghia.com/TheTopics/Tarkovsky_Rondi-1980.html

Rubenstein, Roberta. *Virginia Woolf and the Russian Point of View*. New York: Palgrave Macmillan, 2009.

BIBLIOGRAPHY

Ruiz, Raúl. *Poetics of Cinema*. Vol. I: *Miscellanies*. Tr. Brian Holmes. Paris: Éditions Dis Voir, 1995.

Ruiz, Raúl. *Poetics of Cinema*. Vol. II. Tr. Carlos Morreo. Paris: Éditions Dis Voir, 2007.

Sadoul, Georges. *Histoire du cinéma mondial: Des origines à nos jours*. Paris: Flammarion, 1961.

Sadoul, Georges. *Histoire générale du cinéma*. Paris: Denoël, 1946.

Sadoul, Georges. "Notes sur Jules Verne et le cinéma." *Europe* 112–13 (April-May 1955): 99–103.

Sand, George. *The Story of My Life*. Ed. Thelma Jurgrau. Albany: State University Press of New York, 1991.

Scarpetta, Guy. "Réflexions sur *Le Temps retrouvé*." *Positif* 463 (September 1999): 66–72.

Scorsese, Martin. "Foreword" to Peter Kobel, *Silent Movies: The Birth of Film and the Triumph of Movie Culture*. New York: Little, Brown and Co., 2007. Ebook.

Scorsese, Martin, and Kate Shaw. *Hugo*. Lucasfilm Speaker Series. January 17, 2012. https://www.youtube.com/watch?v=xZ6w3f4v4oU

Scorsese, Martin. *Interviews*. Ed. Robert Ribera. Jackson: University Press of Mississippi, 2017.

Scorsese, Martin. "Martin Scorsese on *Hugo*: A Very Personal Film." CBS News, April 23, 2012. https://www.cbsnews.com/news/martin-scorsese-on-hugo-a-very-personal-film

Scorsese, Martin. "Proust Questionnaire." *Vanity Fair*, March 2010. https://www.vanityfair.com/news/2010/03/proust-scorsese-201003

Selznick, Brian. *The Invention of Hugo Cabret*. New York: Scholastic Press, 2007.

Serper, Zvika. "Kurosawa's *Dreams*: A Cinematic Reflection of a Traditional Japanese Context." *Cinema Journal* 40.4 (2001): 81–103.

Servillo, Toni [Jep Gambardella]. "La grande bellezza agli Oscar, Jep Gambardella intervista Sorrentino." *Vanity Fair*, March 2, 2014. https://www.vanityfair.it/show/cinema/14/03/02/oscar-2014-la-grande-bellezza-jep-gambardella-intervista-sorrentino

Sicinski, Michael. "Paolo Sorrentino: A Medium Talent." *Cinema scope* 58 (2014): 17–21.

Skakov, Nariman. *The Cinema of Tarkovsky: The Labyrinths of Space and Time*. London: I.B. Tauris, 2012.

Smith, Alexandra. "Andrei Tarkovsky as Reader of Arsenii Tarkovsky's Poetry." *Russian Studies in Literature* 4.3 (Summer 2004): 46–63.

Sorrentino, Paolo. *Hanno tutti ragione*. Milan: Feltrinelli, 2010.

Sorrentino, Paolo. Umberto Contarello. *La grande bellezza*. Lausanne: Skira, 2013.

Sorrentino, Paolo. *Toni Pagoda e i suoi amici*. Milan: Feltrinelli, 2012.

Spila, Piero, and Bruno Torri. "Paolo Sorrentino: il cinema, il divertimento, l'ossessione." Interview. *CineCriticaWeb*, February 13, 2010. http://www.cinecriticaweb.it/panoramiche/paolo-sorrentino-il-cinema-il-divertimento-l%e2%80%99ossessione-intervista/

Stam, Robert. *World Literature, Transnational Cinema, and Global Media: Towards a Transartistic Commons*. London and New York: Routledge, 2019.

Synessios, Natasha. *Mirror: The Film Companion*. London, New York: I.B. Tauris, 2001.

Tarkovskaya, Marina. *Осколки зеркала*. Moscow: Dedalus, 1999.

Tarkovsky, Andrei. *Sculpting in Time*. Tr. Kitty Hunter-Blair. Austin, TX: University of Texas Press, 1989.

Tarkovsky, Andrei. *Time within Time: The Diaries: 1970–1986*. Tr. Kitty Hunter-Blair. London: Faber and Faber, 1994.

Tarkovsky, Arseny. *Poetry and Film: Artistic Kinship between Arsenii and Andrei Tarkovsky*. Ed. and tr. Kitty Hunter Blair. London: Tate Publishing, 2014.

Teo, Stephen. *Wong Kar-wai: Auteur of Time*. London: British Film Institute, 2005.

The Book of Chuang Tzu. Tr. Martin Palmer with Elizabeth Breuilly, Chang Wai Ming, and Jay Ramsay. London: Penguin, 2006.

Titze, Anne-Katrin. "Achieving greatness." Interview with Paolo Sorrentino. *Eye for Film*. https://www.eyeforfilm.co.uk/feature/2013-10-26-interview-with-paulo-sorrentino-about-the-great-beauty-feature-story-by-anne-katrin-titze

Tolstoy, Leo. *Anna Karenina*. Tr. Richard Pevear and Larissa Volokhonsky. New York: Penguin, 2002.

Trilling, Daniel. "Dream Tickets." *New Statesman*. December 5, 2011, 44.

Turovskaya, Maya. *Tarkovsky: Cinema as Poetry*. Tr. Natasha Ward. Ed. Ian Christie. London: Faber and Faber, 1989.

Ungureanu, Delia. *From Paris to Tlön: Surrealism as World Literature*. New York: Bloomsbury Academic, 2018.

Van Gogh, Vincent. Letters. http://vangoghletters.org/vg/letters.html

Verne, Jules. *The Moon Voyage: From the Earth to the Moon & Around the Moon*. Auckland: Floating Press, 2010.

Vigni, Franco. *La maschera, il potere, la solitudine: Il cinema di Paolo Sorrentino*. Firenze: Aska Edizioni, 2017. Ebook.

Vodolazkin, Eugene. *Laurus*. Tr. Lisa C. Hayden. London: Oneworld Publications, 2016.

Wai-ming Lee, Silver, and Micky Lee, eds. "Introduction." In *Wong Kar-wai: Interviews*. Jackson: University Press of Mississippi, 2017. Ebook.

Walkowitz, Rebecca. *Born Translated: The Contemporary Novel in an Age of World Literature*. New York: Columbia University Press, 2015.

Wang, Jing. *The Story of Stone: Intertextuality, Ancient Chinese Lore, and the Stone Symbolism in* Dream of the Red Chamber, Water Margin, *and* The Journey to the West. Durham, NC: Duke University Press, 2000.

Welch, John W. *Chiasmus in Antiquity: Structures, Analyses, Exegesis*. Provo: Maxwell Institute Publications, 1998. https://scholarsarchive.byu.edu/mi/22

Wells, H.G. *The First Men in the Moon* (1901). Project Gutenberg; NetLibrary, 1990.

Wild, Peter. *Akira Kurosawa*. London: Reaktion Books, 2014.

Williamson, Colin. *Hidden in Plain Sight: An Archaeology of Magic and the Cinema*. New Brunswick: Rutgers University Press, 2015.

Wong Kar-wai. *Wong Kar-wai: Interviews*. Eds. Silver Wai-ming Lee and Micky Lee. Jackson: University Press of Mississippi, 2017. Ebook.

Wood, Gaby. "How Britain Became the Toast of Broadway." Interview with Stephen Daldry. *The Guardian*, June 14, 2009. https://www.theguardian.com/culture/2009/jun/14/stephen-daldry-billy-elliot-tonys

Wood, Michael. "Other Eyes: Proust and the Myths of Photography." *The Strange M. Proust*. Ed. André Benhaïm. London: Routledge, 2009, 101–12.

Wood, Michael. "Parallel Lives." *The New York Times*. November 22, 1998.

Woolf, Virginia. *A Room of One's Own*. Eds. David Bradshaw and Stuart N. Clarke. New York: Wiley Blackwell, 2015.

Woolf, Virginia. *Mrs. Dalloway*. Oxford World's Classics. Ed. David Bradshaw. Oxford: Oxford University Press, 2009.

Woolf, Virginia. *Orlando*. Ed. Maria DiBattista. New York: Harcourt, 2006.

Woolf, Virginia. "The Cinema." In *The Captain's Deathbed, and Other Essays*. London: Hogarth Press, 1950. In *The Complete Works*. MyBooks Classics, 2018. Kindle edition.

Woolf, Virginia. *The Complete Works*. MyBooks Classics, November 19, 2018. Kindle edition.

Woolf, Virginia. *The Diary of Virginia Woolf*. Ed. Anne Oliver Bell with Andrew McNeillie. London: Hogarth Press, 5 vols., 1977–84. In *The Complete Works*. MyBooks Classics, 2018. Kindle edition.

Woolf, Virginia. *The Letters of Virginia Woolf*. Ed. Nigel Nicolson with Joanne Trautmann. London: Hogarth Press, 6 vols., 1975–80. In *The Complete Works*. MyBooks Classics, 2018. Kindle edition.

Woolf, Virginia. "The Russian Point of View." In *The Common Reader I*. London: Hogarth Press, third ed. 1929, repr. 1951. In *The Complete Works*. MyBooks Classics, 2018. Kindle edition.

Woolf, Virginia. *The Waves*. In *The Collected Novels of Virginia Woolf: Mrs. Dalloway, To the Lighthouse, The Waves*. Ed. Stella McNichol. London: Macmillan, 1992.

Wootton, Adrian. "Interview with Paolo Sorrentino." BFI London Film Festival. October 16, 2015. https://www.youtube.com/watch?v=DetZNqkGK0I

WReC (Warwick Research Collective). *Combined and Uneven Development: Towards a New Theory of World-Literature*. Liverpool: Liverpool University Press, 2015.

Yourcenar, Marguerite. *Dreams and Destinies*. Tr. Donald Flanell Friedman. New York: St. Martin's Press, 1999.

Yourcenar, Marguerite. *Le Temps, ce grand sculpteur*. Paris: Gallimard, 1983. Kindle edition, 2015.

Yourcenar, Marguerite. *Mishima: A Vision of the Void*. Tr. Alberto Manguel. New York: Farrar, Straus and Giroux, 1986.

Yourcenar, Marguerite. *Oriental Tales*. Tr. Alberto Manguel. Ninth ed. New York: Farrar, Straus and Giroux, 1997.

Yu, Anthony. *Rereading the Stone: Desire and the Making of Fiction in* Dream of the Red Chamber. Princeton: Princeton University Press, 1997.

Zonta, Dario. "Paolo Sorrentino: La scena del potere." In Emiliano Morreale and Dario Zonta, eds. *Cinema vivo. Quindici registi a confronto*, 211–30.

INDEX

2046 (film), 191–226
  closing scene, 198
  conception, 194
  editing, 204, 206
  feminine presences, 221–5
  filming, 193
  framing, 207, 212–14, **214**, 219
  love stories, 203–4
  and *In the Mood for Love* (film),
    194–5, 202, 205, 210, 217, 218
  music, 207, 222–3
  opening scene, 198, 205–6, 206–8
  Orient Hotel, 217–19, **217**, 219
  plot, 193
  poetics of repetition, 225–6
  the red chamber, 202, 219–21
  secret story, 198–203
  sequel, 193
  structure, 203–11, 217–19, 222
  and Tarkovsky, 214–16
  temporal layers, 204–5
  temporalities, 220
  see also In the Mood for Love
2047 tale, 213–14, 214

A Thousand and One Nights, 33, 34,
  35, 36
Abbas, Ackbar, 196n
adaptation, 153–5
adoption, 153–5
Allen, Woody, 90–1
alternative logic, 24–5
analogy, miracle of, 165–6
Anderson, Melissa, 167
Andrew, Dudley, 2–3, 4, 6, 8, 15,
  207–8
appropriation, 93
Apter, Emily, 47

Ardant, Fanny, 255–7, **267**
Auriol, Jean George, 18
automatic art, 38
automatic creation, 38–9

Bal, Mieke, 157n
Barr, Alfred, 24–5
Bazin, André, 2, 5–7, 10, 11, 12,
  13–15, 17, 18, 33, 49, 92–3,
  114, 115, 116, 121, 154, 263,
  266–7, 268, 269
beauty, 258–9, 259–63
Bergman, Ingmar, 75
Beugnet, Martine, 171, 174, 181–2
birds and bird metaphors, 76–82, **81**,
  85–7, 148–9, 252–3
Blake, William, 6
Borges, Jorge Luis, 136, 137
Bourget, Jean-Loup, 167
Bovier, François, 151
Bowen, Elizabeth, 131n
Brassaï (Gyula Halász), 25
Bray, Patrick, 184, 185
Breton, André, 1, 38, 43, 56, 91, 96,
  152, 188, 254, 255
  and beauty, 260–1
  Clair de terre, 18–19
  First Manifesto of Surrealism, 17,
    131, 157, 234
  Gradiva Gallery manifesto, 43–4
  Mad Love, 136, 169–70, 182,
    186
  Nadja, 88, 89–90, 154, 166, 172,
    176–7, 186, 234, 240, 241,
    250–1
  notion of realism, 10–11
  Orientalism, 91
Buñuel, Luis, *L'Âge d'or*, 253–4

286 INDEX

Cahiers du cinéma (magazine), 18, 152, 184–5, 191, 231
Calas, Nico, 91
Cao Xueqin, *The Story of the Stone/ The Dream of the Red Chamber*, 9, 198–201, 205, 206, 208–10, 213–14, 217, 218–19, 220–1, 221–2, 224, 225
Cardullo, Bert, 139
Casanova, Pascale, 15, 265
Céline, Louis-Ferdinand, *Journey to the End of the Night*, 228, 233–4
chance encounters, 184–5
Chapman, Mark A., 101
Cheah, Pheng, 21, 23
Chevrier, Jean-François, 11
Chikovani, Simon, 79
Christie, Agatha, 218
Christie, Ian, 32, 53
Ciment, Michel, 198
circulation, 2, 4–5
Cocteau, Jean, 11, 12, 33, 165–6
Cohen, David, 120
Cooke, Paul, 23–4, 119, 139
Crisp, Deborah, 142
Crowdus, Gary, 232–3
Cyprès, Amandine, 154, 181
Cytheras, 235

Daldry, Stephen, 8, 9, 265
   conception of cinema, 120–1
   on theatre, 144–5
   and Woolf, 131–2
   see also Hours, The
Dalí, Salvador, 39, 42, 43, 102, 254, 267
   Meditative Rose, 174, **175**, 176
Damrosch, David, 2, 3, 4
de Chirico, Giorgio, 39
de Medeiros, Ana, 108
death masks, 12–13
DeBona, Guerric, 23, 38, 38–9, 40
Denby, David, 120, 126–7
Dennison, Stephanie, 3
Destino (film), 267
DiBattista, Maria, 131n
Disney, 267
Doniol-Valcroze, Jacques, 18
Doran, Gregory, 268

Dostoevsky, Fyodor, 125–6, 126–7, 259
dreams, 75, 82–3, 95–6, 162
   alternative logic, 24–5
   films as, 23, 23–5
Dreams (film), 10, 75, 94
   Blizzard vignette, 97, 113
   Crows vignette, 86–7, 88, **89**, 90, 91, 95, 110, 111–13, **112**
   cultural references, 92–3
   Mount Fuji in Red vignette, 97, 100, 113
   music, 111
   Peach Orchard vignette, 97, 113
   reception, 92
   structure, 105, 108, 108–14
   Sunshine through the Rain vignette, 96, 113
   Tunnel vignette, 97, **98**, 99–100, 113
   Village of the Watermills vignette, 88, **89**, 97, 106, 107, 109–11, **110**, 113
   water imagery, 113–14
   Weeping Demon vignette, 97, **99**, 113
Durišin, Dionýz, 3

editing, 142–4, 146, 204, 206
Edwards, Gale, 268

Fantastic Art, Dada, Surrealism exhibition, 8, 24–5
Ferrante, Elena, 267
ffrench, Patrick, 164
Flaubert, Gustave, 241–3, 244
Fontaine, Anne, 268
Forster, E.M., 131
framing, 207, 211-4, **212, 214**
Freedman, Doris, 37
Freud, Sigmund, 39

Galasso, Michael, 195
Galt, Rosalind, 3, 4–5
Gambardella, Jep, 227–8, 233, 260
genre, 47
ghosts, 59–62, 65, 77, 95, 135, 136, 151
Gilson, Paul, 18
Glass, Philip, 118–19, 122, 137, 139–42, 148, 265

INDEX

Gorfinkel, Elena, 3
Green, Peter, 59
Guérard, Albert, 269
Guerra, Tonino, 10, 47, 76–7

haiku, 50
Hamlet (Shakespeare), 45, 151, 268
Hare, David, 120, 127, 128, 139, 140, 140–1
Harrison, Thomas, 82
Hawkes, David, 198, 199, 202, 219, 220
Hayashi, Osamu, 91
Hennessey, Brendan, 232, 253
Hillman, Roger, 142
Hiramatsu, Naoko, 91
Hollywood and Hollywood production, 23–4, 118–19, 139
Hours, The (film), 9, 153
    authorial control, 145–50
    background, 119–20
    closing scene, 125, 128–9
    editing, 142–4, 146
    ghosts, 135
    as Hollywood production, 118–19
    opening scene, 122, **123**, 124–5
    Oscar nominations, 118
    portrayal of Proust, 127–8
    portrayal of Woolf, 118, 127, 133, 149
    reception, 118
    rhythm, 135–6, 137, 141–2
    score, 118–19, 122, 124, 137, 139–42
    script, 120, 121, 129–30
    structure, 122–9, 135–6, 139, 144–50
    Woolf's suicide, 122, **123**, 124–5
Hugo (film), 8, 9, 21–37
    authorial masks, 27–33
    as automata, 41
    the automaton, 30, 37–45, **42**
    cinematography, 25
    the Director-God, 28
    escapement mechanism, 30–1
    flashback scenes, 30
    flipbook effect, 35, 41
    and *Le Livre magique (The Magic Book)*, 32–3, 41

Méliès disappearing act, 36
metatextual dialogue with Méliès, 36
narrator, 37
Paris, 24–5, **26**, 38
point of view, 35, 37
as surrealist object, 32
time reversal, 30–1
use of overhead shots, 30
visual sources, 25–7, **26**
voyeurism, 34
Hugo, Victor, 53, 158
Hutchinson, Rachel, 93
hybrid cinema, 15
hybrid works, 267–8

imprinted time, 52
In the Mood for Love (film), 190, 203
    and *2046*, 194–5, 202, 205, 210, 217, 218
    the black hole, 207–8
    corridor scene, 210–11
    filming, 193
    final scene, 195–200, **196**, **197**
    framing, 211–12, **212**
    last scene, 199, 205, 206
    music, 195, 223
    plot, 191–2
    poetics of repetition, 225–6
    the red chamber 2046, 210–11, 224
    secret story, 195–200, 202
    and Tarkovsky, 216
    see also 2046
Invention of Hugo Cabret, The (Selznick), 8
    Alcofrisbas, 17
    as automata, 41
    the automaton, 22, 38, 40
    black frames, 23
    as flipbook, 28, **29**, 34–5
    Méliès gala address, 1929, 28
    see also Hugo
involuntary memory, 164–5
Ivens, Joris, 153

Jaquet-Droz, Pierre, 38, 41
Jarry, Alfred, 16–17
Jesus Christ Superstar (film), 268

288 INDEX

Johnson, Vida T., 52, 58, 67
Jullien, Dominique, 32–3, 34, 183n

Kertész, André, 25, **26**, 33
Kluge, Alexander, 266
Kobiela, Dorota, 267
Kurosawa, Akira, 10, 265
  appropriation, 93
  Bazin on, 92–3
  and painting, 93–5
  and Proust, 115–16
  and *The Mirror*, 105
  Rhapsody in August, 103, **104**
  The Seven Samurai, 92, 93
  Something Like an Autobiography,
    94
  and Tarkovsky, 75, 105–7, 114
  and van Gogh, 94–5, 96–7, 99–108,
    100–8, 109–15
  and Yourcenar, 88–9, 97, 99–100
  see also Dreams

La Grande Bellezza (film), 9
  Andrea's suicide, 250–1
  and beauty, 258–9, 259–63
  cultural references, 232–3
  disappearing giraffe scene, 251–5
  Fanny Ardant in, 255–7, **267**
  intertextual dialogue, 241–2
  Jep Gambardella, 227–8, 233
  Jep's pursuit of phantoms, 248–51
  journey, 228, 230, 234
  lantern, 240–1
  last scene, 228, 258–9, 259–63
  museum scene, 235–43
  music, 230, 240, 245, 247, 251,
    255, 258
  opening scene, 241
  relation to Proust, 243–5
  sea scenes, 245, **246**, 247–8
  surrealist apparitions, 251–5
  use of Raphael, 239–40, 259
  and writing, 229
La Revue du cinéma (magazine), 18,
    19
L'Âge d'or (film), 253–4
Lane, Anthony, 154, 155, 161, 170–1
language, 49, 56, 82

Le Livre magique (The Magic Book)
  (film), 32–3, 41
Le Temps retrouvé (film), 9
Le Voyage dans la lune (film) , 16–19,
    20, 24, 266
Lee, Vivian, 193
Leonardo da Vinci, 96
Lim, Song Hwee, 3
Logan, John, 35
Loving Vincent (film), 267
Lowenstein, Adam, 11
Lumière brothers, 26

MacGillivray, James, 76
Magic in the Moonlight (film), 90–1
Magritte, René, 25–6, 101, 159, 176
  La femme cachée, 186, **187**, 188
Malausa, Vincent, 231
Man Ray, *Proust on his deathbed*,
  12–13, **12**, 165, **165**
Manea, Norman, *The Hooligan's
  Return*, 267
Marker, Chris, 81
Martini, Alessia, 253
Mauclaire, Jean-Placide, 18
Mayoux, Jean-Jacques, 134
Méliès, Georges, 16–19, 27, 75, 144, 266
  *Arrival of a Train at Vincennes
    Station*, 26
  disappearing act, 35–6, 90–1, 168,
    176, 177, 253
  gala address, 1929, 28
  The Hat with Many Surprises, 182n
  *Le Livre magique (The Magic
    Book)*, 32–3, 41
  The Merry Frolics of Satan, 168
  Ruiz and, 157
  Scorsese and, 8, 44
  surrealists and, 8
  see also Le Voyage dans la lune
memory, 51–2, 67, 164–5, 191, 219,
  235–43
metaphor, 63
Mirror, The (film), 45, 55, 57–71, 124,
  158, 162, 267
  Aleksei house scene, 57–64, **63**
  authorial mask, 59
  cast, 155

ghosts, 59–62, 65
Kurosawa and, 105
mirror scene, 65–9, **66**
music, 65
narrative structure, 70–1
spiralling time, 62–4, **63**
mirrors, 65–9, **66**, 162, 172, 215
mixed cinema, 5–7, 44, 154
Moretti, Franco, 2, 15
Morris, Nick, 268
Mrs. Dalloway (Woolf), 9, 119–20,
126, 150
authorial control, 145–50
opening, 134
and *Orlando*, 133, 134, 135
rhythm, 136, 142, 143
Murder on the Orient Express (book
and film), 218
music, 6, 148
2046, 207, 222–3
Dreams, 111
The Hours, 118–19, 122, 124, 137,
139–42
La Grande Bellezza, 230, 240, 245,
247, 251, 255, 258
The Mirror, 65
In the Mood for Love, 195, 223

Nagib, Lúcia, 3–4
Nerval, Gérard de, 13
Niogret, Hubert, 198
Nochimson, Martha, 199
Nostalghia (film), 10, 90, 107, 178,
211, 260, 261, 267
authorial mask, 49
birds and bird metaphors, 76–80, **78**
central scene, 78
double identities, 67
intertextual references, 55–7
last scene, 53–5, **54**, 79, 195
location, 47
opening scene, 74–6
and time, 71–3, **73**
tracking shots, 71–2, 83

objectivity, 14
observation, 50
Orientalism, 91

parallel time threads, 67
Paris, 24–5, **26**, 38
Pauchon, Luc, 108
Péret, Benjamin, 38, 41
Petrie, Graham, 52, 58, 67
phantom-objects, 180–3, **181**
photography, 6, 12–13, 13–14, 163–6,
165
Picasso, Pablo, 19, **20**
Pisani, Giuliano, 239
poetry, 47, 49, 49–50, 54–5, 55–6,
76–7, 83–4, 130, 231
Posnett, Hutcheson Macaulay, 3
Prince, Stephen, 92
Proust, Marcel, 1, 6–7, **238**
The Captive, 148–9, 150, 185–6,
243–4
Céline and, 234
death, 165–6
on the end of the world, 129
filmic imagination, 33–4
The Fugitive, 177–8
The Guermantes Way, 115–16, 152,
250, 258–9
Kurosawa and, 115–16
the madeleine scene, 51, 64
Man Ray deathbed photograph,
12–13, **12**, 165, **165**
miracle of analogy, 166–7
notion of realism, 10
optical devices in, 157n
phantom-objects, 182
and photography, 163–6
poetic prose, 49
on Renoir, 100–1
Ruiz and, 151–3, 154, 161
on the self, 39–40
Sodom and Gomorrah, 60–1, 68,
132, 146–7, 234, 261, 263
Sorrentino and, 243–5
"Souvenir", 247–8
statues, 185
Swann in Love, 249
Swann's Way, 32–3, 52, 53, 55, 56,
154, 163, 173, 185, 260
Tarkovsky's relation to, 50, 51–3,
53–4, 60–1, 69–70
vision, 45

voyeurism, 33–4
Within a Budding Grove, 164,
164–5, 224, 226
on women, 224
Woolf and, 134
see also Time Regained

Quignard, Pascal, 268

Rabelais, François, 17, 32
reality, 62, 234, 255
hidden, 189–90
invisible, 87
real, 14
redefining, 10–16
Red Inkstone, 202
Reider, Noriko Tsunoda, 92, 94, 108–9
Resnais, Alain, 95, 101, 107, 114
Richie, Donald, 92
robots, 41
Romney, Jonathan, 154, 161
Rubenstein, Roberta, 143
Ruiz, Raúl, 9, 15, 33, 69, 151–3
on films, 161–2, 188
François le Champi, 157
La Maleta, 153
and Méliès, 157
and Proust, 151–3, 154, 161
reading of Proust, 156
see also Time Regained (film)
Russian Ark (film), 236–7, 249
Russian cinema, 47–8

sabi, 51–2, 69, 195
Sackville-West, Vita, 132
Sadoul, Georges, 11, 24, 27
Scarpetta, Guy, 184
Schlöndorff, Volker, 256–7, **257**
Schoonover, Karl, 3, 4–5
Scorsese, Martin, 91
and dreams, 24–5
on film making, 44–5
interest in the surrealists, 26–7
and Méliès, 8, 44
and Proust, 34
use of paintings, 27
Vanity Fair Proust Questionnaire, 21
see also Hugo

Selznick, Brian, 7, 8, *see also Invention
of Hugo Cabret, The*
Serper, Zvika, 92
Servillo, Toni, 234
Shakespeare, William, 45, 151, 268
Showalter, Elaine, 143
Sicinski, Michael, 232
Simmonds, Posy, 267–8
Skakov, Nariman, 70n
Smith, Alexandra, 50
Sokurov, Alexander, 236, 249
Sorrentino, Paolo, 9, 69, 172, 190,
227, 265
artistic models, 229–32
Everybody's Right, 227
Jep Gambardella, 243, 244
music, 230
relation to Proust, 243–5
understanding of cinema, 232–3
and writing, 228–9
see also La Grande Bellezza
Soupault, Philippe, 152
Springer, Nancy, 267
statues, 183–6, **184**, **187**, 188, 238
*Story of the Stone/The Dream of the
Red Chamber, The* (Cao
Xueqin), 198–201, 205, 206,
208–10, 213–14, 217, 218–19,
220–1, 221–2, 224, 225
surrealist objects, 32, 43–4, 177–8
surrealists, 1, 11–12, 91
and automatic creation, 38–9
cinema, 8–9
deep history, 18
mannequins, 39
and Méliès, 8, 18–19
Scorsese's interest in, 26–7
Synessios, Natasha, 52–3

tableaux vivants, 167, 176
Tarkovsky, Andrei, 45–50, 94, 144,
151, 265
Andrei Rublev, 80, 114
character names, 57–8
on circulation, 2
diary, 45, 47, 47–8, 51
on dreams, 83
on genre, 47

Ivan's Childhood, 267
and Kurosawa, 75, 105–7, 114
on language, 49
notion of cinema, 52–3
poetics of cinema, 73
poetry, 49
poetry analogy, 49–50
relation to Proust, 50, 51–3, 53–4, 60–1, 69–70
Russian cinema, 47–8
Solaris, 62, 64, 72–3, 75, 106, 113, 160, 214
Stalker, 214
Tempo di viaggio, 47
and time, 51–73, **54, 63, 66, 73**
and van Gogh, 101, 105–7
Wong and, 213, 214–16
see also Mirror, The; Nostalghia
Tarkovsky, Arseny, 47, 49, 50, 54–5, 55–6, 64, 66–7, **66**, 68, 77–8, 79, 82, 83–4, 106–7
Taurand, Gilles, 154, 155
Teo, Stephen, 194, 198, 207
time
embalmed, 6
flow, 72–3
imprinted, 52
imprints of, 195
irreversibility of, 14
irreversible, 156
irrevocable, 148
made visible, 20
materiality, 184
non-linear, 167–70
passage of, 41
as sculptor, 73–4
seeing, 218–19
spiralling, 62–4, **63**
Tarkovsky and, 51–73, **54, 63, 66, 73**
Time Regained (film), 153, 214, 243
adoption, 153–5
analogy, 166–7
the Callipygian Venus, 183–6, **184, 187**, 188
cast, 155, 190
dinner party, 178–80, **179**
ending, 157–60, **159, 160**, 162–3, **165**, 167–70, **168**

Gilberte's name, 176–8
Marcel and Gilberte love story, 173–4, **175**, 176
opening shots, 156–7
phantom-objects, 180–3, **181**
the red book, 160–1
statues, 183–6, **184, 187**, 188
structure, 156, 167, 176
surreal rose, 174, **175**
top hat scenes, 180–3, **181**
train compartment scene, 188–90, **189**
treatment of objects, 170–3
versions of Proust, 157
Time Regained (Proust), 10, 20, 44–5, 56, 150, 161, 190, 235, **238**, 245, 262
on art, 45
and death, 249–50
ending, 156
the madeleine scene, 51
on memory, 164
and networks, 2
statues, 185
voyeurism, 33–4
Time within Time (Tarkovsky), 45, 47–8, 51, 83
Tolstoy, Leo, 126
tracking shots, 71–2, 83
The Trail of the Octopus (film), 89–91, 91
translation, 5, 7
Trilling, Daniel, 23
Turovskaya, Maya, 50, 76

Un Amour de Swann (flim), 256–7, **257**
untranslatability, 46

van Gogh, Vincent, 267
Berceuses, 107–8
The Bridge at Courbevoie, 101–2, **102**
Head of a Woman, 97, **98**
Kurosawa and, 94–5, 96–7, 99–100, 109–15
Langlois Bridge at Arles, 111–12, **112**

letters, 95, 96, 104, 107–8
Pollard Willows and Setting Sun, 97, **102**
Roadway with Underpass. The Viaduct, **98**
Self-Portrait (1887), 109, **110**
Starry Night over the Rhone, 114
Sunflowers, 97, **99**
and sunflowers, 101
Tarkovsky and, 101, 105–7
Wheatfield with Crows, 85–7, 95, 105, 110
Yourcenar and, **103**
Vanity Fair (magazine), Proust Questionnaire, 21
Venuti, Lawrence, 5, 6
Verne, Jules, 16, 17
visionary process, 21
Vodolazkin, Eugene, *Laurus*, 69, 71, 267
Voltaire, 17
voyeurism, 33–4

Walkowitz, Rebecca, 4
Warwick Research Collective, 4
Welch, John, 108–9, 205
Welchman, Hugh, 267
Wells, H. G., 17, 18, 27
Wild, Peter, 95
Williams, Tami, 3
Williamson, Colin, 36, 37, 38
Wong Kar-wai, 9–10
    approach to time, 193–4
    architectural principle, 202–3
    literary sources, 198–201
    poetics of repetition, 225–6
    and Tarkovsky, 213, 214–16
    see also 2046; *In the Mood for Love*
Woolf, Virginia, 6–7, 8, 129–39
    A Room of One's Own, 118, 130, 131, 133, 136
    "The Cinema", 143–4
    cinematic imagination, 143

Daldry and, 131–2
final diary entry, 117–18
Orlando, 124, 129, 131, 133–5, 162
and Proust, 134
"The Russian Point of View", 125–6
suicide letter, 128
treatment of time, 136–9
The Waves, 138–9, 141, 146
see also Hours, The (film); *Mrs. Dalloway*
Wootton, Adrian, 229
world building, 23
world cinema
    definition, 3, 3–4, 119
    definition of circulation, 4–5
    and world literature, 2–3
world literature, 21
    definition, 3, 4
    definition of circulation, 4–5
    visual, 8
    and world cinema, 2–3
Worne, Duke, 89

Young-hae Chang Heavy Industries, 4–5
Yourcenar, Marguerite, 7, 10, 53, 73–4, 75
    and dreams, 82–3, 95–6
    Dreams and Destinies, 82–3, 91, 95, 96
    "How Wang-Fô Was Saved", 87–91, 100, 103, 105, 106, 107, 108, 111, 112–13
    Kurosawa and, 88–9, 97, 99–100
    links to the surrealists, 91
    Orientalism, 91
    "Our-Lady-of-the-Swallows", 79–83, **81**
    "The Sadness of Cornelius Berg", 91, 108, 109
    and Van Gogh, 102–3, **103**
Yu, Anthony, 206, 209, 216, 225–6